DR. KANE'S
ARCTIC

Is now being read by more tha
young, learned and unlearn
be owned and

500 N]

have each pronounced it the mo ..... velous work ever
p

THE FOREIGN JOURNALS

and the most distinguished *savans* of Europe are extravagant in its praise. It is more interesting than

ROBINSON CRUSOE;

being a faithful account of privations and hardships, the narrative of which cannot be read without a shudder.

OUR MOST EMINENT MEN

have vied with each other in extolling its merits. Read the opinions of a few of them.

W. H. PRESCOTT, the Historian, says—

"It is one of the most remarkable records I have ever met with, of difficulties and sufferings, and of the power of a brave spirit to overcome them. No man has probably done more than Dr. Kane to lift the dread veil of mystery which hangs over the Arctic regions. His sensibility to the sublime and the beautiful gives a picturesque effect to his descriptions of the wonderful scenery by which he was surrounded; and he tells the occurrences of his daily life, enveloped with the most frightful perils, with a good-humored simplicity and air of truth that win our confidence, and must have a fascination even for the youngest reader."

WM. C. BRYANT, the Poet, says—

"The merits of Dr. Kane's recent work are so universally acknowledged, that it seems superfluous to praise it. It is a record of one of the most daring—and, so far as the interests of science are concerned, one of the most successful—enterprises of modern times, and it is written in a most interesting manner,—a manner which gives the reader a high idea of the intellectual and moral qualities of the author."

Hon. GEO. BANCROFT, the Historian, says—

"His expedition—in view of the small number of his party, the size of his vessel, (which had not even one companion,) the extent to which he explored the Polar regions, the length of time he remained there, and the marvels of his escape—seems to me without a parallel.

"His constant self-possession during his long trials, his quickness of judgment, his unshrinking courage in danger, his fertility of resources in the hours of greatest difficulty, give him a very high place in the very first rank of Polar navigators as a leader, and commander, and man; and no one of them all has told the story of their adventures so charmingly as he has done. For execution, so far as the publishers are concerned, the volumes are among the handsomest that have issued from the American press."

WASHINGTON IRVING says—

You ask my opinion of his work. What can I say that has not been already said by more competent critics? I do not pretend to critical acumen; being too much influenced by my feelings: still I may give some opinion in this department of literature, having from childhood had a passion for voyages of discovery, and I know of none that ever more thoroughly interested and delighted me than this of Dr. Kane. While I read the work I had the author continually in my "mind's eye." I was present when he lectured in the Smithsonian Institution in 1853, on the Arctic Expedition, which he had already made; when we all wondered that one of a physique apparently so slight and fragile, having once gone through such perils and hardships, should have the daring spirit to encounter them again. I saw him after his return from that second Expedition, a broken down man, broken down in all but intellect, about to embark for Europe, in the vain hope of bracing up a shattered constitution.

It was this image of the author, continually before me, that made me read his narrative, so simply, truthfully, and ably written, with continued wonder and admiration. His Expedition, and his narrative of it, form one of the most extraordinary instances of the triumphs of mental energy and enthusiasm over a frail physical organization that I have ever known. His name, like that of Henry Grinnell, will remain an honor to his country.

Hon. EDWARD EVERETT says—

"It does the author equal credit as a man of science, and an energetic, skillful and courageous adventurer, and a true-hearted philanthropist. In conjunction with his former publication, it will secure him an abiding-place on the rolls of honest fame among the heroes of humanity. The style of typography and illustration is of superior excellence."

G. P. R. JAMES, the Novelist, says—

"I read the two volumes with deeper interest than I ever felt in any work in my life; and I concluded them with love and admiration for the man who wrote them. I only wish there were a dozen volumes more."

Gen. LEWIS CASS says—

"The expedition is a monument of human energy and endurance, originating in the most honorable and commendable motives, and conducted with rare courage, sagacity and perseverance. To the severity of truth it adds the romantic interest of perilous adventure and of the extremity of exposure and suffering. I never read a narrative which took firmer hold of my feelings, nor which excited to a higher degree my commiseration for the heroic men whose terrible calamities it records, nor my admiration for the fortitude with which these were met. It was a contest between man and nature—between the stern power of an Arctic winter and the human frame to resist it. And it is wonderful to see that in their worst extremity the objects of the expedition were never abandoned by the hardy explorers, but they seemed to triumph over the icy desolation whose broad expanse was marked by no animated being but themselves. All other life had fled before its power of destruction."

Hon. CHARLES SUMNER says—

"It is a book of rarest interest and instruction; written with simplicity, ease and directness; possessing all the attractions of romantic adventure elevated by scientific discovery, and, as we sit at our warm firesides, bringing under our eyes a distant portion of the globe, which, throughout all time until now, has slumbered unknown, locked in primeval ice."

Prof. LOUIS AGASSIZ says—

"It will give me the greatest pleasure to write a scientific review of Dr. Kane's last expedition, which I have read with the deepest interest, mingled with admiration for his energy and the warmest sympathy for his sufferings

ELISHA KENT KANE, M.D., U.S.N.

E. K. Kane

BIOGRAPHY
OF
ELISHA KENT KANE
BY
WILLIAM ELDER.

PHILADELPHIA
CHILDS AND PETERSON,
602 ARCH STREET.

BIOGRAPHY

OF

ELISHA KENT KANE.

BY

WILLIAM ELDER.

PHILADELPHIA:
CHILDS & PETERSON, 602 ARCH STREET.
LONDON:
TRÜBNER & CO., 60 PATERNOSTER ROW.
1858.

Entered according to Act of Congress, in the year 1857, by
CHILDS & PETERSON,
in the Clerk's Office of the District Court of the United States for the Eastern District of Pennsylvania.

STEREOTYPED BY L. JOHNSON & CO.
PHILADELPHIA.
PRINTED BY DEACON & PETERSON.

TO THE READER.

THIS book was announced as forthcoming in May last, and was expected by the subscribers for over thirty thousand copies about midsummer; but, notwithstanding a persistency of effort which threatened to exhaust every thing in me except my patience and hope, I was not able to secure the narrative material for the third chapter until the end of August; and that which was required for all after the eighth was delayed till the 7th of November.

I have worked hard, under pressure of a clamorous impatience for the publication. The toil which does not appear in these pages, I think, amounts to ten times more than the reader will discover,—unless he has some time written a biography out of the raw material. I have not been unpunctual. Moreover, I have had so very, very little help that my only temptation to affect thankfulness would be a division of the responsibility, which, in the strictest justice to all parties, rests exclusively upon myself.

My aim was not to write a *review* of Dr. Kane's writings, but a memoir of the man, which might serve to make his readers personally acquainted with him. I would do this, or I would do nothing; and, working steadily to this end, I think I have not diluted my narrative with any thing except my own personality,—for which I respectfully refuse to offer either justification or apology.

It will be observed how largely, and how freely too, I have quoted from Dr. Kane's private letters and memoranda. Bless the memory of the man for the happiness I have this day in declaring that I have not been obliged to suppress a letter or a line for the sake of his fame! I struck out only one word in all my quotations from his manuscript, and altered one in the report of him by a correspondent; and these only because they would have been misunderstood.

May I not well be glad that nothing has discovered itself, in all this scrutiny of the character and conduct of my subject, which could affect my regard for him, or leave me with a shade of doubt or discomfort after all I have said of him?

The "Obsequies of Dr. Elisha Kent Kane," appended to the biography proper, and making so large a part of the volume's value, were prepared by the Honorable Joseph R. Chandler, of this city. His name is a sufficient voucher for their worth.

W. E.

PHILADELPHIA, December 14, 1857.

CONTENTS.

CHAPTER I.
                                                                    PAGE

GENEALOGY—The Maternal Line through a Century—Birth—Baptism—Childhood—Hardihood—Pugilism and Polar Practice—School-Cramps—Juvenile Polytechnics—Drift of Nature under Direction of Providence.. 13

CHAPTER II.

The Boy's Battle with the Books—His Studies at Play—Reconciliation on his own Terms, and at Work with a Will—His Collegiate Course—Civil Engineering—System Suiting the Subject—Dangerous Illness—Self-Culture, its Limits and its Authorities—Life in a New Light—The Study of Medicine—A Student at Blockley—Character at Twenty-One—Celibacy, and a Reason for it... 29

CHAPTER III.

Senior Physician at Blockley—Duties and Studies—Inaugural Thesis—Verdict of the Profession—Physiological Exploration, Methodology, Apparatus, Certitude—Unrest, Cause and Cure—Assistant Surgeon United States Navy—Better Health—China Mission—First Voyage—"As it is written"— Studies Aboard—Around Bombay—Ceylon—Tropic Life.. 44

CHAPTER IV.

The Forethought of Travel—Luzon—The Negritos—A Grand Ramble—A Vagrant Souvenir—Volcano of Tael, Description and History—Descent of the Crater—An Indignant Idol—Skirmish with the Pygmies—The "Treaty Fortnight"—Ki-ying and Cushing—Antipodal Gentlemen—A Dinner—Celestial Health-Drinking—Attachés—Diplomatic Dance—Disappointment.. 57

CHAPTER V.

Testimony of the Secretary and Chaplain of the Mission—Professional Practice in China—Rice-Fever Attack—Homeward—Borneo—Singapore—Sumatra—Interior India—Persia and Syria—The Nile, from the Sea to Sennaar—Professor Lepsius—Life at Thebes—Egyptology—Nilotic Diluvium—Boat-Wreck—Skirmish with Bedouins—Attack of the Plague... 74

CHAPTER VI.

Statue of Memnon—The Ascension, Risk, Escape—Greece traversed afoot—Germany—Switzerland—Paris—Surgical Practice in the East—A Letter—Italy—England—All the World over—A Winter at Home—Repugnance to the "Service"—Waiting Orders—Mis-sent—Coast of Guinea—Dahomey—Pattern of a King—Birthday Ode—Prerogative Royal—Magnificence—The Slave-Trade—Human Sacrifice—The Coast-Fever—Sent Home—The Fleet-Surgeon's Report.................... 90

CHAPTER VII.

A Summer of Suffering—Opportunity lost—The Last Chance seized—Despatched to Mexico—Shipwreck in the Gulf—The Spy-Company—Affair at Nopaluca—Rescue of his Prisoners—Hard Fighting and Rough Surgery—Wounded—Typhus Fever—Newspaper History—Surfeit of Patriotism—Irksomeness of the Livery—Charges against Domingues—The Horse-Claim—How it was proved, and what it proved—Gratitude of his Prisoners 108

CONTENTS.

CHAPTER VIII.

Colonel Child's Letter—Compliment to General Gaona—His Reply—"The Flag of Freedom"—Complimentary Sword—Dr. Kane's Acceptance—Colonel Gaona's Wound—Dr. Kane's Prisoners—Palasios shot—Domingues missed—Hand-to-hand Conflict—Loss and Gain upon "Relic"—To Head-Quarters—Invalided—Homeward—Despondency—Bureau-Favor refracted—Tread-Mill Régime—To the Mediterranean—Lockjaw—Dying Experience—Recuperation—Coast-Survey—An Interlude—Lady Franklin's Appeal—American Response—Dr. Kane volunteers—Ambition's Last Gasp—Amusement and other Refreshments—Off to the Arctic.. 127

CHAPTER IX.

Franklin's Voyages—Search-Expeditions—United States Grinnell Expedition—Lieutenant De Haven—Arctic Rose-Plucking—The Captain's Doubts—The Doctor's Decision—The Personal Narrative—Horrors of Authorship—Dietetics and Drugs—Public Lecturing—Expeditions of 1852—Estimate of Buttons—Second Voyage postponed—Little Willie—In Memoriam—Grinnell Land—Arrowsmith and the Admiralty—Adjourned Justice—Dr. Kane and Colonel Force—Comity and Equity. 146

CHAPTER X.

Mr. Kennedy's Alacrity—Sympathy of the Savans—Confidence strengthened—Exciting the Officials—Hopes on a See-saw—Drudgery of Boring—Kennedy Channel—Cash Contributions—Lecturing-Business—Mr. Peabody—Deficiencies of Outfit—Laborious Preparations—Patriotic Enthusiasm—The Honors in Danger—Race against Time—Admiralty Chart—A Time to be Sick—Daily Prayers—Christian Heroism—Special Providence—Worship among the Hummocks—Vindication of Faith—"How readest thou?"—Saving Faith.. 166

CHAPTER XI.

Motives and Objects—Declaration *in extremis*—Working up the Coast of Greenland—Good-bye—A Father's Testimony—Franklin's Chances—

Refuge with the Natives—Supporting Authorities—Sir R. Murchison—
The Brave trust the Brave—Contributions to Science—Inedited Manuscripts—The Open Sea—Logical Demonstration—The Discovery—The Last Throw—William Morton—Facts and Theories—Lieutenant Maury—Kane's Official Report—British Achievements—Results of Exploration—Washington Land—Within the Polar Ice-Ring.................,......... 187

CHAPTER XII.

The Natural Sciences—Glaciology—Relief-Expedition—Captain Hartstene—Dr. John K. Kane—The Knight and his Squire—The Three Captains—Authorship again—Pains and Penalties—Author and Publishers — The Unwritten Book—Engravings—Mr. Hamilton—Dr. Kane's Drawings—Artistic Skill—Facility and Fidelity—Congressional Subscription—Popular and Public Patronage—The Author's Involvement—The Secretary's Commendation—Testimonials and Medals... 209

CHAPTER XIII.

Kane's Sea—The Chart—Summary of Operations—Last Will—Voyage to England—Hoping against Hope—Reception in London—Last Letter—Disease of the Heart—Voyage to St. Thomas—On his Way to Cuba—Attack of Paralysis—At Havana—Longing for Home—Last Scene of all—He sleepeth—Interpretation—Church Relations—Free-Masonry—The Obsequies—Legislative Resolutions—Learned Societies—English Testimonial... 229

CHAPTER XIV.

Personal Description—Social Bearing—Spirit-Power—Portraits—Hypertrophy—Kindness for Animals—Gun-Murder—Dog-People—Man and Beast—Godfrey—North British Review—Withdrawing Party—Manners and Customs—Toodla-mik—Tastes and Antipathies—Novels and Plays—Prose-Poetry—Mental Method—Medical Skepticism—Benefits of the Study—Governing-Power—The Outside Passage—Routine and Organization—Esquimaux Allies—Fondness for Children—Justice to Subordinates—All else submitted—The End................................ 249

CONTENTS. 9

LETTER FROM DR. HAYES.

PAGE

Dr. Kane's Plan of Search—Adventures of the Depôt-Party—Return of Part of them—Starting of the Relief-Party—Inadequate Appliances—Special Providence—Their Return—Death of Baker and Schubert—Dr. Kane's Sickness—Want of Dogs—Appearance of Esquimaux—An Exchange effected—Breaking down.. 269

LETTER FROM AMOS BONSALL.

Early Acquaintance with Dr. Kane—Volunteering for the Expedition—Character of the Sailors—Dr. Kane's alleged Cruelty to his Men—His Leniency—His Self-Denial and Kindness to the Sick—Death of Jefferson T. Baker and Pierre Schubert—Character of Baker.................... 273

LETTER FROM HENRY GOODFELLOW.

Dr. Kane's Sea-Sickness—His Habits on Board—Failing Health—The Rescue-Party—A Bad Restorative—Government of the Crew—Allowance of Food—Dr. Kane's Abhorrence of Corporal Punishment—His Attention to the Sick—His Spirit of Scientific Inquiry—His Social Demeanor and Conversation—Exercise—Dietetics......................... 276

REPORT OF OBSEQUIES.

Introductory Remarks.. 287
Proceedings of City Councils of Philadelphia...................................... 288
    Mr. Cuyler's Remarks and Resolutions..................................... 288
    Message of Mayor Vaux... 289
    Remarks of Mr. Perkins... 290
    Resolutions offered by Messrs. Holman and Henry....................... 290
Meeting of Citizens... 291
    Mayor Vaux's Remarks... 291

CONTENTS.

	PAGE
Remarks of Hon. William B. Reed	292
Major Biddle's Speech	294
Professor Frazer's Address	296
Mr. Chandler's Speech	297
Remarks of Rev. Dr. Boardman	298
Corn Exchange	299
Committee's Resolutions	300
Remarks of Mr. Busby	300
Proceedings at Havana	302
Communication from the Captain-General	302
Resolutions adopted at the Meeting of American Citizens	303
Remarks of Don José J. de Echavarria	304
Response of Consul Blythe	305
Ceremonies at New Orleans	306
Ceremonies at Louisville, Ky.	307
Programme for Reception of Remains	308
Ceremonies at Cincinnati	310
Programme	310
Relatives of the Deceased : Colonel T. L. Kane, Robert P. Kane, John K. Kane; William Morton	313
Reception of Remains by the Cincinnati Committee	315
Remarks of Mr. Monroe, on behalf of the Louisville and New Albany Committees	315
Remarks of Mr. Anderson in reply	317
The Coffin	319
The Procession	320
Ceremonies at Columbus	320
Remarks of Mr. Anderson, on behalf of the Cincinnati Committee.	322
Religious Exercises at the Capitol	327
Prayer by Rev. J. M. Steele	327
Substance of a Discourse by Rev. James Hoge, D.D.	329
Concluding Prayers and Benediction	336
Order of Procession to Railroad-Station	338
Ceremonies at Baltimore	339
Crossing the Ohio	339
Disappointment at Wheeling	341
Crossing the Mountains	341

CONTENTS. 11

	PAGE
Reception of the Remains by the Baltimore Committee	341
Arrival at Baltimore	342
The Procession	343
Appearance of the City while the Remains were passing through it	345
Meeting of the Maryland Institute	346
Remarks of Mayor Swann	346
Resolutions	348
Remarks of William H. Young	349
Remarks of Hon. John P. Kennedy	350
Proceedings of the Companions of Dr. Kane at Philadelphia	358
Deputations from New York and other Cities	360
Arrival of the Remains at Philadelphia	361
Programme of Procession to Independence Hall	362
Remarks of Messrs. Dukehart, Chandler, and Parry	363
The Funeral Procession	365
Exercises in the Church	368
Invocation, by Rev. Charles Wadsworth, D.D.	368
Funeral Discourse, by Rev. Charles W. Shields	370
Prayer, by Rev. Dr. Boardman	380
Conclusion of Exercises	381
Remarks and Acknowledgments of Committee	382
Proposed Erection of a Monument to Dr. Kane	386

MASONIC OBSEQUIES.

Resolutions of Arcana Lodge, of New York	391
Meeting of Lodge of Sorrow	392
Ode by Brother Herring	393
Address by Grand Master John L. Lewis, Jr.	393
Letters to the Masonic Grand Lodge of New York	395
Commodore Stewart, U.S.N.	396
Commodore Perry, U.S.N.	396
Commodore Read, U.S.N.	396
Lieutenant Maury, U.S.N.	397
Major-General John E. Wool, U.S.A.	397

CONTENTS.

	PAGE
Honorable Judge Kane	397
Honorable Edward Everett	398
C. Edwards Lester, Esq	398
Washington Irving, Esq	398
Fitz-Greene Halleck, Esq	399
J. D. Evans, P. G. M. of Grand Lodge of New York	399
R. L. Schoonmaker, Grand Chaplain of Grand Lodge of New York, &c. &c.	399
Hymn, by Brother George P. Morris	403
Eulogy, by Grand Master Honorable E. W. Andrews	404

ELISHA KENT KANE.

CHAPTER I.

GENEALOGY—THE MATERNAL LINE THROUGH A CENTURY—BIRTH—BAPTISM—CHILDHOOD—HARDIHOOD—PUGILISM AND POLAR PRACTICE—SCHOOL-CRAMPS—JUVENILE POLYTECHNICS—DRIFT OF NATURE UNDER DIRECTION OF PROVIDENCE.

ELISHA KENT KANE derived his blood from the common source, immediately through the Kanes and Van Rensselaers of New York, and the Grays and Leipers of Pennsylvania.

His family, in all branches, dates American for more than a century. The Kane blood is Irish, the Van Rensselaer Low Dutch, the Gray English, and the Leiper Scotch. A hundred years ago his male ancestors of these names were respectively Episcopalians, Dutch Reformed, Quakers, and Presbyterians.

His great-grandfather, John Kane, who came from Ireland about the year 1756, married Miss Kent, a daughter of the Reverend Elisha Kent, by unbroken descent and dissent a Puritan from the earliest settlement of Massachusetts. His other great-grandmother,

Gray, varied the faith of the family with all that was practically best and most beneficent in the religion of the Moravians. This lady, born Martha Ibbetson, was in London in 1749, under the tuition of an apothecary-surgeon. After acquiring so much of his art as qualified her for the Lady-Bountiful life to which she had devoted herself, she emigrated to America. A year after her arrival in Philadelphia, she married George Gray, of Gray's Ferry, a man of great wealth, a liberal gentleman, and a zealous Whig. He was born a member of the Society of Friends, but at the earliest period of the Revolution he was a member of the Council of Safety, and a representative of the resistance party in the Assembly of the Province. On the 4th of July, 1776, he appears, as a delegate from the county of Philadelphia, at "a meeting consisting of the officers and privates of the fifty-three battalions of the Associators of the Colony of Pennsylvania, held at Lancaster, to choose two brigadier-generals to command the battalions and forces of the Province." He was, of course, among the proscribed by the British authorities.

Mrs. Gray was as decided a patriot as her husband, and as actively devoted to the service.

During the occupation of Philadelphia by the British forces, the sick and wounded American prisoners, amounting at one time to nine hundred men, were confined in the old Walnut Street prison. They were not treated as prisoners of war, but as rebels under arrest. Hunger, thirst, cold, and every species of personal abuse and

HIS ANCESTORS. 15

indignity which the malignity and neglect of a brutal subordinate could inflict upon them, made their condition intolerable. Mrs. Gray constantly ministered to their wants,—enduring the insolence and overcoming the resistance of their keeper, as only a woman of high character and determined zeal could meet and manage such difficulties. Food and medicines were supplied at her own expense; and the indispensable services of the surgeon and nurse, for which she was so well qualified, were rendered by her own hands. Her courage and constancy overcame all resistance that could be offered to her as a benefactress. The baffled officer of the prison charged her with being a spy, and she was ordered to leave the city. She appealed to Lord Howe: he withdrew the order, and she held her ground till the British evacuated the city. The American officers who had witnessed and experienced her generous services to the prisoners acknowledged them in the strongest terms of gratitude and admiration.* Afterward, when the tide of affairs turned, and British prisoners needed her aid, it was given as freely and effectually as she had before ministered to the sufferings of her own party. Through all these labors and

---

* "We, the subscribers, officers in the American army, now prisoners in Philadelphia, think it our duty in this manner to testify the obligations we are under, and the respect we entertain for Mrs. Martha Gray, wife of George Gray, Esq., for her unwearied attention to the distresses of the numerous sick and wounded soldiers in confinement, supplying them, at a great expense, with food and raiment, constantly visiting and alleviating, by her attention, their wretched condition, and in every cir-

trials of heroic benevolence, her daughter Elizabeth, afterward Mrs. Thomas Leiper, was her chief assistant.

Of Thomas Leiper, it is recorded, in the chronicles of the times, that he was 1st Sergeant of the 1st City Troop of Cavalry raised for the Continental service; that, as treasurer and quartermaster, he carried the first money from Congress to General Washington, then on the Heights of Boston; that he was at the side of the Commander-in-chief at the battles of Trenton, Monmouth, Princeton, New Brunswick, and Brandywine, and in the field generally, from the beginning to the end of the War of Independence.

Warmly attached to Robert Morris, and ardent in the support of his financial policy, he was one of those patriots who, each lending one-third of his personal estate to the old Bank of North America, enabled him to make provision for the march of the army to Yorktown.

---

cumstance interesting herself in their behalf. As we have been eye-witnesses to the above, we have hereunto set our hands.

Philadelphia, January 29th, 1778.

JOHN HANNUM,
Chester Co. Militia.
PERS'N FRAZER,
Lieut. Col. 5th Penna. Regt.
LUKE MARBURY,
Col. 4th Bat. Maryland Militia
W. TALIAFERRO,
Lieut. Col. 4th Virginia Battal.
O. TOWLES,
Major 6th Virginia Battal."

When the two great parties of 1799 were forming, he became the partisan, as he had long been the personal friend, of Mr. Jefferson. In Mr. Jefferson's letters to Mr. Leiper there is a remarkably free communication of opinion and feeling upon all the political questions, foreign and domestic, of the time. Their correspondence was constant and frequent until the death of Leiper, which occurred in 1822. He was long President of the Common Council of Philadelphia, invariably the head of the Democratic electoral ticket for Pennsylvania, and, by prerogative of his party position, the chairman of all the large Democratic meetings and conventions of the city and State. But he never held any office of emolument,—always refusing such appointments for himself and his family. At the end of the Revolutionary War he and his troop accepted, for all their services in the field, a letter of thanks from General Washington. Their money pay they transferred to the Pennsylvania Hospital, to found a lying-in department, and, by this noble donation of their toil-and-danger-earned funds, that charity was established.

John K. Kane, son of John Kane and Miss Van Rensselaer of New York, was a member of the Philadelphia bar when he married Jane Leiper, and has been judge of the United States District Court for the Eastern District of Pennsylvania since 1845.

Mrs. Kane's blood descends from Martha Ibbetson and George Gray, through Thomas Leiper and their daughter, and ELISHA was, emphatically, her son.

He was born on the 3d of February, 1820, in Walnut Street, between Seventh and Eighth, Philadelphia.

He was the eldest of seven children. Three brothers and a sister, his father and mother, survive him.

He was baptized in his infancy, in the Presbyterian church, of which his parents are members, ELISHA KENT, after the old Puritan clergyman of Massachusetts.

He went through the diseases and the training of infancy vigorously, having the clear advantage of that energy of nerve and that sort of twill in the muscular texture which give tight little fellows more size than they measure, and more weight than they weigh.

His frame was admirably fitted for all manner of athletic exercises, and his impulses kept it well up to the limits of its capabilities, daring and doing every thing within the liberties of boy-life with an intent seriousness of desperation which kept domestic rule upon the stretch, and threatened, as certainly as usual with boys whose only badness is their boldness, to bring down everybody's gray hairs in sorrow, &c. It was not the monkey mirthfulness nor the unprincipled recklessness of childhood that he was chargeable with, but something more of purpose and tenacity in exacting deference and enforcing equity than is usually allowed to boyhood. To arbitrary authority he was a regular little rebel. There was nothing of passive submission in his temper, and he did not overlay it with the little hypocrisies of good-boy policy. He was absolutely fearless, and, withal, given to indignation quite up to his own measurement of wrongs and insults,

PUGILISTIC FEATS. 19

and he had a pair of little fists that worked with the steam-power of passion in the administration of distributive justice, which he charged himself with executing at all hazards. In right of primogeniture, he was protector to his younger brothers, and was not yet nine years old when he assumed the office with all its duties and dangers.

At school, about this time, with a brother two years younger under his care, the master ordered his protege up for punishment. Elisha sprang from his seat, and interposed with a manner which had rather more of demand than petition in it, "Don't whip him, he's such a little fellow—whip me." The master, understanding this to be mutiny, which really was intended for a fair compromise, answered, "I'll whip you too, sir." Strung for endurance, the sense of injustice changed his mood to defiance, and such fight as he was able to make quickly converted the discipline into a fracas, and Elisha left the school with marks that required explanation.

When he was ten years old, four or five neighbour boys, all bigger than himself, who had climbed upon the roof of a back building in his father's yard, were amusing themselves by shooting putty-wads from blow-guns at the girls below. Elisha, attracted to the spot by the outcry of the injured party, promptly undertook the defence, and in the firm tone of a young gentleman offended, required them to desist and leave the premises; but he of course, was instantly answered by a broadside levelled at himself. Fired at the outrage, he clutched the rainspout, and climbed like a young tiger to the roof, and was among them before they could realize the practicability of the feat; and then he had them, on terms even enough for a handsome settlement of the case. The roof was steep and dangerous to his cowed antagonists, but safe to his better balance and higher courage, and they were at his mercy; for no one could help another, and he was more than a match for the best of them, in a position where peril of a terrible tumble was among the risks of resistance. Forthwith he went at them *seriatim*, till, severally and singly, he had cuffed them to the full measure of their respective deservings. But not satisfied with inflicting punishment, he exacted penitence also, and he proceeded to drag each of· them in turn to the edge of the roof, and, holding him there, demanded an explicit apology. Before he had finished putting the whole party through this last form of purgation, little Tom, who had witnessed the performance from the pavement below, greatly terrified by the imminent risk of a fall, which would have broken a neck or two mayhap, called out, "Come down, Elisha! oh, 'Lisha, come down!" Elisha answered the appeal in the spirit of the engagement, "No, Tom, they an't done apologizing yet."

He took no "sauce" from anybody. He couldn't understand why he should, and it was hard and risky to make him know that he must; for he was equally fertile in expedients and bold in execution. On the wharf, one day, when he was not yet twelve years old, an insolent ruffian, big enough and wicked enough to break every bone in the lad's body, aroused his wrath by an intolerable piece of rudeness. Resistance and redress seemed impossible, but submission was completely so. He saw his opportunity,—a rope fixed to the end of a crane hung within his reach, and the ruffian stood fairly in the track of its swing. He seized it, and running backward till it was tightly stretched, he made a bound which gave him the momentum of a sling, and planted his knees like a shot in the fellow's face, levelling him handsomely, and with a spring he put himself under the protection of the bystanders, who had witnessed and admired the performance.

So Elisha earned the character of a bad boy, while he was, in fact, exercising and cultivating the spirit of a brave one. Goody-good people, very naturally, did not understand him then,—they do now. Elisha never reformed: he just persisted until he performed what was in him to do. The rills, so tortuous and turbulent near the springs, rolled themselves into a river in time, and regulated their rush without losing it.

It is said that "education forms the common mind:" it is more certain that "as the twig is bent, the tree's inclined." This boy, at least, was the father of the man. It was utterly impossible to fashion his young life by veneering it with the proprieties which are supposed to shape it into goodness. He may not have known what he should be in the future, but he knew what he must be in the present, and he, happily, did not limber himself by forced compliances. Difficult, daring, and desperate enterprises, not only useless, but recklessly wild, under the common standard of judgment, worked in him like one possessed. At ten years of age he studied the weather, watched the moon, and carefully scanned the opportunities afforded by the nights for scaling fences, clambering over out-houses, and getting into the tree-tops, all round the square that was overlooked by his dormitory. Wherever a cat could go, he would; and escapes from the sky-light, by way of the kitchen-roof and through the trap-door to the yard, and thence abroad to enjoy an unwatched and unmolested rambling, clambering and tumbling, afforded him a seriously high-toned delight. He took nobody into his confidence except his bed-fellow; but this was voluntary and generous, for he was bent upon training him for similar achievements. One instance will illustrate:—

The back-building was two stories high, the front three, and the houses which flanked the kitchen were, also, three stories. To relieve the draft of the kitchen chimney from the eddy of the buildings which embayed it, it was carried up like a shaft sixteen feet above the roof. There it stood at the gable, in provokingly tempting altitude, and the point that concerned our little hero was, how to get to the top of it?

"How should he get to the top! Bless me," exclaims some considerate personage of correct habits and cautious judgments, "why should he?" Elisha would have answered him, "I must, and I wonder why I should not?" Very certainly there would have been two opinions on the matter, if any wise body had been consulted. But the little desperado needed no advice. The thing was to be done, and it was done. It required some engineering, but—it was all the better for that. It is not mere muscle and hardihood that will carry a man to the North Pole. He must have some science and some tackling along with him; and the boy that is practising upon a chimney-top for arctic service, must put his wits to work, quite as much as his muscles and his courage. He made his observations and his calculations,—his determination was long made. The preparations were perfected, and his younger brother taken into the enterprise.

When all in the house were asleep, and the stars gave just light enough to guide, and none to expose the performance, with prevention and punishment among the chances, the two little fellows left their bed, and descended the roof of the front building till they dropped themselves upon that of the kitchen. Here the clothes-line, providently stowed away during the day for the purpose, was lying ready in coil, with a stone securely tied at one end.

"What is the stone for, Elisha?"

"Why, you see, Tom, the stone is a dipsey. I call it a dipsey, (a young science of exploration, and a nomenclature to match, already,) because I'm going to throw it into the flue, so that it will run down into the old furnace, carrying the line down with it, and then I can slip down and fasten it there. Now for a heave. The chimney-top is almost too high for me. It is pretty near twenty feet, I should think; but I'll do it."

Failures to reach the height, then failures to direct the dip of the falling stone, followed in long succession; but this gave practice, and practice makes perfect. At last one throw more lucky than the rest, and the rumble in the chimney and the run of the line announced success. Down through the trap-door went Elisha, and, after securing the end at the furnace, he ascended to the roof again, and was ready. But stop a little,—the chimney is a very narrow stack; it stands outside of the gable, and there is a chance that the climber may swing out and get forty or fifty feet of clear air between him and the pavement below. This must be cared for; and little Tom is duly instructed and planted firmly, with the slack of the rope in hand, to keep Elisha on the right side of the chimney, so that if the bricks on the edge give way and a tumble betide, he may come down all safe and nice upon the roof. All these arrangements made, and the contingencies so well provided for, the rope is seized, the feet planted against the chimney, and, hand over hand, up goes the aspirant, till the top is within reach; but the perch is not so easily attained, even when the full height of the stack is mastered. One hand on a top brick to draw himself up by it, and it yields in its loosened bed! That won't do. With a hard strain he gets his elbow over the edge, and so much of the doubled arm within for a good broad hold, and then daintily and carefully wriggling up the little body, and he's up, seated on the top!

"Oh, Tom, what a nice place this is! I'll get down

into the flue to my waist, and pull you up, too. Just make a loop in the rope, and I'll haul you in. Don't be afraid,—it is *so grand* up here."

But the strength was not quite equal to the will; and Tom's chance had to be surrendered.

The descent was about as dangerous, though not quite as difficult, as the ascent. And then all that remained was to hide the tracks, which required another descent to the basement, a thorough washing of the rope to remove the soot of the chimney; and then, as the business of the night was done, to bed *viâ* the roof and skylight again; and a bright, happy consciousness on awaking in the morning that he *had done it*.

His child history is full of this sort of incidents. Through them all runs the one character of physical hardihood, and steady tense endeavour for doing every thing that seemed difficult of accomplishment, without other aim, or any aim at all, beyond the mere doing.

It might be only the impulse which lifts the lark into the clouds to sing her morning hymn, and leads the chamois to the dizziest heights of the Alps, away above the region where he finds his food; or it might be a habitude providentially induced and adjusted for the after work of his adventurous life. Opinions upon such points as these are not always reason; and reason itself is not quite capable of a solution. Only those who have the like feeling will rightly understand it, and explanation would not explain it to any one else.

From his eighth or ninth till his thirteenth year he

was rather an unpromising school-boy. In the softened phrase of a good authority, (the family physician,) "he manifested no extraordinary love of learning." His manifestations during this period would bear a still severer judgment under the standard which exacts devotion to school studies. He really disliked the lessons systematically imposed upon him; and he was not given to submission or compromise, nor the least inclined to the shabby dishonesty of seeming and dodging. He never complied when he did not consent, and it was an heroic integrity, unbecoming his age of course, that made him a refractory boy first and a noble man afterward, when earnestness and honesty became more seasonable. His teacher put the class into a jumble of classic text-books. Elisha, decided by his relish perhaps, perhaps by his judgment against the assortment, announced his repugnance, and supported it by delinquency in study and deficiency at rehearsal. He thought he could not, and he said he would not, conform. What was that to the teacher? The system was all right, and the order had the warrant of the authorities, and of what consequence was it that it was only not right for the pupil? Many *men* have many minds, but many boys must have only one. The teacher told him that he would rather have him leave the school than stay out of his class. The next day the dissenter took his seat in his place, opened at the lesson, put his finger on it, and closed the book! His mother heard the complaint against him, and exhorted him to obedience. Elisha loved his mother

SCHOOL-CRAMPS. 27

"with his whole heart, and his understanding also;" he went through a struggle,—he yielded. For one week he laboured faithfully, and gained great credit for success. He could go no further; his conclusion was, "I said that I would not, and I will keep my promise. Mother breaks my heart about it, but I cannot do it."

The influence of his example was not good for the established authority of the system; the hypocrisy of apparent submission would have answered better for that; and accordingly, his schools and teachers were frequently changed, although he conciliated the favour of his teachers generally by his readiness in learning whatever of his tasks he was inclined to, and always by his gallantry, fine spirit, and truthfulness.

The mistake was all theirs. It was the period that nature had assigned for the growth of his body and the education of his physical energies. His instincts and his necessities, as well as their resulting tastes, were in just rebellion, and it was well that he was not a sacrifice to the authorities.

In other and happier directions he was assiduous in his own *proper* education. About this time he collected a cabinet of minerals which is still preserved, and exploded any number of chemicals in the out-house, where he tinkered at his own tuition in all the arts, sciences, and polytechnics of the boy-system of self-culture. His stolen reading—all boys who have any thing in them steal the reading which their special capacities require—was Chemistry, Robinson Crusoe, and the Pilgrim's Progress.

He was getting ready, intentionally or unconsciously, for the studies, discoveries, and achievements of his after life.

We propose, therefore, to modify the received report of his school-boy character, and put it :—He manifested no extraordinary love for learning the lessons set him by his teachers. Which very naturally as well as justly turns the point of the judgment, and gives it the right cutting direction.

CHAPTER II.

THE BOY'S BATTLE WITH THE BOOKS—HIS STUDIES AT PLAY—RECONCILIATION ON HIS OWN TERMS, AND AT WORK WITH A WILL—HIS COLLEGIATE COURSE—CIVIL ENGINEERING—SYSTEM SUITING THE SUBJECT—DANGEROUS ILLNESS—SELF-CULTURE, ITS LIMITS AND ITS AUTHORITIES—LIFE IN A NEW LIGHT—THE STUDY OF MEDICINE—A STUDENT AT BLOCKLEY—CHARACTER AT TWENTY-ONE—CELIBACY, AND A REASON FOR IT.

THE name of Elisha K. Kane has passed into history, the history of science and heroic adventure. The youth of his countrymen desire to know him personally, intimately. There is a lesson in his life for them. Hero-worship is a form of devotional faith which may or may not yield its best fruits to the worshipper: the spirit of a generous emulation must work in him to produce them, and for this he needs the directory of the facts and influences which grew his model into greatness.

His father, a scholar, a lawyer, and a literateur, systematic in study, and keen in the pursuit of all useful and elegant attainments, despaired of Elisha's future when the lad was thirteen. He told him then, that he must choose between labour and learning promptly.

Elisha had already chosen both, and both together; but his father had not found the college to suit him. Here lay the whole difference between them, and neither of them understood it. The boy had not a vice or a fault that could spoil the man; but he had scarcely an inclination that promised success in the life designed for him. There was riding at break-neck speed to be done; trees and rocks to climb; pebbles to pick; dogs to train; chemistry, geology, and geography to explore, with his eyes and fingers on the facts; sketching, whittling, and cobbling to do, with other heroics of muscle and mind—all mixed in a medley of matter and system, for which there was no promising precedent, and no prophecy of good. Withal, he was constitutionally averse (he was not exactly incapable of any thing) to continuous allotted labour—so many hours, so many things to do.

It was not until his sixteenth year that he began to feel the deficiencies of his formal education, and addressed himself vigorously to the work of repairing them. The interval of two or three years was occupied with irregular and ineffective efforts to prepare himself for college. His health had given way, he was ill at ease, and he was on bad terms with his stated engagements.

Boys' sorrows do not often break boys' hearts; just as the crudities which they cram into their stomachs do not give them the dyspepsia. Ephemeral despairs and short fits of indigestion relieve them of their troubles of both kinds; for they are not very susceptible of chronic complaints. But there are some fourteen year olds,

AT WORK WITH A WILL. 31

who have character enough to suffer by their mental conflicts. I wish Doctor Kane had himself charted these first encounters of his with the hummocks and icebergs of his life-voyage. It would serve, I think, for guidance in education, as well as his map of the polar regions answers to direct geographical adventure and insure its success.

But, like a brave fellow, he "buckled down to it," and made such progress in the languages, mathematics, and drawing as made him ready for collegiate study in general literature, and civil engineering especially, which was at this time the profession of his own choice.

His father had carried him to New Haven, with the intention of entering him at Yale; but there he discovered the first symptoms of that heart disease, from which he was never afterward entirely free; and besides this, Elisha was behind in certain studies which the ritual of Yale prescribed, and, at the same time, so much in advance in the natural sciences of the college course, that a good year must be sacrificed if he entered under the rules; and his father very wisely decided against Yale under these conditions.

The University of Virginia allows the pupil an election among its courses of study, insisting only upon a certain basis of mathematics and classic literature. Here was the freedom required; and Elisha, in his sixteenth year, glad to avail himself of a happy exemption from arbitrary routine, went ardently at the work to which he was appointed.

Now that he was in "the right place for the right man," he knew how to accommodate himself to the method of necessary rule, and was well inclined to find his own private pathway quietly through the fields of formal study. He made very fair headway in Latin, Greek, and mathematics. What he got he kept, for his memory in all things had the special character given to that faculty by intenseness of impression. He did not take a degree here—he was not a candidate; but the learning of the class-books stuck in him so as to stick out in his style, almost to pedantry: it is the one fault in the diction of his first Arctic book. He had, in fact, a wonderful aptitude for language. Whenever he talked, I must not say lazily, but less intently, he coined words most incautiously, but with a facility wondrously happy; and they were alive with Latin, Greek, French, and grammar. His English was capital always, when he was thinking closely; and he was so nicely critical when he cared to be so, that it was evident enough an eminent linguist had been spoiled to make up a man.

During his year and a half at the Virginia University he devoted himself specially to the study of the natural sciences under Professor Rogers, and of mathematics under Mr. Bonnycastle. Professor Rogers was at the time engaged upon the geology of the Blue Mountains. Young Kane seized this opportunity for exploring nature and resolving her mysteries by the aid of science. In this engagement chemistry and mineralogy, with a

FAC-SIMILES OF GOLD MEDALS,
Presented to Dr. Kane *by the Royal Geographical Society, and by the British Government.*

margin of physical geography, offered him the opportunity for pushing the studies which his heart was set on; and it gave freedom besides for indulging that importunity of muscular activity which possessed him.

At the examinations which closed the terms of study he was distinguished for his progress in chemistry, mineralogy, and the other branches which make up an engineer's qualifications. How well he profited by these studies is amply attested by his published journals of Arctic exploration.

Civil engineering was the drift of all the preparation he was now making. The traveller and the naturalist were striving in him so strongly, that his choice of a profession was determined by these necessities of his nature. But his studies, pressed with too much ardor, were interrupted by an attack of acute rheumatism, of which the symptoms had shown themselves before he left home, and his father was obliged to bring him away wrapped up in a blanket, travelling in pain and difficulty till he reached home, where he was long dangerously and hopelessly ill.

We are now at a resting place, and cannot do better than survey the ground which we have traversed; for we must understand the boy if we would comprehend the man.

His was just the intellect to distinguish between the formalities and the essentials of an education. He had no time, (let this excuse all that was wrong in his refractoriness,) he had no relish, (this justifies him if the laws of harmony have a rightful rule,) for things not pertinent or helpful to his purpose. He was capable of painting, music, or *belles-letters* authorship, and he could have beaten De Foe in his own line of writing. For all these he had the relish that goes with large capability; but, like mathematics to Wesley, they were not to the purpose of his life. He was strongly given to speculative inquiry, but not at all disposed to convert the impulse into a mere intellectual observatory. He could not lobby, he must labor productively, through life. Conventional college studies fell with him into the same category with the esthetics of literature and philosophy; they were judged and settled by their serviceableness to his actual uses. So, he was not a Bachelor, nor a Master of Arts, nor a Doctor in Law or Philosophy; but he was none the less a Monk of intellectual industry, but all the more so.

Where could he find a school for his training and a diploma for his attainments? There is no faculty of Discovery to prescribe its studies and authenticate its qualifications, except the shut world of the unknown which borders and embosoms the realm of established science, and the open world of opinion. They have given him his diploma,—a Master in Scientific Enterprise.

It has been said that "the self-taught has a fool for his teacher." That, however, depends upon whether he is a fool or not; and the maxim, true enough in general, must be applied as Ophelia distributed her rosemary and rue, to be worn "with a difference."

Sir Humphry Davy said that he considered it as fortunate that he was left much to himself as a child, and put under no particular plan of study. But Sir Humphry had genius, and had the command of it. It never made a fool of him; and his common sense worked like a drudge under its guidance. Sir Walter Scott says, that "the best part of every man's education is that which he gives himself." This is universally true. Sir Benjamin Brodie, more exactly to our purpose, "willingly admits that among those whose intellect is of the higher order, there are many who would ultimately accomplish greater things, if in early life they were left more to their own meditations and inventions than is the case among the more highly educated classes of the community." He adds: "A high education is a leveller, which, while it tends to improve ordinary minds and to turn idleness into industry, may, in some instances, have the effect of preventing the full expansion of genius. The great amount of acquirement rendered necessary by the higher class examinations, as they are now conducted, not only in the universities, but in some other institutions, while it strengthens the power of learning, is by no means favorable to the higher faculty of reflection."

Dr. Newman is even more bold. Self-educated persons, he holds, "are likely to have more thought, more mind, more philosophy, than those earnest but ill-used persons who are forced to load their minds with a score of subjects against an examination; who have too much on their hands to indulge themselves in thinking or investigation. .... How much better is it for the active and thoughtful intellect, where such is to be found, to eschew the college and university altogether, than to submit to a drudgery so ignoble, a mockery so contumelious!"

Here are authorities of the highest rank, and points even stronger than our case demands; for young Kane very sufficiently availed himself of the help of the schools, took all their advantages, and kept his peculiarity so well within system as to corroborate and advance his own drift, but without surrendering its freedom or abating its force. Whatever the schools could teach for his use he learned, and he never lost it, because he did not bolt, but digested and assimilated, the nutriment provided.

He was not a radical non-conformist, but a resolute striver after the true ends of all study. His self-culture under his own system was just as far from rebellion in fact as it was from submission in form; and so he grew in strength, and in favor with his helpers. This is the sort of self-culture which we commend, and would enforce by the example of his great success.

He left the Virginia University, as we have seen, dangerously ill. This was in his eighteenth year, and his collegiate studies were at an end. He had scarcely arrived at Philadelphia when his disease developed itself into a very bad case of endo-carditis,—inflammation of the lining membrane of the heart. For a long time his family despaired of his life. He was himself persuaded that there

LIFE IN A NEW LIGHT. 37

was no hope of his ever making himself useful or honored among men. "The doctors tell me," he used to say, "that if I throw off this paroxysm, I may live a month, or perhaps half a year; but they know, and I know, that I may be struck down in half an hour." When he was so far recovered as to sit up, he underwent paroxysms of pain and suffocation that racked his slight frame to the limit of its strength; and one of his physicians told him that an incautious movement might prove fatal. "You may fall," said he, "Elisha, as suddenly as from a musket shot."

This was the period of a new birth to him. Coasting the Infinite so long and so near, it opened its scenery to the eyes of his spirit. He walked in its light thenceforth through his journey to the end. He was let into his own inmost life; he got hold of his destiny, and he ever after governed himself conformably.

He was at one with himself now, and knew how to conciliate order and liberty, to obey and to command, to accept the help of system, and to preserve his individualism under it without conflict; he stood ready to die, but he did not despair.

After a long struggle, which seemed to promise no speedy or certain conclusion, his father saw, without the aid of medical science,—what mere science is not always quick to discover,—that his disease was no longer organic or structural, but neuropathic or functional, and applied the heroic remedy. "Elisha, if you must die, die in the harness." A thousand times after, the doctor met danger and faced death in the harness, and fought his way to victory.

He rose out of the wreck resolutely, and retrieved his life, in a strength made his own by holding it in fee of chivalric service. This is the simple mystery of the man through his whole history. There is nothing else in it that puzzles our judgments.

He recovered, his medical attendant says, imperfectly, and had, all his life after, more or less rheumatic and cardiac disease, abated somewhat, perhaps, while he was in the high degrees of north latitude, by the incompatibility of these affections with the scurvy, with which he was deeply tainted in his last Arctic voyage.

There is the best authority for the opinion that his ailments had always in them a preponderant character of neuropathic disturbance. When he was free, or comparatively free, from the acute form of his rheumatic complaint, his nerves were tingling and rioting with irritation. Add the susceptibility and distraction of this constant besetment to the under-tow of organic disease, and his struggles may be estimated, but only by those who are similarly harassed, and similarly resolute in subduing their demon.

It helps in the apprehension of his vigour of spirit, to find him steady and strong in will and action, firm in purpose, and unwavering in enterprise, all along the years of assiduous preparation, as well as during the whole period, of his great achievements. A brave heart and a sound brain may easily master the mischiefs which

CHANGE OF PROFESSION.

they have the health to hold at bay; but when these bulwarks of resistance and salient points of enterprise are themselves shattered by the enemy, it depends upon the spirit with which they are manned whether the struggle shall be successful. Then it is that the victory is due to the resolution to conquer or "die in the harness."

Instead of fitfulness, capriciousness, and valetudinarianism, our young hero was sedate, earnest, calm, kind, gentle, and steadily industrious.

When he was at the university, while the life in him was as hopeful as it was earnest, he told his cousin that he had "determined to make his mark in the world." After his first critical attack, with death constantly impending, he held on his way till the promise was abundantly fulfilled.

From whatever impulse he then spoke, the ambition of his after-life was of that kind which embraces duty and aims at service,—that kind which seeks power and place for the opportunities they give for heroic and beneficent uses. To such the good Providence intrusts the well-being of the world; and such as are in this spirit faithful in a few things on earth shall be made rulers over many in heaven.

The imperfect and unpromising convalescence from the attack of cardiac disease which terminated his collegiate studies, in the judgment of his friends, made the profession of an engineer altogether impracticable. Believing that he was and would be brooding over the symptoms of his complaint, which was sure to be chronic, they recommended the profession of medicine, in the hope that he would be happier, or less unhappy, if he understood and could manage his own case.

He conformed to his necessity, and in his nineteenth year he entered the office of Dr. William Harris, of Philadelphia, where his preceptor reports him to have "prosecuted his various studies with so much zeal that he made rapid progress, and seemed to have always before his eyes the pledge which he made at the University of Virginia."

On the 19th of October, 1840, he was elected (being an undergraduate and not yet twenty-one years of age) Resident Physician in the Pennsylvania Hospital, Blockley, and entered upon duty on the 25th of the same month. Under the system then in operation in the hospital, he went in as junior to Dr. McPheeters. For six months he occupied the same room with his principal. Their intimacy was close and their friendship cordial. Dr. McPheeters says of him, that "at that time his health was delicate and his appearance even puerile, notwithstanding he was within a few months of his majority. He was laboring under a serious organic affection of the heart—dilatation with valvular disease, which gave rise to a very loud *bruit de soufflet*, (bellows sound,) accompanied by the most tumultuous action of the heart from any violent exertion. He was unable to sleep in a horizontal position, but was under the necessity of having his head and shoulders elevated, almost to a right angle with his body. He was fully aware of the gravity of his disease, as he often remarked to me that he never closed his eyes at night in sleep without feeling conscious that he might die before morning; yet this consciousness did not seem to affect his spirits, or to check his enthusiasm. The habitual contemplation of a sudden death seemed not at all to affect the buoyancy of his spirits, or to abate the ardor with which he pursued the objects of his ambition. I have always thought that the uncertain state of his health had a good deal to do with his subsequent course of life, and the almost reckless exposure of himself to danger."

"At the time that he entered the hospital he had attended one course of lectures, and had been a good student; but, as a matter of course, he was little acquainted with the practical duties of the profession. This, however, he soon acquired in the discharge of his duties in the hospital, which were always performed with more than usual fidelity and earnestness. At first his extremely youthful appearance rather subjected him to a want of confidence on the part of the patients; but his dignity of character, great intelligence, and fidelity, soon overcame all obstacles of this kind, and he rapidly acquired the respect and confidence both of his associates and patients. I regarded him from the first as a young man of fine talents, of more than ordinary cultivation, and remarkably quick perception, accompanied with an ardent devotion to the pursuit of his profession. He was an habitual student, and took particular interest in the numerous *post mortem* examinations made by myself and others—indeed, he manifested a great fondness for pathological investigations."

In the spring of 1841 Dr. McPheeters left the hospital, and his young friend and junior of six months' standing, early in his twenty-second year, and still an undergraduate, became, under the rule, one of the four seniors resident, who had the general charge of the patients. To the system of study and training in medicine, especially as theory undergoes the correction of facts in hospital practice, he gave his consent, and he went through it as he accomplished every thing else he ever gave himself to in his life,—something better than the best of his compeers.

Passing over, for the present, the most important part of Dr. McPheeters' contribution to these reminiscences, I make two other extracts, that we may have our subject before us as he stood in the apprehension of an intimate personal and professional friend during half a year of that period which was to determine his destiny.

"At the time that I speak of," continues Dr. McPheeters, "Dr. Kane was a man of great purity of character. Although surrounded by temptations, I am not aware that he had any bad habits; indeed, I regarded his moral character as above reproach. In his filial relations, too, his conduct was peculiarly exemplary. I have always admired the relations which existed between Judge (then Mr.) and Mrs. Kane and their children as I witnessed them at their fireside, as

REASON FOR CELIBACY. 43

well as they were exhibited in the character and conduct of Dr. Kane. His parents seemed to be his confidential friends and advisers. The relations which subsisted between them were tender and affectionate, and at the same time free from all restraint and embarrassment. This, in my estimation, added greatly to the charm of Dr. Kane's character."

An anecdote which Dr. McPheeters furnishes opens a light in another direction into the mind of Doctor Kane at the time, and prepares us on this point for his future history.

"On one occasion, when going the rounds of the out wards, or almshouse department, with Dr. Kane, we encountered a miserable, squalid, diminutive, and deformed pauper, who had married quite a good-looking woman in the house. As we passed this interesting couple, I jocosely asked the doctor 'what he supposed must be the contemplations of that woman as she beheld that miserable object, and reflected that he was her lord and master?' He paused for a moment, and then replied in a serious tone, 'It is to save some lady just such reflections as these that I have made up my mind never to marry.'"

How heavily the consciousness of physical disease must have hung upon him at twenty-one! How gloomy the future of a youth so finely though slightly formed, who, in full health, would have passed for a model of personal beauty! And how generous, though morbid, the exaggeration of his disqualifying infirmities!

CHAPTER III.

SENIOR PHYSICIAN AT BLOCKLEY—DUTIES AND STUDIES—INAUGURAL THESIS—VERDICT OF THE PROFESSION—PHYSIOLOGICAL EXPLORATION, METHODOLOGY, APPARATUS, CERTITUDE—UNREST, CAUSE AND CURE—ASSISTANT SURGEON UNITED STATES NAVY—BETTER HEALTH—CHINA MISSION—FIRST VOYAGE—"AS IT IS WRITTEN"—STUDIES ABOARD—AROUND BOMBAY—CEYLON—TROPIC LIFE.

IN the spring of 1841, a few months after he attained his majority, and a year before he graduated, he was installed, as we have seen, one of the Senior Physicians Resident at Blockley. The heavy duties and responsibilities of his office were upon him, added to the studies preliminary to his expected graduation in medicine, surgery, obstetrics, chemistry, and all the tributary branches of the healing art which enter into our omnibus system of tuition, under the genuine American notion that nothing less than too much is plenty of any thing. But he found time, as the events of the year showed, for all this, and for a margin of collateral investigations large enough in itself to pack the pages of a year's progress in an ordinary man's work.

In the year 1831 M. Nauche had communicated to the Society of Practical Medicine of Paris some observations upon a new substance found in the renal secretion, which he called *kyestein*, and announced as an indubitable test in cases of suspected utero-gestation. The importance of this discovery made it the subject of a critical examination in Europe, and, at the request of Dr. Dunglison, Drs. McPheeters and Perry, in the spring of 1840, instituted a series of experiments in the Blockley Hospital, the results of which they published in the "Medical Intelligencer" in March, 1841. Dr. Kane, as Junior at the time, had studiously watched the investigation, and when his principal, Dr. McPheeters, retired, availing himself of his apparatus and the insight gained in the preceding six months, "pushed the subject of kyestein," as Dr. McPheeters very frankly says, "much farther than I had done, and wrote his inaugural thesis upon it, the publication of which gave him great celebrity,—and justly too."

With the results at which Dr. Kane arrived we have nothing more to do now than to state their value in the estimation of the profession.

Samuel Jackson, M.D., Professor of the Institutes of Medicine in the University of Pennsylvania, in his valedictory address to the graduating class of that institution on the 28th of March, 1857, says, "It is fifteen years and two days, to the hour, when Elisha Kent Kane stood on this platform, in this room, and received the medical diploma of the University. However sanguine may have been his anticipations of professional success and reputation, (and it is a fair presumption that such were entertained by him,) he was fully justified in that expectancy. He was the foremost student of the class; the thesis he had presented to the Faculty had been honored by a vote of approbation and a request for its publication.* In this treatise, a subject that had recently been brought to the notice of the profession by Nauche, and was still a matter of controversy, was investigated and permanently settled. The conclusions of Dr. Kane were drawn from a series of experiments and observations on one hundred and seventy-nine individuals, and have been entirely acquiesced in. The subject has remained undisturbed in the position in which his publication placed it. This, his first step in medicine, made his name an authority on that question that time has not weakened; it established a reputation that has not been dimmed, and was an augury of professional pre-eminence."

Dr. Dunglison,—the most competent, comprehensive, and critical of our text-book authors,—in his well-known "Physiology," speaking of this investigation, says, "The result of Dr. Kane's observations, which the author had an opportunity of examining from time to time, and for

---

* Extract from the minutes:—"The following resolution was offered by Dr. Jackson, and unanimously passed : 'That the Dean be desired to communicate to Mr. E. K. Kane the approbation of the Faculty for his able and instructive thesis, and that he be requested to have it published.'" Dated March 18, 1842.

the accuracy of which he can vouch, was deduced by Dr. Kane as follows," &c.

M. Simon, of Berlin, Prussia, who had investigated the subject with great zeal and care, refers (in his "Animal Chemistry," English edition of 1846) to our young author thus:—" From the observations of Kane and myself it seems to follow,"—endorsing and affirming the doctrine of the thesis.

A dozen distinguished cultivators of medical and chemical science in Europe and America were engaged in this research; yet among them all Kane made his first " mark in the world," to the effect which our quotations testify.

The general reader is not concerned with the subject-matter of Dr. Kane's inaugural thesis; but there is that in the mind and method of the young naturalist which is much to the purpose of these pages.

Young and enthusiastic as he was, he adjusted himself to his difficult and doubtful inquiry in that spirit of philosophic caution which equally avoids the anticipation and the oversight of facts. His mind was well balanced between the skepticism and the credulity of physical discovery, for which mental integrity is as necessary as mental capacity.

He had witnessed the experiments of highly competent persons, and had observed their confidence in the inferences which they drew from them. Weighty authorities were in the field before him, but he was "careful to avoid the influence which the known opinions of others might have had upon the freedom of his own." He noticed that the aggregate of all the observations made upon the subject in the ten years before he undertook it did not quite number sixty cases. He extended his, not only to the one hundred and seventy-nine cases tabled in his report, but to ninety-two enumerated cases besides, not directly involved in his category, but examined for the corrective cross-lights which they threw upon those that fell fully within the inquiry; and, he adds, in general terms, "numerous others," the subjects of various diseases and of various ages and conditions, which might by possibility modify the results he was aiming at.

Indicating the method of his procedure, and the considerations which controlled it, he says, "My notes were always made upon the spot. If, from any cause, an individual observation, or a series, was unsatisfactory or inconclusive, or if it led to a different result from others, I repeated it at once with increased care; and I was always careful to observe the constitution, habits, and circumstances of each patient." Of all which, indeed, his tabled cases give the most ample and satisfactory proof.

He remarks, upon the caution and comprehensiveness of his laboriously exact inquiries, that, "To justify general conclusions, a large number of cases should be examined, individually and in group, and their progress, changes, and points of difference noted. They should be viewed under different aspects, at regular and frequently recurring intervals. If the indications of a particular case should appear to vary from those of others, repeated observations would become necessary to detect the causes of variance; and the influence of similar causes upon other cases, where they existed, also should then be sought for. And I may be excused for adding that a candid spirit, not too much biassed in favor of theory to admit the existence of observed exceptions—that looks to each clearly-ascertained result as an independent element, and that rejects nothing that appears true because irreconcilable with what was known before—is not less important to the formation of correct opinions than the most careful and varied scrutiny of facts."

"It is not meant by this," he adds, deferentially, "that the gentlemen who have treated on this subject have been regardless of these precautions, or wanting in the proper spirit of inquiry; but it is apparent that their observations have been rather of isolated cases than of classes, that they have not compared a large number of results, and that they have failed to detect any exceptions to their general conclusions."

These paragraphs contain a very complete directory for physical investigation in all its applications. They are a plain translation into specialities of all that is found in Mills and Comté on the conduct of the understanding in philosophic researches,—all that the one means by "the empirical law deriving whatever of truth it has from the causal laws of which it is a consequence," and all that the other intends by "the reciprocal verification of laws and facts carried on *pari passu*,"—with the advantage of being analytically rendered into guide-book clearness, and definitely presented for practical use, and illustrated, moreover, by the method of his own process, of which these abstract directions are but a just description.

It is surprising that a boy in years and experience should thus put himself abreast of the adepts who were in the field of scientific discovery against him; but when we find him working under direction of an unerring method, intuitively his own, the surprise shifts, from the success achieved, to the philosophic spirit of system so early and so fully attained.

The chemical tests employed seem to have exhausted the known resources of that science for the elucidation of his subject; and the doubt which he intimates, of the capability of chemical agents for rendering the secrets of vital phenomena, shows an equally bold and clear apprehension of a truth which concerns the morals as well as the certainties of the Inductive Philosophy.

In the same free spirit he speaks of the microscopic observations, practised with great assiduity and with the best assistance which he could secure: he says, "I do not venture to claim for these the same confidence which is due to my examinations by the unassisted eye."

It is something unusual to find an ardent undergraduate so free from the blandishments of authority and the imposture of apparatus, where all their testimonies, as in his case, make for the very conclusions which he inclines to receive and is tempted to adopt.

UNREST, CAUSE AND CURE. 51

This man was singularly fitted, mentally and morally, for discovery in natural science.

The "die-in-the-harness" resolution was in full play, as we have seen, during the year and a half of hospital service and study at Blockley. Several times it seemed to be near its finishing fulfilment: the doctor was more than once carried home on men's shoulders to be nursed, and returned again to his official duties and scientific pursuits at the earliest moment of adequate strength.

But it was not all desperation that determined him to labor in spite of pain. It had become apparent that his system would not brook repose; rest was not his remedy: unintermitting activity was proved, on fair trial, to be his best medicine. This was true of his whole subsequent life; and his apprehension of this necessity explains and justifies the tension and persistency of his enterprise, otherwise liable to be ascribed to impulses more heroic and reckless than reasonable or even excusable. The current of his life shows convincingly that incessant toil and exposure was a sound hygienic policy in his case. Naturally his physical constitution was a case of coil-springs, compacted till they quivered with their own mobility; nervous disease had added its irritability, and mental energy electrified them. It was doing or dying with him. And it was not a tyrant selfishness, a wild ambition, that ruled his life, but a rare concurrence of mental aptitude, moral impulse, and bodily necessity, that kept him incessant in adventure. If some of his performances which we have to record transcend even the large range which a right regimen dictated, it is only their excess, not their quality or purpose, which invites a candid censure. When anatomy was but little advanced, the sinews were called nerves; and the adjective "nervous" is thence employed by literary people to mean *strong, vigorous;* in colloquial phrase the same word is used for *irritable, agitated.* Put both these senses of the word together, and you will have some notion of the way the nerves were strung in our subject.

His father was so well persuaded of all this, that, when Elisha was about to graduate in medicine, he applied, without consulting him, to the Secretary of the Navy, for a warrant of examination for the post of surgeon in the service. The doctor was not a little dissatisfied with the sudden diversion of his drift, when he learned what had been done and how he was committed. The enthusiasm of his last year's researches was strong upon him; his plans looked to continued occupation in the career he had entered upon with so much success; and, beside this, his hospital-training and habit of mind were rather alien than helpful to the special duties of shipboard practice.

But he resolutely faced about; and the first good fruit of the new endeavor was a decided improvement in his health, under the hard work of preparing himself for his new examination.

He stood the inquisition of the Board of Navy Surgeons handsomely. There were four candidates so nearly equal in the judgment of the examining Board that they settled their relative rank by the rule of seniority. Dr. Kane stood third in the report made under this rule.

Bad health may disqualify a navy surgeon for the performance of his duty, and is properly a ground of rejection, however well he may be otherwise fitted for the place. After Dr. Kane had passed his examination, he frankly told the Board that he labored under chronic rheumatism and cardiac disturbance, and that he knew they could reject him for that cause. But the metal in the man outweighed his physical infirmities in their estimation, and they refused to re-examine him.

There was no vacancy at this time on the roll of assistant-surgeons. Mr. Webster was in the administration, and the public expectation had named him as our minister to China. Dr. Kane's friend, Dr. Chapman, obtained Mr. Webster's promise that he should be the physician of the embassy; and it was arranged with the Secretary of the Navy that he might accept the place without prejudice to his rank in the service. Mr. Cushing, who was ultimately charged with the mission, adopted the friendly purpose of Mr. Webster, and the doctor accordingly sailed in the frigate Brandywine, Commodore Parker, for the Eastern seas, in May, 1843.

This was his first sea-voyage. The vessel, after touching at Madeira, passed on to Rio de Janeiro. There they were just in time to witness the coronation of the Empress of Brazil, and the officers of the legation bore part in the ceremonial. While they remained in port, the doctor availed himself of an opportunity for a trip to the Eastern Andes of Brazil, and he examined with some care the geological character of the region.

Some very brief memoranda of this excursion were transcribed from his diary in letters to his friends at home; but the journal of the grand tour then before him, with all its sketches of objects and scenery, was lost on the Nile, as he returned, by an accident which will be narrated in the proper place; and he never had the leisure to restore his notes even so far as memory might have served to replace the record to any purpose. There was, in fact, not this much in him that would work backward. As in the case of his inaugural thesis, he always took his notes upon the spot, and when he published them afterward his books were scarcely any thing but his journals emptied into type. His writings that have charmed the world are, as nearly as any other man's ever were, his books of original entry. There are several instances, in his three volumes of Arctic Explorations, where his notes seemed to him of questionable accuracy; but a rigid observance of a good rule restrained correction by his memory, and he put them down as they were written. He had a conscience in literary composition, and a habitual respect for the difference between the *litera scripta* and the vestiges of memory in the statement of facts.

The loss of his journal on the Nile makes it difficult to detail satisfactorily the story of his Eastern travels and adventures, and deprives us, besides, of his observations by the way,—a loss even more material; for we could better spare the personal adventures of any year of the fourteen, crowded as they all were with incidents of travel, and peril, and bold achievement, than the fruits of art and thought which he gleaned from them in a day.

The frigate went to Bombay, to meet Mr. Commissioner Cushing, who followed by the overland route.

During the voyage he occupied himself with the severer studies of geometry, algebra, navigation, and in the languages of modern Europe. A young midshipman, Mr. Weaver, for whom he formed a warm and generous affection, became his pupil in these. Among their studies the Bible and Shakspeare had their place. With the admirable idiom of these handbooks of the head and heart few laymen were more conversant than Dr. Kane, and he is a more than ordinary wise man who has profited more in the practical wisdom of their teachings.

Mr. Cushing was delayed by the burning of the steam-frigate Missouri, which had carried him to Gibraltar, so that the legation lay for some months at Bombay awaiting him, and enjoying the hospitalities of the British officials of the station.

During this detention of the frigate Dr. Kane was an active traveller. He visited the caverned temples of Elephanta, excavated from the rock of a mountain-side on the island of that name in the vicinity of Bombay, journeyed by palanquin to Ellorah and Dowlatabad, crossed the Ghauts at Kandalah, and explored the rarely-visited cave-temples at Karli, situated on the coast of the continent opposite the larger island of Salsette.

Returning to Bombay from this excursion, and finding that he had time and opportunity for further research, he passed over to Ceylon, pressed onward to the interior, under the friendly escort of some gentlemen of the garrison, and shared in the elephant-hunt and the rare sports of the jungles. Here, where the wild game is the elephant, which is considered of better quality than in any other country in the world,—not quite so tall as on the continent, but particularly active and hardy,—and where the wooded hills around Candy, the interior capital, which is only a large straggling village, echo continually with the cries of birds and wild beasts, was a field of richly-assorted sports, and a rare chance for the coveted exercise.

He used to refer to this as a time of delightful excitement. The risk edged the relish of the joyance, and he feasted to the full upon the tropical wealth of novelty which everywhere surrounded him, multiplied in its effect by its infinite variety: "here he picnicked in the summer-palace among the hills, took his nooning under the taliput palms, and waked to the wild hazards of the chase."

If the pen and pencil of the Arctic artist had painted Ceylon in the colors of his first surprise, the picture would spare some ineffectual wing-work of the fancy which endeavors to realize it as he saw and felt it.

CHAPTER IV.

THE FORETHOUGHT OF TRAVEL—LUZON—THE NEGRITOS—A GRAND RAMBLE—A VAGRANT SOUVENIR—VOLCANO OF TAEL, DESCRIPTION AND HISTORY—DESCENT OF THE CRATER—AN INDIGNANT IDOL—SKIRMISH WITH THE PYGMIES—THE "TREATY FORTNIGHT"—KIYING AND CUSHING—ANTIPODAL GENTLEMEN—A DINNER—CELESTIAL HEALTH-DRINKING—ATTACHÉS—DIPLOMATIC DANCE—DISAPPOINTMENT.

AFTER a tedious voyage from Ceylon, the legation reached Macao, and the doctor remained connected with it until the negotiations were closed by the treaty of 3d July, 1844. But he was not idle during the six or seven months of the slow proceedings of Chinese diplomacy. He was not attached to the service now as a surgeon of the navy, but as physician to the embassy; and, obtaining Mr. Cushing's sanction, he provided a substitute to serve in his place in case of need, and crossed the China Sea to Luzon.

Before leaving home, he had been furnished by Archbishop Eccleston, of Baltimore, and by his friend Bishop Kenrick, then of Philadelphia, with letters to the Archbishop of Manilla. Under the auspices of this distinguished prelate, he was enabled to make a more complete exploration of the Philippines than any foreigner had at that time effected.

That he had the purposes of the traveller in prospect before he sailed, and intended to avail himself of all the opportunities of the cruise, is indicated by his precaution to secure these and other letters from the Catholic bishops, addressed to the faithful throughout the world, and, along with them, letters in the nature of protections from the Papal consuls of Spain, Portugal, and France. He had been accommodated, to the same purpose, by Mr. George R. Russell to his correspondents in Manilla, and he had similar letters from the Presbyterian Board of Missions, to meet his exigencies at their missionary stations, and from the Lutheran and Moravian officials of the like purport.

The island of Luzon, or Luconia, the largest of the Philippines, is briefly described in the books, quoting Balbi, as having an area of about fifty thousand square miles, and a population of two and a quarter millions,— the western portion under the government of Spain, with Manilla (population one hundred and forty thousand) for its capital, and the eastern or Pacific coast in possession of independent savages. "It is covered," says Murray, "to a great extent with high mountains, among which are several active volcanos, with hot springs in their vicinity, and violent earthquakes have been felt at Manilla and in other quarters. The aboriginal inhabitants consist of two races, the Malays and a tribe of negroes called Negritos. The former have, with some exceptions, submitted to the sway of the Spaniards, and embraced Christianity. The Negritos are generally independent: they are represented, also, as dwarfs or pygmies in stature, and among the lowest forms of humanity in all their characteristics. The native languages of the island are the Tagalic and Bisago."

Dr. Kane traversed the island from Manilla to its Pacific coast, and, with his usual audacity, explored its fastnesses, bathed in the forbidden waters of its asphaltic lake, descended to the very bottom of its great volcano, and perilled his life in a contest with a band of savages who were incensed by his profanation of their sacred mysteries.

A history and description of the volcano, written by a friar in a convent near Manilla, for the doctor, and probably at his request, followed him by a route and with incidents of travel almost as devious and remarkable as his own journeyings. It was carried by a Manilla sea-captain to China, another carried it after him to Calcutta or Bombay, through half a dozen hands it reached New York, thence it went on its way to Illinois, and finally, after a trip of twelve years, it reached its ultimate destination in the summer of 1856. It was put into his hands as he sat at his dinner-table, with the sufferings of all those years recorded in his system and pointing to other interests than those which absorbed him when it was written. He laid it aside, and never opened it.

It is endorsed, "Description of a Volcano in the Island of Luconia. Written by a Friar in a Convent near Manilla, for Dr. E. K. Kane; left with Henry Hesketh for translation." It has the following subscription :—" This is as much as I can relate to my friend Mr. Elisha Kent Kane. T. G. AZAOLA, *Manilla*, 27*th April*, 1844."

This Mr. Hesketh had left Illinois for Trinidad, California, and died there in 1850. The document was forwarded by his administrator to Dr. Kane at Philadelphia, when his celebrity as an Arctic voyageur had made his name a sufficient direction to his residence.

From this description of the volcano and history of its eruptions, which entire would fill fifteen of our pages, we extract so much only as may help to a tolerable estimate of the adventure which makes it a matter of special interest in this work.

"VOLCANO OF TAEL.

" The Indians have no word expressive of this phenomenon, and, as it is situated on an island, they call it *Pulo*, the 'Tagalo' [Tagalic word] for island. This island, which is formed by a mountain from three hundred and fifty to four hundred yards perpendicular above the level of the Laguna de Bombon, is about three leagues in circumference, and in its summit is seen a crater two miles in circumference. The walls which form this crater are fifty to seventy-five yards in perpendicular height from its base, which renders a descent into it impossible without the aid of ropes or ladders. At the

VOLCANO OF TAEL.

bottom of the crater, which is smoking, are seen four or five peaks or cones covered with sulphur. All the rest is a lake of green water which boils in several places, and should contain sulphuric acid. Neither basaltes nor lava are found in all the mountain or volcano, nor scoriæ and burnt clay, nor any pumice-stone.

"The lake in which stands this island, volcano, or *Pulo* has a circumference of thirty leagues: its waters are brackish and bituminous: it is of great depth; the shallowest part is twenty fathoms; the soundings are forty fathoms, forty-five, seventy, one hundred fathoms, and in other parts no bottom has been found with a line of one hundred and twenty-five fathoms.

"The natives call it Bombon, because it is surrounded by mountains of great elevation, more than one thousand five hundred yards above the sea-level, and it is so deep that they liken it to a stalk of cane or bamboo, in calling it Bombon from its narrowness and depth. . . . The waters of this lake issue by a small river, of very little breadth nowadays, whose mouth or outlet is on the southwest of the lake, and it runs a distance of two leagues to empty into the sea, on whose shore now stands the Pueblo of Tael and the hermitage or sanctuary of Casaisay. . . . The situation of the old Pueblo de Tael was nearly on the bank of the lake: it being the capital of the province, and there being an oral tradition that there entered 'Champanes' or 'Pontines' of forty to sixty tons, which traded between it and other Pueblos (*habitations*) of the same lake,—

62   ELISHA KENT KANE.

such as the old Tanauan, Tala and Bauan,—convinces me that the river was not only of greater width, but much greater depth, communicating with the sea by the Gulf of Balayan. The brackishness of the waters of the lake is another indication, having been pent up by the obstructions caused there by the successive eruptions of the volcano, which in the seventeenth and eighteenth centuries were considerable,—especially those of 1736, 1746, and 1749 to 1750.

"When the old Pueblo of Tael was founded, in 1575 to 1576, in the place where *we visited its ruins*, the volcano caused no anxiety, since an old chronicle of the Augustines says that on the skirts or declivities of the mountain the natives had fields of cotton, sweet potatoes, and other crops. Toward the end of the century 1600, the volcano already began to exhibit signs of an eruption, throwing out, says the same chronicle, cinders which destroyed the harvests of the Indians. It also relates that, of every three persons in the island, one died,—without doubt from the gases caused by this. About this time, says the chronicle, were formed (and became visible) within the crater two holes, one full of sulphur, and the other of green water, as at the present day."

Then follow very graphic accounts of the great eruptions of 1716, 1746, and 1754, related by competent eye-witnesses, with very ingenious speculations by Dr. Kane's friend, the friar Azaola, upon the phenomena exhibited and the probable connection of the volcano of Tael with the earthquake which destroyed Lima in 1746, and the

DESCENT OF THE CRATER. 63

shock felt in 1755 at Lisbon, and through Spain, France, Germany, Norway, and elsewhere,—all interesting enough to call for the publication of the paper entire, but only pertinent to our purpose as an introduction to the adventure of our hero.*

His descent into the Tael was a feat which only one European had attempted before, and he without success. Dr. Kane was in company with Baron Loë, a relative of Prince Metternich. They had an escort of natives, provided by the ecclesiastics of the neighboring sanctuary of Casaisay, who pointed out the only pathway to the brink of the crater. The two gentlemen attempted the descent together, but they soon reached a projecting ledge, from which farther progress was absolutely precipitous. After searching in vain for some more practicable route, the baron gave up the project, and united with the rest of the party in efforts to persuade the doctor to abandon it also. But that was out of the question. It was his temper to meet difficulty with proportioned endeavor, and to do his best to master it

---

* A correspondent of the *National Era*, of the 17th of September, 1857, who was at Manilla in February, and made a trip up the Pasig River to the neighborhood of the Tael, describes the water issuing from the springs at Los Banos, on the southeastern extremity of Lake Bay, as boiling hot. He says, "The volcano of Tael, whose crater was explored by Dr. Kane, is twenty miles distant from Los Banos, and it is probable that the subterranean streams which form these boiling springs pass near the fires which communicate with the burning mountain."

before he yielded. The attendants very reluctantly gathered from the jungle a parcel of bamboos, and fastened them into a rude but strong rope, by which, under the guidance of the baron, they lowered him over the brink. He touched bottom at a depth of more than two hundred feet from the platform he had left, and, detaching himself from the cord, clambered slowly downward till he reached the smoking lake below and dipped his specimen-bottles under its surface.

The very next thing in order was to get back again with the trophies of his achievement. This he used to speak of as the only dangerous part of the enterprise. The scalding ashes gave way under him at every step of his return; a change in the air-current stifled him with sulphurous vapors; he fell repeatedly, and, before he got back to the spot where his rope was dangling, his boots were so charred that one of them went to pieces on his foot. He, however, succeeded in tying the bamboo round his waist, and was hauled up almost insensible. When he sank exhausted in the hands of his assistants, the natives protested that the Deity of the Tael had avenged himself for the sacrilege; but the baron, who had less faith in the divinity of brimstone, dashed him with water, and applied restoratives brought by a messenger whom he had despatched to the neighboring hermitage. The remedies were so far successful that he could be carried to the halting-place of the night before. He had saved his bottles of sulphur-water, which he sent home to be analyzed, and with them some fine specimens of porphyritic tufa.

THE TREATY FORTNIGHT. 65

But this was not quite the end of the adventure. As his companion and himself pursued their journeying, the story of the profanation to which the Tael had been subjected went before them. A pygmy mob gathered angrily around them, their escort dwindled away or took part with their assailants, and, before they were rescued by some of the padres, the gentlemen were forced to entrench themselves in a thicket and throw up a dust with their revolvers.

In a letter of the doctor's, dated Whampoa, August 5 and 6, 1844, he gives what he calls "a faithful recollecting history of 'the treaty fortnight.'" Entire, it would fill twenty of these pages: we can afford it only the space of three or four. There is nothing in any published page of his that is richer in all the qualities of his style, nothing more graphic in description, more pictorial in presentment, than this long letter, which, he says at the end, he has "not even time to re-read." Chinese ceremony, costume, architecture, furniture, mandarins, mob, manners, and manoeuvres are rendered as if Retsch had sketched and Diedrich Knickerbocker written them.

In the extracts which follow, it will be seen that the fun of the thing may have been a pleasure pretty fairly divided between the two parties. But our object is to show what manner of man the writer was at twenty-four, and get him in all-sorts before the reader in his own drawn likeness.

THE TWO COMMISSIONERS.

"Ki-ying is a *man;* and, lest this should not be considered sufficiently definite, I would say, in the true cant of a describer, that he is a man above the medium height, stout rather than corpulent, with an easy walk, and a stand perfectly unconstrained. His face, chinese enough to modify the tartar, had a rather sleepy expression; and yet the smile, though nearly sneering, was animated and expressive. The eye had less of the oval at its inner canthus than a southern Chinese, and its pupil, nearly hidden by a heavy eyelid, was bright and even intellectual. Such was the blood-relation of the reigning emperor of the 'Flowery Land,' the successor of Lin, ex-viceroy of Canton, and martyr to a powerful moral sense unsustained by the information of the age.

"Except by powerful proclamations and admirably written protests, poor Lin was, in accordance with the Chinese policy of an Imperial commissioner, aloof from all personal intercourse with the stranger. With Ki-ying it was just the reverse. He had played dignity with the Portuguese, and baffled them; played the jolly companion with Sir Henry Pottinger, and floored him; and now, fresh from a drunken frolic at the Bogue, he met upon terms of cold yet equal and gentlemanly courtesy the Hon. Caleb Cushing, of the United States of North America.

"One feature the two commissioners had in common,—

an artificial one,—the mustache. With the American envoy brown, wiry, truncated, and protruding; with the Imperial dignitary gray, waving, unclipt, and curling around the mouth. The one a wire terrier, the other a dew-lapped mastiff. Which caught the rat? You shall see. . . . . . .

"Dinner was announced by a single servant, who walked up to Ki-ying, and, without any vulgar obsequiousness, did his errand.

"Ki-ying, very much in the same style with which a gentleman of the old school would take by the hand a youngish lady, led in Mr. Cushing."

THE TWO GENTLEMEN.

"Wong led in Commodore Parker; and, before I leave these two, who in every formal visit played a distinguished part, I may say of them, that Wong was, by universal consent, the most gentlemanly, self-relying, and handsomest Chinaman we had any of us seen; and Commodore Parker, in every respect his superior, sustaining himself fully, wherever he might be placed, with an innate, inherited gentility, which extracted marked respect from the mandarins, and placed his American associates instantly at their ease. An opinion, this, only to be valued because derived from the universal voice of the American community in China."

THE DINNER.

The pen pauses long upon the decision, but it must be pretermitted,—all but the summing up.

"People here say it was a noble feast, and many an old merchant has gone into affected raptures at Ki-ying's bounty. Your son can only borrow Uncle P.'s quotation of the Frenchman's climax, which marks, with pretty tolerable accuracy, the seeing, sitting, and rising stages of the banquet:—'Superbe, magnifique, pretty well!'"

THE HEALTH-DRINKING.

"The liquor, warm sam-shou, a distillation from rice, and, as Ki-ying told us, flavored with a Northern grape most highly prized. We took to it quite naturally, and the dear little silver oil-cans from which it guggled were in constant requisition. The grape-flavor was remarkable. Had we not known otherwise, we should have thought it a Madeira with the bouquet of Moselle: it had none of the empyreumatic taste of distilled spirits.

"Health-drinking with the Chinese is a rather serious matter. First, the person chin-chined, or complimented, grasps the stem of the glass with both hands, and stares smilingly at his complimented adversary. Next, they point glasses one at the other, and, if near, they hobnob, then raise slowly and drain to the very drop, turning their glasses upside-down.

"Ki-ying began with the plenipotentiary; then glided easily to Commodore Parker, who, temperate and gentlemanly always, raised the full glass to his lips, smiled, and emptied it in his plate,—thus escaping the perils of the bumper system.

"There was among the Chinese gentleman a smallpoxed mandarin,—not that either smallpox or mandarins are scarce in China,—but there was a smallpoxed mandarin, a man of might: he sat near your first-born. When, in the routine of the civilities, all the mandarins had samshoued the higher dignitaries of the Stars and Stripes, the aforesaid mandarin with the dotted face returned to one of them 'Chin-chin you *wan*,' (wine.) 'With pleasure;' and over went the glasses. 'I chin-chin you two *wan*,' (two wines.) Tip, and over went the glasses. 'I chin-chin you' (holding up three fingers) '*wan*.' The responding smile was more sickly; but, too gallant to flinch, the challenge was met, and over went the glasses again,—about the eighth already emptied.

"Seeing this, Webster, myself, and some others, in revenge, began a similar game with Ki-ying. It was, I mourn to say, but a suspending and temporary digression from the general epic of our smallpoxed hero. Once more he filled his steaming glass and chin-chined to the charge again." . . . . . .

"I would here wander from the Richard and Saladin of this desperate encounter, and turn to a race of nobodies known as the *attachés*. These devoted men—those who had beards and those who hadn't—rallied to a man and to a boy. The duties of the class have been, like themselves, under-estimated. In the case of our embassy to the land of flowers, they had to dress at least three times a day, to talk with the light, or rather heavy, morning visitors, to drink wine with the supernumeraries at the legation-table, and even to answer *all* the invitations,—

previously enclosing them in scented envelops, and sealing them with exceedingly thin-sticked sealing-wax. And now they had still higher duties. Could they remain spectators of the unequal fight? They rallied to an individual. Bristling glasses pointed from every quarter at the smallpoxed hero, and chin-chins were uttered in every gamutine graduation from thorough-bass to treble. Reluctantly he forsook his higher game, and turned upon his new assailants. The battle raged. The reprieved nose of his antagonist of the duello gradually regained its wonted pinch, and the indomitable mandarin, resigning for a time his incipient victory, proceeded to immolate on the spot three of the presumptuous attachés whose devotion had hurled them within the vortex of his civilities.

"And so the dinner passed away. No speeches were made with a more direct bearing upon the commercial interests under negotiation, than a well-expressed remark from our chief that 'this *biche de mer* was really not so bad,'—a proposition which Ki-ying, not understanding, received in courteous silence. After which we toasted the Emperor of China, hip-hipped him, hurraed him, hiccupped him, and withdrew."

A DANCE,

Which was a diplomatic device. The device having been neatly dodged by Ki-ying, the dance had to come off, nevertheless.

"At last, on the 25th of June, another interview

A DIPLOMATIC DANCE. 71

must be had with Ki-ying: every thing was ripe for it. Mr. Cushing did not personally see the subordinates. How should the interview be made available? for it was to decide much."

"The American ladies! What have the American ladies to do with it? Listen. It was determined that Ki-ying should again *Tiffin*,—*i.e.* in the language of the Eastern world, take a dinner-luncheon; that the ladies should meet him; and that informally, but in goodly numbers, and in less than two hours, they should all be there.

"Mr. C. gave me a *carte blanche*, and, with the characteristic modesty which I inherit, your interesting eldest paid an accidental morning call to *all* Macao, and collected, for the good of his country, thirteen ladies and a child. Distinguished services, for which I received a cholera morbus and the thanks of Mr. Cushing.

"O'Donnell and myself presided. Mr. Cushing, Webster, Wong, and Ki-ying were, with the interpreters, in close confab in the forward parlor. Strange, how little things are mixed with big: that trivial ante-dinner interview decided the entire object of the Chinese legation!

"Dinner now one hour on the table: thirteen ladies with *seven* husbands are no trifles to keep amiable. 'Why didn't Mr. Cushing show them Ki-ying and be done with it?' Mrs. R. would not have stood it, (she was not there;) and as for my friend Mrs. T., she thought it quite rude. *Two* hours passed by: small talk entirely run out. A half-hour more, and the fold, whose humble office of diplomacy it had been mine to bring together, were on an ear-pricking *qui vive*. They had heard from James, who had heard from the Chong, who had heard from the sentry, that Mr. Cushing had said, 'And now let's go to Tiffin.' They were all on intelligent tiptoe for the exhibition of five living Chinese mandarins, 'nobles of high degree.'

"The 'now let's go to Tiffin' of Mr. C. was soon followed by a familiar sound saboting along the hall. The two Excellencies, Wong, Pownting-gua, and the three other attachés, were ushered in *en groupe*. The ladies were introduced, and after some interesting conversation, confined, with much tact, to an examination of shawls, necklaces, dresses, caps, and teeth, Ki-ying was taught the European absurdity which converts the arm into a pothook. Mrs. P. made a link with the viceroy, and, the minor men and minor maids following their example, we walked in to dinner.

"It has been my lot, in some few of the many dinners which I have of late attended, to be a seated companion of seated statues: and so we were, all of us, at the well-remembered Ki-ying dinner of the 24th. Our attempts to look jovial were as ludicrous as our attempts to look comfortable; yet, occasionally drinking healths, and sometimes inwardly laughing at the contortions which Château-Margaux induced in Chinese features, we sat out our sit.

"Mr. Cushing was anxious, nervous, not quite at home;

Ki-ying dignified; Dr. Bridgeman chop-fallen : something had gone wrong.

"It had been settled, in that 'ante-dinner confab,' for the hope of visiting the Imperial palace and seeing the Majesty of the Celestials in his own proper person: in Mr. Webster's phrase, 'No Pekin.' Ki-ying had put it squarely to Mr. C. 'Should you negotiate with me, Pekin is a second matter, and that either he (Ki-ying) was a negotiating envoy and Pekin unnecessary, or Pekin the primary object, and he (Ki-ying) unnecessary.'

"Two hours after, I was in a chartered boat, armed to the teeth, and threading the ladrone dangers of the Canton River. I was a freed man."

CHAPTER V.

TESTIMONY OF THE SECRETARY AND CHAPLAIN OF THE MISSION—PROFESSIONAL PRACTICE IN CHINA—RICE-FEVER ATTACK—HOMEWARD—BORNEO—SINGAPORE—SUMATRA—INTERIOR INDIA—PERSIA AND SYRIA—THE NILE, FROM THE SEA TO SENNAAR—PROFESSOR LEPSIUS—LIFE AT THEBES—EGYPTOLOGY—NILOTIC DILUVIUM—BOAT-WRECK—SKIRMISH WITH BEDOUINS—ATTACK OF THE PLAGUE.

THE negotiations terminated, the frigate left her station at Macao, homeward bound, in August, 1844. Dr. Kane, not intending to return with his companions, had resigned his post of physician to the legation, and was even meditating a resignation from the navy, in which up to this time he had been an unpaid, though otherwise a kindly-requited, laborer. It is believed that he intended to practise his profession in China long enough to put himself in funds for a long run of travel in the East. Fifteen months' indulgence and enjoyment through a range so large and rich as he had made it, fully revealed his destiny to him; and all other occupation must now be only subsidiary to this leading object of his life.

What we have been able to gather of the incidents of his sojourn in China, after the departure of his friends, will be given when we have first secured the brief but valuable contributions to these recollections made by two of his associates in the diplomatic voyage.

Fletcher Webster, Esq., was secretary to the legation. From his letters, in which he intended rather to assist than to answer our inquiries, we take a few helpful extracts:—

"I first met Dr. Kane, as physician to our mission to China, on board the Brandywine, at Bombay, in November, 1843. I was secretary to the mission, and an intercourse sprang up between us which rapidly grew into a warm friendship.

"Dr. Kane had, I think, just returned from a trip into the interior of India as far as Poonah and the cave-temples at Karli, which he had an opportunity to make while the frigate lay in port waiting the arrival of Mr. Cushing. I was at once struck by the activity and energy of the doctor, who was never for a moment idle, or seemed enervated by the climate; and the officers of the ship remarked that he could never keep quiet. . .

"We left Bombay for Ceylon; and we had hardly touched at Colombo before he was off on an expedition to Kandy, the former capital-city of the island, some sixty miles distant in the interior.

"On our long voyage from Ceylon to Macao I had an opportunity of learning Dr. Kane well. . . . . Highly accomplished as a physician and surgeon, he seemed to think very lightly of his acquirements in the profession, and to be continually looking forward to something beyond.

"He was very fond of the exact sciences, and was an indefatigable student,—evidently annoyed when not engaged in something, and always restless unless busy,—for hours in the state-room buried in mathematics, and then next seen at the mast-head or over the vessel's side.

"On our reaching Macao, Dr. K. and the rest of us established ourselves on shore; and, while waiting the slow proceedings of the Chinese authorities, he made flying visits to Hong-Kong and Canton, returned to examine the environs of Macao and the islands in the harbor,—excursions always attended with a good deal of personal danger,—and had explored the whole town itself before we, of slower motions, had commenced. . . .

"He remained but a short time with us at Macao, but on leave of absence went to Luconia. He landed at Manila, and thence proceded entirely across the island to the shores of the Pacific, saw all its greatest curiosities, and, on his return to Macao, established himself as a physician at Whampoa Reach, in the Canton River, where he soon acquired an extensive practice among the shipping which usually lies there in great numbers. When I left Macao, in August, 1844, he was still there. . . . .

"Dr. Kane was a person of very nice modesty,—not given to much talking, and not eminently social,—that is, as I found him. In social intercourse, although agreeable and very bright when called out, he still seemed to be thinking of something above and beyond what was present.

"To his great scientific taste and knowledge, and his energy and resolution, he added a courage of the most dauntless kind. The idea of personal apprehension seemed never to cross his mind. He was ambitious, not of mere personal distinction, but of achievements useful to mankind and promotive of science."

The Rev. Geo. Jones, of Brooklyn, chaplain to the China mission, speaks of him, as he knew him on the voyage and at Macao, thus:—

"He was then very youthful-looking, with a smooth face, a florid complexion, very delicate form, smaller than the common size, but with an elastic step, a bright eye, and a great enthusiasm in manner, which also mixed itself with his conversation. He seemed to be all hope, all ardor, and his eye appeared already to take in the whole world as his own. He was very gentlemanly in his appearance and conduct. His conversation showed a great deal of such intelligence as is gained from books, and a great desire to learn on all topics. I soon found he was also ready and skilful with his pencil as well as quick in the use of his pen. All the elements of the subsequently distinguished man were there, only waiting to be brought into use.

"I had very good opportunities for observing him, as I was attached to the ship as chaplain, and as the letter of introduction, (from our mutual friend Elisha Chauncey,

Esq., of Philadelphia,) together with some affinities in taste, brought us frequently together during the voyage, and subsequently to our arrival in the China Sea. I was often struck with his simplicity of manner; for, with his good sense, he had often also, in worldly things, almost the simplicity of a child. This led him to be undervalued by those who could not see the strength of character and energy that underlaid the outside covering, but which showed themselves whenever any thing was to be done, any enterprise to be undertaken, or knowledge to be gained. All this shone out whenever our ship touched at any port; for he was then everywhere, with an activity that seemed to take no rest. His journals, I suppose, will show all this. His visit to the interior of Luzon is especially remarkable; but at Rio, at Bombay, and at Ceylon he visited every thing that was worth seeing, often in distant excursions from the ship.

"His attachments were very strong, and his labors to benefit those he took an interest in were self-sacrificing and enduring. He was very unselfish. His morals, I believe, were good, and his religious sentiments, though now standing for the first time the test of a commingling with the world, stood it very well."

All that we know of his fortunes in China for the succeeding six months is, that, while engaged in very successful practice as a physician and surgeon at Whampoa, he was stricken down at the close of 1844 with the rice-fever. Mr. Ritchie, of Canton, took him to his hospitable home, where he was nursed with the kindest care. It was a hard struggle; but the life-power had the mastery. This illness broke up his plan of professional practice there, and he resolved to come home.

Mr. Dent, the son of a British official at Madras, was also in delicate health, and it was arranged that the two should take the overland route for Europe together. They sailed in January, 1845. The next month they were at Singapore, a flourishing commercial settlement belonging to the British, situated on an island at the southern extremity of the peninsula of Malacca, and, as nearly as may be, under the Equator. In his "First Arctic Expedition" he speaks of Borneo and Sumatra as two of the places in the East which he had visited. It is probable that while at Singapore he availed himself of the facilities afforded by this great emporium of the trade of these seas for excursions east and west to these two islands. He was at Upernavick, on the west coast of Greenland, distant six years of time, seventy-three of north latitude and one hundred and sixty-five of west longitude, when one of those worldwide contrasts which were so frequent in his experiences enlivened the relish of a dwarfed *radish* with the remembered "mango of Luzon and the mangostine of Borneo, the cherimoya of Peru, the pine of Sumatra, and the seckel-pear of Schuylkill Meadows;" and he journalized his enjoyment of the first fresh vegetable he had seen for a year, and gave us our data—all that we have—for this stage of his Oriental journey.

From Singapore they crossed the Bay of Bengal to Ceylon, and thence to the Anglo-Indian peninsula.

Some months were spent in a tour of exploration through the interior of India, including the ascent of the Himalaya Mountains. The Zemindar Dwakanoth Tagore, by courtesy styled Prince Tagore, one of the wealthiest of the native nobles of Calcutta, was preparing for a visit to the court of Queen Victoria; and, Mr. Dent's health having been so far restored as to allow a change of their plan of travelling homeward together, Dr. Kane passed, with his consent, into the prince's suite. The interval before the party started for Alexandria was passed in travelling wherever historical memorials or scientific research invited him. He had every facility that the ample means of the prince, most generously dispensed, could supply; but we have no record of his Indian explorations.

He reached the shore of the Mediterranean in April, 1845, and, bidding a reluctant good-by to his friend and patron, under whose safe-conduct he had traversed Persia and Syria, he bent his way to the regions of the Upper Nile.

Pasha Mehemet Ali, the politic, if not the liberal, reformer of Egypt, to whom the doctor was introduced by Prince Tagore, gave him a special firman for his protection; and under the auspices of the Egyptian Association of Grand Cairo, which had elected him a member, he hoisted the American flag and headed his little boat toward the Pyramids, and Thebes, and the second Cataract.

A letter dated at Thebes, May 2, 1845, covering half a dozen pages foolscap, contains all the memoranda of his Egyptain tour which we possess. Our extracts must serve for its history, with the exception of a characteristic adventure, for which we are indebted to other authorities. He writes :—

"I have been for some days (three) wandering about in a state of amazement, unable profitably to see any thing. Perhaps it may to you seem an absurdity; but there is something so vast in the dimensions of these colossal ruins that I cannot embrace details; and, indeed, I almost fear that I shall leave Thebes without a definite impression of any thing but magnitude.

"My paper is resting upon the enormous foot of one of the Osiride columns in the Memnonium; my breakfast, yet awaiting me, is on the other. Forty-eight columns are behind me, grouped around my bed; and the roof which they support throws its shadow upon this respectable epistle. I have taken lodgings in the palace-temple of Sesostris.

"Thanks to Dwakanoth Tagore and the very meagre influence of my China title, I have been elected a member of the Egyptian society,—a somewhat dubious honor, which has converted my boat into a library, and condemned me to a fee of two pounds six. It has, however, enabled me to wade through the complicated trash of such men as Stevens, and to read, with the country itself for my atlas, the noble labors of Cailliaud and Wilkinson.

"This is very delightful for a sight-seer, but very mortifying to an ignorant man like myself, for my boundary is fixed and limited as my own information. Nothing can be more exciting than the intelligent study of Egyptian antiquities.

"Since Champollion gave tongues to stones, by clothing these wonderful remains with the interest of a recorded history, Egypt has undergone a complete revolution. It is no longer a place for sage Mr. Oldbucks and ingenious gentlemen of the Bill Stumps class. It is nothing more nor less than a great library of monumental history, where all that is wanted is the patient labor of a reader.

"You will be glad to hear that I have had a coresponding acquaintance (now a personal one) with Professor Lepsius, of Berlin and Rome. . . . I met him, seated cross-legged in the great temple of Karnak, supping coffee and copying hieroglyphics. He is at the head of the great Prussian commission; and it gratified me not a little, during our long talks, to find that he knew the Recording Secretary of the American Philosophical Society; and it required a very tolerable strain of my tolerably plastic countenance to sustain myself in the scientific position which, by reflection or inheritance, I was supposed to occupy.

"I dare say that Mr. Gliddon has crammed you sufficiently to make my own literal descriptions useless; or, if he has not, I yield me to mosquitos and this awful khampsin, and spare my imagination. As, however, my portfolio contains but two sheets of paper, and as I have determined to fill them both, I deliver my brain by an easy labor, giving you, as I had it repeated in frequent conversations, the outline of the labors of the great Prussian commission."

An exact report of the expedition of Lepsius and his suite, with their labors, journeyings, and dates, from July, 1842, till the date of this letter, follows.

It is filled with valuable information which was news then; but it is replaced now by the publications of this greatest of all the Egyptologists, in works familiar to all the students of archæology.

Mingled with the narrative of the journeyings of the commission, the doctor gives an occasional intimation of his own. "Lepsius left the Fayoum, (a most interesting region, which I entered at Benisouef,) . . . passed through the great (Nubian) desert to Abou Ahmed and Berber, a journey of twelve days, with fifty-two camels. . . . Accompanied by his chaplain, he ascended the Blue Nile—the scene of poor Bruce's toil—as far as Seso, in 13° north latitude, and rejoined his expedition on the 5th April, '45, at the pyramids of Meröe.

"My own journeying in the desert was not nearly so extended." Yet he elsewhere says that he had "eaten locusts in Sennaar," as far south, if not otherwise as extensive, "and if, as I am nearly determined upon, I make my détour from Esneh (Upper Egypt) to the oasis-wells and Abydos, this poor, scabby, sun-burnt economist will ride on top of a water-skin, with a retinue of two dromedaries instead of fifty-two. . . . .

"From this moment (the professor's return from the Blue Nile) he rested, or rather labored, at Thebes: the great temple of Karnak became his lodging-house, and Joseph's sanctuary his kitchen; and here, dear father, *I*, supping coffee in the temple of Sesostris, would scribble notes to my Karnak friend on the other side of the river, or pay running visits to a couple of Germans who lodged up the hill in an excavated tomb.

"My Thebes life is a very wild one: I am in native dress, with a beard so long that I have to tuck it in. My lodging is on the hot ground, and I walk on an average twenty-six miles a day. Cartilaginous pigeons —delicious young squabs—form the basis of a meal or series of meals, which, numbering five per diem, commence at four A.M. and end at nine in the evening, coffee being the great diluent,—tea without sugar."

Sitting in the temple of Rameses II., whose reign Lepsius puts in the fourteenth century before Christ, or about the time when Jael the wife of Heber drove a nail into the temple of Sisera, and nearly two centuries before Samson pulled down the temple of Dagon upon the aristocracy of the Philistines, it was but natural for him to give himself up for a while to the wonderment of that eternity past which bewilders the Egyptian traveller; but the brain that would not freeze at the North Pole did not melt at Thebes, and he came away as little intoxicated by the thirty-six thousand five hundred and

EGYPTOLOGY. 85

twenty-five years of the Egyptian dynasties which ended three hundred and fifty-nine years before the Christian era began, as if he intended to wait till Lepsius, and Wilkinson, and Gliddon should agree with themselves and each other, within a few hundreds of years at least, about the date of the fourth dynasty.

His deference for the authorities seems to have secured his assent to the date 2300 B.C. for Menes the first Pharaoh; but he turns from the chaos of chronology and cosmogony with instinctive avidity to the terra firma facts of time's changes which lay before him and practically concerned his specialty of study and enterprise.

"One of the most remarkable discoveries is, as to the physical conformation of the old mother-river's capacious offspring,—the Valley of the Nile. Mention this to Mr. Rogers, unless his correspondence may have preceded you. Lepsius paid particular attention to some hieroglyphic inscriptions on the rocks at the narrow defile of Semna; for, in a country as old as this, antiquity is engraved upon antiquity, and the scribbling inscriptions of travellers often give information of the highest value. He saw here the highest rise of the Nile, at that place, during eighteen different years under the government of Menes and his successors, from which we learn that nearly two thousand two hundred years before Christ, or four thousand and forty-five years ago, the average level of the Nile at that place was twenty-two feet higher than at present; while below the first cataract at Silsilis, as appears from the grottoes in the rocks, the level of the river was at least three feet, and probably more, below its present condition.

"This struck me as especially curious, for my own observations at Manfalout, (27° north latitude,) and the excellent conclusions drawn from the great Colossi of Thebes, prove with almost absolute certainty that the Valley of the Nile at Luxor is nearly seven feet higher than at the date of their construction. . . .

"The changes which have occurred in this belt are of the highest interest; for, after all, whether it be the coast-line of the Delta, or the beautiful Fayoum, or the narrow strip which leaves by-gone cities crumbling in the encroaching sands, the source is the same: the great mother scatters her blessings and her curses at each inundation, and a fixed rate of increase or decrease would be of practical importance almost beyond calculation.

"Your society will be the gainer if I succeed in passing my collection at Alexandria. I have two royal ovals in colors as fresh as my Chinese miniatures; and yet their groundwork is the limestone wall of an excavated sepulchre, and the artist some Pharaonic worthy of three thousand years' antiquity. The statue trunk, coming, as it does, from Tel-el-Amaina, will be of great interest."

The accident by which his journals and baggage were lost is thus related :—

"I wrote from Gizneh by special messenger, informing you of the melancholy loss of my baggage. Sympathize with this poor, very poor, devil, who, alone in a sandy desert, rejoices in three shirts, a pair of slippers, and a boat-cloak. I rehearse in duplicate its details.

"Dendera is but six miles from the ancient Tentyrus, a pleasant walk, which intending to enjoy before the sun heated the sands, induced me to bivouack on a slope of the river-bank, in order to start in the small hours of the morning. Preparatory to a house-cleaning during my absence, I drew the boat upon the land-slope, and then, as was my custom, placed my baggage on a platform of boards,—one end of which rested on the shore, the other, dry and comfortable, on the gunwale of the boat.

"My pilot laid his huge carcass over this little isthmus of household goods; and your son, cloaked and carpeted, went to sleep upon the sands. In the morning—Lord help me!—I was the first to rise; but boat, platform, baggage, all was gone. Nothing met my eyes but sleeping boatmen, naked wind-drifts, and complete desolation.

"I cannot fill up an old woman's letter, of the how and the why and the when,—how I felt and what I did. All that I can say is that my boat was recovered two miles down the stream, and that, as far as my mystified senses can account for the affair, the rapid current, aided by a partial quicksand, undermined my boat, tilted the side weighed down by my trunks, noiselessly canted them into the stream, and then, relieved of the weight, floated silently away.

"I am heart-sick at this loss. Nothing in the great scale of ups and downs which I have experienced, you would say; but most depressing in its consequences. Only one thing remains to comfort me; and that is, that, taught by persecution a little foresight, I had previously sent to England my best clothes and—thank Heaven!—my diplomas. But still my list of losses is more than enough to try my well-tried purse and better-tried philosophy.

"The idle hours of the sleepy Nile I had devoted to the arrangement of my collection, papers, &c. They are all gone: even Dr. Morton's skulls have sunk in the quicksands. One thing more, (it ends my story: how shall I say it!) I have lost my watch. Remaining are dear mother's battered writing-desk, containing my business correspondence and my money, my legation sword, valued for old associations, and a carpet-bag of shirts. No jackets, no boots, and no pantaloons."

Whether this was the true, or, at least, the whole explanation of his loss, he had afterward good reason to doubt. Some days after it occurred, as he was landing from his boat, borne through the water on the shoulders of his interpreter, he caught a glimpse of his watch-chain suspended round the fellow's neck, and he succeeded, after a severe tussle and a good ducking, in recovering a part of the chain, and with it the watch itself. The rascal made his escape with the rest of his plunder, which most probably amounted to all that he coveted of the swamped cargo.

He had been before this wounded in the leg in a *mêlée* with a party of Bedouins who attempted to rob him, and was glad on his arrival at Alexandria to put himself under surgical treatment. But a new visitation awaited him here. He had an attack of the plague; and during his illness, which nearly cost him his life, the collections which he had made and sent down the river from time to time by his occasional opportunities, were dissipated and lost.

CHAPTER VI.

STATUE OF MEMNON—THE ASCENSION, RISK, ESCAPE—GREECE TRAVERSED AFOOT—GERMANY—SWITZERLAND—PARIS—SURGICAL PRACTICE IN THE EAST—A LETTER—ITALY—ENGLAND—ALL THE WORLD OVER—A WINTER AT HOME—REPUGNANCE TO "THE SERVICE"—WAITING ORDERS—MIS-SENT—COAST OF GUINEA—DAHOMEY—PATTERN OF A KING—BIRTHDAY ODE—PREROGATIVE ROYAL—MAGNIFICENCE—THE SLAVE-TRADE—HUMAN SACRIFICE—THE COAST-FEVER—SENT HOME—THE FLEET-SURGEON'S REPORT.

BEFORE Dr. Kane could take his departure "from the river unto the ends of the earth," it must needs be that some adventure characteristic of the man, and in keeping with the wonders of the region, should signalize his visit.

The volcano of Tael had tempted him to brave the perils of its descent by the mysteries of nature hidden away in its depths; and here the towering wonders of human art, as tempting for the hidden things which they expose to dubious and difficult research, were all around him. An army of antiquaries were busy disinterring the mummy-history of Egypt from the ruins at their feet, and deciphering the hieroglyphics every-

STATUE OF MEMNON.

where within easy reach of inspection. They brought science and patience to their task, and sat " cross-legged" at their work. Was there any margin of exploration among these labyrinthine ruins and colossal monuments for an athlete who, at the risk of his neck, might wring the heart out of some mystery beyond their daring? We shall see.

The statue of Memnon, of marvellous fame, is the northeastern of the two colossal granite figures which stand on the plain near Medinet-Abou, on the west side of the Nile, opposite Luxor and Karnac. It is ascertained to be the musical statue which greeted the sunrise, by the multitude of inscriptions that testify its miraculous powers and the credulity of the witnesses.

It stands now in the category of obsolete miracles; but it is still a wonder that needs not the help of a superstitious faith to secure admiration.

Professor Lepsius measured it in February, 1845, and in his Denkmäler, (Monuments,) published in 1850, we have a splended engraving of the statue. From these sources—" the Denkmäler" and his " Discoveries in Egypt"—our description is drawn.

The statue is credited by the *savans* to Amunophis III., whom Gliddon, following Birch, places in the eighteenth Theban dynasty, 1692 B.C.; but Lepsius has since transferred him to the seventeenth, an earlier dynasty, and dated his reign in 1530 B.C., or one hundred and sixty-two years later,—an instance of the uncertainties of Egyptian chronology, but which in no wise affects the points with which we are now concerned.

It is in the sitting posture, and measures from head to foot, without the tall head-dress it once wore, forty-five and a half feet in perpendicular height. For its entire height above the level of the temple the base must be added,—thirteen feet seven inches, of which about three feet is hidden by a surrounding step. Thus the statue originally stood, or sat, nearly sixty feet (perhaps seventy with the head-dress) above the plain.

The measurements which specially interest us are those which are obtained by estimating the proportions observed in symmetrical statuary, and by calculations made upon the scale of the portrait given in the Denkmäler, the results of both methods agreeing exactly.

The height from the sole of the foot to the top of the knee is twenty feet. The breadth of the base or block on which the throne and the feet of the figure sit is twenty, and the length thirty-six feet, nearly covered by the sitting statue.

Dr. Kane, observing from below a tablet or lapstone which had never been specially described, suspected that its under-surface might have hieroglyphic inscriptions of value, and determined upon an inspection. This could be accomplished only by ascending from the base between the legs to the point to be examined; and that must be done by climbing,—a feat as yet unattempted, and, therefore, just the thing for him to undertake.

ASCENSION — RISK.

But, as the leg at the calf is about four and a half feet in diameter and thirteen in circumference, to climb it, as one grasps the bole of a tree in his arms to ascend it, was clearly impracticable. There was but one way of working his way up to the knees, which was by bracing his back or neck (as the varying interspace required) against one of the legs, and his feet against the other, and so to wriggle his way upward. His attendants protested that the feat was impossible; and at first it seemed so, for he failed in several attempts. But, stripping himself to his pantaloons, which were no encumbrance in climbing, he was at last successful.

It was slow and weary work: but he made good his ascent to the point he aimed at.

He had counted upon examining the lower surface of the tablet somewhat leisurely as he should lie stretched out in the nook below the knee-joints, and then, by climbing up to the top of the thighs, make his descent to the plain by taking advantage of the irregular projections at the back of the figure,—a route practicable enough for travel under direction of a practised guide. But he had sadly miscalculated the projection of the lapstone. He could not reach it from the position which he occupied; and there he hung, in painful horizontal extension, unable to ascend between the knees, where his passage was effectually blocked; and, as he discovered by the first attempt to return as he had come up, the least relaxation of his brace for that purpose would let him down with a run, and as certainly add another relic to the ruins of Thebes.

We must leave him here till the measures necessary for his relief, and an inquiry which is as necessary to extricate us from a difficulty of our own, are effected.

The figure of the vocal Memnon, as it is given in the books commonly accessible,—such as Chambers's Information for the People, Murray's Encyclopædia of Geography, and Frost's Ancient History,—show no sign of this lapstone or tablet, or, indeed, any other impediment to the continuous ascent of a climber who aims at reaching the lap of the sitting figure, when he has reached the position in which Dr. Kane touched the butt and boundary of his upward tending; and even the large and otherwise accurate drawing of Rosellini gives no hint of it. In his Memnon, as in the popular sketches, the hands lie spread upon the thighs, and the apron of the figure falls at least three feet short of covering the knees. So, the difficulty of finding the difficulty turned out to be almost equal to the alleged difficulty of surmounting it.

But the Denkmäler delivered us from the dilemma. There, as plain as any other feature of the statue, is the obstructing block,—neither an apron nor a lapstone exactly, but a tablet ten inches thick, jutting out flush with the knee-caps, but fixed *between* the knees, not lying on them. The end of this block is obviously quite beyond the reach of a man lying extended midway between the gigantic knees, and too thick to be clutched availably, if it were within the reach, and the climber could raise the courage, and run the risk of trusting to the grasp of one hand for his support and safe ascent by it.

The suspense of this explanation is a shorter one, and probably much less straining, than that which our adventurer had to endure; for he had to wait till a boatman mounted his horse, galloped away over the sands, and brought the Arab guide, who knew the backway ascent of the statue. But happily the messenger brought relief: the Arab climbed to the lap of the figure, and, planting himself firmly for a strong, steady pull, threw the end of his sash over the projecting stone and swung it in till the doctor grasped it, when, swinging himself out boldly, in the faith that a stout fellow could haul in a light one, he was drawn up safely, and then quietly descended by the customary pathway to the plain.

Quite unexpectedly, he had abundance of leisure to transcribe the inscriptions he was in search of,—if there were any; but, for reasons which we make bold to say were probably sufficient ones, he never reported any discoveries, or prospects of making any, likely to tempt future explorers to a rehearsal of his enterprise.

The visit to Egypt, and its engagements, like those of his residence in China, were concluded by an attack of the disease distinctive of the climate. This was his uniform experience in every grand tour of his life, as we shall see in the sequel. The anemometers, hygrometers, barometers, and thermometers of the scientific traveller are no better indicators and registers of climatology than the varied sensitiveness of the constitution he carried with him in all his journeyings.

Scarcely recovered from the plague, or well enough to travel, he set out for Greece in company with a lieutenant of the British army. From a mere scrap of a letter, it appears that he was at Athens on the 10th of June, 1845. He made the tour of Greece on foot, which, in consequence of his weakness, was a slow one; but the exercise was restorative, and he managed to visit all its scenes of ancient story and classic interest.

He left nothing of this trip behind him but a brief itinerary, and some memorials gathered by the way to present to his friends at home.

He went from Athens to Eleusis, thence to Platæa, to Leuctra, to Thebes, to Cheronæa, to Livadia; then to the top of Mount Helicon, and there cut a walking-stick from the brink of Hippocrene, which he brought home for his father, with the motto engraved upon the ring, *Fonte prolui Caballino*. Thence he passed on to Thermopylæ and the Zietoun Gulf, returned by Parnassus to the Delphic oracle at Castri, bathed in the fountain in which the Pythoness was wont of yore to plunge before she mounted the tripod to utter her thrice-sacred oracles, and descended to the plain by Galixidi and Salona, crossed the Gulf of Lepanto in an open boat, visited Megaspelion and Vostitza, traversed the Morea thoroughly, and then took a steamer from Patras for Trieste by the Adriatic Sea.

Here Germany and Switzerland lay before him. He travelled through both, and in the latter so carefully examined the glaciers of the Alps that his ice-theories of the Arctic regions are enriched with frequent and critical allusions to them.

On the 13th of July he was in Paris.

A letter of the doctor's from which we obtain this date discovers that at this time he was intent upon obtaining a license from the Spanish authorities to practise his profession at Manila, in the island of Luzon.

He had made three thousand dollars by his half-year's practice in China, and promised himself an outfit in cash, from a short term of practice among the Philippine Islands, which would give him a free foot for a tour of the world.

Six months had been spent in travel since he left Macao; and it is only now that he confesses how desperately ill he had been there, and how much he had endured in the interval.

The letter is an elaborate defence of his destiny against the solicitations of his family for his return and settlement at home. Its topics and tone are too deeply personal for publication; but we may be allowed to say of it that any page in it would amply justify the warmest admiration for his heroism, his feeling, and his authorship, that all his works and all his achievements have won for his memory.

He was a mere skeleton, he says, when he sailed from China, and his yearnings for home and his mother's nursing are poured out, pulsating with the heart-throbs of a hungering affection; yet he could not consent to surrender the plan of life to which he had so resolutely devoted himself.

This letter, moreover, discovers that he knew himself well, and that his life was not led by an irreflective impulse, but by a purpose as well considered as it was boldly resolved; and it is, moreover, a piece of characterization that might safely challenge a parallel among the gems of æsthetic literature.

He failed in his application to the Spanish authorities, or he yielded the purpose to other considerations; for he soon after passed over into Italy, and returned through France to England, and from England came home.

It will be seen how meagre our materials are for the history of his European travels. A scrap of this story appears in Mr. Snow's journal of the Prince Albert's expedition to the Arctic regions in 1850 in search of Sir John Franklin. The writer met Dr. Kane in Lancaster Sound, and gives him a place in his book. He says of him:—

"Dr. Kane, the surgeon, naturalist, journalist, etc. of the (first Grinnel) expedition, was of an exceedingly slim and apparently fragile form, with features, to all appearance, far better suited to a genial clime and to the comforts of a pleasant home than to the roughness and hardships of an Arctic voyage. I found that he had been in many parts of the world that I myself had visited, and in many others that I could only long to visit. There, in that cold, inhospitable, dreary region of everlasting ice and snow, did we again, in fancy, gallop over miles and miles of lands far distant, and far more joyous. Ever-smiling Italy, and its softening life; sturdy Switzerland, and its hardy sons; the Alps, the Apennines, France, Germany, India, Southern Africa. Then came Spain, Portugal, and my own England: next appeared Egypt, Syria, and the Desert. With all these he was personally familiar, in all these he had been a traveller. Rich in anecdote and full of pleasing talk, time flew rapidly as I conversed with him and partook of the hospitality offered me."

The range of this single trip was, however, something larger, as our readers will remember, than this catalogue of Mr. Snow records: Madeira, Brazil, Ceylon, Luzon, China, its islands, Borneo, Sumatra, Persia, Nubia, Sennaar, and Greece must be inserted into the round trip before it is completed; and at the time of these remembrances he had been in Mexico and in the West Indies, and had just then arrived out, by way of Nova Scotia, Newfoundland, and all Western Greenland, in Lancaster Sound, in latitude north on the Western hemisphere as high as civilized man had till then reached, and was at the time but thirty years of age!

At home through the winter of 1845–46, he must be busy, whether his ultimate purposes could be furthered by the occupation at hand or not. It is probable that, with his usual earnestness, and to give play to his restless energies, he, for the time the way seemed closed upon his travelling propensities, turned his ambition upon professional eminence, with a view to the practice of medicine and teaching as a lecturer in Philadelphia. He took a house in Walnut Street, and furnished an office in it with taste and elaborate care. With his medical brethren he kept a full round of engagements,— chemical, anatomical, quiz, and soirée.

It must be recollected that, although he had now been for nearly four years a titular assistant surgeon of the United States navy, he had not been commissioned and put upon the pay-roll.

His repugnance to the service was decided: it would not be too much to say he detested it. From his first cruise to the end of his voyaging he was always sea-sick in rough weather. But this was as nothing to the routine life of a subordinate to which it subjected him. The distinctions of rank which our naval service tolerates, without justifying, outraged his frank democracy of feeling. All manifestations of masterdom were abhorrent to him. He had no feeling that forbade the taking of human life; but he could not endure the bullying spirit which violates its common rights. An insult, or a blow that carries one with it, he regarded as worse than death if it must be passively endured. And it was just as hard for him to witness as to receive such indignities. There was nothing in him that fitted him for naval service except his capacity for the performance of its duties: its *régime* was his abhorrence. Yet now, when his family urged him to resign his official relations to it, he refused; for at this time there was a speck of war on the horizon, and he insisted that it would not be honorable for him to leave the navy with that chance impending.

Mr. Bancroft, Secretary of the Navy, intended to station him at the Navy-Yard or Naval Asylum of Philadelphia; but, upon an intimation from the head of the Surgical Bureau, that, according to the etiquette of the service, this post should be given to some one his senior in rank, he put himself upon the roll of the Department, "waiting orders,"—curtly justifying himself for the decision with—"What else does the country pay so many idle louts in time of peace for?"

The order came three weeks before Congress declared that "war with Mexico already existed by the act of that power;" but it was to the coast of Africa, in the frigate United States, under Commodore Reed, that he was despatched. This was, as he would phrase it, bitterly bitter to him. It was to the active service of the expected *war* that he looked when he put himself under marching-orders; but he was too proud to retract his submission, or by a word attempt to modify his destination, although it would have required but little beyond his own consent to have it effected. For, in the greatest as in the smallest actions and interests of his life, he stood unflinchingly the hazards of the die which he voluntarily cast: a purpose of his, once fixed, was his fate. *He* never reconsidered or amended a resolution after he had passed it through the forms of enactment.

The vessel sailed about the 25th of May, 1846. In the middle of June it reached Cape Verd.

When the doctor was at Brazil in 1843, he had made the acquaintance of the famous Da Souza, a Portuguese merchant largely engaged in the slave-trade, and, in return for some professional services, received from him introductory letters to his commercial representatives on the Coast. Presenting these letters when ashore with a party of officers, he was entertained with very liberal hospitality, and admitted to the freest confidence that his position would allow him to accept.

He availed himself of the facilities which he could command to visit the slave-factories from Cape Mount to the river Bonny in the Gulf of Guinea.

While the frigate lay in harbor, a caravan was ready to set out from one of those factories on the coast for Dahomey, the great slave-mart of the interior, carrying a magnificent tribute of jewelry and ornate furniture from the factory to his sable majesty. Dr. Kane procured the commodore's permission to join the party, and, it seems, became quite a favorite with the sovereign while the embassy remained at court. A semi-diadem of feathers, and a number of baskets decorated with the royal crimson dye, which are still preserved at Fern Rock, were among the testimonials of regard which he brought home with him.

Notwithstanding all the courtesies received and the impressions they were intended to make, the recollections of the highly-favored guest were not, on the whole, complimentary.

The monarch of Dahomey, in his report, was every inch a king,—as magnificent as the best of them in his retinue, and somewhat more opulent in wives and absolute in authority. A pattern of a prince was he, and a worthy successor of that illustrious predecessor of his, of happy memory, who received an English traveller sitting naked upon a tiger-skin, greased all over with palm-oil and powdered with gold-dust, his hand resting upon a skull, while his poet-laureate sang a birthday ode which is freely rendered thus :—

> " Ho, tam-a-rama bo now,
> Sam-a-rambo jug!
> Hurrah for the son of the sun!
> Hurrah for the brother of the moon!
> Buffalo of buffaloes, and bull of bulls!
> He sits on a throne of his enemies' skulls;
> And, if he wants more to play at football,
> Ours are at his service,—all, all, all."

His majesty, magnificent and munificent in all things royal, amused himself occasionally, or oftener, with cutting off his enemies' heads,—and sometimes his courtiers', with or without reason, and about as rightfully, perhaps, as the same things are done elsewhere for what are called "reasons of state." His munificence was in feathers and baubles, and the favors of his harem, dispensed to such of his worthy guests as had the taste to accept them.

The manner of selecting his host of sultanas was

right royal: applying the Norman doctrine of *tenure* in the lands of England to the ladies, the entire sex of his realm, by a species of domesday practice, the women of Dahomey are annually mustered, the king seizes a few hundreds of them in right of eminent domain, and grants the refuse to his grandees in fee of knight-service, which they are bound to receive with the most humble gratitude.

Nor is his majesty a whit behind the most renowned of his craft as a killer. The large court-yard near the palatial shanty was literally covered with skulls, the memorials of his sabre-skill; and it was only at the pressing solicitation of his christian visitors that he adjourned an exhibition of his prowess in that line.

Dr. Kane returned from Dahomey with the impression that, whatever may have been the case in the early periods of the trade, the slaves that are driven to the coast for shipment may very well congratulate themselves upon the commutation of their fate, even with the "middle passage" before them. Indeed, he believed that the predatory wars of Inner Africa, though now stimulated in some degree by the cupidity of the chieftains, had their origin in a dark fanaticism that sought for prisoners as victims for sacrifice. He was convinced that very many of those whom he saw caged in Dahomey were too young and too infirm to be merchantable.

It is well known that they have two annual festivals of slaughter, in which the king and chief men propitiate the manes of their ancestors by a crowd of victims.

The walls of the palace and, temples are ornamented with skulls; the king has his sleeping-apartment paved with them; and war and glory, after the manner of kingship, are grander and even more merciless with him, as they are elsewhere, than the passion for foreign traffic.

Dr. Kane had not been long on the coast when the pestilence of that region made its appearance on board the frigate. "I am sitting," he writes, "in my little cockpit state-room. Fumes of mouldy boots and molasses are exuding from the dirty deck below me; and heaven's breath comes to me through a long canvas tube. This grateful conductor of vitality is called a wind-sail. Its funnel has been pointed opposite my kennel, and I am thankfully enjoying the wet-towel smell of the scanty breeze. The jaundiced-looking spermaceti candle on my table has been gasping so at the scanty oxygen that I have even put it out of its misery, and I am writing by the beams of the hatchway-lantern. The weather above is rainy, and it is night there as well as here. The thermometer is at eighty-five degrees. Our voyage from the Cape de Verds,—oh! that sleepy period of stagnation,—it was a nearly continuous calm. Six cases of the dreaded fever broke out before we had been a week from port; and I am now in the midst of the true responsibilities of a navy surgeon. We are on our way south. A London homeward-bound may deliver this note: if so, let it assure you of my continued health and determination to make the best of my bad bargain.

Tell mother not to be uneasy. The fever is not contagious, and one never loses by attention to duty."

In less than three months after this he was himself prostrated by the "coast-fever." His attack was exceedingly severe. For three weeks the active virulence of the disease held on without check: in three weeks more he was only strong enough to allow of his being lowered over the ship's side and sent home in one of the Liberia transport-vessels.

A letter of Dr. Dillard, the fleet-surgeon, written at the port of St. Jago, one of the Cape de Verd Islands, to one of the doctor's friends, serves a purpose which warrants its insertion here.

(COPY.)

"U. S. FRIGATE UNITED STATES,
PORTO PRAYA, March 9, 1847.

"Dr. Kane returns home on account of ill health. His disease was the *coast-fever*, and the attack exceedingly severe. It manifested itself on the 1st of February, and continued with unmitigated violence for ten days. The abatement of the fever was not then complete, but greatly diminished, and finally left the patient on the twenty-first day worn out and exhausted. His recovery and convalescence have been slow, his present prostration and debility great. He gains strength tardily; and I fear that if he be kept in this baleful climate he may relapse and die, or suffer in his constitution. Under this view I have thought it best to send him home. He goes in the 'Chesapeake and Liberian Packet,'—a new and comfortable ship,—and will have every possible attention extended to him. May he soon reach his country and rejoin his family in renewed health! God bless him!

"I part with him with regret, and shall miss him much. I lose not only a useful and necessary assistant, but a valued and esteemed young friend. Our association, both official and social, has been of the pleasantest kind. Very truly, your obedient servant,

"T. DILLARD."

To this attack of the coast-fever he was accustomed ever afterward to ascribe the most serious breach that disease had made in his constitution. He carried this feeling with him to the last as a complaint against the administration which condemned him to a field of service ill suited to his constitution and his aspirations.

CHAPTER VII.

A SUMMER OF SUFFERING—OPPORTUNITY LOST—THE LAST CHANCE SEIZED—DESPATCHED TO MEXICO—SHIPWRECK IN THE GULF—THE SPY-COMPANY—AFFAIR AT NOPALUCA—RESCUE OF HIS PRISONERS— HARD FIGHTING AND ROUGH SURGERY—WOUNDED—TYPHUS FEVER —NEWSPAPER HISTORY—SURFEIT OF PATRIOTISM—IRKSOMENESS OF THE LIVERY—CHARGES AGAINST DOMINGUES—THE HORSE-CLAIM— —HOW IT WAS PROVED, AND WHAT IT PROVED—GRATITUDE OF HIS PRISONERS.

DR. KANE reached Philadelphia on the 6th of April, 1847, a broken-down man. He had sailed for the pestilential coast of Africa ten months before, with a reluctance that nothing but a despotic self-government could have subdued. He returned in the condition and with the feeling of a sacrificed man. Knowing that he held his life by the most precarious tenure, and certain that it must be a short one, he yearned to crowd it with activities which might compensate by their worthiness for its brevity. His opportunity seemed now to have escaped him; and the weary weeks of the ensuing confinement in his sick-room were among the worst for him of his hard lifetime. The arm of the service to which

A SUMMER OF SUFFERING. 109

he was attached, and which was odious to him except for such opportunities of adventure and patriotic service as it offered to him, had, while he was absent, entirely performed its share of duty in the Mexican War. Both on the Pacific and in the Gulf, all the strongholds of the enemy against which the navy could be engaged had been reduced, and there was nothing that he desired left for him to expect in the routine of the chances which it offered.

He *must* repair his hopes; and he made the endeavor with an almost desperate tenacity of purpose. As soon as his strength permitted him to travel, and long before his physician and his family had recognised his convalescence, he hurried off to Washington for the purpose of soliciting a transfer of his commission to the military staff, or, if that might not be, a position in the line of the army. He had secured letters from the Governor of Pennsylvania, and from other influential friends of the President, enforcing his application, and he would have been successful; but his health gave way again, and he remained for some weeks dangerously ill at the seat of Government.

One more long term of watching and nursing gave his mother the companionship of her son, under the only conditions in which she had ever enjoyed it since his infancy; and, under her care, by the ensuing month of October he was able to meet his friends again.

One Saturday night, at the close of the month, he attended the Wistar party at his father's house, and passed the evening as if its enjoyments sufficed him. The company congratulated him upon the prospect of a speedy and complete recovery from his long illness: many good wishes and much good advice were bestowed upon the valetudinary, and the festivities went on as if his prudence could be relied upon and all solicitude might now be discarded, for he looked just as if he were clearly pledged to a conformable behavior. But he was missed at the close of the entertainment, which was readily accounted for by the supposition that he had crossed the street to escape the fatigue of late hours, and would spend the night in the quiet which he needed.

He did not return till the middle of the week. He had taken the night train for Washington City, effected his object there, and announced to his friends that he was under orders for the seat of war.

He had pressed his application for worthier service upon the President, and enforced it by the complaint which he had to make of his African appointment. Mr. Polk afterward said that he had this in his mind when he gave him the opportunity of seeing service in Mexico.

The city of Mexico had surrendered a month before to General Scott; but Colonel Childs was at the time besieged in Puebla, and the communication of the commander-in-chief with the Gulf coast was otherwise interrupted by the presence and hostilities of the enemy.

An important despatch which had been forwarded in triplicate by the Secretary of War had each time failed, or its reception at head-quarters had not been acknowledged; and the President had resolved to confide it orally to Dr. Kane, who engaged to thread his way to the Mexican capital as best he might.

He was charged, besides, with orders from the chiefs of the medical staff of the army and navy.*

---

* These orders ran thus :—

"NAVY DEPARTMENT, BUREAU OF MEDICINE AND SURGERY,}
November 5, 1847.

"SIR :—I take the opportunity afforded by your departure for the seat of war under special orders from this Department, to urge upon you the necessity and advantage of collating and preserving such facts relating to field and hospital organization, and especially such surgical cases and statistics, as may come under your observation; and it is my wish that you make a full and accurate report of all such information to this Bureau.

"Respectfully, T. HARRIS,
"*Chief of Bureau of Medicine and Surgery.*"
"Assistant Surgeon E. K. KANE, U.S.N."

"SURGEON-GENERAL'S OFFICE, November 5, 1847.
"*To the Officers of the Medical Department serving in Mexico.*
"GENTLEMEN :—The bearer of this—Dr. Kane, of the navy—impelled by a laudable zeal for professional improvement, and a desire to participate in active field-service, has obtained an order from the Secretary of the Navy to proceed to the head-quarters of the main army and report to the commanding general for duty.

"Dr. Kane is instructed to visit the general and field hospitals, &c. on his route; and I feel assured that the courtesy of the medical staff in the army will afford him all the facilities necessary to promote the objects he may have in view.

"I beg leave to commend him to your friendly consideration.

"I have the honor to be, very respectfully, your obedient servant,
"H. L. HEISKILL, *Acting Surgeon-General.*"

With these official and numerous private letters from Washington friends, he set out on the 6th of November for Mexico. On his way he procured a horse, bred by Colonel Shirley, of Kentucky, every way worthy of the adventurous service which lay before him. The doctor was a brilliant horseman, and no knight-errant could have been better matched with a charger. He bore his master bravely through a hotly-contested fight; and in a very curious way, by a posthumous service, he has been as serviceable to that master's biographer in a field as stoutly debated. If the reader knew exactly how we have been beleaguered, he would see clearly how the "gallant gray" bears his friends through a guerilla skirmish.

The horse and his rider reached New Orleans on the 22d, and sailed for Vera Cruz, in the United States steamer Fashion, on the 23d. Their companions were a mixed multitude,—ladies, officers, gentlemen, volunteer soldiers, followers of the camp, horses, and all the lumber of military equipage. Colonel Seymour, of the Georgia regiment, and Major Roth, of the volunteers, then holding a subordinate rank, were among the passengers.

They had a rough time of it in the Gulf,—encountered one of its severest northers, and were for some days in imminent peril. Their bulwarks were stove, the hull strained badly, and the pumps all broken or choked. The doctor took a very active part in backing the deck-load of dragoon-horses overboard, and was in the act of

ARRIVAL IN MEXICO. 113

immolating his own noble steed, when he was respited by the solicitations of some officers, whose admiration the fine points of the animal had secured. He escaped the submersion, and had his name changed, *in memoriam*, on the spot, from Tom to Relic.

The gale continued: the steamer was sinking; scuttle-holes were cut in her deck, and all hands were employed, under Dr. Kane's supervision, in baling below-decks with camp-kettles. The storm had scarcely even moderated when, driving before it, the Fashion passed between two sets of reefs and found herself near the Castle of San Juan. It was a miraculous escape; for she had no other access to port, and she could not have survived outside.

Landing at Vera Cruz, Dr. Kane learned that a corps of the army, under General Armstrong, of Tennessee, had moved to the interior a few days before. He passed a single night, or part of the night, after landing, and then, with a party of officers who had been prevented from accompanying their regiments, galloped off through the enemy's defiles to overtake their columns. They reached the marching body in safety, and moved on with it as far as Perote.

The rest of this story is so full of the romantic as to require a close shelter for its facts under the authentic data in our possession. We must go roughly, that we may get safely through it.

Dr. George E. Cooper, assistant surgeon of the United States army, writing at Philadelphia, December 1, 1848,

8

says, "When stationed in the castle of Perote in the month of January, 1848, I was visited by Dr. Elisha K. Kane, of the United States navy, who was then *en route* for the city of Mexico, being, as I learned from him, the bearer of despatches from our Government to the commander-in-chief. He was unable to proceed on his journey, for want of an escort, and remained with me until the contra-guerillas or spy-company, commanded by Colonel Domingues, arrived at the town of Perote *en route* for the capital. The doctor had with him at the castle of Perote a full-blooded gray gelding, the finest animal I ever saw in the Republic of Mexico. When the doctor left the castle to pursue his journey, I accompanied him on the Puebla Road until we overtook the rear-guard of the spy-company, which had started some short time before us."

This, as appears from other sources, was on the 3d of January. Immediately before this date, a scrap of a letter written by Dr. Kane on a piece of cartridge-paper, (which, however, was not received in Philadelphia until long after the period of anxiety for his fate had passed,) says, "I have determined to trust myself to the tender mercies of the renegade spy-company, Colonel Domingues, and thus reach Mexico (the city) in time for reputation or not at all."

On the 6th, at a place near Nopaluca, and about twenty-five miles from Puebla, the escort—about one hundred and twenty mounted lancers, all Mexican skinners, bandits, and traitors—encountered a body of

AFFAIR AT NOPALUCA. 115

Mexican guerillas who were escorting a number of Mexican officers to Orizaba, among whom were Major-General Gaona, former Governor of Puebla, his son and aide-de-camp Maximilian, General Torrejon, who led the charge at Buena Vista, and others of less note.

The conflict which ensued was short but severe. Generals Gaona and Torrejon, Colonel Gaona, with two captains and thirty-eight rank and file of the Mexican party, were taken prisoners.

In the first notice of this affair which reached Philadelphia, published in "The Pennsylvanian" of the 8th February, 1848, it was stated that "*Dr. Kenny* comes up (to Puebla) with the escort as bearer of despatches from Washington to General Scott." Dr. Kane's friends at this time knew nothing of his connection with the spy-company, and were not alarmed for his safety. The earliest news in which his name was correctly given was in the "Pennsylvania Inquirer," written at Puebla, January 17, postmarked at New Orleans, February 18. It ran thus:—

"The encounter was quite unexpected; and they did not see each other until within twenty or thirty yards of the advance on either side, as they were at the same time ascending the opposite sides of a steep hill, and met upon the top. After a sharp encounter, which lasted but a few minutes, the spy-company, having killed three or four privates, and wounded Colonel Gaona with a lance in the lungs, and a major with a ball through the thighs, succeeded in making prisoners General Torrejon, General

Gaona, two colonels, three majors, and thirty-eight privates.

"But for the gallantry and magnanimous exertions of Dr. Kane, they would have killed General Gaona, the father of the colonel of that name, and several other officers. Dr. Kane, with the utmost intrepidity, rode from one to another of the spy-company, ordering them to give quarter to all. Dr. Kane is still at the house of General Gaona, who said yesterday to Colonel Childs, the Governor of Puebla, when he called on the illustrious prisoners who are quartered with Colonel Gaona at the palace, that he owed his life to Dr. Kane, and would be glad at any time to die for him. General Torrejon said that he too owed him his life; and so did others of the officers."

In "The Pennsylvanian" of the 24th of March, 1848, the following account of the Nopaluca affair appeared:—

"It seems that in anticipation of the American attack upon Orizaba, since signally successful, a column of Mexicans was hastening to reinforce that place, a considerable distance in advance of which rode on their way a bevy of distinguished officers with a troop of lancers. Dr. Kane and his escort, hastening to the city of Mexico with important despatches, encountered these on the high-road near Nopaluca, about thirty miles distant from Puebla.

"It is not clear to us how the doctor ranked in the party, which was the contra-guerilla or Mexican spy-company of the notorious Domingues; but it appears

RESCUE OF PRISONERS.

that it was at his instance, if not at his order, that they engaged the enemy. The two corps met at the summit of a steep hill, which the escort reached a moment in advance of the Mexicans. The affair was brilliant but brief. The Americo-Mexicans evidently fought with the reckless bravery of men who knew that halters were hanging ready for them if taken. A few of their foes escaped,—a colonel and two captains among the number: the rest were either killed or captured, and carried to Puebla. It is some satisfaction to learn definitely that General Torrejon, who led the Buena Vista charge,— the Torrejon who has been reported out of harm's way so often,—is one of the prisoners."

This is the sum of the military report of the matter: now for that which smacks of romance.

"At one period of the charge, when Dr. Kane was some distance ahead of the rest of his company, his fine horse carried him in between a spirited young major and his orderly, who fell upon him at the same moment. The lance of the latter failed at the thrust, except so far as to inflict a slight flesh-wound upon the doctor, who, being able to parry the major's sabre-cut, ran that officer through the bowels. The fight over, Dr. Kane was attending to his own hurts, when the poor wounded youth seized him by his arm, crying, 'Father! my father! save my father!' The renegade Mexicans, having determined to slaughter their prisoners, had commenced operations by attacking their chief man, an aged person, who had surrendered to Dr. Kane. He was at the moment defending himself, bare-headed and unarmed, against his assailants. Dr. Kane saved him and numerous others; but it appears that he did so with great efforts, and at considerable personal risk."

A writer at Puebla, in the "Inquirer," under date of the 26th January, says, " He parried four sabre-cuts that were made at him, and did not succeed in enforcing obedience to his orders until he had drawn his six-shooter—which all Mexicans hold in mortal dread—and fired at Colonel Domingues, the commander of the squadron; and the doctor received a thrust from a lance in the lower part of his abdomen. They also killed his horse."

The correspondent of "The Pennsylvanian" continues:—

" As soon as the old general was rescued, he sat down by the side of the major, his son, to comfort his last painful moments. When the doctor observed that that individual was bleeding to death from an artery in the groin, he made an effort in his behalf. With the bent prong of a table-fork he took up the artery and tied it with a ravel of packthread, and the rude surgical operation was perfectly successful.

" When they all arrived safely at Puebla, the gratitude of the Mexicans saved was extravagant. They publicly declared to Colonel Childs, the American Governor of Puebla, that they owed their lives to Dr. Kane; and the governor thereupon returned him thanks for his gallantry and humanity. General Gaona proffered him the choice of his stables to replace his Kentucky stallion untimely butchered in the conflict, and some sort of honorary festival was in preparation, when the doctor, from the effect of the wound in the abdomen, joined, probably, to great physical exhaustion, fell deadly sick. His disease took the form of Calentura typhoidea,—the worst of typhus,—and, after lying in a state of insensibility for twelve days, symptoms of approaching dissolution made their appearance, and he was given over by his medical assistants. . . . .

"His life was spared through the gratitude of the noble old Spaniard who owed his own to him. On the second day of Dr. Kane's illness he insisted upon carrying him to his own princely residence, and gave him the benefit of every comfort and luxury which a refined sensibility could suggest and ample means provided. The general, with his distinguished lady and accomplished daughters, took upon themselves all the offices of menials, suffering the care of nursing and attending him to be shared only by the physicians, four of whom they had in waiting night and day."

We have given these newspaper-reports of the affair at Nopaluca for the substance of truth there is in them, because we have no narrative of the incidents from the principal actor himself. Once only in all our personal intercourse the skirmish of that 6th of January was alluded to, and then only to correct one of the exaggerations of his surgical service to young Gaona. He said, "His wound was not in the groin: it was in the chest; and the artery was one of the intercostals."

By way of necessary explanation, I may as well say here, where it is most required, that he never stood questioning on his own achievements, and he could not be ransacked by the most adroit endeavors of even a warrantable curiosity. He has scores of times turned me from the narrative of his experiences to such points of scientific interest as they suggested. He never would "sit" a moment still under scrutiny, or allow *himself* to be the subject of conversation.

This fight with the Mexican generals and their escort, and the subsequent struggle with his own scoundrels, was of all others the very one on which he was indisposed to speak. His personal involvement, his danger, and the resulting suffering, which put him under the deepest obligations for personal kindness to the very party to whom he had been in the same hour a foe at sword-point and a friend at even greater risk, and afterwards an object of care and solicitude for so many weary days, mixed his emotions only too painfully for agreeable reflection. Moreover, he had been in Mexico long enough, and was too well acquainted with the men and events of the last winter of that war to feel comfortable under the reflection that either his country or himself had any thing to answer for concerning it.

If he had lived a century after that experience, he would not have been caught doing any more patriotism, unless it had first been warranted well principled, and its governing councils were somewhat more intent upon manly service to the country than the promotion of their

CHARGES AGAINST DOMINGUES. 121

own paltry interests. His after-life fairly expressed this feeling, for it was resolutely guided by it. He never sought or enjoyed a particle of Government favor from that time till the end of his career.

All that we have from himself on this matter comes indirectly but clearly enough from a formal charge which he made against Domingues for criminal maltreatment of his prisoners, and from the testimony with which he fortified his claim upon the War Department for compensation for his horse killed in the defence which he made for those prisoners against the murderous assault of Domingues and his bandits.

The statements of fact made in these documents were carefully prepared from the testimony ready for their legal proof.

The accusation against Domingues was made to General Butler, then acting commander-in-chief: General Scott had been superseded a month before its date. It ran thus:—

"CITY OF MEXICO, March 14, 1848.

"SIR:—On the 6th of January, while proceeding to the city of Mexico, accompanied by an escort of lancers under command of Colonel Domingues, we fell in with a body of Mexican troops near Nopaluca.

" In the action which ensued, Generals Gaona and Torrejon, Major Gaona, and two captains, were taken prisoners, together with thirty-eight rank and file. I would now respectfully submit to your notice the following facts, which I am able to sustain by satisfactory testimony,—viz.:

"I. That, after the formal surrender of the Mexican party, Domingues, with his Lieutenants Pallasios, Rocher, and others, did, in cold blood, attempt to sabre the prisoners.

"II. That an American officer, upon interposing his person and horse, was similarly menaced and assaulted,— receiving thereby an injury of a most serious character and losing a valuable animal."

[The remaining charges were for robbing the prisoners of their personal effects, and afterwards exposing them to cruel and ignominious treatment on their way to Puebla; and for a second attempt to shoot them, thirty-six hours after the surrender, which was prevented only by a resolute resistance, which succeeded by intimidating the ruffians without resort to force.

The accusation concludes by demanding the punishment of the colonel and the restoration of the stolen property.]

(Signed,) "E. K. KANE,
"*Marine Detachment.*"

The horse-claim furnishes us with the rest of the authentic data in our possession.

Dr. Kane writes to the Secretary of War under date of

"PHILADELPHIA, July 21, 1848.

"SIR:—I left Perote fortress on the 3d of January, 1848, under orders to report to General Scott at the city of Mexico. My escort consisted of a party of

THE HORSE-CLAIM.

lancers, Mexicans in the pay of the United States, commanded by Colonel Domingues.

"On the 6th of January, at a place intermediate to Ojo de Agua and Nopaluca, some twenty-five miles from Puebla, we encountered a body of Mexicans escorting Generals Gaona and Torrejon and other officers. After a short action, we succeeded in routing them, taking forty-four prisoners. Circumstances having made the two generals my personal prisoners, they claimed my special protection against Domingues's band, who sought to kill them after the surrender; and in the effort to shield them against a charging party, headed by Lieutenant Rocher, I received a severe wound from a lance in the region of the bladder, my horse having immediately before been struck down by a lance under the shoulder from the same party.

"I succeeded in raising him up and keeping him till we reached Nopaluca, when he sank from exhaustion. I was transferred to another animal, but, finding myself unable to ride, was placed in a Mexican car with the rest of the wounded.

"My horse was forced along with difficulty by my servant; but, becoming uncontrollable while making an effort to drink at one of the fountains or shallow wells of the country, in the Barris San Miguel, he was so far precipitated into it as from his weakness to be unable to recover.

"In company with Lieutenant Foster, I saw his body there at the halt. This was on the 7th.

"On reaching Puebla, I was attacked very dangerously by congestive typhus fever, in consequence of my wound and the exposure which followed it.

" My certificate, and the affidavit of Lieutenant Foster which accompanies it, were made at the suggestion of Major Morris, of the artillery,—then acting as judge advocate,—as soon as I was able to write.

" My condition at the time may serve as the apology for the brevity and want of detail of those papers.

" I was subsequently carried in a wagon to the city of Mexico, where I reported, and, having been inspected by the surgeons, was ordered to the United States as invalided. I therefore saw little of Lieutenant Foster after our interview at Puebla, and, his corps having been disbanded, I do not know his residence. He belonged to the Louisiana mounted men, Captain Lewis's company. I am unable for this reason to procure a supplemental affidavit from him, and he was the only American officer on the field with me; but I shall transmit copies of this letter to the principal officers of the United States whom I found in command at Puebla, and shall write them to verify such of the facts as have come to their knowledge either from personal observation or official position.

"I have the honor to be, sir,

"Your most obedient servant,

"Elisha K. Kane,"

" To the Honorable Secretary of War."

In answer to Dr. Kane's circular, spoken of in this

letter to Mr. Marcy, Mr. Morris, at the time (September 13, 1848) residing in New Castle, Delaware, writes:—

" . . . Whilst I was in the Government Palaca Puebla as judge advocate, Lieutenant Foster made oath before me of the fact of your losing your horse at San Miguel in consequence of a lance-wound received in an engagement with the enemy which took place between Ojo de Agua and Nopaluca. Previous to that affidavit, General Gaona, in giving me an account of the battle, had stated that through your instrumentality alone he and General Torrejon were saved from the cold-blooded butchery of Domingues's band; that the engagement was a severe though short one; and your own sufferings in consequence of the wound you received in your exposure whilst shielding the generals are facts publicly understood at Puebla.

"The circumstance of there having been no regular official report must be accounted for by the known character of the commander of our troops on that occasion; but this omission, as I look upon it, has nothing to do with your loss. The horse was positively known to have been killed by hostile Mexicans, and, if not in pitched battle, the case loses none of its weight from that circumstance. I knew the animal well, and his value was full six hundred dollars. He would readily have brought that sum, if not more, at even a forced sale."

Dr. A. B. Campbell, assistant surgeon United States Volunteers, under date Philadelphia, November 3, 1848, answers the circular:—" In reply to your inquiry as to my knowledge of the circumstances of the loss of your horse, I can and do certify, on honor, that I visited you daily during the time you lay sick at the house of General Gaona with typhus fever, the result of the wound received in the action with the Mexicans in the before-mentioned engagement, which occurred near Nopaluca on the 7th of January last; and, moreover, that both during the time of your illness, and subsequently, I have heard both Generals Gaona and Torrejon refer to the fact that your horse had been killed by a lance-wound in the action, and they expressed regret that a person to whom they owed their lives should have met with so severe a loss.

"Colonel Gaona, who was dangerously wounded in the same engagement, repeatedly described to me the proud, prancing position of your horse when he was pierced by the lance. Indeed, the circumstances of his death were matters of town-talk in Puebla, and their omission in the official reports is only to be accounted for by the debased character of Domingues."

The testimony of Assistant Surgeon G. E. Cooper, United States army, is to the same effect, and as full.

CHAPTER VIII.

COLONEL CHILDS' LETTER—COMPLIMENT TO GENERAL GAONA—HIS REPLY—"THE FLAG OF FREEDOM"—COMPLIMENTARY SWORD—DR. KANE'S ACCEPTANCE—COLONEL GAONA'S WOUND—DR. KANE'S PRISONERS—PALASIOS SHOT—DOMINGUES MISSED—HAND-TO-HAND CONFLICT—LOSS AND GAIN UPON "RELIC"—TO HEAD-QUARTERS —INVALIDED—HOMEWARD—DESPONDENCY—BUREAU-FAVOR REFRACTED—TREAD-MILL RÉGIME—TO THE MEDITERRANEAN—LOCK-JAW—DYING EXPERIENCE—RECUPERATION—COAST-SURVEY—AN INTERLUDE—LADY FRANKLIN'S APPEAL—AMERICAN RESPONSE—DR. KANE VOLUNTEERS—AMBITION'S LAST GASP—AMUSEMENT AND OTHER REFRESHMENTS—OFF TO THE ARCTIC.

THE young countrymen of our hero, for whom this biography is principally intended, would not be satisfied with a less carefully authenticated narrative of the affair at Nopaluca, nor would their interest in it be gratified with less detail than we are indulging. It deserves to be written in the tone of its own purely chivalric spirit; but Dr. Kane, as a boy and as a man, living and surviving, was and is a doer of things, a worker in facts; and no one that loves him may violate his own simple, manly taste in reporting him.

At Puebla, upon the spot where the facts were best known, and seven weeks after the occurrence, when the incidents had full time to settle into certainty, the best authorities add their testimony to the facts of this story and record their understanding of them.

Colonel Childs, American Commandant at Puebla, to General Gaona.

"OFFICE OF THE CIVIL AND MILITARY GOVERNOR,
PUEBLA, February 9, 1848.

" GENERAL :—For more than thirty days I have been an eye-witness to the kind and affectionate treatment of yourself and amiable family to Surgeon Kane, of the United States navy, bearer of despatches to the general-in-chief.

" In the name of the general-in-chief of the American army, and especially in the name of the Secretary of the Navy of the United States of America, to whose arm of the service this officer more particularly belongs, I give you my most sincere thanks.

"It appears that Dr. Kane, of the United States navy, was marching under an escort of a native spy-company, when a detachment of Mexicans who were escorting you fell in with said company; that a fight immediately ensued, resulting in the capture of several Mexican officers; yourself and your son, Major Gaona, were of the number of the captives, the latter severely, and for a time considered mortally, wounded,—possibly by the hands of the officer to whom you extended such noble hospitality. It further appears that this officer, after the excitement of the battle was over, and you and your comrades were prisoners of war, interposed his person to save the lives of the captured officers; that in doing so he received from one of the spy-company a severe blow in the side with the butt of a lance, and that the blow, together with the excessive fatigue, produced the sickness that came so near terminating his earthly career; that while smarting under the circumstances which occasioned your capture, as was feared, a mortal wound to your son, and you at the same time a close prisoner, insisted on Dr. Kane being taken to your house, where he was attended by your amiable and accomplished wife and daughters with all the affection that parental kindness and sisterly love could dictate. To this assiduous attention, smiled upon by a kind Providence, Dr. Kane is indebted for the pleasing anticipation of speedily being restored to the service of his country and to the arms of an affectionate family.

"To this noble and magnanimous conduct on your part, I know that I but faintly meet the responses of the general-in-chief, and the Government of my country, when I say that yourself and son are released from your paroles unconditionally, and are at liberty to remain in Puebla or to go wherever else it may be your pleasure.

"As the commander of the department of Puebla, I tender you my personal thanks, consideration, and esteem, and have the honor to be your most obedient servant,

"THOMAS CHILDS,

"*Colonel U. S. Army, Com'g Depart. of Puebla.*
" To Brig. Gen'l ANTONIO GAONA,
 Mexican Army, Puebla."

TRANSLATION OF GENERAL GAONA'S ANSWER.

"PUEBLA, February 12, 1848.

"COLONEL:—In due reply to the very courteous and kind note of your Excellency under date of the 9th inst., I am bound to say that, in receiving Dr. Kane into our dwelling and affording him the aid which the lamentable state of his health required, I did nothing more than to comply with the duties of hospitality and gratitude; for most assuredly I shall always most gratefully acknowledge the inestimable services rendered by Dr. Kane to myself and those of my company, in saving our lives when his escort threatened us with death after taking us prisoners.

"I offer a thousand thanks to Divine Providence for saving the life of the much-esteemed Dr. Kane; for the opposite result would have been a most deplorable and fatal blow to myself and my family, who are now rejoicing in the expectation that ere long, as you say, he may once more have the gratification of embracing his excellent family, and being restored to the usefulness for which his conduct has proved him fit in the service of his nation, which, it is to be hoped, will continue as grateful towards Dr. Kane as I shall ever feel to him, as well as I shall to the general commander-in-chief and the Government of the United States for the distinguished and unparalleled favor with which it has been pleased to honor me. Tendering at the same time, also, to your Excellency, with all the warmth of my heart, unbounded thanks for your kind intervention in the matter, praying you to communicate the same to his Excellency, with my sincere gratitude, and also to the distinguished officers of your garrison, from whom I have received so many attentions, and placing in the mean time at your disposition my person and best services, allow me especially, and with the greatest pleasure, to tender to your Excellency assurances of the grateful attachment with which I have the honor to subscribe myself

"Your obedient servant,

"ANTONIO GAONA.

"*Senior Colonel of the Army of the United States of the North, Commandant of the Dept. of Puebla,*

"Don THOMAS CHILDS."

This correspondence was first published in "The Flag of Freedom,"—a little army gazette issued every Saturday in Puebla for the use of the American troops while they occupied the place. It was first republished in the United States in the "Doylestown (Pennsylvania) Democrat," at the instance of a returned volunteer, who, in his note to the editor, says, among other things, "I am personally knowing to the facts which led to the correspondence. Dr. Kane, justly the hero of the letter, is a son of Judge Kane, of Philadelphia, a surgeon of the United States navy, than whom a braver and better officer does not live." "The Flag of Freedom" has also an editorial note upon the correspondence, endorsing the commendation of Dr. Kane's chivalric service to his Mexican prisoners, and their gratitude to him, and applauding the handsome acknowledgment by Colonel Childs.

The Wistar party which he surprised by his desertion in the midst of their festivities in the autumn of 1847, when he left them for Washington City and wrenched from the President the last chance for distinguished service in the Mexican campaign, had a more pleasing surprise when they met a year afterwards, reinforced by the most distinguished citizens of Philadelphia, to honor the gallant and generous improvement he had made of the slender opportunity which the appointment had afforded. More than seventy gentlemen of the city, the popularly-accredited representatives and exponents of its spirit and feelings, signalized their appreciation of their young townsman's achievement in the manner which the following correspondence displays:—

"PHILADELPHIA, February 8, 1849.

"To Dr. ELISHA KENT KANE, *United States Navy:*

"DEAR SIR:—We are honored in being permitted by your friends and fellow-citizens of Philadelphia to offer in their name, for your acceptance, the accompanying sword.

"This modest testimonial is tendered as a record of their high appreciation of your conduct in the service of our country, whose proud boast is that their sons, in every grade, have proved themselves gloriously prompt

COMPLIMENTARY SWORD. 133

in every emergency. Your casual encounter with the enemy in the Mexican campaign, as romantic as unexpected, was crowned, as an incidental exploit, with the distinction due to gallantry, skill, and success, and was hallowed in the flush of victory by the noblest humanity to the vanquished.

"The eloquent gratitude of your prisoners, and the honorable approval of your superior, will be found in the archives of your country; and those who surround your own home in your native city claim to record their sense of your courage, conduct, and humanity in the memorial now offered.

"With cordial wishes for your happiness in life and your preservation to the service you adorn, we have the honor to be

"Your fellow-citizens,
"T. DUNLAP,
"JOHN M. READ,
"N. CHAPMAN,
"*Committee of the Citizens of Philadelphia.*"

DR. KANE'S REPLY.

"UNITED STATES SHIP SUPPLY,
NORFOLK, VA., February 10, 1849.

"GENTLEMEN:—Your very courteous note on behalf of some of our fellow-citizens, and the magnificent offering it refers to, reached me just as I was leaving home. They are altogether almost painfully inappropriate to any services of mine. But I shall cherish them as memorials of regard from men whom I have always been taught to honor, and whose kind estimation would be an ample reward even for the meritorious.

"I am, gentlemen, very gratefully and truly,
"Your friend and servant,
"E. K. KANE.
"THOMAS DUNLAP, Esq.,
"Hon. JOHN M. READ,
"N. CHAPMAN, M.D.,
"*Committee.*"

Determined neither to write nor compile the narrative of this gallant and generous exploit, but merely and simply to collate its authenticated facts, it is nevertheless due to the reader to supply some of the incidents which are not in the record, but are not the less sufficiently well ascertained.

The wound which Colonel Gaona received in the action is stated as inflicted "*possibly* by the hands of the officer" whom the family were at the time nursing under the same roof with their suffering son. There was really no uncertainty about it; but Colonel Childs covers the fact, which so much enhanced the kindness of General Gaona, with a delicacy of doubt which nobody entertained, because all parties wished it otherwise and avoided all unnecessary allusion to it.

The " circumstances which had made the two generals Dr. Kane's personal prisoners" were that they had surrendered to him personally.

In the desperate defence which he made for his prisoners when they were attacked, after the surrender, by Domingues and his two lieutenants, one of them, Palasios, received a shot from the doctor's pistol; and Domingues would have taken another, if the hurry of the conflict had allowed a little better aim.

"The proud, prancing position of his horse when he was pierced by the lance," described by Colonel Gaona to Dr. Campbell, covers the fact that that lance-thrust was aimed at the rider, and helps to show how close and desperate the brief conflict was, and at what risk it was made successful.

On the 4th of January, 1849, the War Department awarded *payment* for the horse. Two hundred dollars cannot be called compensation, especially after it was withheld for a year, and taxed, besides, with as much trouble to the applicant as was well worth the whole sum. But that trouble has paid by giving us the best-proved piece of history that ever was challenged on the ground of its romantic incidents.

We have not relieved this story of the marvellous,— a professor of mathematics could not do that,—but we have faithfully disenchanted the recital, and may now remit the bare-bone facts to the fancy of the readers whom we have held so long impatient of our conscientious dullness.

His illness at Puebla was so severe that he was at one time reported dead to his friends at home, on authority held unquestionable for many days before the relief of better news arrived.

He was to have started for the city of Mexico on the 16th of February; but learning, as he states it, providentially, that four hundred mounted men under Padre Jaurata were waiting for them, the train, already on the march, was ordered back, and they set out on the 18th with a larger force. On the 25th, at St. Martin, he writes:—
"The good effects of my Mexican interference mingle themselves with the bad. I am twenty miles from Puebla, at the base of Popocatepetl,—the rain falling, the wind howling, and some two thousand poor devils shivering under their tent-poles. I am with General Torrejon, snugly housed, warmly welcomed, and awaiting a call to supper."

From Mexico he wrote:—"My movements unknown: should the doctors, as they threaten, order me home, I will apply for a leave, only for the armistice, so as to return to save my honor and be in at the death." Again, on the 3d of March:—"My surgeons have declared this poor carcass unfit for duty; and yet the carcass will not leave Mexico." On the 14th of March, he says:—"You are aware that the surgeons have condemned me; their opinion is formally written out, signed by the superintendent of the hospitals, and by the surgeon-general of the army; but, in spite of this, Mexico I will not leave until I can do so clearly,—until the armistice is more definite or peace is more prospective."

The armistice satisfied him; the opportunities of the

service were gone, and on the 8th of April he was at Vera Cruz, on his way home. His report here has some telling points:—

"On my homeward trail, and but seven days from the great city! An escort of thirty dragoons, a four-horse hospital-ambulance, and much sympathy, accompanied me in my forced retreat from the scene of my hopes.... My leave is but for three weeks from the 10th of April, —my object a surgical operation,—my health such as to require all the kindly care of the home to which I again return, a broken-down man. My hair would be gray, but that I have no hair. My hopes would be particularly small, but that I have no hopes.... Expect never to see me again, and my *luck* may prevent your being disappointed.... Perhaps the fact of having saved six lives may make me a more important person in your eyes. It was a dear bargain; but I do not regret it.... My very dearest love to mother. Tell her that, although I write so thanklessly, I believe myself to be a better man. My wig, tell B——, is a delicate auburn."

He suffered terribly from his lance-wound after his return. In July he was too ill to attend to any business. His condition in the autumn made him willing to ask the Department for the favor of an appointment at the Philadelphia Navy-Yard.

The question was raised whether the post could be given to an *assistant*-surgeon. Dr. Kane's friends in the medical corps bestirred themselves: they were successful! The appointing officer was delighted to learn from the head of the bureau that the clever thing could be done, and without the least delay he did appoint— another man to the post!

Dr. Kane never fattened on favoritism. With the grand exception of the Honorable John P. Kennedy, Secretary of the Navy, when he was preparing for his second Arctic Expedition, he was left at perfect moral liberty to be as ungrateful for nothing to the functionaries of the Government as he might please to feel.

Dr. Kane was not a West-Pointer: he was only an assistant navy surgeon; and it was not regular nor orderly for him to be always dislocating the honors of the service by illustrating it above his degree.

In January, 1849, we find him at Norfolk, Virginia, attached to the store-ship Supply, Commander Arthur Sinclair,—destination Lisbon, the Mediterranean, and Rio Janeiro. The ship sailed in February.

At sea, "beating tediously between Spezzia and Gibraltar," on the 16th of May, he wrote to one of his friends. The letter has matter in it of much value in making up a medical judgment upon the disease which, never wholly leaving him, was at last fatal:—

"I have been sick, and, indeed, am not yet well. . . . The good people at home—God bless them!—cannot realize, perhaps, that a man riding wild horses and preparing for medical examinations may yet need every hygienic influence to keep him from malignant disease. Yet so it is; and I only blame myself for not acting up to my own convictions. The fact is that I did wrong in going to sea. The exposure and wear and tear have proved too much for a constitution already enfeebled by Africa and Mexico; and now the same miserable controlling tyrant which has kept you so long a slave is about to extend his claws over me. The 'sentimental buck' is fast lapsing into a confirmed valetudinarian!

"I do not state all this in a puling, unmanly spirit of useless regret, but because to you, my confidential friend, I feel that the naked truth is a sort of duty. Mexico, or indeed any other scheme of life, is denied me, save the navy; and, if my cough does not leave me, I shall have to leave home as soon as its blessings are tasted, and spend my winters in the tropics.

"Tell my father—the dear judge, of whom I oftentimes think, and for whom in vague, spirit-yearning petition I often pray—that I really believe I behaved like a man when the first spasm of tetanus seized me: I certainly behaved like a medical man. It was about eight o'clock in the evening: I had for some hours had a stiffness in the muscles of the neck, but locked-jaw never struck me; when, suddenly, a sense of tightness, as if every flesh-fibre of my body was a fiddle-string and some hosts of devils were tuning me up, came over me. This lasted a fraction of a minute, and was gone. Of these foretastes of Tophet I had four during the night, and three on shore; and I give you my word, dear ——, that I had no more hope of ever seeing home. There was an utter, unqualified conviction of inevitable death. Once before, during the shipwreck of the Fashion, I had the same feeling, but in a less degree. This feeling was neither fear, nor penitential reminiscence, nor unprofitable analysis of the dreamy after-time, but simple concentrated sadness. I thought of all of you, including poor Gaona, and of myself only as connected with you. Once, thinking I was about to choke, I penned a 'God bless you!'—which, as an instance of calligraphy during a tetanic spasm, I enclose for Pat's museum. That done, I a second time bled myself and fainted, and, according to the shore-doctors who saw me next morning, saved my life. For my own part, placing Providence and the dispensations *primero*, I look upon opium as my sheet-anchor."

Writing again, three days after, in a spirit of marked consideration for the feelings of his friends at home, he reports himself well again. In his own phrase, he says, "That remarkably poor devil, your son, although, in common with the weakest and the strongest of the race to which he belongs, surrounded by hostile elements, has, as a great inherent quality of his splendid organization, a principle of resistance which almost makes him think himself 'reserved for better things.' . . . . I lost forty ounces of blood, and took twenty-two grains of opium, and then, bleached to the color of city milk,—a pale whitewash tinge,—got up to thank Heaven for the prospect, however distant, of seeing again my very well and dearly beloved mother."

The lock-jaw, and the debility which followed, made even a Mediterranean cruise a hard one to him.

RECUPERATION.

They had a prosperous voyage to Rio, however, reaching that port on the 29th June. There he "went out into the fields, drank milk, saw kindly faces, and grew better."

The Supply arrived in Norfolk towards the close of September. In October he was at home, recuperating.

In February, 1850, he completed his thirtieth year. For the last seven he had been pursuing his destiny with fiery-footed haste, and it had evaded him! January had crept away in eventless tranquillity: he had joined the coast-survey and subsided into routine-duty in the service. How he bore this calm in the centre of his whirlwind is not recorded. He perhaps thought within himself that he had submitted. That he had turned his ambition out to play, and almost abandoned himself to poetry, is openly betrayed by a letter dated

"1st of May, SHORT'S HOTEL!

"Who ever heard of Short's Hotel? A perfect little paradise, looking out upon the Bay of Mobile, and containing a four-post bedstead. Destitute of paint or whitewash or wash-basin is Short's Hotel; and yet it is the dearest, sweetest little abode of honeysuckled comfort that ever hung from the boughs of a live-oak. Short's Hotel is about the size of our discarded washhouse. Short's Hotel floats on a velvet-lawned magnolia-studded clearing on the bluff bank. Short's Hotel, to give the climax to its beauties, is *completely invisible.* The limbs of a great gnarled live-oak, all covered with long gray moss, overhang it like the reliquary of a patriarch; and, save when the sea-breezes thrust away the venerable screen, you would think yourself looking at a thicket of Cherokee roses. And here, dear fellow, am I.

"I wish, dear, sick, working friend, that you could enjoy the climate, which just at this moment is preaching to me its sermon of thankfulness; for the only sermons that now reach my gizzard-plated bowels are those of the dear outer world of nature. Summer, of a perennial but sluggish sort, is mellowing every thing around me. God bless you!

"The breeze comes to me purple-stained with the sunset, rippling over the bay with an eloquent crescendo of wavelets and a cadenza of tiny surf. God bless the breeze, too, for I know that that great jungle of glaucous-leafed magnolia (t'other side of Short's) would stifle me with a sirocco of fragrance could it drive its perfume to leeward. Cows, too, have left their impress,—the specific mark of cow-some-where, and I smell a presentiment of milk for supper."

For two years before this date the live world had been moved to its depths by the appeals of Lady Franklin for the rescue of her husband and his companions in the search for the Northwest Passage, of whom no tidings had been heard since August, 1845. She had addressed President Taylor, in April, 1849, soliciting aid from our Government. About midsummer, Sir Francis Beaufort had, on the authority of rumor, announced to the Royal Geographical Society that the President was about to fit out two ships for the search; but that hope had failed under Mr. Clayton's letter promising only that "whatever can be done to aid the search by spreading information of the reward offered by Parliament among our whalers shall be done," and the balance in prayers and sympathies. Lady Franklin, with that tenacity of purpose and desperation of hope which have survived seven years more of disappointment, renewed her prayer to General Taylor in December, 1849; and on the 4th of January he transmitted the correspondence to Congress, recommending "an appropriation for fitting out an expedition to proceed in search of the missing ships, with their officers and crews."

The response of the nation had been given with the heartiest good-will. The general expectation had almost mistaken itself for an accomplished fact. Sympathy, gallantry, national honor, had combined and warmed themselves into enthusiasm; and the public with one voice held the Government committed to the enterprise.

No one, in or out of the service, had felt thè impulse and asserted the duty more ardently than Dr. Kane. He volunteered his service, pressed his application, urged the petition by every means in his power, and had been compelled to abandon the hope. On the 24th of March, 1850, at Mobile, he wrote to a friend:—"The Department has given my 'volunteer' the slighting answer of silence, leaving me the simple satisfaction of having done as I did do. Now, however, as I am probably for months a coast-survey incumbent, your health, morale, and every thing else lead me to press upon you my invitation.

"Come to me by the quiet valley of turbulent waters. . . . This quiet sunshine would not be uncongenial: you could stuff alligators, read books, drink claret, or eat French dinners, just as it pleased you. . . . By the latter days of June we travel northward; stopping at the Havana, Charleston, Norfolk, and then journeying, you and myself, from Boston to Philadelphia by the railroads."

But, all unaware of the fact, he had reached the point which evenly divided his life of desperate adventure and manly endurance into two weeks of years by a brief Sabbath of rest,—an isthmus of ease smoothly linking two continents of effort, with the most massive and mountainous before him: he had abandoned himself to his fate as his last disappointment had colored it, and was pleasantly relieving its tediousness with the lyrics of elegant leisure, when, "in such an hour as he knew not," it sprang upon him like a strong man armed, and carried him into the field of a conflict fitting his necessities and fulfilling his hopes and his life.

His "personal narrative" of the first "United States Grinnell Expedition" opens in the tone of this surprise, just as a whirlwind breaks into the calm of a tropic May day:—"On the 12th of May," he says, "while bathing in the tepid waters of the Gulf of Mexico, I received one of those courteous little epistles from Washington which the electric telegraph has made so familiar to naval officers. It detached me from the coast-survey, and ordered me to 'proceed forthwith to New York for duty upon the Arctic Expedition.'

"Seven and a half days later, I had accomplished my overland journey of thirteen hundred miles, and in forty hours more our squadron was beyond the limits of the United States: the Department had calculated my travelling-time to a nicety."

CHAPTER IX.

FRANKLIN'S VOYAGES—SEARCH-EXPEDITIONS—UNITED STATES GRINNELL EXPEDITION—LIEUTENANT DE HAVEN—ARCTIC ROSE-PLUCKING—THE CAPTAIN'S DOUBTS—THE DOCTOR'S DECISION—THE PERSONAL NARRATIVE—HORRORS OF AUTHORSHIP—DIETETICS AND DRUGS—PUBLIC LECTURING—EXPEDITIONS OF 1852—ESTIMATE OF BUTTONS—SECOND VOYAGE POSTPONED—LITTLE WILLIE—IN MEMORIAM—GRINNELL LAND—ARROWSMITH AND THE ADMIRALTY—ADJOURNED JUSTICE—DR. KANE AND COLONEL FORCE—COMITY AND EQUITY.

SIR JOHN FRANKLIN'S first voyage to the Polar regions was made as lieutenant commanding the Trent, under Captain Buchan, of the Dorothea, in 1818; his second was the great overland journey with Dr. Richardson, to the mouth of the Copper-Mine River, in 1819; his third, to the same field of effort, in 1825; and he sailed for his fourth and last voyage on the 25th of May, 1845, with a crew of one hundred and thirty-eight men and officers, in search of the Northwest Passage from Baffin's Bay to the Pacific by way of Lancaster Sound. His ships, the Erebus and Terror, were met by a whaler in the upper waters of the bay, moored to an iceberg, waiting for an opening in "the pack," on the 26th of July following: they have not been seen since.

SEARCH-EXPEDITIONS. 147

Early in 1848, three expeditions were despatched by the British Government in search of the missing vessels: one, a marine expedition, by way of Behring's Strait, consisting of the Herald and Plover, in command of Captain Kellett and Captain Moore; another, an overland and boat party, conducted by Sir John Richardson, to descend the Mackenzie River; the third, two ships, the Enterprise and Investigator, under command of Sir James Clarke Ross, through Lancaster Sound and Barrow's Strait. An admirably devised and vigorously endeavored plan of search, but entirely unsuccessful. Before the beginning of 1850, they had all abandoned it without having reached even the threshold of the field to be explored.

These failures only aroused the sympathy and stimulated the enthusiasm of England to endeavor the rescue of the long-lost explorers. Parliament, in March, 1849, offered a reward of £20,000 for the discovery and effectual relief of the missing ships, or £10,000 for the discovery and effectual relief of any of the crew of the vessels, or for ascertaining their fate.

Two whale-ships were put upon the search in 1849 : they failed as badly as the more promising expeditions of the year before.

The anxiety and the effort grew by these disappointments, and, in 1850, England sent a fleet to the rescue, —the Enterprise and Investigator, by Behring's Strait, the Resolute and Assistance and two screw-propellers, the Pioneer and Intrepid, by Baffin's Bay; and, joined to these, the veteran Sir John Ross went out in a schooner provided by public subscription; and Lady Franklin herself equipped two others, a ship of two hundred and twenty-five tons, bearing her own name, and a clipper-brig of one hundred and twenty tons, named the Sophia; and still another, of which she bore two-thirds of the expense,—a schooner-rigged craft of ninety tons. Besides all this, Dr. Rae, under direction of the Hudson's Bay Company, undertook the same year to complete an unaccomplished part of the land-exploration of 1848, from the northern coast of America. In all, ten British vessels, manned by daringly adventurous crews, commanded by veteran ice-masters, and carrying a gallant band of volunteers to the scene of trial and danger.

Our own Government, urged by a generous public sentiment, and stimulated by the offer of two vessels for the service by Mr. Grinnell, of New York, went into the adventure with zeal and liberality.

By joint resolution of the two houses of Congress, passed 2d May, 1850, the President was authorized "to accept and attach to the navy two vessels offered by Henry Grinnell, Esq., to be sent to the Arctic seas in search of Sir John Franklin and his companions. The President may detail from the navy such commissioned and warrant officers and seamen as may be necessary for said expedition, and who may be willing to engage in it. The said officers and men shall be furnished with suitable rations for a period not exceeding three years, and shall have the use of such necessary instruments as the Departments can provide. The said vessels, officers, and men shall be in all respects under the laws and regulations of the navy of the United States until their return, when the vessels shall be delivered to Henry Grinnell. Provided, that the United States shall not be liable to any claim for compensation in case of the loss, damage, deterioration, use, or risk of the vesssels."

These vessels were two little hermaphrodite brigs,— the "Advance," of one hundred and forty-four tons, and the "Rescue," of ninety-one.

Dr. Kane, whose rank was now passed assistant-surgeon, U.S.N., went in the Expedition as senior medical officer: his berth was aboard of the Advance. Dr. Vreeland, assistant-surgeon, was assigned to the Rescue.

Lieutenant De Haven, the commander, had seen the same kind of service as that now before him, in the Wilkes Expedition of 1838 to the South Polar continent,—a capital officer, a daring sailor, with a dash of extra spirit for exigencies that more than once surprised the hardiest of his competitors in the struggles of the Northern Ocean. In one of their joint scrapes among the hummocks of Barrow's Strait, with the British tars holding their breath in strained expectancy, he gave them a taste of his quality that won for him on the spot the appellation of the "Mad Yankee." With seven feet of solid oak in the bow of his brig, he used her as a battering-ram against the ice-rafts and opened a track for them. They did justice to him. Lieutenant Osborn, of the Pioneer, says of him and his men, "If progress depended alone upon skill and intrepidity, our go-ahead friends would have given us a hard tussle for the laurels to be won in the Arctic regions." The subsequent history of the American cruisers shows that, if the longest and hardest tussle with the Arctic ice on record may decide, they really won the honors of the combined expeditions of that year. But, however the awards for exertion and endurance may be distributed, the American volunteers had been beforehand in securing one handsome advantage over their competitors in the search, which Osborn states in this way:—"As a proof of the disinterestedness of their motives, men as well as officers, I was charmed to hear that, before sailing from America, they had signed a bond not to claim, under any circumstances, the £20,000 reward the British Government had offered for Franklin's rescue: we, I am sorry to say, had acted differently. America had plucked a rose from our brows." Mercury, chloroform, and proof-spirits may freeze in the Arctic zone, but hearts as warm as these would stand the cold of the North Pole itself.

The commander and the doctor of this gallant little crew met for the first time at the navy-yard of Brooklyn the day before they set sail. De Haven had never heard of Kane; and he confesses that when he took his measure, as a captain looks at the men he must depend upon in great emergencies, he thought he was not the pattern for the place. If he had had but the time, he would have asked the Department to exchange him for a more promising man; but that was impossible, and he concluded that the battered little body would have enough of it by the time they should reach Greenland, and then he could send him back.

De Haven, you are a fine fellow, but you haven't the infallible measure for men. That slight figure has a preternaturally big heart in it; and the "soul, mind, and spirit" of the man is still beyond your estimate, though your admiration for his manliness *now* is as much as your own stout frame can well bear.

To sea they went; and the trial began. That inevitable sea-sickness which persecuted the doctor like a demon, laid him up forthwith, to work away at the feat of turning himself inside out at every pitch of the brig.

After thirty-one days of this exercise, they touched at Whale-Fish Island, and, pat to the purpose so benevolently entertained, and now, by the experience of the trial-trip to the Greenland coast, so abundantly justified, De Haven found an English transport, chartered by the Admiralty, that could carry the completely knocked-up young doctor to England on his way home; and he very kindly, but resolutely, proposed it. All that was required was that the doctor should certify his own unfitness for further service, and he would be sent home invalided, on full pay, rank saved, and all parties handsomely accommodated! The doctor looked at him a moment in almost blank dismay. There was a consciousness of substantial truth and right in it; but, after a spasm of painful feeling which melted the captain's very heart, he turned suddenly, and answered, firmly, "I won't do it." The captain could not insist, and a fortnight afterwards the doctor was fit for the hardest duty of the voyage, and for many months the busiest and most efficient man on board.

His personal narrative of the Expedition shows what a world of work he did in that voyage, the most remarkable for risk, adventure, and actual achievement of that season of search. Of this cruise, styled "The *United States Grinnell* Expedition in search of Sir John Franklin," to indicate the mixed governmental and private enterprise which it represented, it is well known Dr. Kane became the historian. The vessels left New York on the 22d of May, 1850, and returned to the same port on the 30th of September, 1851, a voyage of sixteen months, during nine of them ice-locked and adrift in a frozen ocean.

It is alike impossible and unnecessary for us to follow the doctor in his personal adventures throughout this period which he has himself journalized and published. We have not the temerity to rehearse or abridge a narrative so absolutely perfect in substance, form, array, and effect. It was given to the world from the press of the Harpers early in July, 1853, with the following advertisement:—"It may apologize, perhaps, for some imperfections in this book, to mention that the greater portion of it has gone through the press without the author's revisal. While he was engaged in preparing it, the liberality of Mr. Grinnell, of New York, and Mr. Peabody, of London, enabled him to set on foot a second

Polar Expedition, which sailed under his command on the 31st of May last. It was his purpose to remodel some of the chapters, and to add one or two on collateral topics, if his time had not been engrossed by the preparations for his journey."

This "note" was by the gentleman who supervised the closing sheets of the book as they passed through the press.

Book-authorship was an unexpected and a trying avocation to him. There was nothing in all the multitudinous and immensely varied engagements of his life which fretted, worried, and exhausted him like it. His strength was not adequate, and sedentary occupation was at once unfriendly to his health and repugnant to his habitude of mind. Hotspur, in his worst temper, could not have felt more disposed to "divide himself and go to buffets" over an uncongenial job than our man of manifold capacities over this unwonted work. He *would* write a book for his peers in science and adventure; but he *must* address himself to the multitude, and adjust himself to the trade. He would enlist the public sentiment in support of the private enterprise of search and exploration which he was endeavoring to inaugurate; but he could not constrain his spirit into a conformable address. He doubted his capability most libellously; yet he felt that he could do it if he might execute it as he would, if allowed to follow the leadings of his own mind; and his friends—some of them, at least, and they the most influential—friends to whose judgments he looked one moment with the docility of a child, and at the next resisted with the temper of outraged taste,—well, it may be said in a word, they badgered him till he escaped into the field of that freer fight and even less formidable toil which he encountered in his second voyage to the Polar circle.

At one time during the early summer of 1852 his bodily strength fairly broke down and his brain wellnigh gave way. In diet and drink he was habitually abstemious; in labor he was terribly intense; and when his nervous system broke up under this weakening regimen and wearing work, and he apprehended an attack of apoplexy, paralysis, or some other form of cerebral explosion, to meet the danger he put himself under a reducing drug-treatment, and was on the very verge of a fatal issue when he was arrested by the advice of a friend. Upon a more generous system of living, and some relaxation of toil in book-making, he escaped the imminently impending catastrophe. Add to all this a voluminous correspondence in which he engaged to forward the interests of the second Expedition, and the wearing solicitude of preparation for so great an enterprise, and some idea may be formed of his first experiences in authorship.

He had been lecturing, too, in the principal Eastern cities, creating a public sentiment wherever he went, and had the unfamiliar responsibilities of public speaking to add to the repugnant work of authorship. That he was eminently capable of both, everybody knew but himself; no success in results, no unanimity of public opinion, would ever persuade him to believe a word of it for himself.

The book, indeed, held a secondary and a subsidiary place in his thoughts. It was to be set aside if it could not be finished in time for starting on a second cruise to the North in 1852. He had been straining every nerve, since his return in the autumn before, to get up a private expedition for the ensuing spring.

The unexpected return of the British squadron, and the compulsory drift which had brought the De Haven brigs ice-locked almost to our own shores before they were released, had increased the universal desire to determine the fate of Franklin. The discovery, in 1850, of his winter-quarters at Beechey Island in 1845-46 revived the hopes which had begun to fade rapidly away. Five ships, under Sir Edward Belcher, were sent out to renew the search in the spring of 1852, all bound for Beechey Island; and, in consequence of a report of the murder of Sir John and his crews by the natives of Wolstenholme Sound, on the west coast of Greenland, 76½° N., Lady Franklin refitted the Isabel screw-steamer for the investigation of this story.

The field of search was to be explored more vigorously than ever; and Dr. Kane panted to participate. On the 7th of May, 1852, he wrote to Mr. Grinnell:—"The letters of Lady Franklin and Miss Cracroft (her niece) move me. Their views coincide with my own. I am convinced that an expedition could be carried out under private auspices without feeling the absence of an artificial discipline. If you will send for Penny, I will act either conjointly with him, or in any other position in which I can be of use. . . . The feelings which lead me to this offer forbid the intrusion of any thought of technical dignity. He may have my buttons, and I will go as *cook*. . . . The book will be done in the middle of June: we might be off before the 1st of July. . . . You ought not, and are not, to advance one cent. The great tax upon you will be the 'Advance.' I will go strenuously to work and raise the funds, giving my own salary as a start."

In the afternoon of the same day he wrote again:— "Upon reconsidering my letter of this morning, it seems to me that if you knew of any good, practical man who could act as sailing-master, there would be no necessity for the delay and expense of Penny; and I could readily undertake the exploration proposed."

Again, 9th June, 1852, he says:—"I am still too unwell to undertake a long letter. If it pleases Providence to restore me to robust health, I will gladly form a part of the Behring's Strait expedition, should the 'Advance' join Lady Franklin's steamer. My judgment, however, is averse to the plan."

He did not get off that season. His efforts through the winter and spring to accomplish this wish were disappointed: his offers, unreserved as they were, were not accepted. The book was not finished in June. His health had badly failed him; and in June, when it was tolerably re-established, another task absorbed his thoughts, feelings, and time through all the summer months of the year.

His brother, little Willie, a lad of fifteen, was taken ill in the spring, of disease induced, I think, by excessive assiduity in study. He suffered long and severely, and bore it heroically. While he was yet speechless, after a paroxysm of pain, he wrote on a slate, "Did I bear that as well as you bore your lock-jaw?" At another time he said, "I am pretty well on with my music; selecting all the good pieces and restoring them, and putting the right words to them, so that they may do their good work in every parlor; but if any thing is going to happen to me you must tell me. Don't be afraid. I'll bear it well: and—and—I want to say something to comfort mother."

The doctor was his nurse and bedside-companion till he sank to rest, on the 25th of August.

Natural affection, brother-love, sympathy for extreme suffering, were not the only ties that bound Elisha to Willie's bedside, displacing, while the struggle lasted, every other engagement, and suspending every other solicitude: Willie held him by the independent claim of personal worthiness.

No falsities of fashion or form were permitted to intrude at that brave boy's funeral. There were no *chief*-mourners there: strangers to his blood, who knew him, claimed an equality of grief with those who shared it.

It was not mere precocity of development, nor childish

sweetness of person and temper, which gave Willie his place in our hearts and holds him still in their memories. That youngest of the family bade fairly and surely, we thought, to rank with the eldest in all generous and noble achievements,—in another sphere of life, indeed, but not less excellent or beneficent.

Willie was neither the copy nor the contrast of Elisha. They were unlike enough to love each other like brother and sister; they were like enough for all the reciprocities of friendship. Tears sadly sweet for our loss in the early death of Willie; solemn exultation over the nobly completed life of Elisha. . . .

It seemed, while we looked at their mother, as she stood, in the composure of a great grief ruled by a strong spirit, at the margin of her child's grave, that there was one consolation for her in his premature death:—*He* would never go away, out of her arms, away into the world. She had now one child safe in heaven,—a child unchanging to her until her own change should come. Since then the wandering one has returned, and they rest together. Maternal solicitude is released from its painful vigils, and in the spirit of Christian hope the mother sits now by their tomb as once she watched by their cradles for their gladsome waking.

I would not have ventured to speak of this sweetly sad episode in the epic of Elisha's life, if his portraiture could have been completed without it. Those who know him only as a hero may herd him with the crowd who have in their thousand ways worked their names into history,—men of blood or men of brains,—men of chivalric spirit and distinguished achievement, whom fame amply repays for all they give or have to give to the world. Our man of mighty enterprise and world-wide notoriety had a heart and a soul in him—all nerve to the demands of duty, but, in the deepest and dearest sense, all tenderness, devotion, and tact in the offices of affection and the services of suffering humanity. It may seem strange, but it is true, that he was at once a man, a woman, and a child to those who could receive in full communion the life he had to give them.

The summer went by: the autumn mellowed the sorrows it had brought, and the man sprang to work again. The Book, the Book, and the Expedition,—only postponed, not abandoned,—engaged him; and, among other things, the task of defending De Haven's priority of discovery of the Grinnell Land at the head of Wellington Channel.

It cannot, and there is no reason why it should, be disguised, that our "friendly allies" in the search for Franklin did not behave handsomely, nor fairly, nor respectfully, nor justly, in this matter, which so nearly touched the honor of the American wing of that service. It is all settled now rightly, but it was not done gracefully, by the Lords-Commissioners of the British Admiralty.

De Haven, at the northernmost point of his involuntary drift up Wellington Channel, did, on the 22d of September, 1850, discover land extending from N.W. to N.N.E. of his position, to which he gave the name of

Grinnell. On the 4th of October, 1851, immediately after his return, he made his official report, claiming this discovery, backed by all the evidence that could be required to establish the claim; and the newspapers of the day carried the announcement to England, along with the earliest intelligence of the safe return of the gallant and generous crews who had gone upon the search at their own country's expense and under a pledge to decline the reward which had been offered by Parliament to induce the endeavor.

On the 12th of May, 1851, eight months after the discovery of De Haven, the same land was seen by Captain Penny, of the English squadron. He knew nothing at that time of De Haven's ascent of the channel in the preceding September, and in ignorance of that fact named it "Albert Land," in compliment to his Royal Highness. This name, thus excluding the American discovery, appeared on the map of the Hydrographic Office published in September, 1851, and in Arrowsmith's map of "Discoveries in the Arctic Sea," dated 21st of October, 1851, but not published for several weeks afterwards,—for some of the discoveries of Dr. Rae, which were not announced to the Admiralty till the 10th of November, appear on it.

It is probable, as well as possible, that the Hydrographic Office map of September, 1851, was innocent of any information of De Haven's discovery; but Arrowsmith's loses all right to a respectful construction, not merely by the fact that it was not issued until after news

MRS. ALMY'S HOTEL, HAVANA.

of De Haven's discovery must have reached England, but by the fact, open on the face of the document, that Mr. Arrowsmith, sitting in his office at No. 10 Soho Square, London, did, himself, then and there, discover Albert Land, *nunc pro tunc*, on the 26th of August, 1850, in honor of Prince Albert's birthday, and in dishonor and discredit of De Haven's discovery, made, in latitude 75½° N. and longitude about 93½° W. of the position of No. 10 Soho Square, twenty-seven days true time after the computed time of Mr. Arrowsmith's map.

But, if both these unwarranted claims are to be overlooked in the complaint which we make, the Hydrographical Map of the British Admiralty, dated 8th of April, 1852, stands fully exposed to the charge of insisting upon an unwarranted assumption. This document, issued so long after De Haven's report was published, which was entitled, under any circumstances, to greater consideration, and, in the peculiar relations of the parties, to some international courtesy besides, cannot claim the same forbearance. This map of "Discoveries in the Arctic Seas to 1851, London, published, according to Act of Parliament, at the Hydrographical Office of the Admiralty, April 8, 1852," reasserted the name of "Albert Land" for that tract of country which the Grinnell Expedition had discovered and claimed by naming it after the gentleman who represented the American title to that honor.

Here was an involvement, with an impeachment lying under it; and Lieutenant De Haven, commanding the

"Advance," Mr. Griffin, commanding the "Rescue," and Dr. Kane, the historian of the cruise, were all committed for the vindication of their personal credit and the honor of the service to which they belonged.

The Secretary of the Navy called upon Dr. Kane for a statement of the facts by which the discovery was supported; and he made, also, an official call upon Lieutenant De Haven for a report. Dr. Kane replied under date of 28th of December, 1852. The Secretary sent De Haven's chart to the Admiralty on the 12th of January, 1853, which was received on the 31st of the same month. The Lords-Commissioners, on the 1st of March, replied that "the whole Wellington Channel will no doubt be materially changed by Captain Sir E. Belcher's observations: it would be better to let this matter remain in abeyance until his return, when it will be their lordships' first duty to do the fullest justice to the enterprising efforts of Lieutenant De Haven and to the noble liberality of Mr. Grinnell."

Moreover, the Admiralty had received "an engraved sketch of the region round the Wellington Channel, and a tracing of the Grinnell vessels' tracks up that channel nearly to $75\frac{1}{2}°$ north latitude," forwarded from New York on the 18th of November, 1851, which was laid before the board by their hydrographer, Sir F. Beaufort, as appears by his acknowledgment bearing date the 5th of December.

Well, Sir E. Belcher, returning from his tour of exploration at the head of Wellington Channel, landed in

England on the 28th of September, 1854; and Sir F. Beaufort, Rear-Admiral and Hydrographer of the Admiralty, writing to Mr. Grinnell on the 24th of January, 1855, says, "On carefully comparing all the logs and journals of Captain Austin's squadron, it is manifestly impossible that any of his vessels could have seen that land till the year after its discovery by Captain De Haven."

These logs of Austin's squadron had been in the possession of the Admiralty ever since the autumn of 1851. Sir E. Belcher had discovered no inaccuracies in De Haven's report which could touch his pretensions; and the grace of crediting him and his officers was finally conceded, not to their claim, but to the manifest impossibility of discrediting it after four years of incredulous scrutiny.

Had it been earlier it had been more courteous. The British claim was from the first, as Dr. Kane held it in a letter to Mr. Grinnell, dated May 10, 1852, "utterly indefensible." There were but two questions in the controversy: one touching the capacity of the American officers to observe and understand what they saw, the other affecting their veracity in reporting it. The concession was not made to either claim.

The substance of Dr. Kane's demolishing argument against the English assumption, made for the use of the Navy Department, is reproduced in the twenty-fifth chapter of his Personal Narrative of the First Grinnell Expedition. Lieutenant De Haven's official report is in the Appendix of the same volume, p. 494. Colonel Peter Force, of Washington City, during this period of long-delayed justice, or, rather, the adjourned question of our squadron's honor, brought to the rescue of his countrymen's claims the great resources and ample powers in his possession, and, in a series of papers distinguished for their frankly severe criticism, completely established the De Haven discovery.

Even when Dr. Kane sailed for the North on the 31st of May, 1853, he seems to have felt no assurance that the honor of the Grinnell Land discovery at the head of Wellington Channel would ever be frankly conceded to De Haven by the Lords-Commissioners; for this, to our understanding, is the clear meaning of one paragraph of his letter to Mr. Kennedy, written before he landed at New York on his return. He says, "I have a Grinnell Land *now* which any one is welcome to take who reaches it."

The *now* in this sentence is underscored in the autograph letter. The emphasis upon the word "take" is referred to the judgment of the readers of this brief narrative of the affair, with great confidence that there is no danger of its being put on too heavily. Dr. Kane had put the name of Grinnell on a newly-discovered coast so near the Pole that his priority was not likely to be disputed.

Mr. Kennedy, quoting the same letter,—from memory doubtless,—makes the doctor say, "I have found another Grinnell Land, which any man is welcome to who will go after it." *Another* Grinnell Land, without any difference of name to distinguish it on the map of the Polar region, and requiring a periphrase to determine its locality every time it must be used! No: Dr. Kane did not know or believe that he had two; else he would have ear-marked them better, to prevent confusion in his nomenclature.

Believing that Dr. Kane's characteristic forbearance in the management of this controversy cannot rightfully be construed into any thing like satisfaction with the conduct of the Lords-Commissioners, we have conscientiously endeavored to vindicate the truth of history, leaving the international comities of kindred blood, language, and Anglo-Saxon partnership in the patronage of our planet to take care of themselves, under correction of even-handed justice to the "high contracting parties" and "the rest of mankind."

CHAPTER X.

MR. KENNEDY'S ALACRITY—SYMPATHY OF THE SAVANS—CONFIDENCE STRENGTHENED—EXCITING THE OFFICIALS—HOPES ON A SEE-SAW—DRUDGERY OF BORING—KENNEDY CHANNEL—CASH CONTRIBUTIONS—LECTURING-BUSINESS—MR. PEABODY—DEFICIENCIES OF OUTFIT—LABORIOUS PREPARATIONS—PATRIOTIC ENTHUSIASM—THE HONORS IN DANGER—RACE AGAINST TIME—ADMIRALTY CHART—A TIME TO BE SICK—DAILY PRAYERS—CHRISTIAN HEROISM—SPECIAL PROVIDENCE—WORSHIP AMONG THE HUMMOCKS—VINDICATION OF FAITH—"HOW READEST THOU?"—SAVING FAITH.

FROM this parenthesis of impatience with the Lords-Commissioners in the matter of Grinnell Land—for which, be it understood, Dr. Kane is in no wise responsible*—we return to his unremitting labors through the

---

* In a letter dated May 17, 1853, in which he mentions several presents, valuable for service in the Arctic regions, from Sir F. Beaufort, Captain McClintock, Captain Inglefield, Mr. Barrow, and the Admiralty,—letters to him from Parry, Ross, and Sabine, containing helpful suggestions for his Expedition, and other letters from Captains Penny and Kennedy, in purpose and matter friendly and useful, he says:—

"It will gratify you to see my letters from Sir F. Beaufort and others of Arctic reputation across the water. To me England has always been a seat of sympathy and pride; and I am glad that I never permitted

winter of 1852–53 in the wearing work of getting up the expedition of the ensuing spring.

In a personal interview with the Honorable John P. Kennedy, Secretary of the Navy, he unfolded the plan and purposes of his second Polar voyage. Mr. Kennedy— perceiving that, with all the liberality of Mr. Grinnell and Mr. Peabody, the outfit would be very limited, and believing that he could aid it by some valuable additions through the ordinary means of the Navy Department— suggested to the doctor that he would issue an order to place him on "special duty" with reference to the Expedition, and direct him to report to the Department. This enabled the Secretary to increase his pay to the "duty-rate," and to add many facilities for his voyage, besides giving the Expedition something of the advantages of a Government connection, which might serve a good purpose in its prospective necessities. This order was accordingly issued on the 27th of November, 1852; and, when the time came, ten men belonging to the navy were attached to the doctor's command, under Government

---

myself to use an uncourteous expression in connection with 'Grinnell Land.'

"I hope you will not think me self-adulatory when I say that my lectures and scientific papers have been of practical service in giving our Expedition character among those whose opinions are calculated to advance its permanent reputation. Every thing seems to point to a prosperous commencement; making it only the more incumbent upon us, as Americans and men, to sustain the expectations of those who are watching our course. On this head I feel gravely my responsibility."

pay. Apparatus from the Medical Bureau, "rations and commutations" for the volunteers detached from the navy, and such other necessaries for the voyage were added as were within the Secretary's very liberal construction of his powers. And to these helps the Smithsonian Institute and the National Observatory contributed liberally for scientific purposes. Professors Henry and Bache, and Lieutenant Maury were alike zealous in yielding whatever of assistance was in their power to bestow.

With an appropriation from Congress the Expedition could have been made much more effectual, and much suffering might have been avoided; but the hope of such aid was so slight that it was believed to be almost useless to apply for it.

The gentlemen just named, who are respectively at the head of the Smithsonian Institute, the Coast Survey, and the Observatory, joined in a formal and ably-argued application to the Secretary of the Navy for the assistance of the Department, warmly commending him for the zeal he had already displayed by his orders in behalf of the enterprise, approving its objects, and as warmly endorsing Dr. Kane's "peculiar qualities as an explorer, and his varied resources of knowledge, exhibited, as they had been, in his contributions to the De Haven Expedition," which, they said, "point him out as eminently fitted for the task which he proposes to undertake under your auspices."

In November he received the intelligence of Captain Inglefield's reported discoveries in Smith's Sound,—the

CONFIDENCE STRENGTHENED. 169

track of his own proposed search. In August that officer had entered the Sound and seen a great open sea, cumbered more or less with loose ice, and picturesquely furnished with an island in the distance, to which he gave the name of Louis Napoleon.

This peep into the "great Polar basin" was performed in the space of a few hours, in a heavy gale which blew the vessel out of the Sound. It was, however, duly charted; and Dr. Kane received it as "an entire confirmation of the soundness of his plan of search," and expected that it would probably cause Lady Franklin to add her little steamer, the "Isabel," to his party in the following spring. "Indeed," he says, "every thing points to a successful resolution of the much-vexed question of an open Polar sea."

In the event the "Isabel" did not join his party, and Inglefield's sea was so tight under ice when the "Advance" entered it the next year, that she was stopped by it; and "the same ice is round her still."

Two years of careful observation of that region resolved the island into a mistake; and the coast-lines, longitude, distances, and open sea of Inglefield went into the list of "illusory discoveries."

Lecturing and book-writing went on through the winter, amid the racking toil and anxiety of preparation for an early start for the North.

A hope of Congressional aid—one of those hopes that are born of want to die of fatigue, or, rather, the conscientious duty of endeavoring to secure it—cost weeks of incessant labor.

Of one of those weeks, ending the 30th of January, he gives, in brief, this account:—"In order to excite an interest, I accepted an invitation, hastily given by Professor Henry, to lecture at the Smithsonian, and invited thereto the Senate Committee and Heads of Departments. I gave them a full exposition of our plans, state of organization, and requirements. The Secretary (of the Navy) was present.

"I have not hesitated to call personally on any member of either House whose interest was of peculiar importance; and all this, together with the task of drawing up requisitions, &c. &c., has completely used me up. I have not averaged more than three hours' sleep a night since I left."

It seems that he obtained a promise from the proper parties to append a grant of fifteen thousand dollars, for the use of his Expedition, to the General Appropriation bill. He adds to the statement the ominous remark that "this will require more work."

The issue appears in his record of another week's work in April, after Mr. Kennedy had gone out with the Fillmore administration and Secretary Dobbin had come in with General Pierce:—

April 7th, by telegraph: "Things look black."

8th: "Still seeing Senators."

11th: "Every thing that my poor efforts could do is now done; and I anxiously wait an answer."

"General Pierce favored me with a private interview yesterday at 9 A.M. I talked nearly one hour, and he seemed more than interested; asking many questions, and promising his concurrence, and even preliminary aid with Mr. Dobbin.

"After that interview I drew up a full letter to the Secretary, and presented it through a couple of Senators, who would take care to tell him of the President's sentiments. To this letter I anxiously wait an answer, sick and tired, and anxious to get away. I have written letters enough to carry Collins' lines."

11th, by telegraph: "A bare ghost of a chance."

Same day, by letter: "I have completed a long argumentative paper, by Mr. Dobbin's request, placing the matter in the light of a public obligation." And, after detailing a host of auxiliary efforts and agencies employed, by which he left no stone unturned that might have a worm under it, the *gentleman* breaks out, as with a critical sweat,—"All this is very disgusting."

12th: "The result of a week's hard work is—a sacrifice of time, money, and influence! I will be with you by Thursday night."

The sum total of Government help is given and credited in a letter to Mr. Kennedy, of the 19th of May:—"Your successor, Mr. Dobbin, has given me the kind assurance that he would not undo your work,—an assurance which, while it showed very clearly that he was indisposed to add to it, at least enables Mr. Grinnell and myself to recognise you alone as the centre of obligation. In fact, Loco-foco as I am, I cannot but feel that my little party belongs to another Administration; and I hope that you will not be bored if I show my recognition of your personal agency by a regular bulletin from the land of ice."

"Kennedy Channel," connecting the Arctic ring of perpetual ice with the open sea near the Pole, is the appropriate fulfilment of this purpose.

It will be recollected that the doctor was decided against a "strictly naval expedition." His strenuous but unavailing endeavor to secure for the private one which he conducted every needed assistance from the Government acquits him of responsibility for the deficiencies of outfit which he could not, by all the efforts in his power, prevent.

His personal contributions to the expense-fund cannot be given; but we know that he devoted at least twenty months of unremitting toil, his own pay, (which must have been about three thousand dollars,) and the proceeds of the lectures which he delivered through the winters of 1852 and 1853 in the Atlantic cities. We have the evidence of one item only,—the amount thus raised in Boston. Writing to Mr. Grinnell, 26th of February, 1853, he says, "Mr. George R. Russell, of Boston, forwarded to me the funds resulting from my Boston visit. These I have deposited in the Farmers' and Mechanics' Bank, and, as soon as I get time to run over the accounts, will send you a check for the amount. I wish I could afford to give my travelling-expenses; but I am so out of pocket already with my perambulations, that, in the case of Boston, I had to charge them. These, however, refer only to such as are absolutely incidental to my object.

"Including the several sums of $78 75 and $58 received from New Bedford, and those added to my lectures in Boston, the gross sum is somewhere about $1400."

While at Boston the lecturing-business gets this characteristic touch:—"The fund which I sought to raise works hardly, for I will not accept personal contributions, as I regard them as interfering not only with my own dignity, but that of the Expedition. . . . A letter has been circulated by the first men, inviting me to lecture; and, by the aid of the ladies, all the best of whom I have pressed into the service, I hope to succeed. Every day is the scene of some rival attraction, and I have to do all I can to distance my rivals,—Blitz, Alboni, and Emerson: we are all of one feather. No matter: so that I get my money, I do not care."

The amount of his gatherings from all quarters we do not know, nor the sum of his givings from his own purse before sailing, and especially after his return, when his private resources supplied him with abundance of money.

Mr. Peabody, an American gentleman residing in London, well known for his liberality, paid in ten thousand dollars; Mr. Grinnell gave the brig which was left in Smith's Sound, and how much besides we know not; the Geographical Society of New York, the Smithsonian Institution, the American Philosophical Society, and a number of scientific associations and friends of science besides, came forward to help him: but we have some grounds for the belief that there was no larger cash-contributor, first and last, to the Expedition, than Dr. Kane himself,—if the funds raised by his own labor may be as fairly credited to him as to the parties from whom they were received. And we think they may; for the proceeds of his lectures were justly his own, and the larger part even of his travelling-expenses came from his own pocket.

If he had failed, either in labor or sacrifice, in preparation for this voyage, all the reputation he has won for courage, endurance, and achievement would not shelter him from censure for recklessness and the suspicion of a selfish ambition. But can the most exacting spirit ask more from mortal man than he did to insure the good fortune of his great adventure?

He speaks to the point in his own way, (Second Grinnell Expedition, vol. i. p. 25:) "No one can know so well as an Arctic voyager the value of foresight. My conscience has often called for the exercise of it, but my habits make it an effort. I can hardly claim to be provident, either by impulse or education. Yet for some of the deficiencies of our outfit I ought not, perhaps, to hold myself responsible. Our stock of fresh meats was too small, and we had no preserved vegetables: but my personal means were limited; and I could not press more severely than a strict necessity exacted upon the unquestioning liberality of my friends."

Every word of this apologetic sentence is entitled to its utmost weight, except the generous-spirited exaggeration of his *improvidence*. A mountain of letters before me, written during the last months of preparation for the voyage, prove an amount of foresight, provident care, and thoughtful solicitude and labor which would do honor to the head and all the hands of the Commissary Department of the Navy. Their details are microscopically minute, and their compass thoroughly complete. Page upon page of memorandum and calculation—with their firstlies, secondlies, up to twentiethlies, exact as mathematics could make them, methodical as an adept could contrive, and simple and clear enough for a bullet-headed clerk to comprehend—are here to confront his self-depreciation. At one time the guns are being made under his own eye, that their quality may be insured while economy is consulted; at another, the order is withdrawn because the funds will not reach the outlay, with the protest, "I hate to borrow a gun." Again, he offers to go to New York to superintend the preparation of the "pemmican" required for the voyage. "If we could procure a malt-kiln for a single week, I would undertake the matter; and I think we could prepare it more economically and of more certain quality."

At this time his pen was running, his telegraphs flying, he was worrying the Department, examining recruits, inventing cooking-stoves, pricing rounds of beef, rummaging the Medical Bureau at Washington till he had "succeeded in begging some $2000 worth of outfit," and was all the while up to his elbows in a batch of Department-dough that was only souring while he was trying to make it rise.

No human quantity of omniscience and providence would have been a full match for the duties with which this one man was burdened, and no other man would have performed them half so well. It was a "perfectly thought-out organization" and a wonderfully endeavored preparation. Moreover, it must be recollected that he was well warranted in relying upon Mr. Grinnell's ability, generosity, and responsibility for all those arrangements of the vessel and outfit which did not appropriately and especially devolve upon himself.

In a note to the first page of this chapter, the doctor's English sympathies are indicated; his American enthusiasm is as well entitled to a presentment: the one sprang from the generous breadth of his liberality; the other rooted itself in a patriotism as intense as ever was covered by the banner of his country.

England had almost monopolized the honors of Arctic exploration on the American continent. The Northwest Passage was her achievement. Under De Haven, Dr. Kane had helped to plant the stars and stripes upon the most northern land then discovered upon the Western hemisphere; and now he would carry it to the open sea, if it was in the power of man to accomplish that feat.

He had announced his plan of search for Sir John Franklin, and his prospect of reaching the open Polar waters by the route of Smith's Sound, early in the autumn of the preceding year; but, three months before he can be ready for the enterprise, he is aroused by the fear that England may pluck the honor of this achievement from the American service. Let us see how it affected him.

On the 26th of February, 1853, confined to his room and too ill to write, he dictated the following letter to Mr. Kennedy:—

"MY DEAR SIR:—I take the liberty of sending for your perusal a letter which I have just received from Lady Franklin, to assure you of the gratitude with which she regards your kindness.

"The same mail, to my great mortification, brings me the news that the British Admiralty have adopted my scheme of search, and are about to prosecute it with the aid of steam. Nothing is left me, therefore, but a competition with the odds against me; and for this, even, I must hasten the preparations for my departure. I will be in Washington, with this object, without the delay of an hour, and shall do myself the honor of reporting to you."

6th of March, he writes to Mr. Grinnell:—"Your news that the 'Advance' is in dock came pleasantly in accordance with my wishes. The only means by which we can compete with the screw-steamer of Inglefield is by an early presence in Melville Bay, which may, by a fortunate season, enable us to enter the North Water with the whaling-fleet by the June passage. I am very anxious to reach the Duck Islands by the last of May.

"My own impression as to Smith's Sound is, that it is seldom open until late in the summer,—say last of August, —unless the winter be what is termed an open one.

Should this latter good fortune be the case this season, we may, by an early presence, get the start even of a steamer: but I am discouraged.

"Should the ice, however, be 'fast' across the Sound, and my plan of sledge and boat progress come regularly into play, I ask no favors: steamer or no steamer, we shall do well."

17th of May: "Every hour saved is of importance with regard to Inglefield."

19th, to Mr. Kennedy: "You will be glad to hear that my delay has not as yet interfered with our prospects. My late letters from Lady Franklin speak of Inglefield as not yet leaving, and the Baffin Bay ice as probably still fast."

Two weeks before sailing: "It seems to me, taking Inglefield's departure into consideration, that we cannot be off too soon. . . . If we start at once, and are favored with a fair passage, we may yet meet Inglefield."

Even the log of the first officer shows that the trip up the coast of Greenland was a chase,—a steeple-chase; the Advance on the heels of the Isabel, *doubling* the Bay of Melville to get the inside track, and, for a week, running with iceberg tugs against steam, and in at the winning-post handsomely, to learn at last that she had been running against time!

For all this apprehensiveness was a mistake. Inglefield was not bound for Smith's Sound. He was ten days ahead at Sukkertoppen; but he was despatched to Lancaster Sound, as Dr. Kane learned on his return two years afterwards. The mistake was like many another that has set the world agog: it was a mistake of a *word*. Lady Franklin had informed him that the Admiralty had *adopted* his plan of search. They had only *approved* it; and they had no intention of prosecuting it with steam.

Captain Inglefield's "great Polar basin, visible from 78° 28' 21" North, and extending through seven points of the compass," was not sufficiently persuasive; but the Admiralty lost nothing by waiting for better advices, and Dr. Kane gained nothing by the faith which he so frankly gave to the report. His journal says, "There can be no correspondence between my own and the Admiralty charts north of latitude 78° 18'. Not only do I remove the general coast-line some two degrees in longitude to the eastward, but its trend is altered sixty degrees in angular measurement. No landmarks of my predecessor, Captain Inglefield, are recognizable."

Since the publication of these corrections, the newspapers have announced that "The British Board of Admiralty have notified our Government that they have accepted Dr. Kane's charts, thus throwing overboard the charts of Captain Inglefield and other Arctic navigators belonging to the British navy, as well as the works of all of Dr. Kane's predecessors on the coast of Greenland."

Dr. Kane had every other motive for hastening his departure for, and early arrival in, the Polar sea, which the purposes of his voyage required; but the desperate struggle which he made to secure the honors of Arctic discovery to American enterprise deserves a record here, and a generous appreciation in the minds of his countrymen. His heart was moved to its depths by the hapless fate of the lost mariners of England, and the helpless sorrow of the friends they left behind them; the governing impulse that sent him out twice upon the search was sympathy for the sufferers; but a patriotism as ardent and enthusiastic as a pilgrim's religion devoted him to his country's glory.

About the middle of April he went to New York, to give his personal attention to the outfit of the ship, and to hasten her departure. Immediately after his arrival he was taken ill, and, for three weeks, was bedfast under the kind care of Mr. Grinnell's family. Writing to Mr. Kennedy, from Philadelphia, on the 19th of May, he says, "After a cruel attack of inflammatory rheumatism, and three weeks of complete helplessness on my beam-ends, I find myself ready to start."

To Mr. Grinnell he writes:—"I am so much better that I hope to be able in a day or two to ask you to name a day for our departure; whereupon I will so leave Philadelphia as to give myself a week in New York.

"The enemy still hangs by me, and it requires several hours to thaw out my night's stiffness. The doctors, however, tell me that I must expect this until I get off soundings:—no very comforting opinion to a man who has so much hard work ahead.

"When I review my sickness, its time and place, your own devoted hospitality, and the pleasant store of recol-

A TIME TO BE SICK. 181

lections which it has engendered, I cannot say that I regret my attack. Providence, who watches over our Expedition, has his own wise ends to fulfil in this affliction to myself; and, while I feel that we have as yet lost nothing *practically* by our delay, I regard it as a positive gain that my disease should have manifested itself before my departure."

Those six weeks of suffering and incapacity for the work of preparing for his departure were indeed a heavy drawback then, and their burden and embarrassment followed him in painful memories through the voyage. After journalizing the ghastly merriment of the party, on the next Christmas day, in the ice of Smith's Sound, he makes a significant allusion to the terrible struggle which it had cost to break away from home under circumstances so forbidding.

"So much," he says, "for the Merrie Christmas. What portion of its mirth was genuine with the rest I cannot tell, for we are practised actors, some of us; but there was no heart in my share of it. My thoughts were with those far off, who are thinking, I know, of me. I could bear my own troubles as I do my eider-down coverlet; for I can see myself as I am, and feel sustained by the knowledge that I have fought my battle well. But there is no one to tell of this at the home-table. *Pertinacity, unwise daring,* calamity,—any of these may come up unbidden, as my name circles round, to explain why I am still away."

Did he turn from this sad remembrance, and the

equally sad prospect before him, to make with his own hand an entry in the log kept by the first officer, as a man of faith plants an anchor in a storm of trouble? It reads thus:—"Sunday, December 25. The birthday of Christ."

The following letter to Mr. Grinnell, written two weeks before sailing, serves to show that we may read in this epitomized creed of Christianity, a profession of his faith, and not a mere confession of dependency induced by the weakness of suffering:—

"MY DEAR SIR:—All the expeditions in search of Sir John Franklin have accompanied their daily inspections with a short form of prayer suited to the emergencies of their peculiar service.

"The isolated state of our little party, together with its probable trials, call strongly for a similar exercise; and, as the time of our departure is at hand, I write to suggest that you take the matter into consideration."

The "march of mind," demolishing another mystery of *nature* at every step in its conquering pathway, has wellnigh banished *faith* from our philosophy of life. Inductive science rejects the supernatural. Chivalry, the religion of egotism,—which substitutes daring for duty, generosity for charity, and honor for godliness,—is our explanation of heroism in its grandest manifestations. That a holier Spirit "works in any man both to will and to do of His good pleasure," is an assumption which opinion in this nineteenth century of Christianity is shy of admitting.

SPECIAL PROVIDENCE.

Dr. Kane's heroism would have been reckless if it had not been reverent: he believed that whatever God wills a man may do: he believed in special providence. His life was full of this confidence. In the journal of his first Arctic voyage there are such evidences of it as these:—
"April 21.—I have *more than common* cause for thankfulness. A mere accident kept me from starting last night to secure a bear. Had I done so, I would probably have spared you reading any more of my journal. The ice over which we travelled so carelessly on Saturday has become, by a sudden movement, a mass of floating rubbish."

"11th of June.—One thing more: a thought of gratitude before I turn in. This journal shows that I have been in the daily habit of taking long, solitary walks upon the ice, miles from the ship. Suppose this rupture to have come entirely without forewarning!"

In the journal of his second voyage to the Arctic region, among twenty-two striking instances of clear recognition, I quote an example or two.

On the 10th September, 1854: "It is twelve months to-day since I returned from the weary foot-tramp which determined me to try the winter search. Things have changed since then, and the prospect ahead is less cheery. But I close my pilgrim-experience of the year with devout gratitude for the blessings it has registered, and an earnest faith in the support it pledges for the times to come."

Speaking of a time when things were at the worst, he

says, "I look back at it with recollections like those of a nightmare. Yet I was borne up wonderfully. I never doubted for an instant that the same Providence which had guarded us through the long darkness of winter was still watching over us for good, and that it was yet in reserve for us—for some; I dared not hope for all—to bear back the tidings of our rescue to a Christian land. But how, I did not see."

Prayer, both in its acknowledgments and petitions, implies such reliance upon interpositions. Wilson, one of the rescue-party in that ice-journey which has engraved its record upon the millions of hearts that have followed its terrific details with their sympathies, says, "Just before we started, [on the return with the rescued men,] while the rest of the party surrounded the sledge with uncovered heads, Dr. Kane rendered thanks to the Great Ruler of human destinies for the goodness he had evinced in preserving our feeble lives while struggling over the ice-desert, exposed to a blast almost as withering as that from a furnace. The scene was extremely solemn, as, deeply impressed by the situation, our commander poured forth ready and eloquent sentences of gratitude in that lonely solitude, whose scenery offered every thing to depress the mind and nothing to cheer it. Not a word fell from his lips that did not find a ready response in our own hearts when we reflected upon the dangers we had undergone, and the certainty of death which would have followed a continuance of exposure for even a few hours."

Journalizing the incidents of a day of severest trial, danger, and despondency, he "rendered to every man a reason for the hope that was in him," covering under the form of common words the still higher grounds on which it rested for himself. He puts its vindication thus:—

"I never lost my hope: I looked to the coming spring as full of responsibilities, but I had bodily strength and moral tone enough to look through them to the end. A trust based on experience as well as on *promises* buoyed me up at the worst of times. Call it fatalism, as you ignorantly may, there is that in the story of every eventful life which teaches the inefficiency of human means and the PRESENT control of a Supreme agency. See how often relief has come at the moment of extremity, in forms strangely unsought,—almost, at the time, unwelcome; see, still more, how the back has been strengthened to its increasing burden, and the heart cheered by some *conscious* influence of an unseen Power."

We have underscored the words which must be read "with the heart and with the understanding also" to find the emphasis which his own faith and practice gave them.

"Read, mark, learn, and inwardly digest" them, if you would know what they meant for him and what they may be to you.

This Christian heroism that served him for his own great trials, fortified, by its outraying influence, his crew for theirs. Within the sphere of his life they lived above the level of their own. One of them answered me, when I questioned him upon this aspect of his government:—"Well, it kept us human when we were nearly desperate. While we stood with uncovered heads in an atmosphere far below zero, his prayers brought up the spirit of society and civilization in us; and, although we, perhaps, had very little religion in us, we always had some about us."

CHAPTER XI.

MOTIVES AND OBJECTS — DECLARATION *IN EXTREMIS* — WORKING UP THE COAST OF GREENLAND — GOOD-BYE — A FATHER'S TESTIMONY — FRANKLIN'S CHANCES — REFUGE WITH THE NATIVES — SUPPORTING AUTHORITIES — SIR R. MURCHISON — THE BRAVE TRUST THE BRAVE — CONTRIBUTIONS TO SCIENCE — INEDITED MANUSCRIPTS — THE OPEN SEA — LOGICAL DEMONSTRATION — THE DISCOVERY — THE LAST THROW — WILLIAM MORTON — FACTS AND THEORIES — LIEUTENANT MAURY — KANE'S OFFICIAL REPORT — BRITISH ACHIEVEMENTS — RESULTS OF EXPLORATION — WASHINGTON LAND — WITHIN THE POLAR ICE-RING.

"ENTERPRISES of great pith and moment" command our admiration, sympathy, and emulation with the varied force which the quality of their motives and objects deserves. The agility and courage of a rope-dancer on his perilous balance do not affect us in the same way as the generous daring displayed by a fireman in the rescue of a child from a burning house. There is natural nobleness enough in anybody to feel the difference between a hard day's journey on an errand of benevolence, and the feat of walking a hundred successive hours for a wager. A novelist, an orator, or a player, may work upon the sympathetic emotions of virtue until our heart-strings answer like echoes to his touch; but we are not deceived nor cheated into an admiration unworthy of ourselves. We were not made in the Divine image to take seemings for things. Our instincts stand by the real interests of the world and of the universe, and we will not meanly surrender our souls to any imposture. We say to every man who challenges our admiration for his deeds, "Stop! worship touches the life of the worshipper. If your objects are nothings, expect nothing for them: if your motives are selfish, pay yourself for them. We will not make fools of ourselves: we will settle the account justly to you and honorably to us."

"No man knoweth the things of a man, save the spirit of man which is in him." Dr. Kane speaks of the motives which thrust him out upon his last Arctic voyage, under circumstances as solemn as those which govern the wording of a last will made within the shadow of death. I quote from letters written as he was about to enter the fearful passage of Melville Bay:—

"July 14, 1853.

"DEAR BROTHER AND FRIEND:—Things look so Arctic, and the big responsibilities of my undertaking are so crowding around me, that I sit down from very impulse to give you a brother's letter of confidence.

"It is the quiet hour at which you and I begin to live; lacking midnight not over-much, yet in a full glare of day. The bergs of Omenak's Fiord are marching down from their glaciers; and Proven, our last connecting port with the white man's world, is but a few miles ahead of us. Melville's Bay will bid me its third welcome before three days have passed; and, if it bids me God-speed again, you will have no more letters until I announce success or failure.

"Now that the thing—the dream—has concentred itself into a grim, practical reality, it is not egotism, but duty, to talk of myself and my plans: I represent other lives and other interests than my own.

"The object of my journey is the search after Sir John Franklin: neither science nor the vain glory of attaining an unreached *North* shall divert me from this one conscientious aim."

Then follows a long, minute, and exact programme of his intended operations by boat and sledge after reaching the farthest point to which the brig could be pushed,—an equally careful directory for any searching party who might, perchance, be sent to relieve him after a second winter's absence: and the letter concludes:—

"God bless you, my own dear brother. Do justice to my motives, and believe neither in unmixed good or unmixed evil in this world of medley. Good-bye!"

"GOVERNOR'S HOUSE, UPERNAVICK, July 23, 1853.

"MY DEAR FATHER:—Looking through the port-holes of this house-hulk, I see two hundred and sixteen icebergs floating in a sea as dead and oily as the Lake of Tiberias; yet I cannot warm my thoughts to talk about them. Time was when I could have piled epithets upon such a scene: but that time has passed; facts only are my aim now. The last week has been spent by me almost constantly in an open boat, striving to overcome the delays of an everlasting calm by making my purchases without coming to anchor. This is a somewhat novel service to routine naval men; but I have saved precious hours by it, and now write to bid you share with me congratulations.

"I have all my furs,—reindeer, seal, and bear; my boot-moccasins, walrus lashings, my sledges, harnesses, and dogs,—and all of these without delaying the brig an hour upon her course! Dogs are here, as horses are with you, matters of negotiation, and oftentimes not to be obtained. He (the dog) is the camel of these snow-deserts; and no Arab could part with him more grudgingly than do these Esquimaux. Congratulate me; for I have *all my dogs*, and the tough thews of the scoundrels shall be sinews of war to me in my ice-battles.

"In quest of them I have threaded the fiords between Kangeit (about twenty miles south of Proven) and Karsiek, and thence to Upernavick, once fifty miles at a single pull. During this hard labor we cooked birds upon the rocks, and slept under buffalo-robes. Human destitution—the filthy desolation of the Esquimaux settlements—was contrasted with glories beyond conception. I had never before realized the grand magnificence of Greenland scenery. It would be profanation to attempt to describe it."

After speaking of other and unexpected helps, of a character that promised greatly more than they fulfilled, he continues:—"I feel that something must be achieved; and, if your son fails to bring back his often and hard-battered carcass, he will at least send back a record of manly effort and hardly-tried-for success.

"Our brig is only fifteen miles from the harbor, trying to fan her way with a feeble off-shore breeze, which has, since I began to write, ruffled with cat's-paw tremors the surface of the dead waters. Our course is now directly for the bay; and, as far as my ice-knowledge can predict its condition, every thing is in favor of a safe and easy passage. Say this to mother, but to no outside person, as I do not wish to hazard an opinion. Say to mother to have no fears on Arctic account. I am not entirely well, but as well as I would be at home, and so trusting in the Great Disposer of good and ill that I am willing to meet like a man the worst that can happen to one secure of right, and approving, heart and soul, of that in which he is engaged. Good-bye. E. K. K.

"'Love' ☞ my last word is 'Love.'"

Dr. Kane's published journals are full of the evidences of his faith in the survivorship of at least some of Franklin's party, and of his hopeful devotion to their rescue. His father, speaking from that intimacy and certainty of knowledge which an unreserved confidence afforded, in a note published in the papers of the day, says of him, "His characteristic with us was his sensibility to conscientious impulse. It was this which carried him the second time to the Polar sea, and, had God spared him, would have made him return there again; for he believed, as none but the true-hearted can believe any thing, that some of Franklin's party were still alive, and that it was the mission of his life to reclaim them. He had a child-like fondness for the affections of home; but this, and zeal for science, and ambition for fame, and all else that could connect itself with motive, was subordinated to his one great conviction of duty."

The grounds of this confidence not only held against his own terrible experiences of Arctic exposure, but arose out of those experiences. In May, 1854, after testing the ability of his party to endure a temperature as low as 67° below zero, or 99° below the freezing-point of water, he says, "How can my thoughts turn despairingly to poor Franklin and his crew?

"Can they have survived? No man can answer with certainty; but no man, without presumption, can answer in the negative.

"If, four months ago, surrounded by darkness and bowed down by disease, I had been asked the question, I would have turned toward the bleak hills and the frozen sea, and responded, in sympathy with them, 'No.' But with the return of light a savage people came down upon us, destitute of any but the rudest appliances of the chase, who were fattening on the most wholesome diet of the region, only forty miles from our anchorage, while I was denouncing its scarcity.

"For Franklin every thing depends upon locality; but, from what I can see of Arctic exploration thus far, it would be hard to find a circle of fifty miles' diameter entirely destitute of animal resources.

"Of the one hundred and thirty-six picked men of Sir John Franklin in 1846, Northern Orkney men, Greenland whalers, so many young and hardy constitutions, with so much intelligent experience to guide them, I cannot realize that some may not yet be alive; that some small squad or squads, aided or not aided by the Esquimaux of the Expedition, may not have found a hunting-ground, and laid up, from summer to summer, enough of fuel and food and seal-skins to brave three, or even four, more winters in succession."

In the midst of the last winter, long after the daily prayer was changed from "Lord, accept our gratitude, and bless our undertaking," to "Lord, accept our gratitude, and restore us to our homes," his journal reads: —" Please God in his beneficent providence to spare us for the work, I will yet give one manly tug to search the shores of Kennedy Channel for memorials of the lost, and then, our duties over here, and the brig still prison-bound, enter trustingly upon the task of our escape."

In March, 1856, ten full years after the last date of Franklin's record among the living, he wrote to Mr. Grinnell:—

"In my opinion, the vessels cannot have been suddenly destroyed, or at least so destroyed that provisions and stores could not have been established in a safe and convenient depôt. With this view, which all my experience of ice sustains, comes the collateral question as to the safety of the documents of the Expedition. But this, my friend, is not all. I am really in doubt as to the preservation of human life. I well know how glad I would have been, had my duties to others permitted me, to have taken refuge among the Esquimaux of Smith's Straits and Etah Bay. Strange as it may seem to you, we regarded the coarse life of those people with eyes of envy, and did not doubt but that we could have lived in comfort upon their resources. It required all my powers, moral and physical, to prevent my men from deserting to the walrus-settlements; and it was my fixed intention to have taken to Esquimaux life, had Providence not carried us through in our hazardous escape.

"Now, if the natives reached the seat of the missing ships of Franklin, and there became possessed, by pilfer or by barter, of the articles sent home by Rae and Anderson, this very fact would explain the ability of some of the party to sustain life among them. If, on the other hand, the natives have never reached the ships, or the seat of their stores, and the relics were obtained from the descending boat,—then the central stores or ships are unmolested, and some may have been able, by these and the hunt, even yet to sustain life.

"All my men and officers agree with me that, even in the desert of Rensselaer Bay, we could have descended to the hunting-seats, and sustained life by our guns or the craft of the natives. Sad, and perhaps useless, as is this reflection, I give it to you as the first outpouring of my conscientious opinions."

We are concerned now only with the earnestness of Dr. Kane's own convictions, and the reasons which held his judgment in harmony with his heart to his last hour in the dedication of his life to the enterprise of rescuing the missing mariners; but this is the right place to give the opinions of those high authorities who held the same hope, and for the same reasons, after his had gone with him, unfulfilled, to his grave.

Sir Roderick Murchison, President of the Royal Geographical Society of London, delivering the anniversary discourse, on the 25th of May, 1857, holds the following language:—

"Lastly, Dr. Kane performed those extraordinary researches beyond the head of Baffin's Bay which obtained for him our gold medal at the last anniversary, the highest eulogy of our late President, and the unqualified admiration of all geographers.

"At that time, however, we had not perused those thrilling pages which have since brought to our mind's eye the unparalleled combination of genius with patient endurance and fortitude which enabled this young American to save the lives of his associates.

"With what simplicity, what fervor, what eloquence, and what truth, he has described the sufferings and perils from which he extricated his ice-bound crew, is now duly appreciated; and you must all agree with me that in the whole history of literature there never was a work written which more feelingly develops the struggles of humanity under the most intense sufferings, or demonstrates more strikingly how the most appalling difficulties can be overcome by the union of a firm resolve with the never-failing resources of a bright intellect.

"In all these soul-stirring pages there is no passage which comes more home to the Englishmen who are still advocating the search for the relics of the Erebus and Terror than that in which, after judging from the experience of his own companions how men of our lineage may be brought to bear intense cold and trail on their existence among the Esquimaux, he thus soliloquizes:—'My mind never realizes the complete catastrophe,—the destruction of all Franklin's crews. I picture them to myself broken into detachments, and my mind fixes on one little group of some thirty who have found the open spot of some tidal eddy, and, under the teachings of an Esquimaux, or perhaps one of their own Greenland whalers, have set bravely to work, and trapped the fox, speared the bear, and killed the seal, the walrus, and the whale. *I think of them ever with hope. I sicken not to be able to reach them.*'

"These generous and lofty sentiments, as I shall afterwards point out in dwelling on Lady Franklin's final search, are shared by that distinguished Arctic officer of the United States navy, our associate, Captain Hartstene; and they have justly awakened the hope in the breasts of many of my countrymen and myself that some of the fine young fellows who sailed with Franklin may still be alive, and must, for the honor of our country, be sought for, as well as the débris and records of the Erebus and Terror."

THE BRAVE TRUST THE BRAVE. 197

If the events of the search now on foot under the conduct of Captain McClintock, directed as it is, by the thorough but hitherto unsuccessful explorations of all the region round about, to the spot where Franklin and his companions must have gone, shall disprove Dr. Kane's inferences, his mistake will be explained, to all who understand his character, by the tendency of an ardent mind to believe every thing possible which, in the like circumstances, he could himself achieve. Franklin's party could not have fallen into more hopeless circumstances than his own encountered; and why should they utterly perish when he escaped? or, failing to accomplish so grand an enterprise as his retreat to a place of security, how could he believe that they should perish helplessly where he and his little crew could survive? The leader of the retreat from Smith's Sound was not the man to apprehend impossibilities for resolute men.

For the OBJECTS of this voyage, other than the rescue of the Franklin party, and subordinate to it, but in themselves worthy of the man and of his heroic endeavor to achieve them, I must, perforce, refer the reader to the clear and effective display which they have, in the well-known volumes which Dr. Kane has given to the public. Especially would I call the attention of all who are capable of such inquiries, to the *Appendix* of the Kane Expedition: it occupies nearly two hundred pages of the second volume.

The mass of Dr. Kane's million readers has been, I am safe in supposing, only too much absorbed by the narrative of the Expedition to turn patiently to the scientific results so elaborately and yet so attractively presented in the Appendix.

If it were possible, and at the same time conformable to the purpose and limits of this memoir, to digest the results which are in danger of being overlooked by the general reader, it would be a labor of love to endeavor its accomplishment; but that service must be rendered to the public and to the memory of Dr. Kane as an author and cultivator of physical science under other conditions. I expect, as I hope, that it will be done by a more competent hand. The mass of inedited manuscript left by Dr. Kane will some day be material for a work such as he would have executed, whenever the man shall be found to supply the loss which natural science sustained by his early removal from his own great field of labor.

Variously endowed as he was for observing and resolving the phenomena of nature, and skilled as he was, beyond all men equally qualified for collecting the data, in the art of writing for general instruction, the loss to the public in this unfulfilled purpose of writing a book of Arctic science such as would have satisfied himself, is beyond estimate, and, it is to be feared, will never be wholly supplied.

We are concerned now only with Dr. Kane's personal history, and not otherwise with his scientific achievements than as they illustrate the man. This involves his theory of an open sea at or near the North Pole, and his announcement of an actual discovery of such a body of open water, beginning above the eighty-first degree of north latitude and extending to an unknown distance northward. The grounds upon which he rested this doctrine are fully set forth in his lecture delivered before the American Geographical and Statistical Society, at New York, on the 14th of December, 1852, to which we beg leave to refer, because it cannot be condensed effectively for any purpose here. It is published in the Appendix to his "First Expedition," page 543.

The open sea discovered by the party sent out in June, 1854, from the brig lying then ice-bound in Rensselaer Harbor, latitude 78° 37' 10" North and longitude 70° 40' West from Greenwich, is located at a little above latitude 81°; the linear distance from the brig being one hundred and ninety-six miles, and the travel-distance, following the indentations of the coast-line of the bay and channel intervening, about three hundred and twenty miles. William Morton and Hans Christian, a half-breed Esquimaux, constituted the party who discovered and reported it. Dr. Kane and the astronomer, Mr. Sontag, were at the time ill of scurvy; Dr. Hayes had just returned from his survey of the coast of Grinnell Land, worn out and snow-blind; and of the whole crew and officers there were but six well men on the health-roll. Four of these were despatched in advance, with provisions, to the base of the Great Glacier, (one hundred and twenty miles' travel-distance,) to endeavor to scale and survey it; and Morton and Hans were sent with them, under instructions to push to the north across Peabody Bay and advance along the more distant coast.

The period for exploration was passing rapidly away. The party were in the hapless condition described; but the summer and the objects of the voyage must not be lost. The journal has it:—"I am intensely anxious that the party shall succeed. It is my last throw. They have all my views; and I believe they will carry them out unless overruled by a higher Power.

"But I am not without apprehensions that, with all their efforts, the Glacier cannot be surmounted.

"In this event, the main reliance must be on Mr. Morton: he takes with him a sextant, artificial horizon, and pocket-chronometer, and has intelligence, courage, and the spirit of endurance in full measure. He is withal a long-tried and trusty follower."

This character Mr. Morton had earned by every form of trial to which it could be put through four years of close relations, beginning with the Arctic voyage of the first Grinnell Expedition, in 1850, of which they were both members; and the after and equally trying experiences of his worth, which continued unbroken up to the death of the leader, left the faithful follower and friend with an ample confirmation of all this confidence and trust.

He needs no other certificate of character to secure our confidence; and he does not need even this with those who know him well.

THE DISCOVERY.

Both to the accuracy and veracity of his report Dr. Kane gave unreserved credence. But he speaks of the inferences to be drawn from Morton's narrative with his characteristic caution,—the caution of that mental and moral truthfulness which led him to utter the remarkable sentence that closes the introductory chapter to his "First Expedition:"—"I might have done more wisely if I had been content to substitute sometimes the educated opinions of others for those which impressed me at the moment. My apology must be that *I do not profess to be accurate, but truthful.*"

And now, when summing up the points bearing upon the great question of an open Polar sea, he says, "I am reluctant to close my notice of this discovery without adding that the details of Mr. Morton's narrative harmonized with the observations of all our party;" and then continues, "I do not proceed to discuss here the causes or conditions of this phenomenon. How far it may extend,—whether it exists simply as a feature of the immediate region, or as a part of a great and unexplored area communicating with the Polar basin,—and what may be the argument in favor of the one or the other hypothesis, or the explanation which reconciles it with established laws,—may be questions for men skilled in scientific deductions. Mine has been the more humble duty of recording what we saw. Coming as it did, a mysterious fluidity in the midst of vast plains of solid ice, it was well calculated to arouse emotions of the highest order; and I do not believe there was a man among us who did not long for the means of embarking upon its bright and lonely waters. But he who may be content to follow our story for the next four months will feel that a controlling necessity made the desire a fruitless one."

The three following pages of the book* are given to the consideration, or rather to the suggestion for the reader's use, of certain facts involved in the issue; but he betrays no overweening desire to lodge an affirmative conclusion in the minds which he is addressing. On the contrary, he disclaims any such inclination, deferring, gracefully as modestly, the theoretical argument to Lieutenant Maury, Superintendent of the National Observatory, who has made the physical geography of the sea, and the currents of the ocean of air, his own province by the cultivation of their science with such success as has given him a world-wide fame, and an authority among physicists growing, it may be said, daily by the constantly advancing attainments of his labor.

Moreover, in the notes appended to the brief discussion in which he indulges, he takes care to guard the unlearned in Arctic phenomena against the hasty conclusions which they might draw from the imposing array of facts that support the doctrine of an open water from the point observed to the Pole. He says, indeed, "I do not see how, independently of direct observation, this state of facts can be explained without supposing an ice-

---

* Second Expedition, vol. i. pp. 306–309.

less area to the farther north;" but, he interposes again, "How far this may extend—whether it does or does not communicate with a Polar basin—we are without facts to determine. I would say, however, as a cautionary check to some theories in connection with such an open basin, that the influence of rapid tides and currents in destroying ice by abrasion can hardly be realized by those who have not witnessed their action."

In his official report made to the Navy Department after his return, he states the whole matter thus:—

"This precipitous headland, the farthest point attained by the party, was named Cape Independence. It is in latitude 81° 22′ N. and longitude 65° 35′ W. It was only touched by William Morton, who left the dogs and made his way to it along the coast. From it the western coast was seen stretching far towards the north, with an iceless horizon, and a heavy swell rolling in with white caps. At a height of about five hundred feet above the sea this great expanse still presented all the appearance of an open and iceless sea. In claiming for it this character I have reference only to the facts actually observed, without seeking confirmation or support from any deduction of theory. Among such facts are the following:—

"1. It was approached by a channel entirely free from ice, having a length of fifty-two and a mean width of thirty-six geographical miles.

"2. The coast-ice along the water-line of this channel had been completely destroyed by thaw and water-action; while an unbroken belt of solid ice, one hundred and twenty-five miles in diameter, extended to the south.

"3. A gale from the northeast, of fifty-four hours' duration, brought a heavy sea from that quarter, without disclosing any drift or other ice.

"4. Dark *nimbus* clouds and water-sky invested the northeastern horizon.

"5. Crowds of migratory birds were observed thronging its waters."

In his summary of the operations of the Expedition in the same document, thus :—" The discovery of a large channel to the northwest, free from ice, and leading into an open and expanding area equally free. The whole embraces an iceless area of four thousand two hundred miles."

Immediately after his return from the region in question, after closing an extemporized report of his voyage and its results before the Geographical Society of New York, he was asked by Mr. Chauncey, "Is it possible, in your opinion, to reach this open sea with boats and explore it?" He answered, "That is coming rather near home. I think, with a proper organization, it might be reached; and I have no doubt it will yet be reached and be explored."

He never said or claimed more for a circumpolar open sea *discovery* than this. It was not in the nature of the man at thirty-six years of age, who wrote the Kyestein thesis at twenty-one, to confound hypothesis with discovery, or to mistake inferences for facts observed. But

BRITISH ACHIEVEMENTS. 205

that he believed theoretically in a navigable Polar sea is abundantly proved by his adoption of the Smith's Sound route of search, relying, as he did, upon an open pathway from its northern outlet, east and west, to the Greenland Sea or Wellington Channel, as the search might eventually determine. And when, after all his experiences, and his own failure for lack of the necessary means, he said that he had no doubt it would yet be reached and explored, he uttered a prediction, based upon known facts, which, we may safely venture to believe with him, will 'yet be fulfilled.

The best corroboration of this expectation accessible to the general reader to which I can refer is the eighth chapter of Maury's "Physical Geography of the Sea," edition of 1857.

Kane has left this legacy of honorable adventure to his countrymen, and they will yet, and that ere long, prove themselves worthy of the trust.

The magnetic pole in the Western hemisphere has been discovered and definitely located; the NORTHWEST PASSAGE, with a portage *insertion*, has been found,—a channel sealed solid by Jack Frost, or a submerged isthmus of obstructing rock, sheeted with ice,—no matter: the question is solved, and the discoverer duly honored, putting that old worry to rest. But, whether the magnetic pole fluctuates, with the frost-pole for company, or the water between Banks' Land and Melville Island will not, British enterprise has carried off the honors of these achievements.

It is very certain now that this passage will never be

ploughed by the keels of commerce, or otherwise answer to the venerable old hopes which hung upon its discovery. It cannot be made a track for the missionaries of religion, civilization, and learning, nor does it open a gate for military invasion; but the search for it has given us the geography and natural history of almost all the landmasses of the Western hemisphere; and the long endeavor has fully repaid all the incident expenditure of wealth, labor, and life, so generously lavished upon it.

The whale-fishery of the Greenland seas alone has cost a hundred times more of sacrifice; and we dare not even compare the benefits which trade reaps in whalebone and fish-oil with the treasures of useful knowledge gathered by the liberal labors of science led by benevolence in the Arctic regions.

Since 1848, when fears for the safety of Sir John Franklin and his crews began to be entertained, twenty-five expeditions, employing thirty-one vessels and costing four millions of dollars, have attempted to solve the mystery of his fate. The enterprise to which he gave himself is now known to be a vain one, so far as commerce or travel is concerned, and all the hopes of his rescue are still unfulfilled; but the world has not lost the treasure or the lives which have been expended in the search for the Northwest Passage and for the long-lost mariners.

The results of these explorations make up a grand library of useful knowledge. Geography, geology, meteorology, have gained largely by the great undertaking;

and, when the contributions which it has made to our stock of knowledge come to be thoroughly understood, it will be time to estimate adequately the worth of Arctic adventure.

The two American expeditions in which Dr. Kane participated and of which he was the historian, and that of Captain Hartstene, of which he and his companions were the object, have secured some of the grandest prizes of geographical enterprise which the nineteenth century has aimed at: De Haven baptized the most northern land of the American continent with an American name, and Kane has put that of Washington upon the most northern land on the globe!

It is something, surely, to have discovered the position of the magnetic pole and the geographic range of the lowest temperature. It is something to have traced the great current-system of the ocean,—to have demonstrated its circulation from the earth's tropic heart to its polar extremities, bearing out its arterial heat, and returning the great centripetal tides, as the veins return the life-currents to their source for revivification.

Arctic exploration has, within the last forty years, done as much for physical geography as the labors of the same period have accomplished in any other department of natural knowledge; and, much as it has yielded of mature fruit, it has brought us, besides, to the open portal of a new world of terrestrial discovery. The Polar sea opened to observation by the Kane Expedition of 1854 promises still more than all that has yet been secured.

For there, within the barrier of perpetual ice, is the treasury of the ocean-tides; there is the nursery of that migratory life which fills the seas and air of the northern temperate zone; there the wondrous compensations of polar and tropical forces are displayed; there stands the observatory of the globe, its chemical laboratory, the theatre of its meteoric exhibitions, and a thousand secrets besides, to enrich the natural sciences, and to correct and adjust all that we already know of the system of our planet in accordance with the truth and beauty of its paramount laws.

None of these things are so remote as the movements of the solar system. They cannot be of less moment to us. They must be available for extending the control of man over the material agencies by which he is surrounded; and they are all here put within our reach. The way is opened; the route is charted; its practicability is proved; and it is impossible to doubt the grand results of a well-appointed expedition, guided by the successes, and guarded by the failures, of that one whose first-fruits are the assuring promise of the full harvest.

CHAPTER XII.

THE NATURAL SCIENCES—GLACIOLOGY—RELIEF-EXPEDITION—CAPTAIN HARTSTENE—DR. JOHN K. KANE—THE KNIGHT AND HIS SQUIRE—THE THREE CAPTAINS—AUTHORSHIP AGAIN—PAINS AND PENALTIES—AUTHOR AND PUBLISHERS—THE UNWRITTEN BOOK—ENGRAVINGS—MR. HAMILTON—DR. KANE'S DRAWINGS—ARTISTIC SKILL—FACILITY AND FIDELITY—CONGRESSIONAL SUBSCRIPTION—POPULAR AND PUBLIC PATRONAGE—THE AUTHOR'S INVOLVEMENT—THE SECRETARY'S COMMENDATION—TESTIMONIALS AND MEDALS.

It has been my proper business to *study* Dr. Kane's published journals with care. Whoever will do the same thing with the interest in their contributions to natural science which they deserve will feel something of the reluctance with which I forego their presentation in this work. But it was not until I was alarmed by the vast range of these topics to which the drift of the last chapter had well-nigh committed me, that I felt at once the full force of the onward impulse, and the severity of those restraints of my plan and limits which compel me to break away from the seductive entanglement.

There are treasures of tribute here to the sciences of physical geography, zoology, meteorology, climatology, and anthropology, which their cultivators will do well to avail themselves of. Some acquaintance with the present state and requirements of these departments of physical philosophy warrants me in directing attention to these books,—more especially to his first journal of exploration, which, after all, is *the* book of the two.

The *savans* are just now very earnestly engaged, as upon a fresh field of inquiry, with that branch of physical geography which may be called glaciology. They may find in Dr. Kane's publications a mine of wealth ready and available for their use. For nine months of his first voyage the "Advance" lay docked in an ice-cradle, and at the same time adrift, making a tour of a thousand miles on the Arctic sea under bare poles. The daily study of the ice, through this long period, by a man qualified as he was to observe, digest, and report, is necessarily full of instruction. In his second voyage he had the opportunities of two winters nearer to the Pole than any other observer with his means and capability for exact observation has ever been. His zeal and industry in the study of the phenomena presented, and his exactitude in recording the results, have no parallel in the history of Arctic exploration. We venture, for these reasons, to advise those who have gone through his volumes under the influence of their other fascinations, to read and re-read them till they can see through the enchantment the substance of the physical truths which the genius of the writer has veiled with its brilliancy.

Even the principal incidents of the last voyage must be allowed to pass without a record here. Indeed, they may well be trusted to his own report, which has been, and will be, read by millions who will never open the lids of this mere supplement to the *Life* of Kane unconsciously written into the texture of his own publications.

There are some things, however, omitted in that "epic of manly endurance"—things which he would not record: they are those which wholly concerned himself. Something of all this has been supplied by three of his companions in the Expedition, and they are given at the close of these chapters, for their importance as the testimony of men well qualified to speak to the points, and worthy of all reliance.

It is due to these gentlemen to say here that these letters were not prepared for publication; but I use my liberties at my own discretion. The reader will thank me for presenting, and I will thank the writers for furnishing, them; which must settle the account between all parties, as it must settle all the others which I have opened so freely in the compilation of these pages.

In our narrative we left Dr. Kane and his party, on their way to the unknown North, on the verge of that fearful ice-ring which environs the mystery kept secret since the world began, but now made manifest, and by the revelations of its prophet made known to all nations.

This allusion is neither irreverent nor unwarranted; for the courage and virtue which inspire the knight-errants of noble adventure are the selfsame qualities which made Israel to prevail with the angel, and gave Paul his victories over the spiritual foes which beset him. The good purposes of a great soul rise orderly into the supernatural: they are always sacrificial; they have ever the tone of devotion and the spirit of martyrdom; and they take its risks, too. Why should they be levelled in our apprehension to the plane of a commonplace life, or be muddied with its low-pitched motives, or be measured by its standards?

When the second winter set in without bringing home the Advance and her crew, the most serious alarm for their fate was felt by the friends of the adventurers and by the whole mass of their countrymen. These forebodings were darkened beyond the ordinary apprehension of danger in Arctic service by the fact that their first winter had been an unusually severe one, and by the known deficiencies of their outfit for the endurance of a second one in the ice. Congress was memorialized by the learned societies who stood sponsors for the undertaking; and the general sentiment of the people pressed upon their representatives and public servants for a relief-expedition in the spring. It was frankly accorded, and well provisioned, and better manned and officered.

Two vessels, the bark Release and the propeller Arctic, under command of Lieutenant Hartstene, U.S.N., with a brother of Dr. Kane,—Dr. John K. Kane,—and Lieutenant W. S. Lovell, an Arctic expert and former companion of Dr. Kane, among the volunteers. They left New York on the 31st of May, 1855, exactly two years after the Advance had taken her departure from the same port.

DR. JOHN K. KANE.

After a run round Baffin's Bay, including encounters with icebergs, ice-fields, hummocks, and the usual assortment of circumstances which characterize that sea of troubles,—made in the best time, in the best style, and to the best purpose of all the voyages into that region,— they picked up the lost adventurers on their homeward way, after they had achieved for themselves a deliverance from all their dangers.

For the story of this relief-trip by Hartstene we refer to Putnam's Magazine for May, 1856, written by Dr. John K. Kane. It is well worth the reading for all the usual and unusual reasons, and for this besides: that it is rich with the relish of the Kane pluck which there is in it, and for those relief-touches of happy authorship which distinguish the style and movement of his elder brother's pen.

A word of our own gossip, to mark the conjunction of things at Lievely, where Hartstene found the Kane party just on the eve of making their way home in a Danish vessel by way of the Shetland Islands, and we finish this voyage of suffering and success, defeat and victory, strangely mixed till they landed in safety at New York, on the 11th of October, 1855, after a thirty months' absence.

When the first news of the relief-vessels of Hartstene were announced to the forlorn survivors of the Arctic crew, McGary, Dr. Kane's "iron man," sore with the toils and dangers of a thirteen-hundred-mile trip in an open boat through Smith's Sound and Melville Bay, said,

"There, now! we have had all our hard work for nothing."
"What!" said Dr. Kane, turning sharply on him; "are you sorry that we owe our deliverance to our own exertions?"

It was the knight and the squire, the seer and his servant, over again,—the joint adventure, the equal peril, the fellowship of daring, doing, and enduring, with all the difference between the spiritual and natural in the respective characters of the inspiration and impulse.

The parties to this brief dialogue, alas! knew not then how much they had yet to pay for the honors which they had purchased. McGary, who once stood to his oar for twenty-two unbroken hours, without relaxing his attention or his efforts, in a frenzied sea, and his commander, who stood at his unresting toil for thirty months, have both paid with their lives the price of the strength they borrowed for the demands of that terrible service.

De Haven commanded the first American expedition to the icy ocean of the North; Dr. Kane, the second; Hartstene, the third and last: the navy lost no honor by either of them.

When Hartstene was on his way, with all the dangers of his search immediately before him, he wrote to the Secretary of the Navy, "To avoid further risk of human life in a search so extremely hazardous, I would suggest the impropriety of making any efforts to relieve us if we should not return."

That will do for the character of the man: a single incident will serve for a sample of his conduct. When

AUTHORSHIP AGAIN.

his ship was in peril he *conned* her for thirty-six hours, without a moment's rest. His position was at the masthead: he had a sprained ankle and a lame arm,—his only diversion through the long and anxious watch!

Our readers by this time will be thinking that there are some chances for heroism in the navy without bloodshed. If they do, they may hurrah, without reserve or protest, for Hartstene and De Haven, who still adorn the service.

Dr. Kane announced his safe return to the Hon. John P. Kennedy by letter written before he landed in New York, dated "Entering Sandy Hook, Bark Release, October 11, 1855." He says, "We are back again safe and sound, after an open-air travel by boats and sledges of thirteen hundred miles." Soon after this, when he met his friend he told him, "My health is almost absurd: I have grown like a walrus."

This stock of unwonted strength was now to be employed in the composition and illustration of the book which he entitled "Arctic Explorations: The Second Grinnell Expedition in Search of Sir John Franklin, 1853-54-55."

The labor upon it was soon commenced and long sustained. The toils and risks under which its materials were gained were not greater to him than this task of artist-authorship in which he was now engaged. Nine hundred pages of book-matter carried through in little more than six months is, in his own language, "no fun;" but add to this three hundred engravings made from his own sketches, whose execution, from the moment they went into the hands of the designer till the last proof-impression came from the printer, required his own supervision, and complicate all this with the thousand demands made upon his time and toil by the celebrity-tax levied upon him at this time, and an Arctic voyage will appear almost as nothing to the travail of his last cruise in the troubled waters of "authordom."

The narrative was finished some time in June; but the Appendix was a worry till September, when the book was issued.

The pains and penalties are graphically rendered in his letters to Mr. Childs, of the publishing firm of Childs & Peterson. Brief extracts, grouped in the order of their dates, are expressive enough, and sufficiently explain themselves:—

"The wretched book! there is no reason that the whole *incubus* should not be off our hands this week.—3½ A.M."

"The rest of your requests shall be complied with. At present the letters are dancing up and down, and I think that bed is the best place for me.—3 A.M."

"My wish is to make a centre-table book, fit as well for the eyes of children as of refined women."

"Now that the 'exploration' is over, I attempt to be more popular and gaseous: this latter inflated quality in excess. Most certainly my effort to make this book readable will destroy its permanency and injure me. It is a sacrifice.—May 25."

"Very glad the poor book meets your views. Authordom has again overdone me. I will have to take a spell soon.—June 7."

"My health is nothing extraordinary under this extreme heat; but I think that I have accumulated enough of nerve-force to carry me through to that ominously pleasant word, 'Finis.'—June 14."

"With little spirit of congratulation, and much weariness, I send you the preface, which completes my text. I am not the first who has manufactured an antecedent *ex post facto;* and there is a sort of moral conveyed by this ending of my labors. Now that the holy day is at hand, I am ungrateful enough to complain that it finds me without the capacity to enjoy it.—July 4."

"Do send in rapidly the proofs of the Appendix, and thus shorten my slavery.—July 23."

"My health goes on as usual. Something is the matter, for I get weaker every day. I tried Long Island bathing, but I could not stand it.—July 30."

"I am now convinced that my enemy is a combination of rheumatism and the Arctic scourge of scurvy.—August 9."

"My motion being impeded by my maladies, I would regard it as a favor if you could come to me for a few minutes.—August 21."

"I am unable to announce any improvement in my health.—September 18."

"At present I see no possible chance of being able to work in any way; and the unanswered letters which crowd around me might well appall an abler man. I leave in a fortnight, probably for Europe, as a sort of last resource, to catch my lost blessing. The book, poor as it is, has been my coffin.—September 23, 1856."

His own unaffected opinion of the book is to be gathered from what we have quoted, and from another equally private and earnest utterance which the letter-book of Mr. Childs furnishes. Mr. Childs took the liberty of striking from the proof-sheet of the preface the following paragraph, after it had passed through the author's hands to go into type :—" I might excuse myself for the thousand imperfections which haste and official preoccupation—and something, too, of the indisposition which a weary man may feel to retrace in the closet what was either exciting or irksome in the field—have no doubt impressed on my pages. But my apology would be of little worth; for I know how imperfect the book is while I am giving it to the public."

His fight for freedom in the preface, which he innocently supposed to be the author's preserve,—his own absolute domain,—was a vigorous one; but the autocracy of the press would not allow the modesty of the author to depreciate the book in the market.

He has his last word with them in another note. He says:—"After the *opus magnum* now in your hands, I hope to publish, either through the Smithsonian or the Government, a work on Ice, for reputation sake."

This purpose and its motive put its whole meaning into the first sentence of the published preface :—" This book is not a record of scientific investigations;" and it makes us understand, besides, how much of the best fruits of his life's studies and achievements were reserved for a fitting presentment to the world.

Of the engravings of the work, Dr. Kane says, in his preface, "Although largely, and in some cases exclusively, indebted for their interest to the artistic skill of Mr. Hamilton, they are, with scarcely an exception, from sketches made on the spot."

Their excellence has had a large share of the admiration given to the work. Reviewers have turned aside from the drift of their argument to give them due commendation. Taking one from a hundred criticisms entitled to high respect, that of Blackwood's Edinburgh Magazine may stand for the whole of them:—"The engravings of Dr. Kane's book," says this high authority, "are eminently happy as the productions of a man who is a real poet in art, Mr. Hamilton, whose good taste scatters beautiful vignettes like gems through the two volumes, and invests the whole work with a halo of romance mysterious as the effects of light in those Northern regions, and which could scarcely have been produced by the power of words or the letter-press."

For more than a month of the time during which the artist was engaged upon these illustrations, he occupied the doctor's own rooms, that night and day might be given to their execution. Such were Mr. Hamilton's opportunities for forming an opinion of the author's capabilities as a sketcher: his competency is attested by his admitted pre-eminence as a landscape and marine painter.

He has kindly and cheerfully furnished me with the following letter:—

"July 1, 1857.

"DEAR SIR:—Your note requesting me to transmit to you my impressions respecting the late Dr. Kane's sketches is received.

"Although fully conscious of the very small importance which can attach to any thing I can say in reference to any matter connected with the illustrious explorer, it nevertheless affords me great pleasure to communicate to you my 'opinion' on this subject.

"One of the most prominent features of the doctor's sketches, and one which I think must strike the most cursory observer at all conversant with art or nature, is the air of simple, earnest truthfulness which pervades them. These qualities, without which the most labored efforts are comparatively worthless, exist to an extent which confers importance on the most insignificant of them,—the great bulk of them being directly from nature, and embracing scenery and incident not only from the Arctic regions, but from the four quarters of the globe, made during his various journeys and explorations.

"In glancing over Dr. Kane's drawings and sketches, it will be perceived that, whether executed with every appliance and facility which modern ingenuity can

ARTISTIC SKILL. 221

furnish, or with the half-thawed ink and greasy paper or pasteboard accidentally picked up among the rubbish of the ship's store-room, there is distinctly traceable in all the ever-present influence of one all-absorbing object, —*the faithful record of the most essential features and qualities of the subject or scene before him.*

"Hundreds of illustrative instances might be readily selected from his well-filled folios and note-books. I will refer to a few of those which furnished the material for some of the illustrations of the 'Arctic Explorations.'

"First, we will select that of 'the great green minaret,' *Tennyson's Monument.* The original sketch is of the slightest description, and in lead-pencil.

"Now, every one accustomed to study nature practically is aware of the extreme difficulty of rendering the peculiar texture and tone of old, time-worn, weather-beaten rock, sandstone, crushed débris, &c. Its successful rendition is one of the most difficult achievements of landscape art. In the sketch of the subject alluded to, these qualities (notwithstanding the 'coldness and sickness' suffered at the time of executing it, mentioned by the lamented navigator in his journal) are secured to an extent that would be creditable to the most skilful artist: every fragment is jotted down with a perception and feeling which seize the special character of the minutest particle defined, and yet its minutiæ in no way conflicting with the grandeur of the subject.

"In the subjects of the Three Brother Turrets, the Look-Out from Cape George Russell, Cape Cornelius Grinnell, Northumberland Island, Thackeray Headland, The Cliffs, Glacier Bay, Beechey Island, and in scores of a similar kind, he has been quite as successful.

"With the exception of the shattered ice-belt and the piles of frozen rubbish which are incessantly accumulating on the Arctic shores in the most picturesque combinations, ice and its numberless formations present fewer difficulties to the draughtsman (owing to its sharply defined forms and striking contrasts) than any of those mentioned. Yet in this department we find the doctor exercising the same observance of local peculiarities as in others presenting more complicated difficulties.

"Most of his ice-studies are in pen-and-ink outlines, with a wash of the same material—common writing-ink—for background. Some of them are extremely good and imposing in their effects.

"The Icebergs near Kosoak, the Great Glacier of Humboldt, Weary Men's Rest, are all done in this manner; together with numberless others, such as Ice-foot, Ice-hills, Ice-rafts, Ice-belts, Ice-plains, &c. &c. Many of them are far better adapted, pictorially, for engraving than any in the 'Explorations.' This applies especially to some of the great glacier-scenery.

"I have no hesitation in saying that, could his sketches be placed before the public, they would add still further, if that were possible, to his reputation as an Arctic explorer.

"From these few straggling and imperfectly expressed ideas you can infer my opinion of Dr. Kane's abilities as an amateur artist, which is, as I understand you, the object of your inquiry."

In a postscript Mr. Hamilton adds:—"Another very note-worthy feature of the doctor's sketching was the extreme rapidity with which it was executed. In illustrating his wishes upon any particular subject, I have frequently seen him make slight drawings which required but a very few additional touches to render them complete."

Mr. Hamilton has given the deserved emphasis to Dr. Kane's artistic fidelity. His moral veracity was akin to it, if not its source and spring. There is a wide difference between them, or there may be; but they were but one in him: he frequently exacted as many as a dozen successive drawings of the same subject before he was satisfied with the accuracy and truth of the representation. In a note at the end of the first volume he repudiates two of the prints for the reason that his sketches had been modified by the artist.

I need add nothing to Mr. Hamilton's opinion of the sketches, which number hundreds, running up into the thousands, except that many of them were made in the open air, under a killing temperature, by a sick man, with the broad shoulders of Morton, Stephenson, or McGary for his easel, and lead-pencils for his implements.

Have we given an adequate idea of the artist and author work that went into the book?

When the publication was so far under way as to insure

its early completion, the publishers undertook, with the author's assent, to secure a subscription from Congress for a certain number of copies. A bill, under the conduct of the-Honorable J. R. Tyson, and with the hearty co-operation of Colonel Florence, of Philadelphia, Judge Pettit, of Indiana, Governor Aiken, of South Carolina, Speaker Banks, of Massachusetts, and many others among the leading men of the House, was passed. In the Senate it was ably supported by Governor Bigler, Judge Douglas, Governor Seward, Mr. Sumner, and Judge Butler, but was not passed.

The reports of other explorations had been published at a lavish expenditure of money by the Government: the publishers thought that the purchase by Congress of a limited number of copies would come within the rule of these precedents, and Dr. Kane felt like asking it on the plain grounds of justice to his enterprise; but he was governed by the interests of the firm which had undertaken the publication at an expense exceeding seventy thousand dollars for the first edition of the work, in giving his consent to the application, more than by any other motive. He could not persuade himself that they would be able to replace their liberal outlay by the unassisted sale of the book; and he could not, therefore, withhold his consent from a measure which they thought so important to their security.

If he or they had dreamed that the first year's sales would reach the enormous number of sixty-five thousand copies,—one hundred and thirty thousand volumes,—at

THE AUTHOR'S INVOLVEMENT. 225

the retail price reaching the sum of three hundred thousand dollars, and affording sixty-five thousand dollars copyright to the author, neither of them would have given a fig for any thing that the treasury of the nation or the endorsement of Congress could do for it. The issue proved that the patronage withheld was no loss to the parties interested: the purchase solicited would not have added a dollar to their income, as its refusal did not take one from it.

A letter of Dr. Kane's to Mr. Childs puts this affair upon its right grounds:—

"I had, like a fool, looked upon my approaching narrative as that of a voyage of discovery undertaken by order of the Government, and it seemed to me, under the circumstances, open to purchase or adoption by our National Legislature. With this view only, I had sanctioned an indirect connection with your movement, feeling that it was not a pecuniary recompense, but a direct transaction, for which a full equivalent was extended in the work itself. But Mr. Broadhead's* letter implies that I am acting with you to carry out a Congressional act of pecuniary reward, which is in every respect repugnant to my instincts as a gentleman and an officer.

"The late Expedition I have taught myself to consider as a matter of humanity; and I cannot forget that, whatever it may have done for mere geography, it involved

---

* A Senator, at that time, from Pennsylvania, who did not surprise *his acquaintances* by his conduct in this affair.

the risk not only of my own life, but that of my companions. It gives me pain to look back upon it; one-sixth of our little party perished in the field, and, of those who survive, a majority are mutilated or broken down. I cannot mingle with the associations of this cruise any thing so degrading as that of a pecuniary recompense; and I can only trust that my hard-earned labors will establish their own and best claim to the sympathy and consideration of good men. An honorary testimonial would have gratified me; but even that I now desire not to have mooted.—April 30, '56."

"I beg of you to leave unmolested the action of Congress; for this coupling of my name with the book will interfere with any expression of *disinterested* feeling on the part of the Senate, and thus stand in the way of that which I value far beyond either books or money,—viz., an honorary testimonial in recognition of our party, and such as has already been extended to me by England. —July 30, '56."

Mr. Dobbin, Secretary of the Navy, in his annual report of 3d December, 1855, speaks of the cruise, explorations, and report, in the following language:—

"It was well known that Dr. Kane left the United States in the humane search of Sir John Franklin, in June, 1853, under orders from the Navy Department, and at the same time under the patronage of distinguished philanthropists. His report is brief, but full of startling incidents and thrilling adventures. A more detailed and elaborate report will ultimately be made. The discoveries made by this truly remarkable man and excellent officer will be regarded as valuable contributions to science. He advanced in those frozen regions far beyond his intrepid predecessors, whose explorations had excited such admiration. His residence for two years with his little party far beyond the confines of civilization, with a small bark for his home, fastened with icy fetters that defied all efforts for emancipation, his sufferings from intense cold, and agony from dreadful apprehensions of starvation and death for that space of time,—his miraculous and successful journey in open sledges over the ice for eighty-four days,—not merely excite our wonder, but borrow a moral grandeur from the truly benevolent considerations which animated and nerved him for the task.

"I commend the results of his explorations as worthy of the attention and patronage of Congress."

How the attention and patronage of the Government acted upon these "results" has been seen: those of the public have been a full compensation. "The sympathy and consideration of good men," to which their author appealed, have abundantly supplied the plentiful lack of inspiration under which the responsible functionaries of the Federal Government disposed of the great claim.

Even the extra pay and emoluments made to the officers and men of the like rating in the Exploring Expedition to the South Seas, and granted also to the officers and crew of the De Haven Expedition, have never yet been extended to the poor fellows of the Kane party. Who is responsible for this excuseless neglect?

Mr. Dobbin handsomely put Dr. Kane on full pay while he was engaged in writing his "more detailed and elaborate report." This, indeed, was but a common grace, dispensed to the historians of all the national expeditions; but it deserves to be especially acknowledged in a history of relations to the Government of which it is the single example of a personal indulgence.

Congress, having failed at its first session after his return to appropriate, by a national recognition, the honors he had won for his country, had no other opportunity for repairing the neglect till after his death; then a gold medal was ordered,—of which, I believe, nothing has been heard since the passage of the resolution.

But resolutions duly honoring the enterprise and achievements of the Expedition were unanimously passed by the Legislatures of his native State, Pennsylvania, and by those of New Jersey and Maryland. A large gold medal was voted by the Legislature of New York, which was not finished till after his decease. The Royal Geographical Society of London gave him their gold medal and an honorary membership. The Queen's medal, designed for the Arctic explorers and searchers between the years 1818 and 1856, was presented; and a handsome testimonial, appropriately and specially executed, was given to him by the British residents of New York City.

CHAPTER XIII.

KANE'S SEA—THE CHART—SUMMARY OF OPERATIONS—LAST WILL—
VOYAGE TO ENGLAND—HOPING AGAINST HOPE—RECEPTION IN LON-
DON—LAST LETTER—DISEASE OF THE HEART—VOYAGE TO ST.
THOMAS—ON HIS WAY TO CUBA—ATTACK OF PARALYSIS—AT HA-
VANA—LONGING FOR HOME—LAST SCENE OF ALL—HE SLEEPETH—
INTERPRETATION—CHURCH RELATIONS—FREE-MASONRY—THE OBSE-
QUIES—LEGISLATIVE RESOLUTIONS—LEARNED SOCIETIES—ENGLISH
TESTIMONIAL.

THE narrative of the book was finished, as we have seen, before the 4th of July, the Appendix at the close of August, and the work was published in September. The chart exhibiting the discoveries of the Expedition was put into the hands of the printer, and appeared in all the copies issued before Dr. Kane's departure for England, without his own name attached to any of the lands, channels, capes, or bays which it embraced. Colonel Force, in the exercise of an authority held by right of undisputed pre-eminence in Arctic science and sound discretion in the distribution of the honors won in its service, printed the words KANE'S SEA with his own hand upon a copy of the chart, covering the large body of water which lies between Smith's Strait and

Kennedy Channel; and the publishers, without hesitation, altered the plate accordingly.

The discoveries and surveys embraced in the chart are, in brief:—

1. Nine hundred and sixty miles of coast-line delineated; which was effected by two thousand miles of travel on foot or by the aid of dogs.

2. Greenland traced to its northern face, where it is connected with the farther north of the opposite coast by the Glacier of Humboldt.

3. The survey of this great glacial mass,—"the mighty crystal bridge which connects the two continents of America and Greenland,"—sixty miles in length.

4. The discovery and delineation of the coast-line of Washington Land, separated from the American landmasses by a channel of but thirty-five miles in width, while the Great Glacier puts at least sixty between it and Greenland, and therefore regarded as in geographical continuity with the American continent.

5. The discovery and delineation of a large tract of land forming the extension northward of the American continent.

6. The discovery of a large channel to the northwest, free from ice, and leading into an open and expanding area equally free,—the whole embracing an iceless area of four thousand two hundred miles.

Of these surveys he speaks in this confident language, which from him is a sufficient assurance that they will not disappoint the utmost reliance which they invite:—

HIS WILL.

"I may be satisfied now with our projection of the Greenland coast. The different localities to the south have been referred to the position of our winter harbor, and this has been definitely fixed by the labors of Mr. Sontag, our astronomer. We have therefore not only a reliable base, but a set of primary triangulations which, though limited, may support the minor field-work of our sextants."

The unrelenting ice that forms the crystal link between the known and the unknown Northern seas, thus definitely measured and delineated, bears the name of its conqueror. It is poetically appropriate; and the spontaneous consent of the world awards it.

He sailed for England, "in search of his lost blessing," in the steamer Baltic, on the 10th of October, 1856, accompanied by the faithful Morton, who had gone with him to the world's end, and was now to go with him to the end of his life.

Immediately before leaving New York, he made his will. He was at the time entirely unaware of the large pecuniary results which his last work was to yield to its author. His expenditure for his current support, and in his customary liberal givings to the objects of his charity and kindness, left him nothing which may be very well called an estate; and he knew not at the time that he had certainly much of value to bequeath, for he had anticipated the receipts which he might confidently rely upon, and only felt assured that the expenses of his proposed trip to Europe were handsomely provided for, and that he was not in danger of debt.

He never in his life had been restricted in funds for his ordinary or necessary uses, and only felt their limit in his ardor for the great undertakings of his generous ambition and the indulgence of a large-hearted munificence.

It is because the world will be glad to know that poverty was not among his heavy burdens that this piece of very private history is given to it.

On the voyage to Liverpool an ominous change in his constitutional habit was manifested: he was not seasick. This strange exemption is sadly interpreted to us, by the issue, to indicate the strength of disease overmastering his idiosyncrasy. But the menacing symptoms of his malady were perhaps plain enough to any well-informed judgment not controlled by affection and its hopefulness. His wonderful tenacity of life—a sort of heroic vitality of his system—had so often restored him from hopeless illnesses, that his family, who knew his case best, entertained solacing expectations of benefit from the voyage.

His father, writing to Mr. Grinnell on the 1st of December, after the receipt of alarming news from London, says:—

"I need not say to you how heartfully I share your fears, and how grateful we all are for Mrs. Grinnell's sympathies and your own. But—I hardly know why it should be so—I cannot rid myself of a confidence that our son will be spared to us. I have waited in suspense for weeks, when the army surgeon's letter had assured me that he must die before morning of his wounds in Mexico. I have heard of him prostrate and hopeless with the fever of the African coast, and, before that, with the plague; I have twice bidden him a last good-bye, when he sailed upon his cruises for the Arctic; and but little more than a year ago, when he was fairly out of time, I gave him almost up for ten days before he reached New York. And now I cannot realize that so noble a spirit, so well tried in suffering and peril, so full of love and fortitude and daring, is to be the victim of ordinary disease. I cannot but hope, and trust even, that the same wise and beneficent Providence that has shielded him so often and so manifestly has other good work for him to do among his fellow-men."

Providence has *other* spheres of service for the capable; and a good man's work goes on in this one after his death, as the seed grows while the husbandman sleepeth; else this fond trust would have been fulfilled in the form which our human hearts craved.

Dr. Kane himself was far from sanguine of his recovery; yet, after his manner of controlling his apprehensions without betraying the effort, he seemed to enjoy the voyage. Dr. Betton, of Germantown, who was an old acquaintance, and now his fellow-passenger in the Baltic, says that, "when his strength would permit, he seemed to rise above his maladies and enjoy all around him, contributing his share to the general happiness." Even the watchful and well-schooled Morton was half deceived by the well-supported aspect of cheerfulness habitually worn by his friend.

They reached Liverpool on the 24th, and after three days went to London. Of his brief stay in the city, (about eight days,) Sir Roderick Murchison, President of the Royal Geographical Society, says:—"It was a subject of much regret to me that when Dr. Kane visited England the metropolis (as is usual at that season) was not inhabited by many of the persons who most valued his character, and that none of those attentions could then be paid to him which, had his stay been prolonged, would doubtless have been showered upon him, from the sovereign downwards. But, alas! the hand of death was already upon him; and, when I had the honor of an interview, I at once saw that his eagle eye beamed forth from a wasted and all but expiring body.

"As geographers, we were not, however, remiss in our endeavors to honor him; and, although his malady prevented his attendance at our apartments to receive our heartiest welcome, I then proposed that resolution expressive of our admiration of his conduct which you passed with acclamation, and which was communicated to him personally by our lamented President, Admiral Beechey."

While in the city he visited the office of the Admiralty upon invitation, and called once or twice upon Lady Franklin and Mrs. Sabine; but the fogs of London, so thick at mid-day that the street-lamps were invisible and flambeaus were carried before the carriages, overcame him: he grew worse rapidly. Upon the kind and hospitable invitation of Mr. Cross, he removed to his residence in Camberwell, about four miles distant from the Thames, where he remained from the 2d till the 17th of November, recovering a little in its better air, but only to the extent that enabled him to dine with the family, and requiring to be almost carried to the table.

On the 15th he wrote the letter of latest date from his hand which I have seen. It is addressed to his friend and frequent medical adviser, Dr. S. W. Mitchell, of Philadelphia:—

"MY DEAR FRIEND WEIR:—Perhaps it would comfort our dear people at Fern Rock* if you would mention that I have seen and consulted Dr. Watson with Sir Henry Holland. The former ausculted my lungs and pronounced against any *vice* other than the cold on the chest which now so depresses me. My inability to throw it off is explained by my extreme want of power and this wretched land of fogs.

"They all urge the 'exaltation' of vital function to be expected from a warmer climate.

"Talk over this, and add your excellent father to the consultation. You see the effort with which I write this note: I wish you could see the overflowing kind feelings to you and yours with which I close it.

"Your friend,
"E. K. KANE.

"LONDON, November 15, 1856."

---

* His father's residence near Philadelphia.

The opinion of Dr. Watson, formed probably upon a thorough examination, is supported by that of Dr. Mitchell, which, however, he states to be the result of a single exploration, and that a rather slight one, or at least not sufficient to warrant a confident diagnosis.

But the history of the case, running through a period of twenty years, without depending upon the results of auscultation, is perhaps sufficient to confirm this opinion.

It is scarcely conceivable that exercise of the most violent kind, under the most unfriendly circumstances, would be practicable, much less remedial, in a case of organic disease of the heart so considerable as it must have been to account for all the appearances.

The opinion of Dr. Hayes seems to offer a theory that better unites and explains the symptoms manifested throughout the long continuance of the case. It consists well enough with an inordinate volume of the organ and its frequent rheumatic attacks, while it denies any structural derangement greater or other than frequent inflammation supposes; and it accounts, besides, for their intermitting character and for the symptoms—bellows-sound, palpitation, and difficult respiration—by ascribing the paroxysms to serous effusion in the pericardium, or sack which loosely invests the heart; oppressing and disturbing its action until, by absorption, or whatever process nature employs in such exigencies for working her own cures, the fluid was removed.

The facts of the case point in this direction:—Quiet increased, and active exertion decreased, his liability to palpitation and dyspnœa. The surgeon of the "Advance" was called frequently during the winter of 1853–54 to his bedside, to find him suffering with these symptoms without any apparent cause for their occurrence.

These attacks sometimes happened when he had been for hours lying in his bunk; and they were often so violent that he had to be propped up with pillows, and so protracted that they threatened a fatal issue. But the next day he would be moving about with his accustomed alacrity, not hesitating to start off alone upon a two hours' walk on the ice. On his return there would be no reappearance of the symptoms; and never, at any time, did he suffer from them by any excitement or exertion, however violent. The ordinary rules for the management of a patient laboring under organic disease of the heart were not only unsuited to his case, but positively injurious.

His experience of these facts clearly warranted the manner of life to which his impulses prompted him, and the maxim "do or die" was with him a physical as well as a moral necessity.

Nervous excitability was a marked character of his temperament, and may have had a large share in his chronic ailments, as it was the form of their final and fatal exhibition; but the opinion of his case which ascribes his cardiac troubles and their symptoms to serous effusion, occurring either independently, or as a result and resolution of a rheumatic affection of the heart, looks like the better explanation of the anomalous symptoms so often exhibited.

On arriving in London, Dr. Kane had thought at one time of going to Sicily, at another to the South of France; but Cuba was determined upon, as equally promising, and nearer home in the event of requiring its consolations under disappointed hopes of recovery. On the 17th of November he left the hospitable mansion of Mr. Cross, and went down by rail to Southampton. Mr. Cornelius Grinnell and Mr. Wood, both of New York, came down from London for the purpose, and saw him on board the Oronoco, bound for St. Thomas, which he reached on the 2d of December. He remained there, waiting for a passage to Cuba, until the 20th.

Again on this voyage he escaped his usual sea-sickness. But he suffered acutely from rheumatism in his limbs, shifting into every part of his body. At St. Thomas he was hospitably entertained by Mr. Swift. He was able to walk from room to room in the house, and once drove out with his kind host. He had fever here nearly every day, and suffered greatly from night-sweats; but, upon the whole, he was considerably improved by his stay on the island, and this advantage of the climate determined him finally to continue his journey to Cuba. He had provided himself with woollens before he left England, under the feeling that he might determine to go direct from St. Thomas to the United States, risking the coldness of the coast to get home, and there abide the issue.

ATTACK OF PARALYSIS. 239

On the 20th, in the evening, he sailed for Havana. It was blowing a half gale at the time, and the sea was boisterous. The next day he complained of nausea after breakfasting. In the afternoon he slept, and Morton engaged himself in "overhauling their luggage." While thus employed, the doctor waked and sat up, gazing at him for a moment or two, then lay down again, and called "Morton," in a thick voice. He moaned as in great pain, and said "yes" when he was asked if the ship's physician should be called. When he came, the doctor said to him, "Do give me anodyne." A few minutes after, when they were alone, Morton said to him, "What is the matter? you scare me, sir." He replied, "You may well be scared, poor fellow: you will not have me to trouble you long."

About twenty minutes after saying this, Morton discovered that his right arm and leg were paralyzed. He asked him what this meant; but the tongue would not do its office. He was, however, conscious, and only incapable of vocal utterance. By the 24th he had revived considerably; he was able to sit up with support, and looked out with interest upon the shore of Cuba, which was now in sight.

On the 25th, the vessel landed at Havana, where he was received by his brother Thomas, who had gone out to meet him there as soon as the family were advised of his destination. The next day he went ashore, and on the 29th was reported as considerably improved,— able to use the paralyzed leg as well as the other; but the arm remained powerless, and utterance imperfect, yet sufficing for the simple communication of his wants.

On the 7th of January, his mother and his brother John left New York for Havana. They arrived on the 12th or 13th. His mother, having been exposed to the contagion of smallpox immediately before leaving home, abstained from seeing him for four or five days, under fear of communicating the disease; but after that time he had her, his two brothers, and Mr. Morton in constant attendance upon him to the end.

His anxiety to get home was, however, but little abated. It had all the urgency and impatience of a dying man's longings. He was quite able to make the journey, he could stand while he was dressed, could walk with but little support to a chair; he could ride out if the day were but favorable, and they need have no fears for him!

He was a child again in these importunings. He had come back from the long voyage of a lifetime to his mother's knee, with all the pretty little ways and trivial troubles of the nursery. Heroism had not hardened him; the world had not weaned him from his heart's dependency upon home affections; and his very inquietudes were disguised pleasures: they veiled while they indulged his overflowing fondness.

Every day—two or three times every day—he must hear the words of life from the lips that had taught his to lisp his infant prayer; and, if Morton's occupations interrupted her, "Go on, mother: never mind Morton," expressed his interest and its impatience.

A month by the calendar—an age to the watchers— wore away in this manner, and they were ready to sail; but the weather was unfavorable, and the journey was postponed till the next steamer-day. That next steamer brought him—brought his corpse—to his country. *He* had left it for "that undiscovered country from whose bourn no traveller returns."

On the 10th of February, suddenly and without warning, he was seized with "apoplexy,"—inaccurately described, for he was not unconscious nor insensible; only paralyzed, with the power of emotional expression left, the power to indicate his sympathies, sufferings, and wants.

The tenacious vitality of his frame held him to earth till the 16th,* and then released him so gently that the Bible-reading went on for some minutes after the other watchers had been made aware of his departure.

When death invaded the little family at Bethany and struck down the brother, Jesus said to his disciples, "Our friend sleepeth." They answered, not knowing what they said, "If he sleep, he shall do well." They must be told in the language of their own blindness, plainly, "He is dead." How hard it is for mortal man to understand the proper language of immortality! And the sister (not Mary, who had loved herself into the

---

* 16th of February, 1857. He was born 2d February, 1820.

secret of the Savior's life long before his disciples divined it, but Martha, the worldling) hoped only that her brother should rise again in the resurrection of the last day. Jesus said unto her, "I am the resurrection and the life; whosoever liveth and believeth in me shall never die. Believest thou this?"

Yet at the grave of his friend He wept! Neither Faith nor Hope forbids the griefs of Love bereaved. It is their office to heal, not to harden, the heart. They sit by the just-opened tomb, as Mary saw two angels in white, the one at the head, the other at the feet, to answer the plaints of grief-blinded affection. It is sown in corruption.—*It is raised in incorruption!* It is sown in dishonor.—*It is raised in glory!* It is sown in weakness.—*It is raised in power!* It is sown a natural body.—*It is raised a spiritual body!*

Here the real meets the actual, the true confronts the apparent, and Life answers the argument of Death.

One of the incidents of these last days of lingering in life has been reported and received as an act of Christian forgiveness for wrongs he had suffered and was still suffering in their consequences. I owe it to his memory to record here my own apprehension of it.

He had settled that account two years before, forgiving *then* what was to be forgiven, and accepting what was to be borne without blame to the party offending.

It was the indignation and threatened revenges of his attendants that wakened his noble heart with the pang which attested his consciousness, clearness of apprehension, and persistency of purpose to keep the peace he had made. And, when his best-loved and nearest cried out, "Elisha, I will forgive them," his smile of satisfaction was not the clearance of his own heart of a grievance, but the gladness of knowing now that the hearts where his image must rest had been disburdened of an incongruous feeling.

He settled a similar trouble with me, for the same cause, long before; and, if I know any thing assuringly, I know that he did not trail with him to his death-bed a grievance which he had met and disposed of in the spirit of manly justice and Christian generosity when he first encountered it.

The history of these last days is given here with careful reference to its proper effect. Nothing is strained in statement or colored in description for any purpose or to any end. And it is only necessary now to add that no clergyman of any denomination visited him at Havana, and that he never held membership in any church other than that by birthright and baptism, in his infancy, in the congregation to which his parents belong,—the Second Presbyterian Church of Philadelphia.

It is proper also to state that immediately after his return from his last Arctic voyage he requested his pastor, (as he once called him,) Rev. C. W. Shields, to make public thanksgiving for the deliverance of the Expeditionists from the perils of their cruise, attended the service, and warmly thanked the pastor for performing it.

He had requested public prayer to be made in one of the churches in New York for the well-being of the crew and the prosperity of the enterprise, before he set out. He was prayed for by name in one at least of the Catholic churches of his native city during his absence; and he and his party may have been the object of other congregational supplication and thanksgiving elsewhere.

It is safe to say that he valued at its highest worth the devotional solicitude of all men for his welfare who gave it in the spirit which makes prayer acceptable to God and helpful to man.

In the summer of 1852 he entered the Franklin Lodge of Free Masons in Philadelphia.

What Masonry meant to him and he meant by it is apparent from an address, evidently extemporized, on the night before he left New York upon his last Arctic voyage. The occasion was a special one, having reference to his enterprise and search for Sir John Franklin, who was a brother Mason. The whole speech is given in the appendix of this volume; but we call attention to an extract, now that we are on the subject of his religious and societary connections, for the illustration it affords of his character in this aspect.

Answering the address from the Grand Master, he says:—

"With regard to your remarks directly associated with my name, I should be embarrassed could I not refuse to believe them addressed to me in any other capacity than that of the representative of a cause which, perhaps, may claim to associate Christian charity with American enterprise,—the attempt to save a gallant officer and his fellows from a dreadful death, without inquiring whether he or they and ourselves are citizens of the same or of another race, or clime, or nation.

"Worshipful, I have heard upon this floor to-night our party characterized as a Masonic expedition. And is it not this? And is its work not substantial Masonry? Are you, sir, or you, brothers, here, that are gathered around me,—are we blindly attached to this or that ritual of this or that form or order of the Masonic institution? Say, is it not rather that we see reflected in Free Masonry the cause of free brotherhood throughout the world, and that our signs and our symbols, our tokens, legends, and passwords, are only honorable in our eyes, and honored because they are a language in which affection can securely speak to sympathy, and humanity safely join hands with honor.

"Brothers, we are called in our day, perhaps, to make Masonry what it should be,—not a sectarian society, to garb, or rank, or enroll men, to separate them from their fellows, but a bond to unite the good and true in a common union for the common defence and welfare of all who are good and true men."

To the "Obsequies of Dr. Elisha Kent Kane," prepared for publication by the Hon. Joseph R. Chandler, and appended to this narrative, I am glad to refer for all that can be done to report the tribute of sorrow paid by his country to his remains through their long journey to their final resting-place.

The recollection of my readers needs not to be refreshed: they were witnesses, they were the mourners, of that national procession; and they have it by heart, richer, fresher, better than my pen could portray it.

The newspapers and journals of the day echoed the general mourning of the public; the pulpits responded to the common feeling of the worshippers; and the Legislatures of Pennsylvania, New York, Massachusetts, Ohio, New Jersey, and other States, adopted resolutions expressive of the national feeling which honored his life and mourned his death. The flags of the capitols were ordered at half-mast; and the municipal governments of all the principal cities of the Union united in corresponding testimonies of respect.

The Philosophical Society of Pennsylvania ordered his portrait to be painted for their hall, and appointed Professor A. Dallas Bache, one of their Vice-Presidents, to prepare a memoir for publication. The Academy of Natural Sciences of Philadelphia, and the learned societies of the Union generally, joined in their several appropriate ways in commemorating his worth and services. Dr. Hawks, President of the Geographical Society of New York, pronounced a eulogy upon him before that body; and the venerable Dr. Francis paid a similar tribute in behalf of the Medical Society of that city. The Royal Geographical Society of London, through their President, gave the heartiest expression of their appreciation of him as a man and an explorer. A page from this eulogy must conclude—without in any adequate degree completing—the summary of the tributes laid upon his tomb. Sir Roderick Murchison closes his review of the life and achievements of their medallist and honorary member thus:—

"'The long procession of mourners, (as it is written in the Philadelphia Evening Journal of March 12,) the crowded yet silent streets through which they move, the roll of muffled drums, the booming of minute-guns, the tolling of passing bells, the craped flags at half-mast, and all the solemn pageantry of the scene, proclaim that it is no ordinary occasion which has called forth these impressive demonstrations of public respect.'

"Agreeing entirely with this eloquent writer, that few men have ever lived who have earned a better title to the admiration of his race, and also warmly commending to your notice the sentiment proceeding from a great commercial city of our kinsmen, 'that we are not to look to the mere *utilitarian* value of Dr. Kane's labors and adventures for the claim to that bright and unfading glory which must ever surround his name,' let me say that, by re-echoing the voice of America on this occasion, England can best cherish the memory of one who dared and did so much to rescue her lost navigators.

" Having thus imperfectly glanced at the feats which our deceased medallist accomplished in the short lifetime of thirty-seven years, under the impulses of humanity and science, I cannot better sum up his virtues than in the words of the divine* who preached the funeral sermon over his bier. 'He has traversed the planet in its most inaccessible places, has gathered here and there a laurel from every walk of physical research in which he strayed, has gone into the thick of perilous adventure, abstracting in the spirit of philosophy yet seeing in the spirit of poesy, has returned to invest the very story of his escape with the charms of literature and art, and, dying at length in the morning of his fame, is now lamented with mingled affection and pride by his country and the world.'"

---

*Rev. C. W. Shields.

TOMB OF DR. KANE,
In Laurel Hill Cemetery, near Philadelphia.

CHAPTER XIV.

PERSONAL DESCRIPTION—SOCIAL BEARING—SPIRIT-POWER—PORTRAITS—HYPERTROPHY—KINDNESS FOR ANIMALS—GUN-MURDER—DOG-PEOPLE—MAN AND BEAST—GODFREY—NORTH BRITISH REVIEW—WITHDRAWING PARTY—MANNERS AND CUSTOMS—TOODLA-MIK—TASTES AND ANTIPATHIES—NOVELS AND PLAYS—PROSE-POETRY—MENTAL METHOD—MEDICAL SKEPTICISM—BENEFITS OF THE STUDY—GOVERNING-POWER—THE OUTSIDE PASSAGE—ROUTINE AND ORGANIZATION—ESQUIMAUX ALLIES—FONDNESS FOR CHILDREN—JUSTICE TO SUBORDINATES—ALL ELSE SUBMITTED—THE END.

DR. KANE was five feet six inches in height: in his best health he weighed about one hundred and thirty-five pounds. He had a fair complexion, with soft brown hair. His eyes were dark gray, with a wild-bird light in them when his intellect and feelings were in genial flow; when they were in the torrent-tide of enraptured action, the light beamed from them like the flashing of scimetars, and in impassioned movement they glared frightfully. All these phases might be displayed within the selfsame hour that he had laid his head upon his sister's knee, and in a cooing voice, soft as the music of feeling could make it, said, "Pet me, Bessie; love me, darling."

In company, when the talk ran glib and everybody would be heard, he was silent, but tense and elastic as a steel-spring under pressure. He had a way of looking attentive, docile, and interested as a child's fresh wonder; but no one would mistake the expression for the admiration of inexperience or incapacity; yet it cheated many a talker into a self-complaisance that lost him his opportunity of learning something of the man which he wanted to know. This was the thing in his demeanor which people call his reserve: the reserve of absorbed attentiveness he had; but there was nothing of strained reticence in his manner.

An Irishman would not think him a humorist, nor would a Frenchman call him a wit; a Yankee would give him a high character for both; an Englishman would call him clever,—leaving you to guess what that might mean; and almost anybody who met him in the intervals given to easy intercourse would say that he was a delightful social companion.

He was shy of the probe: he shrank like a sensitive-plant from any rude ransacking of his sanctuary of feeling and opinion; but his caution was not cowardly. He only would not be nipped; and he had skill enough among the hummocks and slush of society to find his own lead and keep an even keel. He was a gentleman, and had absolute possession of himself.

Idle curiosity never made any thing of him, and he did nothing at gossip; but inquiry with an aim was never disappointed. Sitting one day at his father's table, after

SPIRIT-POWER.

his return from his last Expedition, some one closed the narrative of a dangerous adventure with the words, " I never encountered any thing so awful in my life." The doctor had been for an hour silently attentive to all that was said. At this point one of the guests turned to him and asked, " What is the most awful thing that *you* ever experienced?" His face took a devotionally deep expression; and he answered, "The silence of the Arctic night!"

His answer may pass for sentiment, poetry, or worship, as you would receive it. His company read it to their own several depths, and all so far aright; for his character lay in him in concentric rings, all concurring and all according, and you could have it in your own measure.

A vein was opened here; and after dinner, alone with him, I asked him for the best-proved instance that he knew of the soul's power over the body,—an instance that might push the hard-baked philosophy of materialism to the consciousness of its own idiocy. He paused a moment upon my question, as if to feel how it was put, and then answered, as with a spring, " The soul can lift the body out of its boots, sir. When our captain was dying,—I say dying: I have seen scurvy enough to know, —every old scar in his body was a running ulcer. If conscience festers under its wounds correspondingly, hell is not hard to understand. I never saw a case so bad that either lived or died. Men die of it usually long before they are as ill as he was. There was trouble aboard: there might be mutiny. So soon as the breath was out of his body we might be at each others' throats. I felt that he owed even the repose of dying to the service. I went down to his bunk, and shouted in his ear, 'Mutiny, captain! mutiny!' He shook off the cadaveric stupor: 'Set me up,' said he, 'and order these fellows before me.' He heard the complaint, ordered punishment, and from that hour convalesced! Keep that man awake with danger, and he wouldn't die of any thing till his duty was done."

Reader, if there is a curl on your lip now, turn over another page: this story is not for you. The doctor with his eye on you would not have made the mistake of throwing such a pearl under your feet.

The most fatal prognostic of the doctor's own last illness was that he said to Mrs. Grinnell, as he was going on board the Baltic for England, "I cannot say that I will come back to you this time."

But we were talking of his personal make and qualities. To my eye he was as handsome as the finest combination of form, features, expression, and action could make a man. His profile portrait in his last work—not the full-face on our first page—presents him as he was best seen. They are both as true as art could make them; but if you loved the man you would see the reason for it clearest in the one we prefer.

His fine head (a feature never wanting in a fine character) was so well set, and his chest was so large, that, as a perfectly proportioned miniature gives the impression of full size, one never felt in his *presence* any deficiency in his stature.

It will be recollected that from sixteen years of age he was reported by medical men to be laboring under hypertrophy of the heart,—a term of art meaning excess of nourishment, and consequently increase of volume, in the organ, and that increase usually implying disease in its muscular tissue.

Dr. Jackson, of the Pennsylvania University, who was one of the earliest and ablest of our physicians who followed Laennec in his method of exploring the chest, is perhaps responsible for this opinion; but he tells a curious story about this case now. He was in Paris some years since, and, observing that the statue of Julius Cæsar gave a similar conformation of the chest, remarked to a young friend who was with him, "Cæsar had hypertrophy." The friend said, "No: on historical authority you are wrong." Soon after he returned to Philadelphia, in company with the same young gentleman he one day met Dr. Kane in the street, was struck with the resemblance, and called the young gentleman's attention to it. But upon subsequent reflection he yields his earlier opinion, and is rather inclined now to ascribe the thoracic fulness of both cases to a disproportionately large heart, without referring either to any *diseased* change of size or form.

No post-mortem examination was made in the case under consideration; and we have none of the facts which it would have afforded for the settlement of this very curious question.

Dr. Kane was a marksman, a brilliant horseman, and a first-rate pedestrian. Foot-tramps, and the chase without the usual relish for its accompaniments, were a passion with him. Horses and dogs were something more than pets and indulgences to him; but, much as he enjoyed the exercise and excitement of the forest and field, he was tender to the objects and instruments of the chase to an extent that verged on sentimentalism; but there was nothing of this in his composition.

His attachment to dogs and horses was a strongly marked feature in his character. He called them by their given names always, with a feeling which kindly, almost respectfully, accorded to them their poor claims to a distinct individuality, if not personality, with its incident rights and the resulting relations with their masters and among themselves. In his journal of "The First Grinnell Expedition" he seems to have been the expertest hunter of the party; yet almost as frequently as the incidents of this service are recorded, some protest is uttered, indicating the activity of this sentiment of fellowship and sympathy with the birds and beasts "slaughtered," as he styles their killing, under necessity of an overruling humanity towards his patients among the crew needing such anti-scorbutic diet.

There are two instances of seal-shooting, or, as he calls it, gun-murder, (at pages 221 and 232 of that volume,) which would help the reputation of Sterne himself for tenderness and beauty of sentiment, and would have given him, moreover, as good a personal character, if he had had the honesty and earnestness of our author.

The diction of these passages, it must be noticed, is used to dash the confession with a little of that evasive deference for unsympathizing criticism to which publication exposed the sentiment. But it is plain enough that the gentle gentleman hoped somebody would find his feeling under its cover, and be encouraged in kindliness to the *poor beasts*. Moreover, there is nothing in it of the floridness of parade sentimentalism. The language has the very tone of conscious misdemeanor in it:— "Scurvy and sea-life craving for fresh meat led me to it," —the commonplace of the police-office justifying misconduct by the plea of a beggarly necessity.

In the year 1848, I think it was, the elephant on exhibition at the Philadelphia circus killed his keeper, and went on a spree generally in the menagerie, making a general jail-delivery among the tiger and lion cages, with such zeal that he broke one of his tusks in the performance of the day. The alarm roused the police, and the Mayor ordered out a company of muskets to kill the enraged animal. Dr. Kane heard the rumor, and went into the excitement, but in his own way. "The cowardly tyrants," he exclaimed, "to call the elephant mad! An animal with the intelligence of an elephant has a right to be *indignant:* that's the word for it. He has been outraged by a brute with less than his own intellect, and nothing of his sense of right; and now he must be murdered to check his just revenge!"

But he had no contempt for any of God's creatures,— not even for men in the depth of their debasement. To a friend who was patting a dog after he had been abusing some of the lowest and loathsomest of our own species and the culprit-side of human nature generally, he said, "I like your kindliness to the poor dog-people: I have that feeling more than moderately strong myself; but I never saw a man who was not higher than a dog." This was after he had seen humanity in its lees in every quarter of the globe.

He was not incapable of taking human life for cause requiring it. He held it at a much lower value than the rights, dignities, and liberties which belong to it. These he scrupulously respected in all his actions and utterances. It was indeed a reverence, as for a sacred thing, which he gave to the majesty of manhood and to its proper defences: he never indulged even in irony, and was as incapable of detraction as of petty larceny. He was always thoughtful—carefully thoughtful—of his action and influence upon the minds of those around him.

He sent a bullet after the deserter Godfrey, "at long but practicable distance,"—whether with the purpose of executing summary justice upon him, or not, is not clear, much less conclusive, in the circumstances; and the statement by no means supports the severest construction of which it is capable, for he was not the man to propitiate illiberal criticism. But take it that he did not count upon the chances of a long distance and a spent ball, and that his aim failed his purpose; then recollect that he afterwards brought the delinquent a prisoner to the brig, at the expense of a desperate journey of one hundred and forty miles, when Bonsall, Petersen, and himself were the only men on board capable of working for the rest; and is it not plain that his motive is found in his duty to prevent the ruinous influence which the wretched fellow would exert over the Esquimaux at Etah, upon whose friendly offices the crew under his command and care at the time depended for their very existence?*

Governed by a magnanimous deference for other men's rights, which was not a weakness or a factitious sentiment, but a ruling principle, with him, he was heroically patient and forbearing towards those whose defection in the hour of his sorest need put his goodness and greatness of heart to the severest proof.

---

* It is worthy of notice here, that of more than a thousand reviews of his book, the North British Review is the only journal that has found fault with his conduct in this affair—or in any other. And it is just as remarkable that this reviewer suppresses the justifying reason, the imperative necessity, in his statement of the case. I say *suppresses*, for he quotes every thing else in the passage which contains it, as by a careful selection. Dr. Kane's language is, "I learned, too, that Godfrey was playing the great man at Etah, defying recapture; *and I was not willing to trust the influence he might exert on my relations with the tribe.*" The reviewer has it, "Godfrey was at Etah with the Esquimaux; and the moment Dr. Kane heard it he resolved 'that he should return to the ship.'" The writer, in every particular of his censorious strictures, was evidently in the condition of a man who does not see what he neither understands nor desires to find in the case before him, however plain it may be to everybody else.

Turn to the first volume of his second voyage, at pages 83 and 348; estimate the pressure of the conditions in which he was placed; and then look where you will for an equally imposing exhibition of generous justice.

He was not a coward; he could bear all his own burdens: he was not an egotist, and did not pile censure upon other people's heads to save his own.

In work, exercise, and mental application, he was intense, and, therefore, not systematic. He was remarkable not only for getting along with very little sleep, but for irregularity also in its indulgence. He was as little as possible subject to habit or periodicity; and he seemed rather to engineer his faculties by his will than to give up any of his conduct to the rule of custom. He fought hard for his freedom from himself, and, resultingly, he had always at command a loose foot, a free hand, and stood in ready adjustment to exigencies. He conformed to usages for convenience' sake, without any struggling, but without any submission; and, having no imperious necessities of his own, he had no conflict with those of other people.

Whether he retired early or late, he rose early, taking long walks before breakfast when no pressure of engagements threw him out. But when he had something on hand which must be done to time,—as writing his last book, —he worked till three in the morning, and then took out the tuck of the long constraint and relieved himself of its weariness by a dashing ride of five or six miles, or by cracking his dog-whips in the yard for an hour or two,

—whips with lashes from sixteen to thirty-three feet long, which not one man in a thousand could unfold; but he could crack them like a pistol. They were the whips used in driving his Esquimaux dog-teams.

And what a wild carouse old Toodla-mik, the leader of his Arctic sledge-hacks, would have with him in the frosty mornings of their last winter's fellowship! It was a rough communion, and not quite a complete one. Toodla was an "Injin," every inch of him,—hyena, wolf, and slave in a mixture,—fierce as the boldest of the types, and cowardly and treacherous as the worst.

At the first call he would look out of his kennel and hesitate a moment; then, without the usual all-hail of the civilized canine,—for he had not learned to bark,—with a bound he was upon the doctor's shoulders, looking a sneaking compound of felony and fondness. Then for the play: the whip was the attraction, not the compulsion. It looked Arctic and Esquimaux enough to see him springing like mad to receive the lash wherever it fell; no fear of the cracker. There was no place exposed to it except the eyes, nose, and fore-feet. Under defence of such a coat of hair, nothing but a cudgel could reach his sensibilities.

Toodla had his virtues, whether he intended them or not. He had rendered services made high and noble by their appropriation. His name is connected with many memories which will not soon perish; and he stands now, his own monument, preserved in that Westminster Abbey of representative animals, the Academy of Natural Sciences of Philadelphia.

In personal habits Dr. Kane was nice even to daintiness; temperate and delicate in diet, and abstinent from wine as a beverage, taking it only as a form of table or social courtesy, nor then, if refusal would cost less than compliance. He had a horror of tobacco in all its forms. When a friend defended its use with the remark, "Its cost is trivial, a mere nothing," he retorted, "But what does your tobacco-function cost your body, and, per consequence, the agent within?"

His intellectual tastes expressed his character and conformed to it. He was not a novel-reader; and for the stage he had no relish. "The theatre," he says, "has always been to me a wretched simulation of realities; and I have too little sympathy with the unreal to find pleasure in it long." His favorite books are in the ice of Smith's Sound: they modified him less than they entertained him.

In fifteen hundred pages of book-matter, he never makes a quotation to assist himself in expression, except one from Bunyan; and even that is used for its allegorical effect as much as for its beauty and power.

He wrote his own poetry in the higher form of prose: for two instances out of many hundreds, read the following gems, wrenched as they are from their exquisite settings:—

"I am afraid to speak of some of these night-scenes. I have trodden the deck and the floes when the life of earth seemed suspended,—its movements, its sounds, its coloring, its companionships; and as I looked on the radiant hemisphere, circling above me as if rendering worship to the unseen Centre of light, I have ejaculated, in humility of spirit, 'Lord, what is man, that thou art mindful of him?' And then I have thought of the kindly world we had left, with its revolving sunshine and shadow, and the other stars that gladden it in their changes, and the hearts that warmed to us there, till I lost myself in memories of those who are not; and they bore me back to the stars again."

He finds a poppy, green under seven feet of snow. A lucidly simple explanation of its securities in a climate that runs down to 50° below zero warms his fancy into poetic sympathy with its delicate life :—" No eider-down in the cradle of an infant is tucked in more kindly than the sleeping-dress of winter about this feeble flower-life."

His logic was nothing akin to the legal method of reasoning. It was amusing to hear him answer a lawyerly argument which had run away from the sharply severe sequence and drift of the facts involved,—" I don't understand you." An edifice of assumption and generalities went down under his touch like a card house, however systematically built. His demand upon his interlocutor was, " What do you know?" and his reservation seemed to be, " I can do my own thinking."

Nor was his method merely the analogical, although it was chiefly by contrast and resemblance. He trusted implicitly to nothing but the accuracy of observation employed upon the subject itself, guarding himself against the risks of resemblance, on the suspicion that the process often unconsciously conceals vicious speculations. And he was as cautious with induction; for he was well aware that it is much given to putting distance over-boldly between the truths which it connects, and is often unsafe both in data and demonstration. Nor did he jumble induction and analogy after the manner of the current philosophizing in which there is so little philosophy. "Then, in the name of all that is rational, how did he think?" Take this for a reply, and in it or by it find the answer:—He believed all that he *knew*, and he trusted his whole weight upon the legitimate inferences as far as they would carry him, but still holding deductions for mere hypotheses until he had proved them by their trial upon the facts, all the while proceeding as resolutely as the simplest credulity could do; and so, his characteristic audacity of belief was never misguided by inferences mistaken for certainties.

His faith in medicine was decidedly thin, but not limber. He says of it, "I am, I fear, heterodox almost to infidelity as to the direct action of remedies, and rarely allow myself to claim a sequence as a result."

For routine-practice and the highest professional success he perhaps had not a just appreciation. He preferred the achievements of an explorer, mixed with adventure, to the reputation of Hunter or Harvey. His skepticism in drug-practice had a basis in his own make, which put life, in his idea, out of and above the reach of chemicals. This feeling, which was to him a fountain of opinion as well as a spring of action, shows itself just in the right place. When the Advance party were reduced to ten men, and four of them were on their backs, the thermometer at 30° below zero, and prospects even lower, he says, speaking of Morton and Hans, " I can see strength of system in their cheerfulness of heart. The best prophylactic is a hopeful, sanguine temperament; the best cure, moral resistance,—that spirit of combat against every trial which is alone true bravery."

Yet he was not unaware of the advantages which his medical attainments gave him. In his darkest day he says, "I am glad of my professional drill and its companion-influence over the sick and toil-worn. I could not get along at all unless I combined the offices of physician and commander."

Anatomical and physiological study, in fact, had done more for him than he knew. There is nothing like the former for art in observing and describing the physical properties of things; and no method of inquiry goes more directly or thoroughly into the phenomena of forces and the dependency of actions than that of the latter. Dr. Kane's descriptive powers gained greatly by his training in the study of anatomy and the practice of the dissecting-room and the laboratory; and his application of the doctrine of *endosmose* to the explanation of Arctic ice-thaw while the thermometer is still below the freezing-point, and its happy help to the understanding of that paradox of fact, the viscous flow of the glaciers, is a splendid example of the extension of physiological science to one of the most remote fields of physical inquiry.

Dr. Kane's trouble with medicine was that hypothesis must be so largely accepted for facts, and agencies hazardously credited with efficiency upon grounds but slightly supported by evidence. In a word, his mental integrity was something too stubborn for the authority of oracles.

His power to govern his subordinates and to lead his equals was not overmeasured by his reliance upon it.

He went out on his last voyage without any of the rules and regulations which govern our national marine, or authority to enforce them. The men were volunteers, and the expedition was a private venture. Yet on deck, in dangerous and difficult navigation, he held the respect of the sailors. Tried every day by the rough standard of these regular-bred routinists, they felt and conceded his superiority. When he bravely ventured upon the outside passage of Melville Bay on his outward-bound trip, Brooks and McGary thought he must be right, though they had never heard of such a thing before; and, when two years of daily trials had habituated them to a frank obedience, they followed him in an open boat through the same perilous passage which the little brig had first found by the instincts of her commander. It was like inviting a score of draymen to make an ascension in a paper balloon through a snow-storm; but they trusted, for they had learned a habit of dependence by a thousand instances of assuring experience.

He was at once indomitable and irresistible; but the spring in his spirit was neither a blind temerity nor an irreflective transport, for he never took a step undirected by forethought: his boldness was reliance upon the anticipations of caution, and just because he looked so carefully ahead he never looked back. It was not as a phrase-maker, but as a law-maker, he uttered these maxims of order :—" I realize fully the moral effects of an unbroken routine." "Whatever of executive ability I have picked up during this brain and body wearing cruise warns me against immature preparation or vacillating purposes. I must have an exact discipline, a rigid routine, and a perfectly-thought-out organization."

But, wonderful as the history of his reign over his own desperately tried crew through all the adventures of the cruise appears, his management of his Esquimaux neighbors of Etah varies, if it does not otherwise enhance, the evidence of his mental mastery over his fellow-men. These animal-men began by robbing the brig, and at one time would have been willing to destroy the crew: they ended by helping them to purpose on their retreat from the scene of their sufferings. He says of them, "As long as we remained prisoners of the ice, we were indebted to them for invaluable counsel in relation to our hunting-excursions; and in the joint hunt we shared alike, according to their laws. Our dogs were, in one sense, common property; and often they have robbed themselves to offer supplies of food to our starving teams. They gave us supplies of meat at critical periods: we were able to do as much for them. They learned to look on us only as benefactors, and, I know, mourned our departure bitterly." Their own statement and explanation of the relations subsisting so long and so happily between themselves and his party has matter in it to dwell upon:—"You have done us good. We are not hungry; we will not take [steal]. You have done us good: we want to help you: we are friends."

Savage superstition and the marvellous six-shooter had some share in this influence; but he observed a justice in his dealings with them which secured their confidence, and exhibited a superiority, in all the qualities of manhood which they understood, that could not fail to impose respect.

His emotions at parting with these poor creatures were the earnings of his admirable management of them through all their strange intercourse:—"I blessed them for their humanity to us with a fervor of heart which from a better man peradventure might have carried a blessing along with it."

The heart so tender and true to objects so repulsive as these could not be insensible to the charm that there is in childhood, in its beauty and innocence, or indifferent to its claims to the consideration and care which may minister to its culture under the influences of Christian civilization.

FONDNESS FOR CHILDREN. 267

Dr. Kane loved children with a woman's tenderness and a man's forethought. When he was about leaving for England, and a course of popular lectures was proposed to him in the event of his early return to the United States, with the tempting assurance of ten thousand dollars for the ensuing winter's work, he answered, "I will not talk about that now; but if I do come back, and have but the strength to deliver one lecture, it shall be to an audience of children."

He was once urged to write a *Robinson Crusoe* story of his adventures. He looked up at first with the surprise of his habitual self-depreciation and despair of strength for such a task; but the idea brightened,—doubtless with this cherished reference to the service of the youth of the country, and said, "But could I do it?" The answer was, "Yes, and without exhaustion, or risk of failure in the effect: that is your style exactly." "I'll do it," said he, and walked off in a glow of pleasure, as if to indulge the anticipation to the full and enjoy it unobserved.

The loss is fellow to the sorrow of all the disappointment which shrouds these buried hopes. His death *was* untimely; for he could have lived to the end of his days, however prolonged.

The liberal spirit and considerate feeling towards the men under his command—all of them—that marks the book which immortalizes all its subjects is in perfect keeping with the character he displayed where his tastes were gratified and his affections secured. It proves that his virtues were not the caprices of feeling, but held the rank of principles in his character. It was magnanimity without its pride. He rendered justice by the rule that exacts little where little is given; and he did not so much forgive as justify the deficiencies of limited capabilities, moral as well as mental and physical; and it was not in disappointment or suffering, however severe, to warp his justice or sharpen his judgments.

But this chapter of *personal* characterization *must* close.

His scientific attainments, great and varied as they were, were as nothing to him except as they could be worked into his practical life. They must be overpassed in his biography; for it must not give them a prominence which he refused them. And his literary acquirements and achievements,—they are rendered by a thousand pens, whose several authorities each one outweighs the worth of my opinions.

Success was the measure by which *he* judged his own strivings. The generation which he addressed and served shall judge the works that survive him, remembering only that, had he lived, he would have written a book of Arctic science for his peers, and a hand-book of natural history, travel, and adventure levelled to the intellectual capacities of childhood and lifted to the rank of its requirements. Credit him with the purpose of such a service to the world as this, and estimate his capability by the evidence he has afforded in that which he has done.

LETTER FROM DR. HAYES,

SURGEON OF DR. KANE'S EXPEDITION.

DR. KANE'S PLAN OF SEARCH—ADVENTURES OF THE DEPÔT-PARTY—RETURN OF PART OF THEM—STARTING OF THE RELIEF-PARTY—INADEQUATE APPLIANCES—SPECIAL PROVIDENCE—THEIR RETURN—DEATH OF BAKER AND SCHUBERT—DR. KANE'S SICKNESS—WANT OF DOGS—APPEARANCE OF ESQUIMAUX—AN EXCHANGE EFFECTED—BREAKING DOWN.

ON the opening of the spring of 1854, Dr. Kane's health was much improved, and his plan of search was fully developed before the return of the summer.

A depôt of provisions was to be established to the northward of the vessel, upon the most northern point of the opposite coast of the strait; and, upon the return of the party sent out for the purpose, it was his intention to push forward at the head of his grand party, and, making this depôt or cache his final starting-point, descend in as nearly the direction of the Pole as circumstances would admit, until reaching the extreme north shore of the American continent, when he would turn to the westward in search of the missing expedition.

This depôt-party was sent out under charge of Mr. Brooks; and, as you know, it resulted only in disaster. They encountered tremendous ridges of hummocks in the centre of the channel, from ten to forty feet in height. After battling with these for eight days, and finding it impossible to pass them, they set out on their return; but on the first day of their retreat four of them were frozen and rendered helpless. Placing the sick in their sleeping-bags within the tent, and leaving Hickey to look after their wants, the remaining three (Ohlsen, Petersen, and Sontag) put off for the vessel, forty miles distant, in a bee-line, which they reached in thirteen hours without a halt.

Immediately upon their arrival, Dr. Kane organized a relief-party,— consisting of all the well men in the ship except myself, I being left behind to be in condition to receive the sick when they should arrive. There were at the time five on board incapable of duty.

The relief-party therefore consisted of eight, besides Dr. Kane. Ohlsen was of the number, and acted as guide, starting back after a rest of but two hours.

This relief-expedition was *the heroic* performance of the cruise; and when we are made acquainted with the plain facts connected with it, when we reflect that it was triumphantly successful against all odds, (and *such* odds,) we are astonished at the endurance of the actors in the drama, and of the responsible person. The leader of the band—he who took them out and brought them safely back—looms up in our imagination as something more than human. At that time we were inured to hardship and scarcely realized the magnitude of the deed. The calmer reflection of later days makes me shudder at the bare thought of the condition of this party when I first saw them, after a march of nearly a hundred miles without sleep or rest, and for seventy hours constantly exposed to a temperature ranging from 20° to 50° below zero.

Dr. Kane had not yet taken the field for exploration, but was preparing himself for his grand journey upon the arrival of the party of Mr. Brooks at the vessel. He was in no condition to hazard such an enterprise; and he certainly would, under the circumstances, have been excusable had he despatched the party under command of Ohlsen or some other competent person. But that was not the metal of the man. He was not the one to shirk danger, greater though it might be to him than to others.

The rescue-party set out in two hours after Ohlsen arrived. They carried only three pounds of lard, twice as many of pemmican, and a small tent (our only one) that barely sufficed for the accommodation of the relief-party. There was one being made which would have held the entire party; but it would have taken eight or ten hours to finish it; and, said Kane, "in those eight or ten hours our comrades in the wilderness may die."

If they had been provided with a good tent, provisions for four or five days, sleeping-fixtures, and a strong guide, they would have been prepared for any emergency. As it was, God only knows how they reached the tent on the ice. The tracks were obliterated; their compass was sluggish; their only guide-boards were the bergs, and these were almost all identical in shape. Every thing depended upon Ohlsen. Had he lost his way, or broken down, or become stupefied with cold and exposure, there would scarcely have been one chance in a hundred that they would ever reach the tent; and in their efforts to find it—groping about without the slightest knowledge of where they were, out of sight of land, ill disposed to give up the search—I saw little chance of their doing other than perish, and the men whom they sought would have died without knowledge that they were remembered.

But Ohlsen did not lose his way, nor break down, nor become stupefied, and my black picture may therefore be called useless. But why he did *not* is to me a mystery. He was the strongest man I ever saw; and, although he had walked double the distance, when at last they reached the tent he was the best man of them all. There was a special providence in it.

I was very fearful—indeed, felt almost certain—that I should never see Dr. Kane again alive. When he set off, he looked the suffering invalid that he was; but now, as always when something was to be done which required nerve and manhood, a sleeping power was aroused within him, which sent palpitating heart, puffed cheeks, rheumatic joints, and scurvy limbs hastily to cover.

They all came back delirious: they were knocked up with scurvy. Two of the rescued—Brooks and Wilson—lost toes; two others—Baker and Schubert—died.

Baker died of lock-jaw a few days after his return, and the circumstances attending his death were the most distressing I ever witnessed. I discovered his disease before the morning watch was called; and in less than twenty-four hours he was a corpse. Dr. Kane was more oppressed by the prospect of Baker's death than he had appeared to be by that of his own. He paced the upper deck during a greater part of the day. He had a tender heart; and he could not bear to witness human suffering if duty did not call him to the bedside, or to administer to the sufferer.

Dr. Kane was then again confined to his bed, from causes which I will presently relate; and so weak was he that I was afraid to announce poor Schubert's death to him. It affected him seriously, and renewed his cardiac troubles.

The greater part of Dr. Kane's dogs died during the winter of 1853–54. This loss caused him, in making out his plans, to rely almost solely upon the physical force of his crew.

On the opening of spring we had but three dogs; and, after the return of the first party and their rescuers, all hands were knocked up completely. With these three dogs, and six men upon whom he thought he might count with tolerable certainty in a week or two, Dr. Kane was preparing to take the field. But, just in time, the Esquimaux appeared,—four men, with four sledges and twenty-four or twenty-six dogs.

I venture to say that this day was one of the happiest of Dr. Kane's life, and certainly the happiest he had seen for many a week. "Esquimaux alongside!" shouted McGary down the hatch. The person for whose ears the words were intended might with great propriety have answered with an interrogative "What?" or stopped to think what good could come of it. But the word "Esquimaux" was enough. It was significant of dogs; and for dogs he had prayed. I would give much to see the picture which shot out meteor-like upon his imagination, transforming him from a weak, quiet invalid lying on his back, reading a volume of the Naturalist's Library, into a strong and vigorous man standing upon the shore of the open sea, or on the floe, with Sir John Franklin's hand fast locked in his own.

He was lying in his bunk. "Esquimaux alongside!" had hardly been caught by the half-slumbering crew; but no such sound could be lost on the ears of Kane. Quicker than a flash he was out upon the deck. His only words were (and these, I believe, he got off between leaving his blankets and alighting upon the deck with an emphasis you will be well able to appreciate) "Thank Heaven! I'll make my journey now." His clothes were on in a twinkling; he was out upon the floes in less time than it takes to tell it; and in half an hour he was richer by a team of dogs, and poorer by a couple of butcher-knives and a few needles. He was a sick man no more, and in a few days was in the field with a train of seven men and a team of seven dogs.

But the spirit and enthusiastic devotion to duty which had carried him through the rescue, and the consciousness of responsibility which bore him up through the trying days which followed, could not give him muscle, nor recharge the over-exhausted electric-battery of his nervous system. To break down at last was inevitable: yet he would not "give in." For two days he was carried forward on the dog-sledge, unable to walk, or stir hand or foot. Sinking, and almost insensible, his party put about, and, by forced marches, reached the vessel at last. We met our commander at the gangway supported by his companions, and apparently dying. At that moment his resuscitation seemed to me impossible.

*   *   *   *   *   *

Truly yours, with respect,

I. I. HAYES.

WEST CHESTER, PA., July 18, 1857.

LETTER FROM AMOS BONSALL,

A MEMBER OF DR. KANE'S EXPEDITION.

EARLY ACQUAINTANCE WITH DR. KANE—VOLUNTEERING FOR THE EXPEDITION—CHARACTER OF THE SAILORS—DR. KANE'S ALLEGED CRUELTY TO HIS MEN—HIS LENIENCY—HIS SELF-DENIAL AND KINDNESS TO THE SICK—DEATH OF JEFFERSON T. BAKER AND PIERRE SCHUBERT—CHARACTER OF BAKER.

DEAR SIR:—Knowing that you are engaged in the publication of a "Life of Dr. Elisha Kent Kane," written by Dr. Wm. Elder, I thought perhaps it would be proper for me to give you some of my impressions of him as a friend, a commander, and a man. In speaking of him as a friend, I shall pass over the earlier period of our acquaintance during my own boyhood, merely remarking that I had a great admiration for his achievements in India, China, and other parts of the Eastern Continent,—incidents and anecdotes of which I had heard from himself and others.

Having expressed a desire, if he ever made a second voyage to the Arctic region, to accompany him, he wrote me early in December of 1852; and I volunteered immediately on his informing me that he could secure me a situation on board his vessel.

From that time I was in daily intercourse with him, and always found him kind and courteous in the highest degree. After I left home for New York, before the sailing of the Expedition, he, during a short visit to Philadelphia, having a few hours to spare, drove out to visit my parents, and gave them my last adieu and brought me their blessing and last charges; and that at a time when he was suffering very severely from chronic rheumatism and scarcely able to rise from his bed.

After we were fairly embarked, he sank for a time from sea-sickness, and was always ill whenever there was breeze enough to create the slightest swell. In fact, I believe no man but Dr. Kane would have persevered in the voyage under the accumulated diseases from which he suffered at that time; and I scarcely think there was one of the Expedition who thought his recovery possible.

On account of his sickness at the time of the fitting out of the Expedition, a great deal was necessarily intrusted to others, and we sailed very imperfectly prepared to encounter the perils and privations of an

Arctic winter; and, worse than all, the men had been shipped from the ordinary class of sailors in port, without regard to their moral character or physical ability; and before reaching Greenland we had difficulties with some which should not have occurred, and others were comparatively useless on account of sickness.

Here I may with propriety speak of a charge which has been promulgated since his decease,—that of " cruelty to his men." I must say that, so far from being cruel, in many instances I considered that the punishment was by no means commensurate with the offence; and had he been more severe at the beginning of the voyage he would have had less trouble at the latter part.

His course was always to incite to exertion with the promise of rewards. To those who had not ambition to exert themselves for the common good, the punishments were, unfortunately, of such a nature as to have no terrors. Indeed, I have known individuals to commit offences for the express purpose of being put in confinement and thereby escape their daily routine of duty.

In many cases of extreme suffering which occurred during our absence on journeys, he always used every means in his power to alleviate the condition of the patients. He gave up his own bed to those who were sick and frozen; and during the second winter, while crowded together in the little cabin of the Advance, by his indomitable energy and activity he prevented the last spark of hope from dying out, and, under Providence, enabled us, by obtaining fresh meat from the Esquimaux, to support life and strength until the season opened sufficiently for us to escape.

At the time of our leaving the brig, by his exertions with the dogs and Esquimaux he not only conveyed the sick (six in number) to the open water, thereby relieving of the burden those who worked at the boats, but carried down a great portion of the provisions, besides returning to the ship several times for bread, by these means saving the provisions we had prepared and packed for the journey. During our passage through the ice in open boats on that perilous journey of more than eighty days, by his judicious management he not only cheered the dispirited and quieted the querulous and discontented, but he so dispensed the provisions as to give no one the slightest cause for complaint, (a most difficult operation, as any one who has had to do with starving men can testify.)

Looking back upon it now, after a lapse of more than two years, with a shudder, I can freely say that it was to his careful organization at the first, and his cautious progress during the journey, that we owe our deliverance and restoration to our homes.

Restraining a party of men on a homeward journey, after undergoing the perils of two Arctic winters, cut off from communication with civilization for such a length of time, is a much more difficult matter than urging them forward at a ruinous rate would be; yet often it was more essential to our safety that we should lie still and recruit our exhausted energies, and await the favorable movements of the ice, than exhaust ourselves in fruitless endeavors to surmount difficulties which, by waiting patiently a short time, would be removed from our path.

In writing, I find a difficulty in avoiding the description of traits spoken of by others, and perhaps would have said as much to the purpose if I had stated that to me he was invariably a kind friend, an indulgent commander, and always manifested a warm interest in my welfare for which I shall be forever grateful.

As you desired, I will endeavor to give you some account of the death of Jefferson T. Baker, which, occurring as it did, (he being the first of those of our comrades who left their bones to bleach on the barren coasts of Smith's Sound,) made more impression upon us than any subsequent death; and, without considering the relations which he bore to me, I may say that every man and officer in the ship felt as though he had lost a brother. It is unnecessary to speak of the occurrences preceding his death, as Dr. Kane, in his "Explorations," has given them to the world in a manner which leaves nothing to be said by me. After the fearful journey which we made to rescue those of our comrades who were frozen on the terrible 25th of March, we were so exhausted, both mentally and physically, that it required several days for us to recover our wonted tone of mind and bodily habit, so violently deranged by exposure and hardship. The sick men, on their arrival at the brig, were kindly cared for by those who were expecting us; and every thing possible to alleviate their intense suffering was done by our skilful and warm-hearted surgeon, Dr. Hayes. All that he could do for us in the emergency was done, and after some hours of rest we began to be comfortable once more. Short respite! The next day Dr. Kane called me to him, and, with tears in his eyes, told me his fears in regard to two of the sufferers, J. T. Baker and Pierre Schubert, as their wounds were worse, and symptoms of aberration of mind in Baker's case were manifest.

I did not realize the frightful result for some hours, and then, after it broke in its full force upon me, (that there was no hope of saving him, and that he must die,) it was necessary to keep every thing as quiet as possible, to prevent those in the same condition in the other berth of the cabin (which had been devoted to the sick and wounded) from learning the truth so long as it could be concealed from them, and then to prepare them for the sad reality.

Every preparation was made for the burial which could be done in our situation; and the next day we carried him to his last resting-place on Observatory Island, and placed him in the snow-house, (where one month after we placed Pierre beside him,) the state of the ground not permitting us to make a grave for two or three months afterward.

Jefferson Baker volunteered as a member of the Expedition, and always bore out the character which he had gained for attention to his duty, and was beloved alike by the officers and men of our little band. He was personally known to Dr. Kane before the time of our departure; and he had always felt more deeply interested in his welfare than perhaps any other member of the Expedition, and had hoped to aid him, on our return, in achieving something of advantage to himself.

Yours, respectfully,
A. BONSALL,
Mr. G. W. CHILDS, Oct. 13, 1857.   Upper Darby, Pa.

LETTER FROM HENRY GOODFELLOW,
A MEMBER OF DR. KANE'S EXPEDITION.

DR. KANE'S SEA-SICKNESS—HIS HABITS ON BOARD—FAILING HEALTH—THE RESCUE-PARTY—A BAD RESTORATIVE—GOVERNMENT OF THE CREW—ALLOWANCE OF FOOD—DR. KANE'S ABHORRENCE OF CORPORAL PUNISHMENT—HIS ATTENTION TO THE SICK—HIS SPIRIT OF SCIENTIFIC INQUIRY—HIS SOCIAL DEMEANOR AND CONVERSATION—EXERCISE—DIETETICS.

WHEN, about a month prior to the sailing of the Expedition, I saw Dr Kane on his return to Philadelphia from New York, where he had been seriously ill for several weeks with, as I was informed, inflammatory rheumatism, he was as much changed in appearance as it is possible for a man to be when convalescent. Instead of the former restless and intense vitality of eye, he had the subdued look of a broken-down invalid. In the interval between this period and that of his departure he had recovered in a great degree the tone of his bearing; but he was far from being either well or vigorous.

He had always been subject to sea-sickness in a very acute and distressing form, manifesting itself in a constant retching without power to obtain relief, and giddiness, which a comparatively slight roughness of the sea—for instance, a four or five knot breeze—invariably brought to him, and which scarcely abated in severity through the longest voyage : it was therefore infinitely worse than the short, violent, and spasmodic form.

The occurrence of this malady increased his general debility, but did not prevent his frequent presence and activity on deck. He superintended the work upon the sledge apparatus and equipments, and interested himself in the course and speed of the brig.

He was fond, on fine afternoons when the sun shone out, of reclining on a large tarpaulin-covered box on the quarterdeck, where, wrapped in a buffalo-robe, he would write his journal or watch the working of the ship, and seem to forget his exhausted frame. At night he would suddenly appear over the combings of the cabin companion-way, dressed in his gown of cashmere, lined with the wool of the fœtal lamb, a favorite garment which he had received from a Hindoo priest. After inquiring the course and examining the log, and asking whether more sail could not be carried, he would return to his bunk, but not always to sleep. The recorder of the watch, descending to write the hourly observations, would generally be met by an inquiry from him.

Indeed, throughout the entire cruise he seldom fell asleep until late in the morning, and four or five hours was in general his maximum of rest. His sleep, too, was very light. It was scarcely ever necessary to more than utter his name to make him open his eyes; and if it was accidentally mentioned in the cabin, within hearing of his bunk, he would awake immediately.

As we advanced along the coast of Greenland, he seemed stronger, and underwent the exposure belonging to boating among the settlements with the alacrity of a well man, without evincing any sign of ill health, except a more than his usual sensitiveness to cold, making him require more clothing than he would otherwise have wanted,—for he seemed to be in need of a heat-making power.

When we reached the waters of Smith's Sound, Dr. Kane spent much of his time in open boat, looking for harbors,—frequently, too, after a previous long exposure of himself in the crow's nest. But a marked change for the worse took place about this time,—perhaps owing to the excessive exertion,—and his health seemed very unpromising for an Arctic winter. In spite of it, he made his fall-journey to investigate the feasibility of sledging over the ice beyond. He returned quite broken down, but thoroughly persuaded that it was his duty to remain, notwithstanding the almost impassable character of the ice around us, and to make an attempt to travel along the somewhat better paths he had reconnoitred.

All winter, though he never relaxed or intermitted his rigid personal supervision of the ship's affairs, it was only too evident that he was struggling with disease. As well as I can describe his case, his circulation was deficient: his face and hands would be swollen,—the capillary action being very sluggish. Sometimes he required Mr. Morton's assistance to enable him to rise; but, once on his legs, he would go about as if he were not seriously ailing, making some facetious remark as he stretched out his swollen hands, or glanced in his glass at his face. His only allusions to his ailments were in a tone of pleasantry or gayly-affected complaint.

A slight apparent improvement was visible in his health about the date of the departure of the first party, soon after the return of the sun in 1854. He took daily drives with the dogs, whom he was training; but his condition was any thing but suitable for the prodigious exertion of the rescue-party; and the training which he had had, since the light returned, of perhaps a dozen drives and as many walks, together with light daily exercise,—these were altogether but a poor preparative for a forced march of forty miles over the roughest possible ice at a temperature of from 40° to 50° below zero.

As is well known, in less than three hours after the messengers, breathless and almost crazy with cold and fatigue, came to the brig, the heroic leader started out with a party of eight men, including Ohlsen, whose senses were bewildered by having had but an hour or two of rest from the journey, to enter the trackless frozen sea. Every man on board accompanied him, except the surgeon, one in the cabin with a leg drawn up with scurvy, two men whose condition was unfit for a sledge-journey, and two out of the three returned party,—making six left behind. Despatch was all-important. But they had to drag a sledge laden with a tent and restoratives, and, part of the way, their exhausted guide. The returned party, with nothing to carry but one rifle, had reached the ship in one march; but they had known no alternative except to perish in the snow.

It was a subject of melancholy speculation in the cabin among those who remained, as to whether the tent could be reached in a single march. The returned travellers thought it utterly impossible. There was a different opinion entertained with equal strength, which was borne out by the result.

The history of that party has already been told. It was not a very good discipline for a sick man who looked forward to starting out again, at a temperature below zero, a month later. The wear and tear of hospital, amputations, and the counteracting of the depressing effect of death, together with the actual privation arising from the recent reduction of coal to an allowance only sufficient for one fire, and an occasional extra one,—all taxed to the utmost the nervous system of the commander, and called for a rare union of firmness with gentleness.

Throughout the entire cruise the government of the crew was truly benign. On board ship, the food—or grub, as it is universally called at sea—is a much more important matter than it is on shore. Food and drink, with tobacco, stand in the place of all other recreations and pleasures for the sailor, and form the great element in Jack's estimate of a ship. After a hard exposure, while working in the cold, a mere cup of coffee has a taste and value which it would be difficult for one whose lot has always been a life of ease to associate with such an apparent trifle.

On board the Advance, the allowance to the crew was varied and liberal to a degree seldom known in ships. There was very little difference between the cabin-table and the forecastle-mess. Sugar and butter of excellent quality were furnished almost *ad libitum*. After we had gone into winter-quarters, the daily fare was absolutely the same at both ends of the ship, in substantial materials, the only difference being the few trifling stores purchased by the cabin-mess, such as Worcester sauce, olive-oil, figs, &c. The dinner of the men was prepared chiefly by the cabin-steward, and consisted of soup, meat, and dessert-courses. If there occurred any dissatisfaction,—and no sybarite can be more critical than the sailor,—the dinner was inspected by the first officers, accompanied by a culinary staff of cook and steward, or by the commander, who always invited the men to make their complaints to him freely. The second winter, as it is hardly necessary to remind you, we had but one mess.

It was remarked more than once by Dr. Kane that the crew in an Arctic expedition were entitled to a great deal of indulgence, as they bore their full share of the work and hardship, but by no means received an equal share of the laurels, and could not be expected to feel quite the same zeal that the officers did.

He could be severe when necessary. He was always firm, but desired to be lenient. The ability in a commander to gratify a kindly disposition must depend in a great measure upon the character and behavior of the crew themselves. But, unfortunately, it does not require a very wide acquaintance with human nature to know that there are men who are at times, and some who seem always, utterly insensible to any arguments or appeals except those of fear and force. It was not until repeated admonition and expostulation, and appeals to the manly instinct of the individual, had failed, and until a second or third offence was committed, that even so mild a punishment as confinement was resorted to; and this means was adopted without the accessory of placing a man in a bolt-upright posture, or mast-heading him, as it is called when a man is compelled to hang on for a long time in the rigging,—punishments which may all be very well sometimes, but which were excluded from Dr. Kane's scheme of government. This mercy was at the expense of the loss of the prisoner's service to the always short-handed crew. When instant coercion was necessary in the extremity of circumstances, Dr. Kane did not hesitate to adopt a proper course.

The idea of tying a man up to gratings and flogging him, as practised in the American marine before the abolition of corporal punishment in the navy by act of Congress, was revolting to every sentiment of his soul; and, when compelled to witness punishment during his naval career, he always had stood by in abhorrence. He had been an earnest advocate of reform in this matter, and always freely expressed his detestation of the practice of corporal punishment.

In the control of others, Dr. Kane evidently exercised a painful conscientiousness. His actions were subjected to severe self-scrutiny.

His generosity led him to a peculiar demeanor toward the Danish subjects in the party. He regarded Petersen (the interpreter) in the light of a guest, and sought to maintain the amenities of that relation in his intercourse with him, while he made it a pretext to extend to him all the indulgences and attentions within his power. Poor Hans he looked upon as his own personal charge, and humored his whims and wishes as he might have done a child's.

His consideration for the entire crew was indeed beneficent. He made constant personal inspections of the men's quarters, and kind individual inquiries respecting their welfare,—sought to promote their amusement and provide for their instruction. The cabin-library was open to them, and instruction in mathematics, &c. offered. His care for the sick was delicate, unremitting, and constant. He never omitted, so long as he could move, his round of visits or relaxed in his efforts to invent some dish out of the reduced resources which might be palatable to them. That he was the nurse as well as physician of almost the entire ship's company at one time or another is well known; but how well he performed the duty can only be known to those who were the recipients or witnesses of his benevolent actions. It was no uncommon thing for him to send away some savory dish of the intestines of a ptarmigan, which the steward had cooked with artistic skill and offered to him in a silent night-watch, and, thus refusing it, to direct it to be given to some sick comrade who could relish it.

The paramount idea of Dr. Kane was the search for Sir John Franklin. A religious anxiety to do something to promote discovery bearing upon the whereabouts of the lost sailor was his ruling passion as a commander. Nothing but the most earnest desire to conduct discovery in person could have prevailed upon him to take the field in April, in his state of health. The result must almost have been foreseen by himself; and he certainly had strong forebodings of it. He was brought back delirious and very ill; but the disease seemed to have reached its crisis on his return to the brig, and soon he began to mend apace.

I think it was in the highest degree fortunate that he undertook the adventurous trip in an attempt to reach the British station at Beechey Island, as nothing within our reach could have so effectually recruited his health as the fresh game, eggs, and cochlearia, and the summer sea-breeze.

To this voyage he owed that recuperation which made him a sounder man on his return than he had been before during the cruise, or at least from the setting in of the first winter.

At the inevitable approach of a second winter, Dr. Kane knew full well the terrible perils from scurvy that it threatened; but he was only nerved to stronger effort, and worked with trebled energy. In combating the scurvy in himself and others, providing for the difficult economy of the ship, and giving the assistance of his own hands in all its labors, his nervous system was wrought to a supernatural tension; and, when we remember the contrivance, invention, and mental labor required for providing the appointments of the sledges and boats of that remarkable journey, and his exposed sledge-travel, the mind is oppressed in the attempt to appreciate his immense power of endurance. To his vigilant foresight and minutely-circumspect providence,—certainly only the more remarkable if *acquired*,—by which all the wants and contingencies of the journey were provided for, no less than to his vigilance and decisive judgment and his genius for prompt action or combination, the success of that remarkable boat-journey was undoubtedly due.

During my sojourn for ten days at Anoatok I had a good opportunity of observing his unwearied diligence in sledging between the boats, Etah, the brig, and Anoatok, conveying flesh to the boats and to our hut from Etah, and bread and baked flour from the ship, as well as his unfailing, kind consideration for the sick at a time when all his energies might have been taxed by the superintendence of the efforts of the main party for escape. From the ship to the hut and back was no unusual journey for him,—a distance of fifty or sixty miles. When he brought me down from the ship with him, notwithstanding his labor in driving and alternately with me running beside the sledge to lighten the weight, and lifting the sledge over high hummocks, or running before the dogs to keep them in the track, he started on his return without sleep. This labor kept up for a week involves no trifling exertion.

The next most conspicuous trait in our commander was his indefatigable scientific research. He never took a walk, much less made a journey,—not even the desperate march for the relief of the first party,—without looking intelligently at the ice, the land, the atmosphere, the effect of the temperature on the men, and obtaining results for his notebook. It may be some proof of his sanguine confidence in the ultimate safety of the party during the most trying periods, that, while he was ever disposed to cheer and encourage the spirits of those around him, at the same time he did not relax in the prosecution of his journals and registers.

His private journal was regularly written by his own hand at the close of each day; or, if unavoidably postponed a few days, it was brought up at the earliest practicable moment. He reviewed the log in the afternoon, and generally added some notes of his own to the remarks of the watch-officer.

His sketches were nearly all made on the spot,—the more elaborate of them finished in the cabin. They bear, I think, an intrinsic truthfulness in their appearance which speaks for itself. They certainly far surpass any illustrations of Arctic scenery which I have ever seen. The landscapes are as faultless for general inspection as photographs. It is difficult to conceive that the picture of Sylvia Headland and the Floe is not engraved from a photograph. The portraits of the Esquimaux are equally excellent. During the first winter Dr. Kane frequently occupied himself with painting in oil; but, during the long night of the second, chart-making was substituted, as being more in keeping with the lack of conveniences.

The social demeanor of our commander was cheerful and affable, even gay. He did his best to devise recreations and promote the most harmonious social intercourse. He patronized the ship's newspaper, edited the first number, and executed the vignette and caption with artistic taste. The best of its articles were by him.

It was his usual practice to play a game or two of chess after supper, the first winter. Cards were permitted only on Wednesday and Saturday evenings. This rule was adopted to prevent too great a devotion to the fascinating pasteboards.

In conversation, Dr. Kane was all that might have been expected from his eventful career and varied attainments. He seldom referred to his personal adventures, and, when he did, it was with delicate reserve; but his descriptive powers were frequently employed for the entertainment of the little circle around him.

He made a great point of urging the use of lime-juice and the other anti-scorbutics, and habitual exercise, upon the officers, and the keeping up of a cheerful tone of mind. His cheerfulness, composure, and self-command never flagged at the worst period. His own custom of exercise was regular and systematic. He frequently took long walks by moonlight, inviting one or two of the mess. One *bitter* cold evening in the middle of the first winter, after expatiating upon the importance of exercise, he playfully challenged the first officer, Mr. Brooks, to go with him and build a fox-trap at the head of a fiord, two or three miles off. Mr. Brooks accepted the challenge, and to the question, "But are you in earnest, Brooks?" answered "Yes, by George, I am, sir," with an earnestness not to be mistaken, and specially characteristic of the stalwart boatswain. They went and accomplished their purpose. But although Mr. Brooks was the largest and perhaps the most powerful man belonging to the Expedition, he ever afterward declined accepting a similar challenge from his commander, alleging that Dr. Kane's powers of endurance far exceeded his own.

Dr. Kane's dietetic habits were the triumph of principle and will over nature. His palate was delicate; yet he accustomed himself to eat puppies and rats, as he had always before accustomed himself to the diet of the country in which he sojourned. He sometimes remarked that he had eaten of almost every animal which is used as food in the various countries through which he had travelled. The advantage of being able to overcome one's repugnance to the flesh of proscribed animals is very evident to any one who has been in situations making its use an imperative necessity. When our Expedition arrived in Greenland, not more than one-third or one-fourth of the ship's company could eat seal-meat with any satisfaction; and, even till the close of the cruise, some of our party ate their raw walrus or seal meat with little zest.

Even during the second winter, with all its squalid discomfort and privation, Dr. Kane's thoughts would revert to the Northern regions of search. His desire to look upon the open water there was unabated; and, when Petersen returned from the south, in December, 1854, he questioned him closely respecting the possibility of obtaining dogs. When afterward he had obtained them, he confidently hoped to pass the limits of the farthest explorations of the previous summer; but the defection of Hans dashed these hopes to the ground. A sight of the Great Glacier of Humboldt was sufficient reward for two days' absence from the brig. He still clung to the hope of passing the glacier, and he started on a fine morning in March or April, while active preparations for escape were going on, accompanied by Morton; but this time the team of dogs was unequal to the task, and the sledge returned, I believe, the same evening.

HENRY GOODFELLOW.

PHILADELPHIA, December 7, 1857.

Honors to Dr. Kane.

REPORT

OF THE

JOINT COMMITTEE

APPOINTED TO

RECEIVE THE REMAINS AND CONDUCT THE OBSEQUIES

OF THE LATE

Elisha Kent Kane.

PHILADELPHIA, April 7, 1857.
HON. JOSEPH R. CHANDLER.

DEAR SIR:—It has seemed to the gentlemen composing the Committees of the City Councils and of the citizens of Philadelphia, which have had the direction of the public solemnities attending the funeral of the late Dr. Kane, that a report or narrative of these solemnities should be written and preserved.

It has been thought that this is due to the constituencies of the respective Committees which have united in directing them, and it has also been thought that thus an enduring record may be preserved of those remarkable and impressive demonstrations of public respect which attended the passage to the tomb of the remains of a citizen so gifted and so renowned.

I have been instructed to request you to prepare this narrative, and I trust that it will comport with your feelings and your duties to comply with the wishes which I have much satisfaction in conveying to you.

I am, dear sir,
Truly, yours,
THEODORE CUYLER,
Chairman Committee of Councils.

PHILADELPHIA, April 27, 1857.
THEODORE CUYLER, Esq.

DEAR SIR:—In compliance with the request which your favor of the 7th instant has conveyed to me, I have the honor to present a report of the proceedings of the Joint Committee appointed to receive the remains and conduct the obsequies of the late Dr. Elisha Kent Kane. All of us who united in those arrangements must feel how eminently due they were to the deceased, and yet how feeble an expression were they of the deep feeling of respect and regret entertained by our fellow-citizens for Dr. Kane.

Very truly, yours,
JOSEPH R. CHANDLER,
Chairman of the Joint Committee.

Report of the Obsequies

OF

DR. ELISHA KENT KANE.

To ordinary record we may safely trust the ordinary occurrence of the day; and the chroniclers of passing events will not fail to do justice to whatever is deemed worthy of commemoration. But the record of unusual occurrences, it may be admitted, is entitled to more than the ordinary means of perpetuation, and especially when public demonstrations denote a full appreciation of great and good acts. The public press reflects, with wonderful accuracy, ordinary and extraordinary proceedings which daily take place; but, with a fidelity that constitutes its excellence and its power, that press reflects all alike, and the perfection of the whole seems to render it difficult to contemplate with desirable abstraction any single event which it presents. There are circumstances, too, which render it proper to make a speciality of some extraordinary demonstration, not merely to augment the honors bestowed upon the person or fame of a distinguished individual, but to do justice to the purity and correctness of public sentiment in which those honors originated, and by which they were made the reward and stimulus to distinguished public virtue.

The deep and general interest manifested in the proceedings relative to the honorable reception of the remains of the late Dr. Elisha Kent Kane, and in the solemn public obsequies which followed, renders it appropriate that those to whom was delegated the duty of arranging and conducting those ceremonies should make public report of the origin of their power and the manner in which it was exercised; and the following statement of the proceedings of the several bodies which were represented in the "Committee of Arrangements" will show the feelings in which the solemnities originated in this city, and the sentiment which it was the duty of the several committees in their joint action to illustrate.

CITY COUNCILS.

At a regular meeting of the City Councils of Philadelphia, held February 26, 1857, Mr. Cuyler, in Select Council, upon unanimous leave, submitted the following preamble and resolutions, prefacing them with the following remarks :—

MR. PRESIDENT :—I beg leave to ask the unanimous consent of the Chamber to an interruption of its accustomed duties, for the purpose of offering a preamble and resolutions. They are expressive of the high sense the city of Philadelphia entertains of the glory and renown which attend the achievements of one of the noblest of her sons in the cause of science and of humanity; and, alas! they are expressive, too, of her sadness at his early death, and of her desire to do honor to his memory. The death of Dr. Elisha Kent Kane has added another name to that list of great and noble men, born among us, whose cherished memories the city of Philadelphia places among her crown jewels.

It has happened to us, sir, often before, that we have been called upon to mourn the death of citizens who have won for themselves a proud distinction, sometimes in military affairs, and sometimes in statesmanship or diplomacy, or perhaps in the higher walks of professional life; but not before this, within my recollection, has it happened to us, as in this instance, where he, whose body is now borne hither that his ashes may mingle with his native soil, was a martyr in the cause of science and of humanity. I do not propose, sir, to speak of the career of Dr. Kane. The great events of his life are known to all of us. They were wrought out by the high faith and the noble impulses of a pure heart and an earnest nature. These steeled his heart to the delights of life, when the sad cry of suffering humanity called him to deeds of noble daring. These raised his feeble frame above bodily weakness, and enabled him to triumph over cold and hunger, and kept bright and warm within his breast the flame of pure humanity amidst the never-melting ice of Polar seas and the dreary horrors of an Arctic winter.

Mr. President, there is something due from the city of Philadelphia to the memory of such a man. He whose eventful life was carried through so many strange vicissitudes in all quarters of the globe will find at last in death that repose which seems in life to have been denied him here among us. Other cities through which his remains have been carried on their journey toward this their place of burial have received them with appropriate honors. I am persuaded that the city of Philadelphia will desire to bestow upon them also her tribute of respect, and

OBSEQUIES OF 289

will feel a melancholy satisfaction in receiving and committing to the tomb the remains of one of her sons, who has in his lifetime shed so much of lustre upon her annals.

The resolutions I offer, sir, are expressive of these sentiments, and I ask of the clerk that he will be kind enough to read them.

Whereas, The body of the late Dr. Elisha Kent Kane, of Philadelphia, who died in a foreign country from disease, contracted or enhanced by exposure to the severity of an Arctic climate, during a journey prompted by a high-toned and chivalric feeling of philanthropy, and sanctioned by the Government of our Union, is on its way to his native city for the purpose of interment, and it seems to be fitting that some expression should be uttered by the representatives of the citizens of Philadelphia, indicative of their sense of the great merit of their deceased fellow-citizen, and of the renown and glory which have attached to the entire country from his admirable achievements in the cause of science and humanity, an expression which is responsive to similar sentiments coming from various parts of the Union : Therefore,

Resolved, That the city of Philadelphia will retain in ever-grateful memory the noble services of Dr. Kane in the cause of science and humanity, which have reflected glory and renown upon his native city, and upon the whole country.

Resolved, By the Select and Common Council of the City of Philadelphia, that a joint special Committee of five members of each Chamber of Councils be appointed, whose duty it shall be to cause such measures to be taken upon the arrival of the remains of Dr. Kane as will comport with the dignity of the city of Philadelphia, and be a fitting testimonial of her respect for the memory of Dr. Kane.

[The above resolutions were adopted by both Chambers and approved by the Mayor, February 27, 1857.]

The following message was received from Mayor VAUX on the same subject:—

To the President and Members of the Select Council.

GENTLEMEN,:—Information has been received in this city that Elisha Kent Kane departed this life at Havana, and that his remains are on the way to the place of his birth for the purpose of burial. A citizen of Philadelphia has made a sacrifice of his life in a service dedicated to philanthropy and science. To honor the memory of such a man is worthy of an enlightened community. In order that the City Councils may

19

have an opportunity to take such action on the subject as to them shall seem appropriate, I have considered it proper to address them this communication.   RICHARD VAUX.

Mr. Perkins rose to second the resolutions, and said :—I know nothing, sir, I can say in relation to the resolutions which have just been offered, and which I rise with some unction to second, that has not already been better expressed; and yet, sir, I cannot but feel I owe it to the high esteem and regard I have ever felt for that distinguished man, to offer my humble tribute to his memory.

Dr. Kane graduated at our University, I think, in 1843, as a physician, but very soon extended his usefulness far beyond the usual sphere of an *ordinary physician*, and in the short space of fourteen years has built up for himself and *for his country* a world-wide reputation which threescore years and ten have rarely attained : this is the condensation of *manly ambition;* and I feel pride in casting my feeble effort to add something to that respect and regard which, as a *fellow-citizen* and *fellow-countryman*, are so justly his due. I trust the resolutions will be unanimously adopted.

In the Common Council, February 26, 1857, Mr. Holman offered the following, which were adopted previous to the resolutions of Select Council being introduced into that chamber :—

Mr. Holman, on leave granted, offered the following :—

Whereas, We have heard with unfeigned regret of the death of Dr. Elisha Kent Kane, a native of Philadelphia, whose brilliant career, as an officer and explorer, has rendered his name dear to every American citizen ;

And whereas, The character of Dr. Kane, his indomitable courage, his untiring zeal, his enthusiastic love of science, and his sympathy for the suffering, have embalmed his memory in the hearts of all who can appreciate the noblest and loftiest qualities of human nature : Therefore,

Resolved, That Dr. Elisha Kent Kane was not only an honor to this city, but to the nation at large, and that his genius, his toils, his selfdenial, his patience, and his perseverance throughout a most arduous career of duty and philanthropy, are calculated to adorn the American character.

Resolved, That we sincerely condole with his bereaved relatives and friends, and that a copy of these resolutions be tendered to his afflicted family.

Mr. Henry offered the following joint resolution :—

Resolved, By the Select and Common Councils of the City of Philadelphia, that a joint special Committee of five members of each Chamber of Councils be appointed, whose duty it shall be to cause such measures to be taken upon the arrival of the remains of Dr. Kane in this city, as will comport with the dignity of the city of Philadelphia, and be a fitting testimonial of her respect for the memory of Dr. Kane.

The joint special Committee appointed under the above resolutions is as follows:—

Select Council.—Messrs. Theodore Cuyler, T. J. Perkins, Isaac N. Marselis, John Welsh, Oliver P. Cornman, and George M. Wharton.

Common Council.—Messrs. Alexander Henry, Andrew J. Holman, Henry T. King, Joshua T. Owens, and D. S. Hassinger.

MEETING OF CITIZENS.

In pursuance of a call issued by Hon. RICHARD VAUX, Mayor of the city of Philadelphia, the citizens assembled in the District Court-room, on Friday evening, March 27, 1857, for the purpose of uniting with the municipal authorities in making arrangements for the reception of the remains of the late Dr. Elisha Kent Kane, and for appropriate funeral solemnities.

At seven o'clock the meeting was called to order by Prof. John F. Frazer, of the University of Pennsylvania, and, on motion, his Honor, Mayor VAUX, was called to the chair.

On motion of Mr. Isaac Elliott, the following gentlemen were appointed

VICE-PRESIDENTS.

HON. HORACE BINNEY,	REV. H. A. BOARDMAN, D.D.
HON. J. R. INGERSOLL,	JOHN A. BROWN, ESQ.
DR. ROBLEY DUNGLISON,	FREDERICK FRALEY,
HON. ELLIS LEWIS,	JOHN WELSH,
HON. ELI K. PRICE,	HON. GEORGE SHARSWOOD,
PROF. A. D. BACHE,	CHARLES HENRY FISHER,
COMMODORE CHARLES STEWART,	SAMUEL V. MERRICK.

On motion of the Hon. Joseph R. Chandler, the following gentlemen were appointed

SECRETARIES.

J. FISHER LEAMING,   S. AUSTIN ALLIBONE,
EDWIN COOLIDGE.

On taking his place as Chairman, Mayor VAUX stated the object of the gathering:—

The occasion of our assembling is to pay, on behalf of this community, a tribute of respect to the memory of Elisha Kent Kane. He lived for his country, philanthropy, and science. He died a victim to the devotedness of his life to his life's purpose. A citizen of Philadelphia, with a fame coextensive with learning and humanity, his mortal remains are about to be placed in a grave of his native soil. The nobleness of his self-devotion, the heroism of his contests, the results of his exertions, the cause of his early death, have placed his name among those of whom it is justly said, "*Dulce et decorum est pro patria mori.*"

REMARKS OF HON. WILLIAM B. REED.

The first speaker of the evening, Hon. William B. Reed, then rose and said :—

MR. CHAIRMAN :—The duty has been delegated to me to offer to this meeting the draft of a few resolutions expressive of the feeling which animates it. I perform that duty with melancholy pleasure. The resolutions are meant to describe in precise and unexaggerated terms the pervading sentiment of this community, of sorrow, of pride, of gratitude.

Two hundred years ago, the greatest poet (save one) that ever spoke the English language said,—

"Peace hath her victories,
Not less renown'd than wars."

And we have met here to-night, in this, the city of his birth, to do honor to him who was emphatically one of the heroes of peace and peaceful enterprise. His victories were won in dismal solitude and amidst silent suffering,—in the gloom of Arctic winter, and the greater peril of Arctic summer. His were peaceful conflicts, away from humanity, while the rest of what is called the civilized world were embroiled in fiercer and more ambitious struggles; for in the three years of Dr. Kane's last adventure, from May, 1853, to September, 1855, when Hartstene (to whom be all honor, too) found the wayfarers at Lieveley, the outer world was either convulsed, or with interest watching the bloody strife in Southeastern Europe. I do not pause to ask whose was the greater heroism: those who fought within and without Sevastopol, or those eighteen American men who, clustered in the little cabin of the Advance, watched and suffered during two Arctic winters, and hoped and struggled for but one reward,—the discovery and rescue of the gallant men who, eight years before, had sought and encountered, and, as the result has shown, had been sacrificed to, the same perils. Our Philadelphia hero was with the heroes of peace, in solitude, in silence, and suffering. Hence, we have reason to be proud of him.

OBSEQUIES OF 293

We have gratitude, too, to express. The wasted frame of the dead is brought back to us, but we, his friends and townsmen, have been made aware that the last hours of his life were passed in foreign lands, among those who were personally strangers, and yet that first in England, where no American gentleman can long be a stranger, and afterward in Cuba, which peaceful affinities are every hour binding closer to us, our Philadelphia man, untitled, undistinguished except by what he has done and suffered for humanity's sake, was nursed, and cared for, and consoled, with as much tenderness and affection as if his bed of sickness had been within the limits of his native land. In this our gratitude is due.

Our sorrow it is not easy to describe, simply because what we as fellow-citizens feel seems feeble in comparison with the sharper grief of relatives and intimate personal friends. The community mourns for an eminent citizen. We mourn with selfish sorrow, because we craved other honors which he might have won for us. The latent hope is frustrated that our American explorer—our Philadelphia adventurer—might, had his life been prolonged, yet have solved the problem of Franklin's fate, and carried back to our fatherland that which would have been more precious than the abandoned Resolute,—some survivor of poor Franklin's band, or some authentic intelligence (for there is really none such) of their actual fate. We sorrow not without hope, while such men as Hartstene, and Simms, and De Haven are left with us.

Let us, then, citizens of Philadelphia, do honor to the memory of the dead—our illustrious dead—in the manner which best becomes him and us; with dignity, with moderation, with decorum, with no exaggerated ostentation, with no effort to make mere ceremonial transcend the limits of actual feeling. Let us show we feel this blow deeply. While other communities may exceed us in display, let Philadelphia—the city of Kane's birth, and education, and manhood—show the deepest and most earnest feeling.

Mr. Reed then submitted the following preamble and resolutions :—

The citizens of Philadelphia, convened in general town meeting, at the call of their Chief-Magistrate, desire to unite with the constituted authorities in doing honor to the memory of their distinguished townsman, Dr. Elisha Kent Kane, who recently died in a foreign land, and whose mortal remains now approach their final resting-place in his native city. With this view, they have

Resolved, That Philadelphia discharges the simplest duty of self-

294   DR. ELISHA KENT KANE.

respect in doing honor to one who, on the great theatre of the enlightened world, has attracted the interest and the applause of all who sympathize with the noblest impulses of humanity and watch the progress of scientific discovery and gallant adventure.

Resolved, That, aside from the debt of gratitude we owe for the fame he has gained for Philadelphia, as Christians and citizens of the world, we honor him for the persevering resolution with which he conducted the second American Expedition in search of Sir John Franklin, with no superior officer to control or direct him, and no other support in long years of trial and privation than his own moral and intellectual resources, and the sympathies of the gallant men under his command.

Resolved, That the English people owe (and we doubt not will gladly pay) to Dr. Kane this especial gratitude :—that he, more than any other, by the power of his pen and the influence of his example, awakened the interest of America to the career and fate of those heroic men whose undiscovered destiny is yet the problem of this age of active enterprise.

Resolved, That Philadelphia, sorrowfully but proudly welcoming the mortal remains of her dead son home again, thanks with earnest sincerity the distant communities whose kindness consoled his latest hours upon earth, those who strove by all the appliances of professional skill and domestic comfort to arrest the progress of disease, and, when in another land the hour of final agony came, those who mourned with tender sympathy around the bed of death.

Resolved, That the citizens now assembled, thus inadequately expressing the general sentiment of the community, will unite with the Councils and the other authorities in such funeral ceremony as may be determined on, and that the Mayor be requested to appoint a committee of sixteen citizens to act as a committee of arrangement.

Resolved, That a copy of the proceedings of this meeting, duly engrossed and authenticated, be communicated to the family of the deceased, and to such of the authorities of the British and Spanish Governments as may hereafter be determined on as best representing those whose kindness to our lamented townsman we desire to commemorate.

MAJOR BIDDLE'S SPEECH.

Major Charles J. Biddle, in seconding the resolutions, said :—I am requested to second the resolutions which have been offered to the meeting. In so doing, I shall not trespass long upon your indulgence, for I see present many gentlemen whose eloquence may find an appropriate theme in the event which now brings us together.

This meeting is not an assemblage of the professional associates or the personal friends of the deceased,—such as are convened on occasions of ordinary bereavement,—but it represents the citizens of Philadelphia, who desire to join with the municipal authorities in paying the last honors to one whose career reflected honor upon the city of his birth. For, at this moment, there is no man, native to our city, whose name and fame are so widely spread as his whose untimely fate we deplore. At an age when a man has done much if he has acquired local distinction, Kane's celebrity extends throughout—nay, beyond—the limits of the civilized world, for even in the ice-bound regions of the North Pole his name is recalled with reverence and affection.

But it will not be inappropriate for me to leave to others those general reflections which his career suggests, and to mention a circumstance of which I had particular opportunities of hearing. During the war with Mexico, Dr. Kane obtained a release from other duties and came out to that country to join the American army. With his ardent and chivalrous temperament, I can suppose him to have heard with regret that battles which decided the issue of the war had been already fought and won. But Providence reserved for him a distinction so appropriate to his philanthropic character, that all will perceive how much more it became him than ordinary military honors.

At that time, there was employed by General Scott, for purposes of communication and intelligence, a company of Mexicans, who had attached themselves to the American cause. Dr. Kane arrived at the city of Puebla at a time when this company was returning from an expedition and on its way to join the army. In his eagerness to reach that destination, he did not wait for a worthier escort, but placed himself under their guidance. Upon the road they met with a Mexican force, and the mutual hostility of the two parties led to an immediate encounter, in which our adherents, aided by Kane and encouraged by his example, were victorious.

But the enmity of these renegades against their own countrymen was not restrained by the rules of ordinary warfare, and their first impulse was to improve their advantage by a massacre of the prisoners. Against this I need not say that Kane remonstrated; and, when his remonstrances proved vain, he threw himself before the intended victims, and made his own body the barrier between them and the death that menaced them. Single-handed, his dauntless bearing prevailed in that struggle;

but when I saw him, not long afterward, he bore upon his person a wound from an intercepted blow aimed at the life of one of the prisoners,— a wound from which he had not then recovered, if indeed he ever entirely recovered from the effects of it.

Here, then, I say, he won an honor consistent with that benevolence of character which was to impel him to those arduous researches the end and aim of which were to carry aid to suffering humanity. Doubtless all of us thought with regret and sympathy of Franklin and his comrades, lost, starved, frozen up in living death, "in the thrilling regions of thick-ribbed ice;" but their cry for aid seemed to reach the very heart of Kane, and he girded himself up, and roused the enthusiasm of others to noble and powerful and persistent efforts for their rescue.

It is in this forgetfulness of self, in sympathy for others, that I recognise the traits of a noble character, worthy, fellow-citizens, of all the honors we can pay to it.

PROF. FRAZER'S ADDRESS.

Major Biddle was followed by Professor John F. Frazer, of the University of Pennsylvania, who spoke in eloquent and impressive language of the scientific attainments of Dr. Kane, and of the name and fame which he had acquired by his industry, his energy, his trials, and his sufferings. My own personal acquaintance with Dr. Kane, said he, dates from comparatively a late period. I became acquainted with him shortly before his first expedition; but I know few persons, and in the course of my reading came across few sources of such abundant, thorough, well-digested information, as Dr. Kane brought back with him from every expedition he made. His was truly, sir, a scientific mind,—a mind quick in its observations,—a mind enthusiastic in its appreciation, —a mind full of that brilliant genius of induction, by means of which he was enabled to see the connection which lay between phenomena which, perhaps, might have been passed unappreciated and been forgotten by others.

But it was not merely in recording science that Dr. Kane excelled, but it was in that beautiful disposition which enabled him to see something beyond what is ordinarily considered science. He was enabled to see that this portion of his study was, in effect, nothing but preparation for a greater and more full knowledge of more grand and sublime mysteries hereafter.

OBSEQUIES OF

MR. CHANDLER'S SPEECH.

The Hon. J. R. Chandler said:—After what has been said, and well said, the object for which we assemble this evening will find its greatest approval. Indeed, sir, the public grief for the cause for which we assemble on this occasion is of a character which words fail to express. I appear, sir, at the request of the gentlemen of the committee, or I would not have trespassed upon your time. While I was without that intimate personal relation with Dr. Kane which others here possessed, I was deeply interested in his public movements, and greatly concerned for his last voyage to the North. And it was my good fortune to concur in a resolution by which the intrepid gentleman should go at the public expense. But, sir, I stand here, as a member of this community, to say how deeply every member of it feels the loss that the nation has sustained in the death of Dr. Kane, and to express our appreciation of his great worth, and his noble, generous daring, and his benevolence, which outstripped all, to give expression to those feelings which such acts and such motives excite,—expression, sir, which will not be complete until every individual benefited or honored by his exertions shall also utter his sentiments, and until impartial history shall have handed to future generations, for admiration, the name and the deeds of one who is so honored by the present generation. His life will be the history of private griefs; it will be the history of many sufferings, and a statement of deep and of abiding interest. But, sir, history will do justice to these, and demonstrate the propriety of any movement to do honor to the memory of one who was so distinguished. It would be scarcely proper in any public meeting to attempt to follow Dr. Kane through his interesting movements by which he has connected his name with the history of this age. The gentleman preceding me has given an edifying anecdote concerning him. It would be interesting to every Philadelphian to follow him upon his track across the frozen ocean, to fancy one's self with him when he looked down on the calm, peaceful Arctic Sea from a point upon which perhaps no man had ever rested, and the existence of which had been recorded by no pen but his, and then to follow him from that cold frozen region down to the sunny climate of the Antilles, and to see there, festering in his heart, the arrow which had been planted there at the North, already wasting his life in disease, and now looking across the barrier of time upon the great ocean of eternity, which he could not describe, making those last discoveries, and the only discoveries made by Dr. Kane that were not for the benefit of those whom he left behind.

I speak now, sir, because I believe it proper on an occasion of this kind to do honors such as this meeting is called to do. I do not suppose, sir, that we shall add any thing to his fame; but it is to our own credit as Philadelphians, it is to our own credit as citizens of the city that gave him birth, that we appreciate his deeds; and it is a source of gratification to every Philadelphian, and the friends of Dr. Kane especially, that while he was busily engaged in those vast pursuits which gave him a world-wide fame, that while he was looking from the Equator to the Poles, and making himself familiar with all that concerned this earth, it was a providential blessing that he was not unacquainted with the fickle tenor in which his life was held.

I will not trespass longer. I have other duties to perform; but this was a solemn one to me. There are those who will do more honor to his principles, but there are none who can feel more deeply the honor and glory that was reflected on our beloved city by such a man.

REMARKS OF REV. DR. BOARDMAN.

Rev. Dr. H. A. Boardman said:—I am here, sir, on the invitation of one of the gentlemen of the Committee. I should have been here under any circumstances, (Providence permitting;) and I am here on that invitation simply to express my concurrence in that object for which this meeting has been assembled, and my sympathy in the great bereavement which an All-wise Providence has seen fit to visit upon us; and, if I rightly interpret the feelings of this community by my own, there can be but very little of the mere pageantry of grief. We are not here simply to express our admiration for Dr. Kane.

There is not a man in this assembly,—no! there is not a man in this broad land, or any other land,—who has read those picturesque and beautiful volumes, whose heart has not gone out in love as well as in admiration for him. It is impossible for a man who is susceptible of any generous sentiment to read the simple and graphic records of his labors and his trials without love, and not feel it to be a privilege to cast if it be but a single flower upon his grave.

Dr. Kane, sir, has established a name and a place for himself among our men of science, and he will be held in high and honorable remembrance by the scientific associations and institutions of Christendom; and they will not fail to pay every homage to his memory, in fitting terms and with becoming honors.

Dr. Kane, sir, has gone down to the grave lamented; and this bereavement will go home to thousands, to millions of hearts, just in proportion as that work—I refer especially to the last work—whose circle throughout the civilized world, like the tide, is continually swelling and swelling to receive new appreciations. Philadelphia may well mourn. Let us not forget the intrepidity, the indomitable energy and perseverance, of Dr. Kane.

Sir, there is not an act recorded in his volumes which is in the least degree tainted with the element of selfishness. He stood among that company not as their leader and captain,—not as their guide and teacher simply,—but as their friend and their father; and it was his daily care—yes, sir, and his daily prayer—that they might be sheltered and protected at whatever hazard of personal inconvenience or peril to himself.

The speaker concluded by referring to the scientific acquirements of the deceased, and in a life of so short duration.

Mr. John A. Brown suggested that the citizens should adopt some measure to secure the erection of a suitable monument to be placed over the final resting-place of the deceased, and something to that effect should be embodied in the resolutions.

Mr. Coolidge moved to refer this to the committee to be appointed under the resolution.

Mr. Brown acquiesced in this motion, and it was agreed to.

The preamble and resolutions were unanimously agreed to.

The Mayor announced the Committee of sixteen, as follows:—

HON. JOSEPH R. CHANDLER,	HON. CHARLES J. INGERSOLL,
ISAAC ELLIOTT,	PROF. JOHN S. HART,
MAJ. CHARLES J. BIDDLE,	WILLIAM B. FOSTER,
HON. WILLIAM D. KELLEY,	EDWARD WARTMAN,
ISAAC HAZLEHURST,	THOMAS S. STEWART,
GEN. GEORGE CADWALADER,	HON. WILLIAM H. WITTE,
ISAAC F. BAKER,	ALEXANDER CUMMINGS,
JOSEPH M. THOMAS,	CHARLES HALLOWELL.

On motion of Hon. William D. Kelley, the meeting adjourned at about 8 o'clock.

CORN EXCHANGE.

A meeting of the members of the Corn Exchange was held February 27, 1857.

Colonel S. N. Winslow, after a few remarks in regard to the decease of Dr. E. K. Kane, moved that Mr. Alexander G. Cattell be called to the Chair, and Mr. W. S. Pierie be appointed Secretary, which was agreed to.

Mr. George L. Buzby moved that a committee of three be appointed to submit a preamble and resolutions expressive of their views upon the subject, which was agreed to.

Messrs. George L. Buzby, John Wright, and William B. Thomas were appointed on the committee, who submitted the following:—

Whereas, It has pleased an All-wise Providence to remove from his earthly career Dr. Elisha Kent Kane; and,

Whereas, The mercantile and commercial community, having a proper appreciation of the eminent abilities of the deceased, and of his enthusiastic and untiring efforts in behalf of science and philanthropy, feel, in common with the rest of our fellow-citizens, the irreparable loss which not only Philadelphia, but Pennsylvania, and every other city and State in the Union, have suffered by his demise : Therefore,

Resolved, That the members of the Corn Exchange Association tender to the parents and relatives their sympathies in the day of their affliction.

Resolved, That the officers and members of the Corn Exchange Association will join with the civic and military authorities in rendering an appropriate mark of their respect to the memory of the deceased, and that a committee of five be appointed to confer with similar committees from other associations upon the subject.

Resolved, That the Secretary furnish an authenticated copy of the above preamble and resolutions to the family of the deceased.

Mr. Buzby, in moving the adoption of these resolutions, appealed to that proper pride which ought to exist in the bosom of every Philadelphian when a distinguished fellow-citizen has won the applause of an admiring world. There certainly was that strength of public spirit in the Corn Exchange Association which insured their prompt desire to render the last tokens of respect to the memory of the remarkable man who has left this world young in years but full of honors. He had, then, he was sure, only to propose the resolutions, without the necessity of any lengthened remarks, which, whilst unnecessary to move them to a proper action on this occasion, must necessarily fall short of the tribute due to the departed. A community which fails to respect the memory of her own great children, and to furnish those outward tokens so appropriate at such a time as this, has lost its own claims to the respect of mankind.

On motion of George McHenry, seconded by E. G. James, the preamble and resolutions were unanimously adopted, and Messrs. James Steel . J. Hoffman, J. J. Black, George Raphael, and James Barratt, were appointed on the Committee.

On motion, Messrs. A. G. Cattell and Samuel L. Ward were subsequently added.

On Saturday, February 28, the Committee from City Councils, and the Committee appointed by the meeting of citizens, and the Committee on the part of the "Corn Exchange," assembled in the Select Council Chamber, with a view of uniting their exertions to promote the objects for which they were severally appointed, when, on motion of Theodore Cuyler, Esq., Chairman of the Committee of the Select Council, Hon. Joseph R. Chandler, the Chairman of the Committee from the meeting of citizens, was appointed Chairman of a Joint Committee, and H. G. Leisinring was appointed Secretary.

The Joint Committee determined to do all in their power, with such means as they possessed, to fulfil the intentions of the several bodies by which they were appointed, and to make such arrangements as would allow to the citizens of Philadelphia an expression of their high regard for the merits of the distinguished dead, doing honor at once to the greatness of his enterprise in the cause of science, and to the beauty of his example in the exercise of benevolence. And the Joint Committee now respectfully report their proceedings under that organization.

At the time of the appointment of the Committee of Arrangement, the remains of Dr. Kane had been brought from Havana, where he died, to the city of New Orleans, where they were received with distinguished honors, which were continued on the whole route from that city to Philadelphia, making the passage of the body of the deceased one continuous display of public regard; and so intimately connected were these demonstrations that each seemed to be one link in a lengthened chain of admiration and affectionate respect: so universally felt and expressed, and so in unison with public sentiment, were they, that the concluding ceremonies in Philadelphia may be regarded as a natural termination of the demonstrations of regard commenced at Havana.

And hence the Committee have deemed it consistent with the objects of their appointment to notice briefly the testimonials by which other communities manifested their respect to the character and services of the deceased.

The death of Dr. Kane, it is known, occurred at Havana, on the 16th of February, 1857; and the citizens of the United States, resident in that city or transiently there, availed themselves of the earliest opportunity to express their grief at the loss and their respect for the character of their distinguished countryman; and it is gratifying to notice that the highest authority of the island of Cuba has commended himself to the grateful acknowledgment of every American by his promptness in offers of aid in the demonstrations of respect to the deceased.

The subjoined is an abstract of the proceedings in Havana on the death of Dr. Kane :— /

PROCEEDINGS AT HAVANA.

HAVANA, 17th February, 1857.

The citizens of the United States resident and transient in Havana were this day called together at the Consulate, by A. K. Blythe, Esq., for the purpose of making a public demonstration of respect to the memory of our much-lamented fellow-citizen, Dr. E. K. Kane.

At two o'clock, a very large number being assembled, were called to order by General Patterson, of Pennsylvania, who, after a few remarks, nominated the Hon. A. K. Blythe, United States Consul, as Chairman, and Henry Tiffany, of Maryland, as Secretary.

Mr. Blythe explained the object of the meeting, which the assemblage heard with deep sensation; and he also submitted the following note from the Governor Captain-General:—

[COPY—TRANSLATION.]

Office of the Governor Captain-General and Superintendent of the Exchequer of the Ever-Faithful Island of Cuba.

(SEAL.)

Government Secretary's Office—Section of Government.

I have received the communication that you have addressed to me, under this date, soliciting permission that the American citizens residing in this city may meet at your residence for the purpose of making a public demonstration on the decease of your fellow-citizen, Dr. E. K. Kane. I have the greatest satisfaction in acceding to the wishes expressed by you, and beg of you to make known to me the result of the meeting indicated, that I may unite with you in the manifestation that shall be resolved upon to the memory of that distinguished man of science. God preserve you many years.

HAVANA, 17th February, 1857.

(Signed,) JOSE DE LA CONCHA.

OBSEQUIES OF 303

To the Commercial Agent in Charge of the Consulate of the United States.

HAVANA, February 18, 1857.

A. K. BLYTHE, ESQ.:—

DEAR SIR:—His Excellency, the Captain-General, having been informed that Dr. Kane's body is to be taken to his native country, and wishing that its transportation to the vessel selected for that purpose may be effected with the respect due to his merit, has resolved to place at your service, and that of his friends, the Government barge, particularly as there are no American men-of-war in port whose boats might perform this sad duty. His Excellency, for this reason, would wish you to inform him beforehand of the day when the ceremony will take place, in order that he may give the corresponding orders to the boat, and that some of the members of the Scientific Corporations of this city may accompany the remains.

(Signed,) MANUEL AGUIRE Y TEJADOR,
Secretary.

On motion of General Patterson, a committee of five was appointed by the Chairman, to present resolutions expressive of the sympathy of the meeting. The committee, consisting of General Patterson, of Pennsylvania, Governor H. W. Cushman, of Massachusetts, C. C. Thompson, of New York, Colonel Robertson, of Havana, and James Battle, of Alabama, reported the following, which were adopted unanimously :—

The late Dr. E. K. Kane, having, by dispensation of divine Providence, terminated his brief but eventful career, we, citizens of the United States resident and transient in Havana, desiring to express our grateful sense of his distinguished services to his country and mankind, do resolve,

FIRST, That in the death of Dr. Kane our country has lost a valuable and world-renowned citizen, who has adorned her annals; science has been deprived of an ardent advocate, ever ready, by self-abnegation, to advance her interests; and humanity a devotee, who yielded his life in obedience to her commands.

SECOND, That, whilst we deeply deplore his loss as a public calamity, we tender our heartfelt condolence to his parents, brothers, and distressed relatives.

THIRD, That these resolutions, with the letter of the Governor Captain-General in relation to this meeting, be presented to the family of the deceased, and a copy of the same be made public through the press of the United States.

To the same committee that had introduced the resolutions was referred the duty of assisting the family, as mourners, in removing to the steamer the body of Dr. Kane, for conveyance to the United States.

On the 20th of February, the body of Dr. Kane was borne on men's shoulders to the Plaza de Armes, followed by upward of eight hundred persons, citizens of the United States and subjects of other countries. At the Plaza, the body was received by His Excellency the Governor of the city and suite; also, by various associations, who joined in the procession to the place of embarkation,—namely:

The Inspection of Public Instruction.—Messrs. Dr. Don Nicolas Gutierrez and Don José Luis Casaseca.

The University.—Dr. Don Antonia Zambrana, Rector thereof; Dr. Don Fernan Gonzales del Valle, Dr. Don Angel J. Cowley, Dr. Don José Joaquin Sibou, Dr. Don José Sanchez, Dr. Don José Ignacio Rodriguez.

The Economical Society.—Don Manuel Ramos Izquierdo, Don Eugenio de Arriaza.

The Preparatory and Especial Schools.—Don Pelayo Gonzalez, Director.

The Royal Board of Improvements.—Don Francisco Campos and Don José Valdes Fauli.

The Superior Board of Health.—Dr. Don Manuel José Valero, Secretary thereof.

The Medical Department of the Army.—The Inspector of the Corps, Don Fernando Bastarreche, Chief of the same in the island.

A band of military music accompanied the procession from the beginning, and another band joined it at the Plaza. The State barge received the body and the mourners at the place of embarkation, and conveyed them to the steamer Catawba. The boats of the steamer and of private American vessels, as well as those belonging to the ships of other nations, followed in solemn procession.

The Spanish flag, which had been hoisted at the Cabaret, was lowered as the body was received into the barge; and, on board of the Catawba, Brigadier Don José Ignacio de Echavarria, Civil and Military Governor of Havana, addressed to the Committee of Arrangements and the persons present the following discourse:—

GENTLEMEN:—Enlightened communities always feel themselves bound to render a tribute of respect and of affection to those privileged beings who, in the elevation of their ideas, are ready to sacrifice themselves to accomplish an object of interest to all humanity. Dr. Kane belongs, undoubtedly, as we all know, to this class of celebrities. His ardent scientific zeal, his fervent enthusiasm for the exaltation of his country, and his love for mankind, impelled him to investigations in the frozen regions, where, through imminent perils, immense privations, and with a self-denial as exemplary as it was enviable, nothing deterred him from the accomplishment of his object for which he offered his health as a sacrifice. He came to this land for the restoration of his health; and, when the hope began to be entertained of accomplishing it, the sad event has occurred which assembles us in this place. All the inhabitants of Cuba would have shared in the satisfaction, if his life had been spared; but Providence, in His high designs, ordained that here he should breathe his last, and to-day all deplore a loss so important. His Excellency the Governor Captain-General, entertaining these sentiments, has wished to offer a public and solemn testimony thereof, of the sympathetic interest that this lamentable event has awakened, and of the share which his Excellency, together with the scientific corporations of the island and the whole country, take in the just grief of the fellow-citizens of Dr. Kane, who will ever be honored by the memory of this illustrious man. May he rest in peace, and may all coming generations be faithful and constant to his memory, to preserve and enhance it as it merits!

Mr. Blythe, United States Consul at Havana, responded to the above, in the following terms:—

SIR:—I regret much that we have not a common language, in which, on behalf of my countrymen, I might express to you our deep gratitude for this, the closing act of so great and generous kindness shown to the memory of our deceased fellow-citizen. I cannot forbear, however, to avail myself of the occasion to declare to the Americans here assembled that his Excellency the Captain-General, and all the authorities, have done every thing suggested by us, and much dictated by themselves, to the honor of him whose loss we all deplore, and who in his life so honored our native land. I rejoice that it has been so, for two reasons: it is a just tribute to him who faithfully served his country and mankind, and is evincive of a spirit of amity on the part of those who have so generously co-operated with us in our sad duties. The mild amenities of life, whether socially or nationally extended, do much to mollify the feelings and create cordial friendships: when to courtesy is added the exalted sentiment of humanity, such actions are the result as command our grateful admiration. With great pleasure I say to you, my countrymen, that for all these benignities we are under great obligation to those in authority here. Again, sir, in behalf of the people I represent, I return to you, and the other officers of your Government who have so generously participated with us in these sad rites, our sincere thanks.

The whole proceedings at Havana, from the arrival of Dr. Kane, sick and suffering, until his remains left the harbor of that city, were marked by delicacy and kindness toward him and his friends while he lived, and, when he died, honors that reflect honor upon the officers and people, and appeal to the finest feelings of the human heart for appreciation and gratitude, were bestowed upon his memory and remains.

CEREMONIES AT NEW ORLEANS.

The Catawba arrived at New Orleans on the 22d of February, and, as soon as the steamer reached her berth, his Honor, Mayor Waterman, promptly proffered to the relatives of the deceased the city's guardianship of the hallowed remains while they remained within its limits; and, that offer being gratefully accepted, the company of Continental Guards escorted the body to the City Hall, where it lay in state under the honorable guard of the company that escorted it thither. Every pains were taken to make expressive the demonstrations of respect; and the manifestations of regard on the part of the citizens of New Orleans were such as to do honor to that city.

The procession to convey the remains to the steamer Woodford, that was to ascend the river, was composed of an unusual display of the military of the two brigades in full uniform, the Sons of St. George, a large and imposing body of Englishmen, the Masonic Order, the corpse, with twelve pall-bearers, being officers of the Army and Navy, and representatives of Civic Societies, the Mayor and Recorder and Foreign Consuls following in carriages. The Keystone Club, composed of Pennsylvanians and citizens in general. The whole proceedings in New Orleans were most expressive and honorable to all.

The progress of the steamer that conveyed up the Mississippi and the Ohio the remains of Dr. Kane was watched with intense anxiety, and whenever it was possible the attempt was made by the people to give expression to the respect which the lofty character and ennobling service

OBSEQUIES OF 307

of the deceased had excited. Only one feeling seemed to animate the public mind through the whole progress of the remains,—deep and abiding respect for the memory of Dr. Kane, and anxiety to give such an expression to that feeling as would be most to the honor of him who had so honored his country and his kind; and many anecdotes are related of gentle and delicate expressions of regard.

At Louisville, Kentucky, preparations worthy the high credit of that city had been made, to do honor to the deceased.

In anticipation of the arrival of the remains, the Mayor of Louisville issued a call for the Councils of the city to meet, with a view of making proper arrangements to do honor to the fame of the hero of peace, and public meetings of citizens were also held to unite in these demonstrations. The Order of Free Masons had also made arrangements to lead in this manifestation of respect.

CEREMONIES AT LOUISVILLE, KY.

At a meeting of the respective committees on the part of the Masonic fraternity, the city authorities, and the citizens of Louisville, held at the Merchants' Exchange, March 2, 1857, for the purpose of making all necessary arrangements for the reception of the remains of Elisha Kent Kane, M.D., Captain Thomas Joyes was appointed Chairman, and John D. Pope Secretary.

His Honor the Mayor presented a communication from George L. Febryir, Esq., Chairman of the Committee of Arrangements, Cincinnati, Ohio, stating that extensive arrangements had been made by the citizens of Ohio for the reception of the remains of Dr. Kane in that State, and asking that a committee of escort from Louisville be appointed, which would be met at the Miami River by a committee from Cincinnati.

Which was read, and thereupon Dr. U. E. Ewing, Col. Thos. Anderson, Col. L. A. Whiteley, Capt. Thos. Joyes, Dr. Palmer, Dr. N. B. Marshall, Dr. Lewis Rogers, James S. Lithgow, and Moses Dickson, were added to the escort heretofore appointed to convey the remains to Cincinnati.

Captain Lovel H. Rousseau was appointed Chief-Marshal on the part of the citizens, and authorized to appoint assistant marshals at his discretion.

The following programme was adopted, and ordered to be published:—

PROGRAMME FOR THE RECEPTION OF THE REMAINS OF DR. E. K. KANE.

Upon the signal being given, the respective committees of reception will assemble immediately on horseback, at the court-house, and proceed thence to Portland, where, in conjunction with Lewis Lodge, No. 205, they will take charge of the remains and accompany them to the intersection of Maine and Twelfth Streets.

At the same signal, all the associate bodies and the citizens who intend to participate in the procession will assemble as follows :—

The Masonic fraternity at their hall, corner of Market and Third Streets.

The firemen at the Union Engine House.

The various other civic associations at their respective places of meeting.

The citizens on foot, in carriages, and on horseback, at the court-house.

Within one hour after the signal for assembling the procession will be formed at the court-house, and proceed, in such order as may be directed by the Chief-Marshal, to the corner of Twelfth and Main Streets, where, upon the arrival of the cortège from Portland, the procession will be formed in the following order :—

Chief-Marshal and Assistants.
Music.
Masonic Fraternity.

Pall-Bearers.  Pall-Bearers.

Family and Relations of Deceased in Carriages.
Reception-Committee and Escorts.
Members of the Medical Faculty.
Members of the Legal Profession.
Municipal Authorities.
Chief of the Police and Assistants.
Music.
Fire Department.
Civic Associations.
Citizens on Foot.
Citizens in Carriages.
Citizens on Horseback.

The signal for assembling will be the tolling of the fire-bells and the firing of the minute-guns.

The citizens generally, and the civic associations of New Albany, Jeffersonville, and the adjoining counties, are invited to join the procession.

Masonic Reception Committee.—M. W. Barr, Frank Tryon, John D. Pope, Syl. Thomas, B. A. Flood.

Citizen Reception Committee.—Col. Thos. Anderson, Capt. Thomas Joyes, Dr. T. S. Bell, Dr. U. E. Ewing, Col. L. A. Whiteley.

Pall-Bearers.—Samuel Griffith, S. Hillman, J. C. Hoffman, G. P. Schetkey, David L. Beatty, David T. Monsarrat, D. Marcellus, C. C. Spencer.

Masonic Chief-Marshal.—Edwin S. Craig.

Assistants.—H. C. Morton, J. H. Shroder.

Citizens' Chief-Marshal.—Capt. L. H. Rousseau.

Route of Procession.—The procession will move, under the direction of the Chief-Marshal and his assistants, up Twelfth Street to Walnut, up Walnut to Second, along Second to Main, down Main to Fourth, and out Fourth to Mozart Hall, where the Reception Committees and Pall-Bearers will take charge of the remains until they are delivered to the escort to accompany them to Cincinnati.

The body of Dr. Kane was received with great ceremony, and conveyed to the Mozart Hall, where it lay in state, attended by a guard of honor.

On the following day the remains were removed to the steamer. The procession was headed by the Masonic Fraternity, and was composed of the city authorities and the numerous associations of the place. The whole arrangement of reception and transmission of the remains in the city of Louisville was of the most liberal kind. From Louisville the remains of Dr. Kane were conveyed to New Albany, Indiana, and appropriately received there.

A Committee from the city of Cincinnati here met the New Albany and Louisville Committee, and received the charge of the sacred remains and conveyed them by steamer to Cincinnati, accompanied by deputations from the cities below. The feelings of deep respect expressed in the remarks of the various Committees, as they resigned or received the charge, were eloquent homages to the great merits of the dead.

OBSEQUIES OF

CEREMONIES AT CINCINNATI.

PROGRAMME AND ORDER OF ARRANGEMENTS.

MILITARY AND CIVIC PROCESSION.

FORMATION AND LINE OF MARCH.

Grand Marshal—Gassaway Brashears.

Assistant Grand Marshals.

General C. H. Sargent,	Colonel John W. Dudley,
Charles Hartshorne,	Captain H. W. Burdsall,
E. N. Fuller,	E. B. Dennison,
J. P. Epply,	W. L. O'Brien,
J. B. Covert,	Theophilus Gaines,
Theodore Cook,	Thomas McBirney,
C. W. Rowland,	Joseph Myers,
Ambrose W. Neff,	General John McMakin,
Joshua H. Bates,	L. Laboyteaux,

George Bogen, Jr.

MILITARY.

In order as follows:—

United States Troops, from Newport Barracks.

Volunteer Uniform Troops, from abroad.

Volunteer Uniform Military of the Third Brigade, First Division, Ohio Volunteer Militia.

Independent Uniform Military Associations.

Clergy, in carriages.

Mexican Volunteers.

Independent Guthrie Grays, Captain W. K. Bosley.

Masonic Fraternity.

Pall-Bearers. *Pall-Bearers.*

Judge James Hall,	N. W. Thomas,
John Swasey,	Judge Van Hamm,
Geo. K. Shoenberger,	Captain George Hatch,
James F. Torrence,	James Wilson,
Dr. O. M. Langdon,	Dr. A. S. Dandridge,
Dr. J. B. Smith,	Dr. J. F. White,
Dr. J. D. Dodge,	Dr. George Fries,
General James Taylor,	Thomas Porter,
Larz Anderson,	C. W. West,
William J. Schultz,	James H. Walker,
Captain C. G. Pierce,	E. S. Haines,
Joseph Jones,	C. B. Smith,
William Hoon,	John D. Jones,
Joseph Raper,	Bellamy Storer,
C. F. Hanselman,	F. Bodman.
C. Moore.	

[FUNERAL CAR WITH REMAINS.]

DR. ELISHA KENT KANE. 311

Relatives and immediate friends of deceased, in carriages.
Officers of the Army and Navy.
Committee of Arrangements.
Physicians and Medical Societies.
Judges and Officers of State and United States Courts.
Governor of Ohio and suite.
Pioneers of Cincinnati and Ohio, in carriages.
Trustees of the Common Schools.
Independent Order of Red Men.
Mayor and Public Authorities of Newport.
Mayor and Public Authorities of Covington.
Mayor and Public Authorities of Cincinnati.
Steamboat Association.
Turners' Society.
Independent Order of Odd-Fellows.
Officers and Members of the Y. M. M. L. Association.
Cincinnati Chamber of Commerce.
United Irish Association.
Butchers' Benevolent Association.
Citizens in procession not attached to any association.

Societies and organizations not yet reported, and participating, will be assigned places by the Grand Marshal.

The procession will form, at eight o'clock on the morning of the general obsequies, on Fifth Street, with the right resting on Front Street, displaying east. Upon the arrival of the remains, they will be received and in procession escorted east on Fifth Street to Western Row, south on Western Row to Fourth Street, east on Fourth Street to Broadway, south on Broadway until the right of the procession shall rest at Front Street, where the column will halt, and, with honors paid the remains, be dismissed by the Grand Marshal.

All associations and organizations designated in the programme of procession, and others intending to participate, will, on the morning of the funeral obsequies, report themselves through each others' own officer, or marshal, to the Grand Marshal, who will be found at the Mechanics' Institute Building, southwest corner of Vine and Sixth Streets, up to the hour of formation of procession. By order of

THOMAS H. WEISNER,
BENJAMIN EGGLESON,
W. S. FLAGG,
JOSEPH TORRENCE,
W. K. BOSLEY,
W. B. DODD,
JOHN D. JONES,

F. LINCK,
JOSEPH DARR,
JAMES C. HALL,
JOSEPH K. SMITH,
G. L. FEBIGER,
C. H. SARGENT,
Committee of Arrangements.

OBSEQUIES OF

At twelve o'clock M., March 6, the Committee appointed by the General Committee of Arrangements for the funeral obsequies of Dr. E. K. Kane, to receive the remains of the lamented dead from the Louisville and New Albany Committee, in whose charge they were, proceeded to the mail-boat Jacob Strader, and, placing themselves under the charge of Captain Blair Summons and Dr. Dunning, at one o'clock the boat slipped her cables, and moved off, like a thing of life, down the Ohio.

The Committee consisted of the following gentlemen :—

THOS. H. WEASNER,   CHAS. ANDERSON,
JNO. C. SCHOOLEY,   GEO. L. FEBIGER,
DR. T. N. WISE,   E. B. REED.

An appropriate badge had been prepared for the Committee, of which the following is a description :—

FIDELIS AD 'URNAM.

WE

MOURN

THE DEATH OF

KANE,

THE

GREAT EXPLORER, RIPE SCHOLAR, AND NOBLE
PHILANTHROPIST.

WHOSE NAME

ADDS LUSTRE TO A MIGHTY NATION.

HIS MEMORY
SHALL BE
IMMORTAL!

About five o'clock, as the boat proceeded on her way, she was met by quite a heavy snow-storm, which soon whitened the shore on either hand, and reminded the Committee forcibly of their mission. They were to receive the remains of one who had battled with fiercer snow-storms and far keener blasts, not on the bosom of the Ohio, but on the rough

Arctic seas,—not in the midst of civilization, and in sight of land, but where on every hand naught but the dreary iceberg and a frozen sea encompassed him. What more fitting herald of the approaching steamer which bore the remains of the great Arctic explorer than this sudden March snow-storm? Each one of the Committee felt there was a significance in it beyond their ken.

The Committee at first disembarked at Warsaw, expecting that it would be the best point to await the coming of the Telegraph, which bore the remains. But Captain Summons assured them that he would place them safely on board the Telegraph, if he did not, as he anticipated, meet her at Vevay, when the Committee again placed themselves under his charge, and in a short time had the satisfaction of reaching Vevay just as the Telegraph was rounding to at that point. They stepped from one boat to the other, and were received by the Committees from Louisville and New Albany, who had the remains in charge. The following were the gentlemen composing said Committees:—

On behalf of the Masonic Fraternity of Louisville, L. T. Sedgwick, Frank Tryon.

On behalf of the City Council of Louisville, Andrew Monroe, D. Sargant.

On behalf of the citizens of Louisville, John Barbee, Mayor, Dr. Flint, Captain P. A. Key.

On behalf of the Masonic Fraternity of New Albany, John R. Cameron, C. M. Johnstone, F. C. Johnson, G. W. Bartlett.

RELATIVES OF THE DECEASED.

The Cincinnati Committee was then introduced to the relatives of the deceased, consisting of three brothers. The father and mother, being well advanced in years, had returned to Philadelphia, it being thought unadvisable that they should bear the fatigue of travelling with the corpse of their son at the slow rate which was rendered necessary in order that, at different points, the people might show their respect and receive the remains with appropriate honors. The eldest of the brothers,

COLONEL T. L. KANE,

Is said to bear a strong resemblance to the deceased. He is rather below the medium height, square but delicately built, with an expansive chest. His hair is dark brown; he wears small side-whiskers, with mustache and goatee. His eye is piercing and dark. Altogether, his appearance is prepossessing, and he looks the thorough gentleman. He is apparently in delicate health. His face is at once sad and impressive. By profession, Colonel Kane is an attorney. His age is thirty-two.

ROBERT P. KANE.

This gentleman is somewhat taller than his brother, Colonel Kane, though not so squarely built. He is rather slender; has light hair, blue eyes, wears a light mustache, and has the air of a gentleman who has mingled much in society; converses fluently and well. His age is about thirty. He is also an attorney.

DR. JOHN K. KANE.

This gentleman is the largest one of the brothers, but is not above the medium height. He has a very fresh look, and is the blonde of the family. He has an open, frank countenance, with a retiring, unassuming demeanor. He is by profession a physician, and is connected with the Philadelphia Hospital. His age is about twenty-three.

The name of

WILLIAM MORTON

will no doubt be familiar to all who have read the account of the last Arctic Expedition under the command of the lamented Kane. This gentleman sailed to England with Dr. Kane, and thence to Havana, and now accompanies the remains to Philadelphia. Mr. Morton was born in Ireland, but left his native land at a very early age, and has now been in America about seventeen years. He first became acquainted with Dr. Kane in California, and, after one voyage to the Polar seas, joined the Arctic Expedition under Dr. Kane, and sailed on the ill-fated "Advance." Mr. Morton was the one who volunteered with the Esquimaux boy to go north in search of the open sea, and after a circuitous and fatiguing route of three hundred miles, dragging their sledges over the icebergs, the great Polar Sea was discovered, and the noble Morton (in whom every one will become interested in reading Kane's account) is now the only living white man who has ever beheld the great open Polar Sea, whose cold waters roll and toss against the icebergs of the far-distant North.

Mr. Morton is now but thirty-five years of age, and has the appearance of one who could well undergo the fatigue of an Arctic winter, and in reply to a question if he had any desire to return, he said, "Never, unless I could have gone with my old comrade the doctor."

DR. ELISHA KENT KANE.

RECEPTION OF THE REMAINS BY THE CINCINNATI COMMITTEE.

The different Committees, after the steamers had got fairly under way, met together in the centre of the cabin, when Mr. Weisner, Chairman of the Cincinnati Committee, notified the Committees of Louisville and New Albany that the Committee which he had the honor to represent were ready to receive the remains of the deceased; whereupon Mr. Andrew Monroe, in behalf of the various Committees, made the following remarks :—

MR. CHAIRMAN :—The people of Louisville and New Albany are moved by the same melancholy impulses which have brought you here, and, joining their voices in that universal wail of woe which has gone up from one end of our bereaved country to the other, in consequence of the death of the distinguished devotee of knowledge and humanity, Dr. Elisha Kent Kane. Influenced by these impulses, and cherishing a holy regard for the now lifeless tenement of a noble soul, and for the mourning surviving friends and relatives who accompany it, they have, by a general meeting of their people, their municipal authorities, and Masonic Fraternity, received the body under their charge, and, after paying that honor which their high appreciation of Dr. Kane's great qualities demanded, have intrusted it to our charge as their Committee, to be by us transferred to the people of Cincinnati. As the organ of the several Committees, the people, municipal authorities, and Free Masons, I now commit the remains to your charge, as the representatives of your city.

Permit me to say, in discharging a melancholy duty, mingled with that pleasure which we always feel in paying our honors to the distinguished dead, that the people of Kentucky, in honoring the dead, have conferred honor upon themselves. Those States, those cities, appreciate the services of the pioneer in discovery and martyr to humanity, and, by the array of numbers which poured forth to meet his remains and escort the body to its place of sepulture, have vindicated their title to all I claim for them.

It is peculiarly appropriate just here to remind each other of the character and extent of the services we are approbating. The thousands who moved in solemn procession through the streets of Louisville to-day were not actuated by party feeling nor by a love for military renown. Other ages and other countries have vied with each other in giving costly honors and grand displays of pageantry to party leaders and military heroes. They would shower wealth and applause upon their living heads, and strew their paths with fragrant flowers and cushions of velvet upon which to press their royal feet, and erect costly and magnificent monuments to the memory of victors upon battle-fields and in senate-chamber when dead. But it is reserved for this age and this country to shower their honors and distinguished marks of esteem and enthusiastic admiration upon one neither prominent upon the battle-field nor in the political arena. Here we have city after city pouring out by thousands to meet, and joining in grand procession to escort from one city to another, the remains of a man who never fought a battle, never held a seat in senate-chamber,—a man who was devoted to no political party. But on account of his assiduous devotion to science, his contributions to the general knowledge of the world, and the pure virtue and indomitable energy displayed in the cause of humanity, in seeking in a far-off land the lost and wrecked inhabitants of another country, their hearts are filled with love for his virtues, and by their acts they evidence their pride in him as their countryman. It speaks well for the taste and character of our people when we see such regard paid the disciples of science,—to honors won in the peaceful but laborious investigations into the earth's formation. It speaks well for us when we join our voices in the sentiment,—

> O Peace ! thou source and soul of social life,
> Beneath whose calm, inspiring influence
> Science his views enlarges, Art refines,
> And swelling Commerce opens all her ports,
> Blest be the man divine who gives us thee !

But, quiet and monotonous as his researches may seem to the vulgar and unappreciating, the labors of Dr. Kane proved full of interest to him in life, and, as connected with his death, momentous and disastrous. The warrior whose heart is pierced by the glittering steel or whose head is laid low by the whizzing ball falls suddenly, and in the midst of an excitement that renders death almost pangless. But toiling and laboring in the bleak and cheerless wilderness of an icy ocean or snow-covered land, where perpetual winter inflicts perpetual pain, and severe hardships induces a slow but certain death, renders the martyr yet more worthy of sympathy as well as esteem. To this climate and these causes Dr. Kane owes his early and melancholy death. The feeble body with which nature endowed him was too frail a support for the vigor and energy of his genius; and thus the mind wore away the body.

DR. ELISHA KENT KANE. 317

Genius! thou gift of Heaven, thou light divine,
Amid what dangers art thou doom'd to shine!
Oft will the body's weakness check thy force,
Oft damp thy vigor and impede thy course,
And trembling nerves compel thee to restrain
The noble efforts to contend with pain.

The people of Louisville and New Albany, having paid all honor the dearest friend of Dr. Kane could desire to his memory, and escorted his remains thus far by the committee, now hand over to you the lifeless body of a noble soul, knowing your desire, and that of the people of Cincinnati, to discharge your melancholy duty; and that from your people the memory of the deceased will be as fully and as freely honored as we have honored it, in the marks of respect we have endeavored to bestow.

REMARKS OF CHARLES ANDERSON, ESQ.,

Upon receiving, from the Louisville and New Albany Committees, the remains of Dr. Kane.

MR. CHAIRMAN AND GENTLEMEN:—In behalf of the Cincinnati Committees, I have the honor to receive from your hands the remains of our deceased fellow-countryman and fellow-man, to whose memory, sir, you have just paid a tribute at once so fit and so feeling. As you have so well said, successive crowds, from cities, towns, and farms, in a long procession wending its solemn way across this wide land, have, of their own accord and as individuals, met together to follow this dead corpse in its last voyage on the way to its tomb. And now, to-night, have we also come together, from different and distant States and cities, midway in a long route of its river-travel, and upon this, at once the dividing and uniting line of those several States,—you to surrender and we to receive this sad treasure of our nation's regard. On such an occasion, is it not meet, my friends, for us to pause a moment to inquire, Why is all this show of ceremony and this general and spontaneous expression of real feeling? This man, whose lifeless form is the object of such emotions and such pageantry, in his life had never distinguished himself neither on the bloody battle-field as a warrior, nor as a statesman in the halls of legislation, nor before listening and applauding multitudes as an orator, nor yet as a founder or leader of any sect or party in theology, politics, or society. And heretofore our countrymen, too much following in the beaten tracks of preceding men and nations, have always paid their deep homage at the graves and to the memories of warriors, statesmen, and leaders of parties,—and, alas! to them alone. But this man was neither of all these, as the world estimates these things: he lived without influence and died without power. He was but a simple and earnest devotee (in all of his short span of life) to the just cause of science and humanity; and he died their common martyr. A quiet student of the laws of nature, he had diligently and most bravely travelled, and explored, and labored, and endured, in order to test and to verify those propositions which preceding searchers after truth had published, and to discover, and, for the benefit of the race, promulge, some of those principles which had not before been revealed. Gentle, self-sacrificing, and, like all truly brave men, tender-hearted, he pitied the lost and frozen navigators of the Arctic deserts, of land or ice or ocean, and, warmly sympathizing with the bereaved widow and their kindred, he consecrated his mind, his labors, his sufferings, his life itself,—so able, so arduous, so painful and protracted, so precious to family, to friends, to country, and to his kind, —to their rescue. And such only was Elisha Kent Kane.

And now, my friends, upon the death of this man whose life was so short and so inconspicuous, what do we behold? Of what scene indeed are we the actors or spectators? Villages, towns, cities, and the intertermediate rural homes, pause from their daily labors or pleasures and pour a long, broad stream of grieved and sincere mourners behind his coffin. How and why is this?

If, my friends, he had conquered great and rich provinces to our commonwealth,—if he had found and poured into our private or national coffers the countless wealth of gold and gems from Californian or Australian mines,—if he had sacrificed himself an eager victim to some idea or passion on which had clustered and crystallized a great and fanatic church or party,—if, pursuing the vain dreams and searches of the classic ages, he had discovered the fountains of perpetual youth and beauty in some sequestered ocean-isle of ceaseless peace and joy,—then, indeed, would our selfish gratitude teach us the secret of our grief. But his voyages and explorations have been, to the exchequers of our temporal and material interests as to the yearning and mourning affections of bereaved kindred, a complete failure. He brought back to the nation only a dreary and chilling account of a far-off country, over whose land and air and waters, amidst wilderness-plains of snow and mountain-icebergs, hoar Winter reigns in absolute and eternal desolation. And to the sad and wearied heart he brings neither Franklin nor his comrades, nor any trace, or clue, or tidings, of the lost and loved ones, save the frightful assurances of that keenest suffering from frost and hunger through which they lived, in which they died. And yet—and yet—we mourn, all true Americans sadly mourn, this man. Nor is it his countrymen alone who shall grieve at his death. England, Europe, Christendom,—ay, wherever, upon isle or continent, or afloat upon the waters of the rivers, lakes, or seas, the story of Kane's voyages and life shall reach, (and where has it not?) every man whose mind has been kindled to a love of knowledge, or whose heart retains its natural love toward his brother-man,—will rejoice to know that he has lived, will mourn to learn that he has died.

Now, therefore, my friends, may we not in some confidence reply to our question? Is it because our country and our age (let croakers say what they will) have grown wiser and better than other lands and former ages of people, that a scholar and a philanthropist is thus deplored? Let us, then, so uniting our sad tones in these funeral rites over the dead, take consolation from these scenes of solemnity, and rejoice to believe in this improvement of our countrymen and our fellow-men.

In conclusion, gentlemen, allow me to express to you, as the representatives of our sister cities, our admiration of the taste and propriety of your proceedings in this most delicate affair, and to invite you all most cordially, as well in your individual as in your official capacities, to accompany and unite with us in those ceremonials which it may be the lot of our city and citizens to control.

At the conclusion of Mr. A.'s speech, the Cincinnati Committee was taken down to the forecastle of the boat, where the remains of Dr. Kane were, and took formal charge of the body from the hands of the Joint Committees.

THE COFFIN.

The coffin which contained the embalmed body of the deceased was enclosed in an ordinary box, on the top of which were insignia of Masonry, consisting of apron, gloves, and a sprig of acacia. Around the whole was the star-spangled banner, whose ample folds covered all that was mortal of the early and gifted dead,—Dr. E. K. Kane.

The Telegraph reached her wharf at this city at her usual hour. At six o'clock, the steamer Champion came alongside, and the remains were transferred to her deck. A pedestal appropriately draped had been erected on the forecastle, upon which the coffin was placed. The steamer then started down the river until she arrived at Ludlow's Point, where she landed and waited until the minute-guns announced that the Committees were ready to receive the remains. She then started for the city, and landed at the foot of Fifth Street, where the Committee who had the body in charge delivered it to the pall-bearers, some twenty-four in number.

THE PROCESSION.

The procession was then formed, and moved in the order as published, through the various streets named. The military was well represented, the Masonic Fraternity, the Pioneer Association, and other societies, as enumerated in programme. The streets through which the cortège passed were lined with citizens, both old and young. Many of the houses were draped in mourning, and in several places banners were stretched across the streets and appropriately draped.

Lieutenant Morton, the faithful friend of Dr. Kane, who stood by him while living, and saw him breathe his last sigh and closed his eyes in death, walked immediately behind the hearse which bore all that was earthly of his dear commander, until it reached the Little Miami Depôt.

The remains will be conveyed to Columbus this afternoon by the cars of the Little Miami Railroad, starting at six o'clock, at which place they will lie in state at the Capitol over the Sabbath. From thence they will be conveyed to Wheeling, and on to Baltimore, where they will be received by the citizens of the Monumental City with fitting honors.

In conclusion, we can but express the gratification we feel in knowing that our citizens have united as one man in showing respect to the mortal remains of one who belonged to no party, was no warrior with sabre stained by blood, or statesman with high-sounding name, but, in the language of one whose lips are wont to breathe eloquent words, was a voluntary martyr to science and to art.

AT THE DEPÔT

The procession reached the depôt of the Little Miami Railroad Company about one o'clock. The remains were placed upon a bier in front of the depôt, where they were honored by the entire column. The pall-bearers then removed the body to the car which was to bear it through the State. It is a magnificent express-car, which was elaborately hung inside and out with mourning-festoonery.

CEREMONIES AT COLUMBUS.

A few minutes before meridian, on Friday, March 6, intelligence was received by telegraph from Cincinnati, that the remains of the late Dr. Elisha Kent Kane would pass through Columbus on their way toward

Philadelphia; that they would reach this city by the 11.20 night train, and remain until the departure of the 10.10 morning train of the Central Ohio Road on Monday.

Immediately on receipt of this intelligence, action was taken on the part of each branch of the Legislature responsive to the deep feeling of all classes of the people, to manifest their regard for the character and services of the lamented dead; and a joint committee of the two Houses was appointed to make the necessary arrangements to accomplish that object.

The Grand Lodge of Free and Accepted Masons of Ohio was convened in special Communication by order of the Grand Master of that Fraternity, and a committee appointed on its part to co-operate with such other committees as might be appointed to make suitable arrangements for the occasion.

At an early hour in the evening, a meeting of citizens of Columbus was held at the Neil House, and a committee selected to act in behalf of the citizens of the capital of Ohio in conjunction with other similar committees representing other organizations.

At eight o'clock in the evening, a joint meeting of all these committees was held at the Neil House; when two members from each committee were delegated to proceed to Xenia on the morrow, and there meet the funeral cortège from Cincinnati, accompany it to Columbus, and thence to Wheeling.

Another like committee was detailed to make suitable arrangements for the reception of the remains, for respectful care for them during their stay in the city, and for appropriate religious exercises on Sunday.

The State Fencibles, Captain Reamy, volunteered such services as might be required of them,—which were thankfully accepted by the Joint Committee.

At Xenia, when the train arrived from Cincinnati, at about nine o'clock P.M., the throng of people was so dense and so promiscuous as literally to take possession of the road and delay the departure of the train, whereby its arrival at Columbus was postponed to a few minutes past twelve o'clock. At London, and other places along the route, notwithstanding the lateness of the hour, and that the train had barely time to halt, the people were out in numbers to offer their spontaneous tribute of sympathy and respect.

At midnight the train arrived at the Columbus station-house, where the Joint Committee, the State Fencibles, and a large concourse of citizens, were awaiting it. The stillness of the midnight-hour, the rolling of the muffled drum as the remains were launched from the car, the tolling of the bells of the city, the solemn strains of the dead-march by the brass band, the display of flags at half-mast, as seen by moonlight, the respectful silence of the concourse of citizens that thronged the street,—all conspired to impart to the scene an air of grandeur and solemnity seldom witnessed. The solemn procession, accompanied by a civic and military escort, proceeded to the Senate-Chamber, where due preparation had been made for its reception; and here the remains were consigned to the custody of the Columbus Committees, in the following very neat address from Charles Anderson, Esq., on behalf of the Committee of Cincinnati:—

Mr. Chairman, and Ladies and Gentlemen:—A few weeks ago, upon a green and golden island of the Caribbean Sea, green with the verdure of perpetual spring, and golden in the warm sunshine of a tropic climate, and with the ever-ripe and ever-ripening fruitage of an eternal summer,—surrounded by every circumstance of nature and of art to promise and to insure the highest and purest state of ease and health and happiness which this our human life can know,—there lay, languishing in feebleness and agonizing in pain, on his bed of mortal sickness, a youth and stranger. And over his starts of keen spasms and the fever-dreams of his faint and flickering mind there watched but three sad sentinels,—his mother, a brother, and a friend, the friend and companion of all his labors and wanderings, who had loved him almost with the fondness and constancy of a mother and with the manly attachments of fraternal feeling.

This feeble and suffering invalid had begun life in a country far distant, under a climate far different, and with a natural constitution which promised a wholly dissimilar state of health. But a spirit of restless though persistent enterprise for knowledge and usefulness and fame had seized upon his earliest youth, and had drawn his swift and willing feet from this our new and Western continent into the far sunrise lands and islands of the olden hemisphere, among our very antipodes. In the cause of knowledge he had searched the tiger-peopled jungles and the dark and dank morasses of India and China, and he had hung suspended mid-air in the gaping throat of a mountain-volcano, over a red-hot lake of liquid and molten metals and minerals, which for ages and centuries uncounted and countless had been seething, unseen by man and unchallenged by science, like a vast caldron of hell, over its infernal fires.

DR. ELISHA KENT KANE.

In the cause of his country he had as it were "taken the wings of the morning and flown to the uttermost parts of the sea." Leaving that land of the East and those pursuits of civic enterprise, he reappeared almost like magic, armed and plumed for war in the Valley of Mexico and upon our side of the Pacific Ocean. And there did he signalize his courage and address in battle as much as his most chivalric humanity and magnanimity to his foes and his prisoners.

And, in the cause of science mingled with benevolence, again and again had he torn himself from the dear land of his birth and from the dear mother who bore him, disparting the prized links which made that chained and charmed circle around the genial warmth of the family hearth and the purest piety of the family altar, to explore among the icebergs of the untracked Arctics and amidst the desolations of a still bleaker barbarism.

From the West to the East, and from the East to the farthest West again, from the Equator almost to the Northern Pole, and from the Pole to the Equator, following and crossing all the latitudes and longitudes, circumnavigating and re-circumnavigating the great globe itself, did this pilgrim of science, this knight-errant of benevolence, thus devote himself to the help of his fellow-man and to the improvement of his fellow-men. And now do we see him, laid panting with his pain, and languishing in his weakness, the tortured and sacrificed victim of his herculean task, the dying martyr to his early passion and his lifelong toils. And so lived and so died Elisha Kent Kane! And then,—a pale, thin, cold corpse, without sense, or pulse, or motion, with no glance to kindle and beam forth from the filmed eye, with no thought to thrill like electricity through the chilled brain, with no kindly emotion to warm and make happy the stilled and silent heart,—there in Cuba lay his remains,—the dust and ashes of that once bright and busy life, now burned out into blank and endless darkness.

And is this, then, all there is of life? Is the scene of this drama now closed forever? And can such a life and death teach us no more than this simple and painful lesson,—that dust and ashes and tears is the end as well of men as of their works? Alas! alas! even so! And yet, my friends, it were not well to submit in dogged despondency to a faith so cheerless and so cold. Let us, with our simple memories, retrace this short story in its mere detail of facts through these last days and weeks to the present hour. Let us, indeed, by our reason and fancy, "follow it, with modesty enough, and likelihood to lead it," through the hours, days, weeks, months, years, ages,—ay, centuries,—to come. We too may find our explorations not in vain. Like the subject of these meditations, we too may find our faith and hope in God and man revived and renewed to a higher and holier reverence and love.

Recurring to that sad scene in Havana, we see these few friends of the departed slowly and silently starting with his remains for their common country and their family home. They bid adieu to the kind strangers of that foreign island. They cross the Gulf and land upon our own shores, among strangers to themselves and to the deceased. And what now occurs? The whole population of New Orleans,—without any appeals from a party press, (for he had been no partisan,) without the incitements of a sectarian zeal, (for he had been of no sect,) without any of that wild and fervid enthusiasm which a victorious war ever excites, (for he had been no conqueror, crowned with that wreath of green and red, of bays and blood, which so stirs the hearts of all men,) without the warm impulses of mere simple patriotism to arouse them, (for his known labors had not been those of a mere patriot, but he had lived and died as a man and for mankind,)—in the absence of all these the usual causes of popular feeling, that entire people, each man, woman, and child acting outwardly from the living sentiment within, all arose as one man to join in the sad solemnities of that funeral train which trails with undiminished woe across a continent. And so, my friends, has it been from that hour to this,—from New Orleans by all the shores of the Mississippi and the Ohio Rivers, and along the lines of the railroad to Columbus; and so will it be from Columbus to Philadelphia. Not the small devoted band who wept and prayed over his dying pillow,— not the absent family, perplexed with various hopes and fears, and grieved by that sorrow which makes the sad heart sore,—not the usual circles of kindred, schoolmates, and friends,—mourn alone for this departed youth. But cities and peopled States—ay, a nation's millions of minds and hearts—have perceived the depth of their loss, and have felt and uttered a spontaneous sympathy with this august and solemn pageant. Our nation has suffered a national bereavement. And, more, the whole nation feels it as such. Not only so : unless we greatly misconceive the signs of these times, civilized mankind, without distinctio of tongue or nation, will feel this loss of a true and real *man*.

And now, my friends, may we not pause to ask ourselves whether this unforced and earnest regret of a whole nation, and almost of the whole race, for the loss of a mere youth, whose fame was only the fresh reward of genius in science and of enterprise in benevolence, does not betoken a new and better era in the world's history ? All nations and

DR. ELISHA KENT KANE. 325

ages have mourned, with grand and gloomy pomp, the dead heroes and monarchs of mankind. But here is the first instance, in all history, where simple mind with simple goodness, guided by zeal and energy to gentle and kindly ends, have been at once recognised as constituting a character worthy to be honored by all when living and to be mourned by all when dead. I know not how others may feel; but, as an American, I am proud of my country, that she has contributed to the world's long line of true heroes and martyrs such a character as Kane. But I am prouder far that all her classes, whether of rich or poor, learned and unlearned, old and young, of both sexes, have been thus proved capable in mind and heart truly to appreciate and warmly to feel a nation's loss. And, as a man, I feel proudest of all that this age is worthy to have had such a real hero, and is both able and willing to recognise and acknowledge him whilst he was with it and of it. Heretofore, such characters have only been fully valued by the generations coming after them.

As for the memorials necessary to perpetuate his fame and purity of character, let us not, my friends, concern ourselves for them. They, like these passing ceremonies in which we now unite, may honor us. They touch not him, nor can affect his fame. His monument is in the imperishable works of his own mind and heart and hands. More durable than marble, more touching than poetry, sweeter than music, hour after hour, day by day, for years and decades and ages—ay, centuries of ages to come (unless men shall cease to read)—shall his glowing pages excite for himself and his theme the enthusiastic admiration and love of mankind. Let these, then, the living, the undying thoughts of his various and mighty mind, let the impulses of his gentle and generous heart, which so inspired him to great activities, to patient endurances, and to bravest deeds,—*be these records* his monument. And if an earthly and material memento more than this love and fame impressed upon the universal mind and heart be necessary to perpetuate, not his glory, but the world's fitting remembrance of him, then let nature, or something most like nature,—let something the most closely associated with his works and life and death,—bespeak at once the world's truest honor and purest taste.

And there, upon the crystalline shores of that Polar sea, that green and liquid solitude, broad as the Atlantic and lonely as Sahara,—shut in, through all the earth's ages, from the uses or the visits of man, by wide wastes of snow and vast mountains of solid and unmelting ice, reposing still, as it has ever reposed, in the calmness of its own cold, serene, primeval purity and peace, with its smooth bosom never furrowed by any keel, never shadowed by any sail, and (oh, sad and sweet exception to the cruel annals of our race!) never stained by human blood,—there, at the margin of that clear mirror of the circumpolar sky, whose blazing constellations, *those stars that never set*, circling in their smooth and constant orbits forever around and above it and its crystal horizon, seem fondly to behold themselves, the brightest glory of all the skies, truly reflected in it, the purest spot of all the earth,—*there*, on such a shore, by such a sea, under such a sky, henceforth and forever so associated in the whole human mind with his name,—there, on some brave precipice, let there stand

> "A pyramid of lasting ice,
> Whose polish'd sides, ere day has yet begun,
> Shall catch the *first* glow of the unrisen sun,
> The *last* when it shall sink, and through the night
> The charioteers of Arctos wheel ever round
> Its glittering point."

And—though few or none of all the myriads of men living and to live might ever have the courage to look up at that sapphire wedge of ever-during ice keenly piercing the calm sky of a semi-annual day, or glistering now in the sheen of the circumpolar starlight, and anon coruscated with the more-than-rainbow beauties and glories of the Aurora-effulgences—to me it would seem a most apt and tender fancy, that, though unseen, mankind should ever

> "*Feel* that it is there."

With this brief and imperfect expression of those thoughts and feelings which have been suggested and excited by these most touching and appropriate ceremonies, at deep midnight, and in this grand and now most solemn temple of our State's majesty, permit me, sir, as the organ of the Committees from Cincinnati, now and here to surrender to your watchful care and to your heartfelt reverence these, the earthly remains of Elisha Kent Kane.

William Dennison, Esq. responded, on behalf of the Columbus Committee, in a very appropriate address.

A detachment of the State Fencibles was then detailed by Lieutenant Jones, as a guard of honor, which remained on duty while the remains were in the Senate-Chamber, except while relieved by a like guard detailed for the purpose from members of the Masonic Fraternity. The remains lay in state in the Senate-Chamber from one A.M. on Sunday until nine A.M. on Monday.

By ten o'clock on Sunday morning, the citizens began to wend their way to the Senate-Chamber, which had been judiciously arranged by Mr. Ernshaw, the draughtsman, for the accommodation of the greatest practicable number of persons. By eleven o'clock, the spacious hall was densely packed, when Colonel Kane, Robert P. Kane, Esq., Dr. John K. Kane, Jr., brothers of the deceased, and Lieutenant William Morton, his faithful companion in his perilous voyages, entered, and were conducted to seats reserved for them.

The religious exercises at the Capitol consisted of—1st, Prayer, by the Rev. Mr. Steele, of the First Congregational Church. 2d. Music, by the choir of that church, executed with great judgment and skill. 3d. Discourse, by the Rev. Dr. Hoge, of the First Presbyterian Church. 4th. Anthem, by the choir. 5th. Collects and Benediction, by Rev. Mr. La Tourrette, of St. Paul's (Episcopal) Church.

Notice was given that the Senate-Chamber would be open from two to five o'clock, to afford the citizens opportunity to pay their mournful tribute of respect to the ashes of the dead; and thousands of all classes and conditions gladly availed themselves of the opportunity,—when the doors were closed, and the silence of the chamber was broken only by the tread of the guard of honor left on duty.

PRAYER

Offered by REV. J. M. STEELE, *on the occasion of the Funeral Solemnities, while the remains of* DR. KANE *lay in state in the Senate-Chamber, Columbus, Ohio.*

O God! thou art not the God of the dead, but of the living. Thou art the God of Abraham, and Isaac, and Jacob. We do not all die: the body perishes, but the soul lives. A day is coming when the earth and the sea, the rocks and the ice, will give up their dead. The scene before us brings to our remembrance the promise of the resurrection. We have come hither to pay our last respects to the earthly remains of one of whom when living we had all heard, and whom we had learned to love and revere. Thy thoughts are not our thoughts, nor are thy ways our ways, Lord God Almighty: thou didst hold him in thy hand when wind and waters and all nature were against him. Thou didst bear him through storm, and cold, and darkness, and famine, and fear, and didst set him down in safety upon the deck of the Release. And, when the cheers of his countrymen welcomed him back to the social world of love which they represented, hope elevated and joy brightened his crest.

Long had he trod the ice-foot in safety. Through two Arctic winters God had kept him. And in the third, under the mild light of a genial clime, before the returning sun had gilded the topmast of the Advance in her ice-bound home, the floes yielded beneath his feet and he passed into the eternal sea.

His sun went down at noon. But age is not measured by the number of years: wisdom is the gray hair unto a man, and an unspotted life is old age.

Bear with us, O Lord, if in our addresses to thee we make mention of the virtues of him whose loss we deplore. For he acknowledged God as the author of his powers, and it was a part of his wisdom to know whose gift he was. Much had he seen, and known, and done. His feet had touched the soil of every continent on the globe, and his temples had been laved in the waters of every sea. His life was a voyage of discovery. Already the benefit of his labors is felt, more or less, in every country. His plans were original, and as full of humanity as they were of genius. He had been endowed with superior powers both of mind and body, and where others perished he survived. But the silver cord is loosed at last, the golden bowl is broken, the pitcher is broken at the fountain, and the wheel is broken at the cistern. The dust will return to the earth as it was; but the spirit has returned unto God who gave it. The shades of a more-than-Arctic night have settled on his dust,—a night that knows no day; but the spirit is bathing in the mellow light of day,—a day that knows no night.

The Advance is in the ice, the Eric is in ashes, the Hope is on a far-distant shore, the Faith—the "precious relic"—is in possession of his country, and Kane is in heaven. He will need the craft no more, for now he walks with the Evangelists upon the crystal and stable sea.

The accurate scholar, the generous commander, the thoughtful Christian, has passed from our sight and beyond all human rescue. The faithful cables which held him through so many storms have yielded their strands at last. He has seen and crossed the "open sea," and already there have burst upon his view the splendors of the city of God. And we trust he has found those for whom he went out to look, safely moored by those happy shores where the sun never sets and the waters never freeze.

And now, O righteous Lord, as we remember the mourners, we must pray for the world. His relatives are the children of men. We seem to see him standing upon the slope of the glacier in the Arctic summer, pointing to the nations and saying, "Behold my mother and my brethren." But his mother has closed his eyes in their last sleep, and the mourners go about the streets of every city in the civilized world. Genius will preside at his obsequies, and Learning will weep at his grave. Oh, let us trust that the stroke of death which has borne him from us has not left science and the dignified charities of human nature, as it were, orphans upon the world.

To-day, for a few minutes, the rays of the sun will fall upon the deck of the Advance; but her master has gone to a land where they have no need of the sun, neither of the moon to shine in it, for the glory of God doth lighten it, and the Lamb is the light thereof.

And now, O God, preside in these funeral solemnities. Speak through him who will address us. And prepare us all for a meeting with those who have gone before us, and with one another, in that future world of which we read in thy word. For it is a bright and happy country, "and the nations of them which are saved shall walk in the light of it."

Most merciful Father, hear our prayer, through the merits and mediation of thy Son Jesus Christ our Lord. Amen.

THE SUBSTANCE OF A DISCOURSE

ON THE

DEATH OF E. K. KANE,

Delivered in the Senate-Chamber, at Columbus, Ohio, March 8, 1857.

BY REV. JAMES HOGE, D.D.

PASTOR OF THE FIRST PRESBYTERIAN CHURCH, COLUMBUS.

"*So teach us to number our days that we may apply our hearts to wisdom.*"

PSALM XC. 12.

We are assembled to remember the life and lament the death of one who has attained high distinction among his countrymen. His name and actions and worth are known, also, far beyond the limits of this nation,—even throughout the civilized world. It is true that the honors we give to his memory cannot affect him; but it will be profitable to us —to the living—to recall to memory his life, and record our impressions of his worth, under the influence of that truth of God which teaches us, and impresses us with a just view of the brevity and uncertainty of life, and directs our attention to a right improvement of the time which is allowed to us in the present state of existence.

Such instruction is given in the text in a few plain words; and it is the more forcible that it is expressed in the form of a prayer to God, who has endowed us with life and all its advantages, for our welfare now, and for our safety and happiness in another and future world. On this subject we ought to think, to reason, to feel, to act, as those who must be judged by Him who now sustains us in life and will ere long call us to a solemn account.

The brevity of life is universally acknowledged; and yet we are apt to feel and act as if it were without an end. In one hour we confess and complain that our days are few and evil, and in the very next hour we forget our confession and live as if we had no apprehension of death. This is not wise. It is not even consistent with worldly prudence. In all our views and feelings, in all our enterprises, we ought to remember that our time is short.

Our days are numbered and appointed to us. And what is their number? "Very many," answers the busy worldling who is immersed in the pursuits and cares of life, the careless spendthrift whose pleasures now engross him, and hopes of other days of gratification lie before him in prospect. "Almost innumerable," cries gay, sanguine, thoughtless Youth. "Why should I now even think their number will ever run out?" And hoary Age, too, can dream of days, and months, and years before him, which may yet serve him for the purpose of gaining earth or heaven, or both. But what is the true account given by experience and confirmed and applied by Holy Scripture? "The days of our years are threescore years and ten; and if by reason of strength they be fourscore years, yet is their strength labor and sorrow." And now, what are these few years in comparison with the thousand years of those who lived before the flood,—or with the long lapse of time from the creation to the final judgment,—or with the far longer duration of eternity? A span; a handbreadth; a passing present hour.

The word of God speaks in this wise respecting our days on earth:— "For what is your life? It is even a vapor, which appeareth for a little time and then vanisheth away." "In the morning it flourisheth and groweth up; in the evening it is cut down and withereth." "The days of the years of my pilgrimage have been few and evil," said aged Jacob in answer to the question "How old art thou?" When we look back, the time which is past seems very short; but when we look forward, the coming time promises to be long. The first view is truth, the latter is delusion. We saw the beginning of the past, but we cannot see the end of the future,—if a future in this life remains to us. As our life is short, so is its movement swift,—rapid as the motion of the earth in its orbit.

How careful, then, should we be to number correctly the few rapid days of our mortal life!

Uncertainty also enters into the correct estimate of human life. That the hour of our death will come, we know with absolute certainty; and we are equally sure that it will soon arrive. We may live the threescore years and ten allotted to man as the ordinary length of old age; but how few continue so long! Perhaps one of a hundred. Often a day, a month, a year, or a score of years, is all that is given us as the number of our days. Death comes, our life is cut off, and we are gone, and shall be here no more forever. In the natural world, very often there comes a frost, a blast,—and the bud is blighted, the flower is withered, the unripe fruit is cast worthless on the ground. The sun rises and sets regularly at his appointed times; but the sun of our short life may go down at noon, or in the morning, and so may not reach the evening of repose and preparation for an eternal day on which multitudes found their resolutions and hopes of happiness in time and eternity. All we can say with confidence is, that the lesson which is taught by the history of the world is true: we may live a day, a year, or a series of years, or we may not. Death will come; and he snatches away budding infancy, buoyant youth, vigorous manhood, as well as decrepit age; and at times and dates unforeseen he bears away all as his lawful prey. Truly, our pilgrimage here is a journey along a way beset with dangers, in a world which is a land of yawning graves,—the one great city of the dead. We may plan and labor for a year, an age yet future; we may calculate for other results than we have secured by our efforts; we may hope for other happiness than we have yet enjoyed: but death, with ruthless stroke, buries all in the dust. The very care we take, the precautions we adopt, the means we employ, that we may live long on the earth, may be the occasion or the cause of hastening us to the end of our portion of time and launching us on the boundless ocean of eternity. Uncertain, indeed, to us, is the tenure by which we hold our life. It is perfectly known to God, fixed and determined in his foreknowledge and purpose, but hidden from us and concealed in the impenetrable darkness of the future. No eye of mortal can see in that darkness, no wisdom search out the inscrutable future. "Go to, now, ye that say, To-day or to-morrow we will go into such a city, and continue there a year, and buy and sell, and get gain : whereas ye know not what shall be on the morrow." "Ye know not what a day may bring forth." "Watch, therefore, for ye know not what hour your Lord doth come." "Be ye ready, also, for your Lord may come at an hour when you look not for him." Life is uncertain; death is certain. "It is appointed to all men once to die, and after this the judgment." Dream not that friends or physicians, strength, or wisdom, or goodness, can delay your departure hence.

Life, short and uncertain as it is, most manifestly is nevertheless long enough for the great end for which it is given, on the condition that we so number our days and consider our end as to improve the present time wisely and faithfully. On this account, the end for which life is given, it is infinitely important to every one of us. It is of incalculable value with reference to ourselves and to others, and to the purposes of God. To ourselves, as we are rational beings, moral agents, susceptible of constant improvement and real enjoyment, even in our present mortal condition, being capable of continued existence, of intellectual and moral cultivation, of vigorous and wisely-directed action, it is desirable to live as long as Heaven shall please to continue us in this condition. We know, we feel, that we differ in this respect from the mere animal, and we are sensible that there is much good in our present state, although we are exposed to dangers and adversities and must bear afflictions. And, in taking aright the number of our days, we should inquire diligently what we ought to be and do in this life for our own proper advantage. If we improve our time, our powers, our opportunities, as we may and ought to improve them, if we choose and pursue the true, the pure, the good, in respect of principle and conduct, and if we reject and avoid the false and the evil, it will be our real advantage. Such attainment will be to us far better than wealth and pleasure.

But especially is life, whether long or short, of infinite worth to every one, as it has a definite, decisive, certain reference to a future life. We are immortal beings, destined to a future and endless existence beyond this life, beyond death, beyond time. As certainly as we die, we shall live again. And we are placed and continued in this world as the introductory stage of our existence. The character which we form here will determine our character hereafter, as certainly as the nature of the infant man shall still be the nature of the mature man. Our conduct, too, in this life, will be the subject of our future and final account and the ground of our endless recompense. A period of probation, however short, may properly be the basis of retribution. And probation under grace may be as justly and certainly decisive as probation under law. Now the gospel is preached to us; we are called to repentance toward God and faith toward our Lord Jesus Christ, that we may be saved,—saved from our sins and delivered from the wrath of God, and be made new creatures and heirs of eternal life. Our eternal happiness depends on thus applying our hearts to wisdom. There is no other salvation, no other way of eternal life, no other Savior, no other method of receiving salvation. If we are thus saved, all is well; if we neglect this salvation, all is lost. And it is now, while life continues,—here, in this world, the place of our gracious probation,—that we may be saved, prepared to die and to enter into that rest which remains for the people of God. "Behold, now is the accepted time; now is the day of salvation." "Hear, and your souls shall live."

During our days on earth we may do much for the welfare of others. God has made us social beings. This is seen in our very nature as moral agents, and in our whole condition as intelligent, active beings. The social principle is universal, and strong, and practical, as a part of our moral nature; and the purposes for which it is implanted in us are manifest in the numerous and various relations among men. These are domestic, and civil, and religious. On this principle it is that men universally are the subjects of reciprocal influence for good or for evil. As no man is made for himself alone, but all, in some important sense, for others also, as for themselves, there are mutual duties, which are obligatory, and by the performance of which we may be useful to each other; or, if we neglect those duties which are founded on these relations, or act contrary to them, we inflict injury and are worthy of blame. How careful, then, should the heads and members of the family be in doing good and not evil to each other in the family according to existing relations! And with what rectitude and truth and benevolence should the members of society act toward one another for mutual advantage! Especially as we have mutual influence, and live together, in this our short uncertain day, with reference to a future, eternal condition, as has been already said, we ought to promote the spiritual and eternal welfare of others, by all proper practicable means, even as our own. "Thou shalt love thy neighbor as thyself." "Do good to all men as you have opportunity, and especially to them who are of the household of faith." Remember, the time is short, the night is at hand wherein no man can work. And who can tell in how great a degree the present and future welfare of children may be affected by the example, the whole conduct, of parents?—to what extent the character and state of neighbor by his neighbor, of inferiors by superiors, of the higher also by the lower, and of future generations by the present generation? Combining such views of our true welfare and our usefulness to our fellow-men, we learn the value of life, short and uncertain as it is, and we become sensible of the necessity of "applying our hearts diligently to wisdom,—that wisdom which is profitable to direct."

This wisdom is taught by divinely-revealed truth, and is to be sought from Him who is the Father of lights. It is designed and suited to secure our fulfilment of the wise and benevolent and holy purposes of Heaven concerning our present and future condition. These designs of God shall all be accomplished. "God's counsel shall stand, and he will do all his pleasure." But it is by means that he ordinarily effects his will; and these means are, in respect of our life and destiny, our own purposes and works. We are instruments in respect of our dependence and subjection to God, and we are agents in respect of liberty and power of choice and action. Fatal necessity, as well as blind chance, is excluded from the administration of the divine government: all is fixed and regular, yet all is just, benevolent, and wise. Of this government we are the rational subjects; under it we have the allotment of our days, and find our duty and happiness in applying our hearts to true wisdom, under the direction of Providence, the instruction of truth, and the help and guidance of grace. Then let us live that we may be ready to die, as those who have wisely lived, hoping for pardon and acceptance and eternal life through our Lord and Savior Jesus Christ. And let us humbly and earnestly beseech God to enable us by his grace so to number our days that we may apply our hearts to wisdom.

Under the influence of such sentiments respecting life and its duties and advantages and responsibilities, let us pause at the side of the grave, and remember the life, while we lament the death, of Elisha Kent Kane, whose mortal remains now lie before us. Why does a nation mourn his removal?—nay, why do the enlightened, the philanthropic, the scientific, throughout the civilized world, lament the loss? His character, his aims, his deeds, although he marched not at the head of armies nor sat on a throne, answer the inquiry.

He was born in Philadelphia, February 3, 1822, and consequently at his death in Cuba, February, 1857, was a few days over the age of thirty-five years. I will not attempt a narrative of his life (this must be left to better-qualified friends) further than to say that, having been liberally educated, and having studied medicine, he entered the United States service as surgeon in the navy, and in this capacity was attached to the first mission from our Government to China. Then he visited also the islands of the Indian Ocean, and some portions of the continent of Asia,—likewise also portions of Africa and Europe. His actions and adventures in his extensive travels I need not recite. On his return,

DR. ELISHA KENT KANE.

avoiding ease and indulgence at home, he entered our squadron on the African coast, and visited the slave-stations, and was about to make a journey of exploration in the interior of Africa, but was hindered by severe disease. Afterward he was connected with the coast-survey, and engaged in the service of his country in Mexico during the war, and after its close returned with a high character for enterprise and humanity and science.

At this time the first Grinnell Expedition was in preparation; and he engaged with characteristic ardor and energy in the enterprise designed generally for Northern exploration and particularly for discovering the fate of Sir John Franklin. In the second Grinnell Expedition for the same purposes, the command was assigned to him, and after an absence of two years he returned, and gave to the public a full narrative of all he had endured and accomplished. The hardships and exposure he suffered during this voyage brought on him the disease which laid him on the bed of death in the midst of his days. His character and his deeds will perpetuate his memory.

He was a man of genius. Possessing in a high degree the powers of conception, comparison, and scientific analysis, with strong imagination and poetic fancy, he was fitted by nature for those enterprises which demand a master-mind. In every walk of life he must have been conspicuous, and especially as he had the power of concentrating his faculties on any object to which he was devoted. Great energy, unresting activity, strenuous effort, always directed by good sense and sound judgment, were manifest in every part of his life from his earliest years. And he was also persevering and patient and hopeful in the greatest difficulties and discouragements.

Courage of the highest kind was a prominent trait of his character,— physical courage which no danger could appall,—moral courage, not often in any high degree united with physical, which no enemies could daunt,— courage such as fits a man for great deeds at the head of armies, on the throne of power, and equally in the labors and difficulties and dangers of discovery by land or sea. And, besides, when exposed to trials and sufferings in which energy and courage avail little, he had fortitude to bear to the utmost limit of endurance. Thus endowed with those qualities which constitute the basis of greatness, he attracted the notice and secured the confidence of those who knew him. He was not, however, stern and rigorous. Kindness entered into the constitution of his character equally with energy and bravery. Generous, humane, compassionate, he who never was overcome by dangers and difficulties and sufferings which were his own was ready to sink at the view of the sufferings of others who were under his care : he could even conquer enemies who were arrayed in battle against him, and then at the risk of his life protect them, when prisoners, from the rage of his own associates in arms.

To complete his character, we may add—and we may be highly gratified to be able to add—that all his high characteristics were elevated and governed by sound and thorough moral principle, and sanctified by the influences of the religion of the Bible, which reveals and offers to us Jesus the Christ of God as in all things a Savior. And nothing can more fully exhibit his true character than the three rules which he established when he began his second expedition :—

Implicit and unvarying obedience to orders.

Entire abstinence from intoxicating liquors.

Daily devout worship of God, in all circumstances.

In conclusion, while we remember with due esteem the life and services, to humanity and science, of Dr. Kane, and lament his apparently-premature death, let us go on to the end of our course fulfilling our duties with diligence and fidelity. And let us all, now and at all times, lift up our hearts to God with the prayer, "So teach us to number our days that we may apply our hearts to wisdom."

CONCLUDING PRAYERS AND BENEDICTION,

BY REV. JAS. A. M. LA TOURRETTE,

RECTOR OF ST. PAUL'S CHURCH, COLUMBUS.

In the midst of life we are in death. Of whom may we seek for succor but of thee, O Lord, who for our sins art justly displeased?

Yet, O Lord God most holy! O Lord most mighty! O holy and most merciful Savior! deliver us not into the bitter pains of eternal death.

Thou knowest, Lord, the secrets of our hearts : shut not thy merciful ears to our prayers; but spare us, Lord most Holy, O God most mighty, O holy and merciful Savior. Thou most worthy Judge Eternal, suffer us not, at our last hour, for any pains of death to fall from thee.

Almighty God, with whom do live the spirits of those who depart hence in the Lord, and with whom the souls of the faithful, after they are delivered from the burden of the flesh, are in joy and felicity : we give thee hearty thanks for the good examples of all those thy servants who, having finished their course in faith, do now rest from their labors. And we beseech thee that we, with all those who are departed in the true faith of Thy holy name, may have our perfect consummation and bliss, both in body and soul, in thy eternal and everlasting glory, through Jesus Christ, our Lord. Amen.

O merciful God, the Father of our Lord Jesus Christ, who is the resurrection and the life, in whom whosoever believeth shall live, though he die, and whosoever liveth and believeth in him shall not die eternally; who hath also taught us, by his holy apostle St. Paul, not to be sorry, as men without hope, for those who sleep in him : we humbly beseech thee, O Father, to raise us from the death of sin unto the life of righteousness, that when we shall depart this life we may rest in him, and that at the general resurrection in the last day we may be found acceptable in thy sight, and receive that blessing which thy well beloved Son shall then pronounce to all who love and fear thee, saying, " Come, ye blessed children of my Father, receive the kingdom prepared for you from the beginning of the world." Grant this, we beseech thee, O merciful Father, through Jesus Christ, our Mediator and Redeemer. Amen.

Almighty and merciful God ! we humbly supplicate thy fatherly compassion in behalf of those parents whom, in thine unsearchable wisdom, thou hast bereaved of their son. Look upon them, O Lord, in mercy. Sanctify this affliction to their good. Deepen within them a sense of the shortness and uncertainty of human life; and let thy Holy Spirit lead them through this vale of misery in holiness and righteousness all the days of their lives. Increase in them true religion; nourish them with all goodness, and of thy great mercy keep them in the same, through Jesus Christ, our Lord. Amen.

Assist us mercifully, O Lord, in these our supplications and prayers, and dispose the way of thy servants toward the attainment of everlasting salvation, that, among all the changes and chances of this mortal life, they may ever be defended by thy most gracious and ready help, through Jesus Christ, our Lord. Amen.

Our Father, who art in heaven, hallowed be thy name : Thy kingdom come : Thy will be done on earth, as it is in heaven : Give us this day our daily bread : And forgive us our trespasses, as we forgive those who trespass against us : And lead us not into temptation : But deliver us from evil. Amen.

BENEDICTION.

The peace of God, which passeth all understanding, keep your hearts and minds in the knowledge and love of God, and of his Son Jesus Christ our Lord. And the blessing of God Almighty, the Father, the Son, and the Holy Ghost, be among you, and remain with you always. Amen.

On Monday, at nine o'clock, a procession was formed in the following order, and, with solemn music by the band from Cincinnati and Goodman's brass-band, with tolling of bells and other appropriate tokens of sorrow, proceeded to the railroad-station, whence a portion of the Joint Committee proceeded with the remains to the city of Baltimore,—where, by an appropriate address by Professor S. M. Smith, M.D., they were delivered to a committee appointed from that city for their reception.

ORDER OF PROCESSION.

Chief Marshal.—Lucian Butler.
Assistant Marshals.—Richard Nevins, H. M. Niel, Walter C. Brown.
Cincinnati Band.
State Fencibles.—Captain Reamy.
Columbus Cadets.—Captain Tyler.
American Flag.

PALL-BEARERS.		PALL-BEARERS.
Medical Profession.		*Masons.*
Dr. Wm. M. Awl,		W. B. Hubbard, P.G.M.
Dr. R. Thompson,	HEARSE.	W. B. Thrall, P.G.M.
Dr. S. Parsons,		N. H. Swayne, M.M.
Dr. R. Patterson,		G. Swan, Esq. P.G.O.
Dr. S. M. Smith,		Dr. L. Goodale, P.G.T.
Dr. John Dawson.		D. T. Woodbury, M.M.

Lieutenant Morton, of the Kane Expedition.
Committee to accompany the remains to Wheeling.
Cincinnati Committee of Arrangement.
Columbus Committee of Arrangement.
Relatives of the deceased, in carriages.
Reverend Clergy.
Goodman's Band.

DR. ELISHA KENT KANE.   339

Grand Lodge of the Masonic Fraternity of the State of Ohio.
Governor of Ohio and Staff.
Heads of Departments, and other State Officers.
The Senate and House of Representatives of the State of Ohio.
Medical Profession.
City Council of Columbus.
Mayor and City Officers.
Firemen.
Judges and Officers of Court.
Citizens generally.

CEREMONIES AT BALTIMORE.

On March 10, Baltimore discharged a solemn duty in honoring the remains of the lamented Dr. Kane. Upon no occasion had her citizens united more generally or with a greater earnestness of purpose in manifesting their appreciation of distinguished worth and eminent services. The arrangements for the obsequies were well designed, and the one purpose that animated those who participated in them and the vast throng called out to witness their occurrence gave to the scene an impressive and grand solemnity.

From the Camden station to the Maryland Institute Hall, the streets were walled with people, whilst windows, balconies, and roof-tops were occupied by spectators. Through this dense mass, preserving, in spite of its denseness, a quiet decorum that was in itself the most fitting testimonial of the occasion, the well-arranged and imposing procession passed, gathering up the good-will, affection, and respect which the population entertained for the noble soul that once animated the cold remains now passing onward to their final resting-place. A juster tribute, more fittingly expressed, never engaged the participation of her citizens.

From the moment the remains reached the Ohio River and were placed in the cars of the Baltimore and Ohio Railroad Company, they have been regarded as committed to the especial guardianship of Baltimore.

CROSSING THE OHIO.

The remains of the distinguished Arctic explorer, Dr. Elisha K. Kane, reached Bellair on Monday afternoon, having come direct through from Columbus, Ohio, where they had lain in state in the Capitol over

Sunday, the use of which had been tendered by the Governor as a mark of respect to the memory of the deceased.

The remains were deposited in a car prepared for the purpose by order of the President of the Central Ohio Railroad, festooned with black inside and out, with white rosettes; and the locomotive drawing the train was likewise trimmed with badges of mourning.

On reaching Bellair, a large number of persons were collected to pay a passing tribute to the memory of the deceased, and the body was removed from the cars to the steamer "Blue Dick," preparatory to crossing to Benwood, amid every demonstration of the kindliest feeling by all present. The flag of the steamer was draped at half-mast, and the saloon hung in mourning, in which a cenotaph was raised on which to rest the coffin. Whilst crossing the river the bells of the steamer, and of all the locomotives at the railroad-stations on either side, were tolled, the scene being one of the most impressive character.

On reaching Benwood, the remains were conveyed from on board the steamer to a car prepared by the Baltimore and Ohio Railroad in which to convey them to Baltimore. It was prepared especially for the purpose, and was shrouded with the badges of mourning both inside and out.

Among those who crossed the Ohio and entered the cars to accompany the remains to Baltimore were the Cincinnati and Columbus Committees, consisting of the following gentlemen :—

Committee from Cincinnati.—H. H. Robinson, G. S. Bennett.

Committee from Columbus.—L. Butler, Dr. S. M. Smith, Dr. A. S. McMillen, S. Long, E. F. Rhinehart, Captain J. O. Remy, E. H. Nichols, Hon. E. B. Langdon, J. G. Neal.

The Committee represents the military, the Masons, and the citizens of Columbus.

There was also, accompanying the remains of Dr. Kane, an uncle of the deceased, and John J. Kane, Jr., his brother.

The officers of the Baltimore and Ohio Railroad, and the Central Ohio Railroad, at both Bellair and Benwood, extended every attention to the family and committee, with the freedom of their roads going and returning.

The Ohio Committees reported that at Zanesville, and all the principal stations on the Central Ohio Railroad, the people assembled in great numbers, and stood uncovered while the train was passing, whilst at some points the station-houses and dwellings by the side of the road were draped in mourning, indicative of the deep and wide-spread feeling of admiration that prevailed for the character and services of the deceased, and the heartfelt sorrow for his early demise.

DR. ELISHA KENT KANE. 341

DISAPPOINTMENT AT WHEELING.

The announcement received at Wheeling, on Saturday evening, that the remains of Dr. Kane would lie over on Sunday at the State Capitol in Columbus, was a sad disappointment, as extensive arrangements had been made to pay a passing tribute to his memory. The Masonic fraternity, the Odd-Fellows, the military, the six fire-companies, and the citizens generally, had, in anticipation of the body passing through that city and remaining there over Sunday, made preparation for its proper reception and an expression of the general feeling of the community in honor of the memory of the deceased. Indeed, there is no doubt that Wheeling would, if opportunity had offered, have equalled any other city on the route in an appropriate expression of the national grief for the loss of so distinguished a citizen.

CROSSING THE MOUNTAINS.

The train, with the remains, and the Committee, and relatives of Dr. Kane, left Benwood at half-past-five o'clock on Monday evening, and amid the darkness of night sped its way across the mountains. There was, therefore, but little opportunity for the people to make any demonstration, though a large number were collected at all the stations to see the passing train.

At Fairmount the train stopped half an hour for supper, at nine o'clock at night; and, notwithstanding the lateness of the hour and the severity of the weather, a large portion of the citizens were at the depôt, and all the bells in the town were tolled whilst the train remained.

During the remainder of the night they passed along through the mountain-gorges without further incident. Cumberland was passed just before daybreak, a large number of persons being at the depôt at that early hour. At the stations east of Cumberland there were various marks of respect shown the train as it passed.

RECEPTION BY THE BALTIMORE COMMITTEE.

At half-past six o'clock on Tuesday morning the train reached Martinsburg, where a large number of citizens with the Baltimore Committee were in waiting. The remains were then formally transferred to the charge of the following gentlemen, comprising

THE BALTIMORE COMMITTEE.

HON. W. GILES,
JOHNS HOPKINS, ESQ.,
PROF. CAMPBELL MORFIT,
COL. THOMAS CARROLL,

BENJ. DEFORD, ESQ.,
WM. H. YOUNG, ESQ.,
SAMUEL SANDS, ESQ.,
WENDELL BOLLMAN, ESQ.

After a short delay, during which a large number of the citizens of Martinsburg viewed the remains with mournful interest, the train proceeded on its way.

At Harper's Ferry there was also a large and silent assemblage of spectators, as was also the case at Ellicott's Mills and all the intermediate stations.

ARRIVAL IN BALTIMORE.

The train which was due in Baltimore at ten o'clock was an hour behind time, and on reaching the Camden Station an immense concourse of persons were assembled to witness the removal of the remains of the distinguished deceased from the cars, among whom were a goodly number of ladies and children, who had remained nearly two hours in waiting.

The car in which the body was deposited was festooned with black, and the locomotive bore a flag draped, whilst black streamers were floating from different parts of the engine.

A detachment of the Independent Grays were in attendance, under command of Sergeant John Gibson, who acted as a guard to the coffin in its transportation from the car to the station-house, where a suitable catafalque draped in mourning was erected in the centre of the large hall, on which it was placed and left in charge of the military detachment.

The anxiety to see the coffin was very great, and it was necessary to close the hall. Marshal Herring was in attendance, with a large force, to preserve the regulations adopted by the Committee of Arrangements.

Immediately on the arrival of the train at the depôt, the bell of the First Baltimore Hose-Company commenced tolling, which was responded to by the bells throughout the city, and continued up to the closing of the ceremonies at four o'clock in the afternoon.

The hall of the new depôt, in which the remains reposed until the moving of the procession, had been appropriately draped in mourning, under the direction of William Prescott Smith, Esq., an intimate and much-loved friend of the deceased, who, being an officer of the Baltimore and Ohio Road, had given his personal attention and effort to all the arrangements for the transfer of the body from Bellair to Baltimore.

DR. ELISHA KENT KANE. 343

THE PROCESSION.

At half-past two o'clock the remains were removed from the depôt-building and placed on a gun-carriage prepared for the purpose and drawn by four horses. On the coffin was the sword of the deceased crossed over the scabbard, (the sword was presented by the city of Philadelphia,) a lambskin apron, and sprig of evergreen. The procession was then formed in the following order, under the direction of Chief-Marshal Anderson:—

City Guards.
Independent Blues' Band.
Lafayette Guards.
Company A of Artillery from Fort Henry.
Grand Lodge of Maryland and Subordinate Lodges of Free and Accepted Masons.
Guard of Honor.
Independent Grays, Capt. Brush, wearing crape on the hat and left arm.

PALL-BEARERS.	FUNERAL CAR.	PALL-BEARERS.
Surgeon W. Mason, U.S.N.		Maj. Donaldson, U.S.A.
Surgeon H. S. Harris, U.S.N.		Surgeon Talbot, U.S.A.
George P. Kane,		D. A. Piper,
Hon. J. P. Kennedy,		Wm. Prescott Smith,
Dr. J. R. W. Dunbar,		Hon. Thomas Swann,
Prof. Campbell Morfit.		Chauncey Brooks.

Detachment of United States Seamen from steamship Alleghany.
Officers of the Army, Navy, and Marine Corps.
Officers of the 1st Light Division Maryland Volunteers.
The Mayor and City Councils of Baltimore.
The Reverend Clergy.
The Medical Profession, Dr. Houck, Marshal.
Judges and Officers of the various Courts and Members of the Bar.
Commissioners of Public Schools.
Officers and Members of the Maryland Institute.
Linhardt's Band.
Male School of Design.
Junior Members of the Maryland Institute.
Fire-Companies.
Marine Band from Washington, thirty-five performers.
Mechanical Fire Company, A. Brashears, Marshal.
Pioneer Hook and Ladder Company, F. H. B. Boyd, Marshal.

Western Hose-Company.
Literary Society of Loyola College.
Faculty and Students of Newton University.
German Turnverein Association.
Citizens.

The family of the deceased were not in the procession, although his brother and uncle were in the city, deeming that it would not have been proper, under the circumstances, for them to have done so.

The Masonic fraternity turned out in great numbers, and made an admirable display, neat and appropriate to the occasion, being dressed in black suits with white gloves and aprons, only the officers of the lodges wearing regalia and insignia of office.

The boys attached to the School of Design attracted great attention. They could not have numbered less than three hundred and fifty, each with a white ribbon in the left lappel of their coats. The officers and members of the Institute were also out in force, and presented a good representation of the solid, substantial, and useful men of the city.

The military display was small; but the three companies of Volunteers, with the Flying Artillery from Fort McHenry, made an admirable appearance.

The officers of the army and navy, with a detachment of seamen from the steamship Alleghany, also formed a pleasing feature of the cortège. The seamen, dressed in naval attire, were especially attractive.

The Mechanical Fire-Company, with the famous band from the Washington Navy-Yard, were, as usual, a prominent and interesting feature. Their foster-children, the Pioneer Hook and Ladder Company, with Lindhart's Band, also made an admirable appearance, and proved themselves not only firemen, but gentlemen in the strictest sense of the word. The Washington Hose-Company were also in line, and made a very fine appearance.

The procession, thus formed, moved up Eutaw Street to Baltimore Street, and thence to the Maryland Institute. On reaching the Institute, the artillery filed to the left, and the men stood with arms presented until the corpse was removed to the main saloon and placed in the catafalque.

The military was drawn up on the east side of the hall, from the south end to the centre, while the Masonic order, the firemen, the members of the Maryland Institute, and other civic societies took positions south of the catafalque and entirely around that portion of the hall. The Independent Grays, the Committee of the Maryland Institute, the officers of

DR. ELISHA KENT KANE.

the army and the field and staff officers of the first, fiftieth and fifty-third regiments of Maryland militia formed an oblong square. The coffin was then covered with the national standard by the seamen from the receiving-ship Alleghany.

At a signal from the Most Worshipful Grand Master, Rev. James McKenney, the Free Masons gave the grand honors; after which dirges were played by the band from the Washington Navy-Yard and the Independent Blues' Band. The procession then retired by companies, leaving a detachment of the Independent Grays in charge.

While the procession was moving, minute-guns were fired on Federal Hill by the Eagle Artillery, and the bells of the fire-companies were tolled.

APPEARANCE OF THE CITY.

There was an immense concourse on the streets to see the cortège, and all the houses on the line were filled. Balconies and windows, and every available spot, was occupied.

The flags on all the public buildings and of the shipping in the harbor were hoisted at half-mast, and several buildings were appropriately and tastefully hung with mourning. The houses of the Mechanical Fire-Company, the First Baltimore Hose-Company, the literary depôt of Mr. Henry Taylor, the buildings of Messrs. Stine Brothers, and the large building of Messrs. Weisenfeld, were handsomely decorated; and there were others wearing the badge of mourning.

The request that business should be suspended on the streets through which the procession passed, was strictly observed and the thoroughfare was cleared of all obstructions.

There has seldom been so large a turn-out in the city, especially of ladies, who numbered thousands in the houses and on the sidewalks. The event will be long remembered; and Baltimore has paid a just tribute to the memory of one who was worthy of her regard.

The remains lay in state at the Maryland Institute Hall last night, in charge of the Independent Grays, Captain Brush, as a guard of honor, and were visited by an immense concourse of persons during the afternoon and evening. We learn that the sword placed on the cenotaph at the Institute was sent from New York for the purpose by Henry Grinnell, Esq., it being the same that was presented to Dr. Kane by the State of New York. It is an exceedingly rich and valuable weapon.

The entire hall wore an impressive aspect. At the front door was a draped arch overhung by the national standard. Reaching the landing the columns at the right and left were hung in mourning. The main saloon, where the remains lay in state, had at each end the American flag, while the gallery was draped throughout its entire length and festooned at each bracket with a white rosette.

The platform in the rear was also draped and festooned, and the desk wrapped in mourning. In the centre of the hall was a catafalque covered with black and trimmed with silver gimp, upon which the coffin was deposited. At each corner of the structure was an American flag, furled upon its staff and capped with crape. On each side, and suspended from the gallery, was a large national standard; and on the left, drooping over the catafalque, was a blue flag covered with white stars, and on the right, in the same position, a small American standard.

The upholstery at the hall was done by Holland and Conradt, and E. A. Gibbs supplied the scarfs and badges. The tasteful and appropriate arrangements in the undertaking-department were made by Mr. A. Jenkins, one of the general committee, and of the firm of A. & H. Jenkins.

As Dr. Kane was an active and most esteemed member of the Maryland Institute, it may not be amiss to give at length the proceedings of that association, preparatory to a demonstration which it made in his honor.

MEETING OF THE MARYLAND INSTITUTE.

Agreeably to announcement in yesterday's papers, the members of the Maryland Institute assembled last evening in the library-room of the building, for the purpose of testifying their regard for the memory of the late Dr. Kane, and to make necessary arrangements for receiving the remains. At eight o'clock the chair was taken by the Hon. THOMAS SWANN, Mayor of the city, and one of the Vice-Presidents, (the President, Hon. Joshua Vanzant, being absent from the city,) who, in a few words, stated the object of the meeting. He then made the following address:—

GENTLEMEN OF THE MARYLAND INSTITUTE:—It has become my painful duty to announce to you the death of our distinguished countryman, Dr. Elisha Kent Kane. This sad event took place at Havana, on the 16th instant, whither he had repaired for the benefit of his health,— broken down by the exposure and toils of his late expedition to the Arctic seas. As a member of this Institute, his presence had become

DR. ELISHA KENT KANE.

familiar to you all, and I need hardly recur to associations which were alike honorable to himself as they were grateful to the members of this body. He was one of its early contributors and most earnest advocates. It was during a recent visit abroad, as I have been informed, that he urged a friend, only less distinguished than himself, if he ever visited the United States, not to overlook the Maryland Institute as a prominent object of interest. His voice has been heard in these halls. It was the theatre of many a noble effort of his genius and his learning; and we may well be permitted to drop a tear over the loss we have sustained, in common with the civilized world.

In the midst of a career such as no man had traversed before him—a career marked by daring and adventure, enriched by useful discovery, and rendered memorable by the most generous impulses of the human heart—he has been withdrawn from the scenes of his earthly triumphs: he had reached the last round of the ladder, and his early exit has only added increased lustre to the brilliant record of that modest and unobtrusive career which has astonished both hemispheres.

Dr. Kane was one of those who seemed to estimate life only as a means of accomplishing some great and useful purpose. When the stoutest hearts quailed, he was unmoved. In the midst of frozen seas, where barriers of eternal ice threatened to shut out forever all hope of reunion with the civilized world behind him, he continued to press forward with the gallant followers whom his own courage had inspired, until he reached a point upon the earth's surface which no human foot had pressed, and which nature herself seemed to have stamped as forbidden ground. The bones of the intrepid Franklin, falling in the same perilous adventure, lay mouldering upon the outskirts of this great field, while the more successful march of the unsatisfied American bore him to the utmost verge of human discovery, beyond which no subsequent traveller is likely to penetrate.

When we look at the extreme youth of this meritorious officer at the time when he entered upon these daring explorations,—when we consider his patient endurance, his untiring energy, his profound science,—we cannot contemplate without emotion his brief career, and the many striking incidents of his past history.

A mere boy, he took upon himself the responsibilities and duties of bearded men; and, at an age comparatively immature, we find him sinking into the grave, crowned with the glittering testimonials of princes and potentates, of statesmen and men of letters, vying with each other to honor themselves in doing homage to this illustrious American.

Such was Dr. Kane. We have met here to-night to pay the last tribute to his memory. He was the friend of this institution; he had endeared himself to us all. May the example he has left stimulate us to increased effort in the useful field of our labors! May we look with renewed pride to the results of his successful life, and always remember such triumphs are to be met with only in the walks of untiring industry and spotless virtue!

Mr. Swann then offered the following preamble and resolutions, which had been prepared by a committee of the membership:—

Whereas, The Maryland Institute has been apprized of the death, at Havana, on the 16th instant, of Dr. Elisha Kent Kane, an honorary member of this Institute; and

Whereas, his name has become distinguished, not only in his own country, but throughout the civilized world, for his contributions to science and useful discovery, placing him in advance of the most chivalric, skilful, and enterprising of the navigators who have gone before him, in all that was calculated to reflect honor upon his country or shed a lustre upon his own fame; and

Whereas, it is proper and becoming that the whole country should recognise the severity of the blow which has deprived us of one of our most illustrious citizens, and especially by the Maryland Institute, whose labors he has shared and whose character he has contributed so largely to adorn by the close and intimate relationship in which he stood toward us:

Resolved, That the members of the Maryland Institute receive with unmingled sorrow the sad intelligence of the death of Dr. Elisha Kent Kane, and that they tender to the family of the deceased their most sincere condolence in this heavy bereavement.

Resolved, That a committee of twenty-five of the members of this Institute be appointed in behalf of this body to take charge of the remains of our deceased brother on their arrival in Baltimore, or at such point on the Baltimore and Ohio Railroad as they may deem most convenient and proper, and that they be instructed to make such further arrangements as may be necessary to represent the feelings of the Institute on an occasion of so much sorrow not only to its own members but the whole community.

Resolved, That the presiding officer of this Institute be instructed to enclose a copy of these resolutions, together with the proceedings of this meeting, to the family of the deceased.

DR. ELISHA KENT KANE. 349

The paper having been read, William H. Young, Esq., arose and seconded the resolutions, and paid the following tribute to the lamented Arctic Explorer :—

MR. CHAIRMAN :—The announcement of the death of Dr. Kane, though not unexpected, comes, nevertheless, right home to all our hearts. I cannot at this moment call to memory the name of any one in all this broad land whose death would strike a chord so sympathetic or so universal as that of this young man. I know no name that has become so fondly familiar in the hearts and homes of the people as his. Admiration at the gallant story of his life, honor and applause for the noble discharge of duty, do not express the deeper feelings with which he was regarded. The affectionate esteem which usually attends only warm personal attachment can alone adequately represent the sentiment entertained for him by those who, though they knew not his person, responsively yielded their affections to the holy instincts of his inner life and nature. His high ambition, his noble zeal, his indomitable energy, were so blended with the honest frankness of his disposition, the tenderness of his love, the generous sympathy of his heart, and all so resplendent, and so enlisted in the success of the enterprises to which he had lent the fulness of his mind, as to distinguish a character to which his friends could desire nothing added. His name will ever be associated with that of Lady Franklin, and with her undying devotion and love. Unto the untiring hope and prayerful perseverance of that noble Englishwoman he seemed almost to have wedded himself. Cordial and tender were the sympathies that had grown up between them; and her widowed heart is yet to grieve over his untimely death as though another of her own best-loved ones has been torn from her arms.

He devoted the early years of his manhood to danger, to toil, and to suffering for a purpose almost hopeless; yet no man called him rash. He sacrificed fortune, health, and life itself, that a very shadow might assume reality; and men looked on amazed yet admiring, silent yet exulting. Never did expedition leave the shores of its home blessed with so many prayers as those which followed the Advance on her last voyage. Never did the public mind more anxiously wait for a result or more ardently hope for its safety. And when those sent to their succor brought the brave crew back to their own land again, the world breathed freer for a while, and the universal heart uttered a prayer of thanksgiving.

And now but a brief year has passed, and we have met here to pay a last tribute to his memory, feebly to express our sense of the loss the world has sustained in his death, and to mingle our heartfelt sorrow with that which the brave and generous everywhere must feel at the event.

Dr. Kane has died early in manhood. His career, though short, was eventful and memorable. Forbearance, devotion, sacrifice, submission to toil and the endurance of privation, were the features of his living; but heroic courage and dauntless energy gave crowning glories to his young life, and now bring hallowed memories to consecrate his early grave. His was an exalted and earnest nature, with an inborn right to immortality. How greatly hath he achieved it! Science had no worthier worshipper, humanity no more devoted spirit. Loyal to duty, he had genius to conceive and power to perform. Pure of heart, truthful and generous, the hearts of those around him gathered close to his. The humblest of the gallant crew who shared his fortunes through the long, frozen nights of Arctic winters felt cheerier in his presence and happier at the sound of his voice. He was unostentatious, and in his manner modest even as became the high behests of his great nature. The friends who knew him best, and the dear ones at home, forget the claims of his mere achievements in the love more precious which these golden qualities inspired. In more than one land his death shall be celebrated by throbbing breasts and tearful eyes; and his memory shall be embalmed in the hearts of the good of both sexes, and of every age and of every clime.

The history of his brief life presents a bright example to his young countrymen,—a beautiful memory for the grateful homage of his brothers in the service.

We could have wished that his enterprises had been crowned with fuller success,—not, indeed for his fame's sake, (for the glory of his name is secure,) but to have made more complete his own happiness. But he heeds not these things now. He hath laid himself down with the brave to sleep. Death hath kissed him with lips colder than the north wind's breath. Life, with its behests and hopes, is over. He lives with the immortal dead.

The Hon. John P. Kennedy, late Secretary of the Navy, and member of the Maryland Institute, spoke as follows:—

I am not willing, Mr. Chairman, to allow the present opportunity to pass without a few words from me to express my hearty concurrence in the object proposed by the resolutions which have been already so

DR. ELISHA KENT KANE. 351

eloquently commended by yourself and other gentlemen who have spoken, and so cordially received by the committee. It is peculiarly appropriate that the leading part of the manifestation of a purpose to do honor to the memory of Dr. Kane should be assumed by the Maryland Institute. He was a distinguished member of this body, whose fellowship he cherished to the latest moment of his life with a most grateful remembrance of the earnest, and, I might say, affectionate, interest which it took in the preparation, the progress, and the consummation of both of his expeditions to the Arctic circle. It was foremost in the study of his grand design,—the first to cheer him onward to its accomplishment, the first to applaud his achievements. In the hall of the Institute he ever found an overflowing audience to listen to his exposition of his plans; and there, too, he found the largest sympathy in the utterance of his hopes. No associated body in the United States, no section of the general community outside of his immediate and most intimate friends, met him with the same hearty appreciation of his purpose, or with such cheerful tones of encouragement, as the Maryland Institute, and the great mass of the intelligent citizens of Baltimore who are accustomed to frequent its rooms. The brave explorer felt, throughout all the hazards and toils of his perilous ventures, that he had a host of friends here who thought hopefully of him in his darkest day, who watched his fortunes with an eager solicitude and listened with anxious concern for the first tidings of his return. It was a source of strength to his resolution amidst the dangers of his path, and an ever-present encouragement to his labors, that he had such friends at home ready to welcome the moment which should give him back to his country, and still more ready to approve and applaud the generous aims of his enterprise. Sir, these sentiments on both sides created an intimate relation between Dr. Kane and the Maryland Institute, and now give a peculiar appropriateness to the purposes of the present meeting.

Nothing that I can say on this occasion can enhance the high esteem which this community entertains for the character and exploits of the young hero to whom the spontaneous feeling of the country at this moment is according such extraordinary honors. I do not speak with the expectation of adding any thing to that esteem: my purpose in uttering a word here is rather to indulge a personal wish to perform a duty to a friend with whom I was connected under circumstances that furnished me many occasions to admire his manly virtues and rare accomplishments. Sir, I think I may speak of Dr. Kane with more intimate knowledge than perhaps any member of this committee. My intercourse with him, both private and official, was of a kind that enables me to recall many interesting particulars touching his last expedition.

It was my good fortune to be brought into a confidential communion with him at a time when my friendship could be made useful in furnishing essential—I might almost say indispensable—aid to the success of that most perilous of his Arctic explorations, that voyage of which the result has been to furnish the most remarkable of all the records yet given to the world of Polar discovery. The liberality of two private gentlemen whose names are already highly exalted on the rolls of munificent and public-spirited men—Henry Grinnell and George Peabody—had contributed the money to the outfit of that expedition; but, notwithstanding their liberality, it still stood in need of many most necessary supplies. Dr. Kane had been invited to take the command. Indeed, I believe the project of this second expedition to the Northern seas had originated with himself, stimulated to it by a correspondence with that distinguished lady whose devotion to a hopeless pursuit of the traces of her lost husband, Sir John Franklin, has for years past been the theme of a world-wide admiration and sympathy. Her acquaintance with Dr. Kane, and her confidence in his extraordinary ability for such an undertaking, had been formed in the progress of his participation in De Haven's voyage; and she was prompt to advise and encourage our friend's overture by the strongest appeals to that generous aspiration of his which was not less ennobled by the benevolence of its object than the gallantry and skill which he was able to bring to its achievement.

He communicated his views and plans to me, sir; but I did not hesitate to say to him that I would assist him with every means I might find myself authorized, by my position at the head of the Navy Department, to put at his disposal. I accordingly suggested to him that I would bring the expedition within the control of the Government by adopting it as a public enterprise, and by giving him a special order to conduct it under the direction of the Department. In pursuance of this purpose, I forthwith issued to Dr. Kane the order "to conduct an expedition to the Arctic seas in search of Sir John Franklin," enjoining upon him to make his reports to the head of the Navy Department. Having thus brought him into this relation, he became entitled to what is understood in the navy as " duty-pay," by which he received a small addition—I wish it had been more—to his means for defraying the expenses of the voyage. I also detailed for him, in the course of his preparation, some chosen men from the service, consisting in all of ten out

DR. ELISHA KENT KANE. 353

of the entire party of seventeen. These were entitled to their pay and rations from the Government. Some other facilities—all that I could grant from the ordinary resources of the navy without a specific appropriation by Congress—were added, in the supply of nautical instruments, maps, and charts, and, I believe, also some preserved meats, vegetables, and other provisions. The Department, however, could not do so much as was needful; and I felt, at the departure of the expedition, that no small risk would attend the comparatively scanty amount of supplies for such a voyage. Never, I believe, in the history of exploration, has a national adventure so full of peril, and so certain of hardships, been committed to the chances of wind and wave and inhospitable shores, so inadequately furnished as this,—never one that had more in it to quell the courage and try the hardihood of its commander, from causes attributable to the insufficiency of its outfit. Kane seemed to have a painful consciousness of this fact. Almost his last words to me were, "My friend, if I am not home before the second winter, keep your thoughts upon us, and get the Government by all means to send in relief. We shall stand sadly in need of help." I promised him I would do my part in such an event; and, sir, when the time came I did not forget it. I rejoice to add that the Government in that emergency needed no prompting, and that the relief, as you well know, in due time went upon its successful errand of grateful duty, under the lead of a gallant captain who sped, with the faith of a true comrade and the characteristic devotion of his profession, to the rescue of that shattered little band whose fate many then thought scarcely less precarious than that of the unhappy adventurers they had themselves gone forth to seek and succor.

Among many letters in my possession I have two from Dr. Kane, which I preserve with scrupulous regard. One, I believe, is the last he wrote on bidding adieu to an American shore. It was written at St. John's in Newfoundland, on the outward voyage. It was to inform me that all was well at that point, and to relieve me of a solicitude for himself which he knew disturbed me at the time of his departure. He had spent the previous winter in Washington in almost daily intercourse with myself; and I had seen with concern the terrible tax he had imposed upon his health in the unremitting study of preparation for his voyage. His incessant labor day and night had made a visible inroad upon his strength; and I was obliged often to caution him against the consequences, and to entreat him to desist from work. Night after night was spent till dawn of day at his desk. He grew thin and pale, and manifestly enfeebled. At length, when all was ready in April for his voyage, and his appointed time for sailing had come, he was struck down with a rheumatic fever, which confined him for some weeks to his bed, and when he was next reported only convalescent I was surprised to learn that he had gone aboard at New York and stood out to sea. Commencing such a voyage under such circumstances, his friends naturally felt a great concern for his success. His letter from St. John's was written to assure me that he had conquered his malady, and he was ready for the sterner contests that awaited him.

This first letter was dated in June, 1853. The second—in October, 1855, two years and four months later—was dated off Sandy Hook, announcing his return. It speaks joyfully of the pleasant days before him, and describes his health as singularly robust. There is in it, too, a playful allusion to a claim made by the British Explorations contemporaneous with the former voyage of De Haven, which had been a subject of remark in the maps of the Admiralty, in which "Grinnell Land" of our chart is described as "Albert Land." He says now, in this letter, "I found another Grinnell Land," alluding to the most remote region of his recent discovery, "which any man is welcome to who will go after it."

It was not long after this when he called upon me. I never saw him looking so well. He said himself, "My health is almost absurd. I have grown like a walrus." I mention these trivial facts to show that it was not his voyage to which we may, with any certainty, attribute his subsequent ill health. The ardor of his spirits and energy of his mind conquered all the difficulties of his expedition; but, I fear, we may assign to that very ardor the unhappy sequence of decaying strength which has now laid him low and caused this general sorrowing in our country. He set himself immediately upon the laborious task of preparing those volumes of surpassing interest which give us the history of his adventures, and which are now in every one's hand. The change from an active life to the sedentary pursuits of his study, his task pursued with that unremitting industry which was the habit of his nature, and which I had so often rebuked and attempted to check in the days of his preparation in Washington,—to this I look as the more probable cause of that decline which advanced with such fearful speed toward the grave. A spirit so eager, determination so intense, overlooked and seemed to forget the repose and the nurture that were essential to health; and Kane, the beloved and the lamented, has fallen a victim to the uncontrollable energy of his own will. What the rigors of the Pole, and the long Arctic night, and the ice-bound prison-house of frozen seas, could not subdue, has been overthrown by the insidious assault of the midnight lamp and the dead wood of the desk.

Stern as were the trials of that Polar voyage, neither they nor the subsequent labors of his study had quenched his zeal in the career to which he had devoted his life. He longed to repeat them in a new endeavor, to which he was instigated by the combined influence of a hope to ascertain something more definite in regard to the fate of Franklin's party, (concerning which the recent reports of Dr. Rea had accounted, in his opinion, only for a portion of the whole number, leaving room to conclude that traces of the remainder might still be found,) and of the attractions of scientific investigation in the great field of geological phenomena which these wonderful realms of ice present.

Soon after his work was published, (September, 1856,) Lady Franklin intimated to him her wish to equip another expedition, and obtained, as I understood, the consent of the Admiralty to invite him to take command of it. This offer fired his imagination with the ardor of new hopes in the cause of humanity and science, and the ambition of still greater achievements. He came to consult me on the subject. I did all I could to dissuade him from further pursuit of an adventure which I thought too hazardous and too hopeless of success. I found that this had been the advice of other friends; and there was a manifest tone of dejection and disappointment in his reluctant acquiescence in these counsels. "I dislike to give it up," he said; "and, if it were not for one consideration that touches me very nearly, I should persist in going. *My mother* is distressed at it," he added, "and wishes me to abandon the thought. I can resist other persuasions, but that must settle the question with me." And afterward, recurring again to it, he said, "It is so flattering an offer to me, coming from a foreign land,—the command of an expedition fitted out in England and intrusted to me upon the invitation of friends there, and sanctioned by the Admiralty: it goes hard with me to decline it."

As I was about visiting England myself at the time of this conversation, he asked me to call on Lady Franklin in London and explain to her why he could not accept this offer, and to say how much he prized the honor it was intended to confer upon him. This was the last interview I ever had with him. I sailed a few days afterward, and when in London I made several visits to Lady Franklin, and faithfully communicated to her what he had desired me to say. At the Admiralty Kane was well known and greatly esteemed; and it was no small satisfaction to me to find there that his character and services were associated, in the minds of the most intelligent men, with sentiments of the highest esteem for our navy in general. I am convinced that his fame reflected a lustre upon our whole naval service, and that he was regarded, in some degree, as the representative and type of the accomplishment, gallantry, and patriotic devotion to duty of the whole corps of American naval officers, whose character, both abroad and at home, is identified with the highest renown of our republic.

Such was the confidence and respect which Kane had inspired in the official ranks of the British navy, and among the scientific men connected with it, that the Admiralty did not hesitate to accept and adopt his charts for the correction of their own, and—with a promptitude which no less does honor to their integrity and sense of justice than it evinces their friendly dispositions toward our country—to acknowledge the claim of our first expedition under De Haven to that priority of discovery of the "Grinnell Land" to which I have alluded as heretofore a subject of discussion. The Admiralty have been wanting in no just and grateful recognition of the results and value of both of our expeditions, nor in the highest commendation of the public spirit of those who originated and conducted them. It is only by such interchange of grateful service and liberal appreciation that two great nations allied to each other by kindred of blood and affinity of ambition in promoting the great ends of civilization may hope to confer upon themselves and mankind that incalculable good which shall make their power a permanent blessing to the world. It should be the desire and policy of both to cultivate this disposition in all their intercourse.

Upon my return to my own country, I found that Kane had just sailed for England. His reception there was all that might have been expected. In the midst of the gratulations that were offered to him, and the happy greetings of his reception, we were afflicted with the startling reports of his failure in health, and the still more alarming tidings that he was obliged to seek a more sunny clime. The next news brought us warning from Havana of his quick decay, and, soon afterward, the report of his death. His body is now upon its way to the home of his youth, attended by mourning friends. In its passage through our city let us receive it with such honors as shall announce our high appreciation of his whole character and service, and express the profound sorrow of this community. The character and services of Dr. Kane are worthy of being preserved in the memory of the nation. A gentler spirit and a braver were never united in one bosom. He possessed the modest reserve of the student in combination with the ardent love of adventure and daring which distinguished the most romantic son of chivalry. With equal zeal and ability he pursued the attainment of science and the hardiest toil of exploration. It was pleasant to contemplate so much defiance of danger, such rugged adventure, such capability for severe exposure to the roughest labor, in a man of such delicate nurture and so mild and gentle in deportment. We saw in these traits a union of Sir Philip Sidney with the endurance and hardihood of Captain John Smith, of our own colonial history. Such a character is a model for the training of youth and a subject for the applause of mature age. The early death of Dr. Kane has been recognised as a national loss; and the honors which have been awarded to his memory, throughout the long journey by which his remains are conducted to their final resting-place, are such as we have heretofore accorded only to the most eminent men of our country. I find a mournful pleasure, Mr. Chairman, in being able this evening to concur with this committee in the measures they have proposed by which this city may unite in this general tribute of respect.

After a few remarks from N. H. Thayer, Esq., the resolutions were adopted.

Upon motion, the Mayor was then directed to appoint the committee of twenty-five, which he did.

On motion of Mr. Kennedy, the chairman was added to the committee.

The following gentlemen compose the committee:—

HON. JOSHUA VANSANT,	JNO. DUKEHART,
HON. JOHN P. KENNEDY,	HUGH A. COOPER,
JAMES M. ANDERSON,	THOMAS TRIMBLE,
JAMES MURRAY,	WILLIAM H. KEIGHLER,
JNO. ROGERS,	WENDELL BOLLMAN,
WILLIAM H. YOUNG,	T. M. CONRADT,
ADAM DENMEAD,	SAMUEL SANDS,
HON. REVERDY JOHNSON,	PROF. CAMPBELL MORFIT,
JOHNS HOPKINS,	HUGH BOLTON,
J. CRAWFORD NEILSON,	LAWRENCE SANGSTON,
SAMUEL HINDES,	GEORGE W. ANDREWS,
GEORGE A. DAVIS,	ROBERT LESLIE,

D. L. BARTLETT.

On motion of John Dukehart, Esq., the meeting then adjourned.

On the morning of Wednesday, the 11th, the remains of Dr. Kane were, with great solemnity, removed from the Hall of the Maryland

Institute, and conveyed with becoming accompaniment to the depôt of the Baltimore and Philadelphia Railroad, under the immediate direction of the following-named gentlemen :—

HON. JOSHUA VANSANT,   JOHN DUKEHART,
HUGH A. COOPER,   THOMAS TRIMBLE,
JOHN ROGERS.

With them was the delegation from the Philadelphia Joint Committee of Arrangements. At Elkton, Md., a committee from the Masonic Order, and the citizens of Wilmington, Del., were introduced to the delegation. This committee consisted of the following-named persons :—

HON. JOHN M. WALES,   CHARLES STEWARD,
CAPT. GEORGE N. HOLLINS,   DR. J. WHITE,
CHRISTIAN RAUCH,   J. S. VALENTINE,
WILLIAM JORDAN,   DR. JOHN SIMMS,
HON. D. W. BATES.

At Wilmington, Del., and at Chester, Pa.,—the stopping places of the cars,—thousands of citizens were assembled to do honor to the deceased.

A hasty glance at the public proceedings of citizens and corporations of cities and States, on the occasion of the arrival of the remains of Dr. Kane, has been taken. No attempt has been made to record all: a volume would not contain them. It seemed sufficient to note the particular points at which it was necessary for the boats or cars containing the body of Dr. Kane to rest, and to refer, in most cases generally, to the proceedings in reference to the distinguished dead.

But demonstrations of high respect were not limited to processions with the body. They were provided for wherever it was supposed the remains would pass,—especially at Pittsburg, in this State. In the Legislature of the State most appropriate and eloquent tributes were paid to the gifted son of Pennsylvania. In the Legislatures of New York, New Jersey, and of Massachusetts, and in almost all the scientific associations of the country, special action was had with regard to the eminent services and early death of Dr. Kane. As among the most touching memorials of deep affection and ineffaceable gratitude for the dead may be cited the resolutions adopted at a meeting of the companions of Dr. Kane in his Arctic Expedition, which are subjoined :—

PROCEEDINGS OF THE COMPANIONS OF DR. KANE.

The surviving members of the late Arctic Expedition met at the La Pierre House, on Friday evening, for the purpose of taking such action as might be deemed appropriate in view of the regretted death of their late commander, Dr. E. K. Kane.

The meeting was called to order by calling Dr. I. I. Hayes to the chair, and appointing Mr. Amos Bonsall Secretary. On calling the meeting to order, Dr. Hayes said, in explanation of their object in coming together,—

We little thought, comrades, when we so often spoke of the meetings we would have upon our return home, that the first would be to mourn the loss of our brave commander. Through dangers he has often led us. Again we are called to follow him; but the circumstances how different! There we followed him through paths forced over a trackless waste by his own energy. Now death is our pilot. It is hard to realize that he is indeed dead. He was one of those with whom you could scarcely associate the thought. But the tears of a sorrowing and grateful people assure us that it is too true. The bright star we have all so often seen just flickering on the verge of the horizon has gone down. The frail force which held it to this earth is broken. That soul so strong, that body so weak, too much in antagonism long to remain together,—alas! we shall never know the one but by its influence upon our lives, nor see the other but by its impress upon our memories.

But I will not anticipate you. Let us show in some way, unitedly, our appreciation of his services while living, and our sorrow at his death.

Mr. George Stephenson offered the following resolutions, which were unanimously adopted:—

Resolved, That we have received with pain the sad intelligence of the death of our late honored commander, Elisha Kent Kane, and embrace this the earliest opportunity of unitedly expressing our sorrow.

Resolved, That while we join with our countrymen and the citizens of his native State in paying tribute to the memory of one who had already achieved so much for the world's good and the nation's glory,— knowing him as we did well through scenes which try men's moral nature,—our hearts mourn the loss of those high qualities which endeared him to us as captain, comrade, and friend. We found him wise in counsel, clear in judgment, bold in danger, fearless in execution; ever alive to the calls of humanity, with a firm faith in the protecting care of an overruling Providence, which gave him moral power to rise above physical weakness, filled him at all times with cheerful hope, and imbued him with almost superhuman strength; and we hold his name in grateful remembrance.

Resolved, That we do deeply sympathize with his bereaved family, knowing full well that, great as is the loss to us of one possessing so many manly virtues, greater still must it be to those who held to him a nearer relation.

Resolved, That, as the only means now left us of showing our respect for the memory that lingers sadly yet brightly with us, we will, in a body, follow his remains to their last resting-place, in such position as may be assigned us by the Committee of Arrangements.

Resolved, That the Secretary be directed to forward to the family of the deceased a copy of these resolutions, signed by all the members.

The meeting then adjourned.

I. I. HAYES, *President.*

AMOS BONSALL, *Secretary.*

DEPUTATIONS FROM OTHER CITIES.

A committee of fourteen members from both branches of the Common Council of the city of New York arrived in Philadelphia to manifest the sympathy of that city in the great loss, and her high appreciation of the services and character of Dr. Kane. This delicate attention on the part of a sister city was beautifully consistent with the liberality of one of her distinguished citizens, to whom Dr. Kane was indebted for much encouragement and liberal contributions of means to undertake and accomplish his great Arctic expedition. These gentlemen, with the committees from other cities, were formally received by a sub-committee, and became the guests of the city of Philadelphia. Such was the expression of respect to Dr. Kane from all parts of the Union, such the proceedings in cities through which the remains of our townsman passed, such the voluntary, the spontaneous expression of regard for the services and memory of the good and great. And while these honors in other places were, to the passing body, thus distinguished, here in Philadelphia, where was his home in life, and where was prepared his resting-place in death, the proper reception of the honorable deposit and the vigilant guard of the sacred remains ought to be followed by such public solemnities as would enable the authorities and people to express their sense of the respect paid to the memory of their townsman elsewhere, and the appreciation of the honor conferred on them by the heroic services of the deceased in the cause of science and philanthropy.

DR. ELISHA KENT KANE. 361

PROCEEDINGS OF JOINT COMMITTEE RESUMED.

The committee, impressed with the importance of complete arrangements and the preservation of order in all the public proceedings, deemed it necessary to make an early appointment of a marshal, who should advise with them in the formation of a procession and execute the plan adopted; and they unanimously selected Peter C. Ellmaker, Esq., as marshal-in-chief, with authority to appoint aids and assistant marshals.

From the many who hastened to offer their services as undertakers, the committee selected for the duties of that place Mr. William H. Moore.

With reference to military escort and guard of honor, the committee adopted the following resolutions:—

Resolved, That the offer of the services of the Artillery Corps of the Washington Grays, by Captain Thomas P. Parry, be accepted, to act as a guard of honor on the occasion, if consistent with the arrangements of the naval and military authorities.

On motion of Mr. Thomas, it was

Resolved, That, if consistent with the orders of the commanding officer, the First City Troop of Cavalry, Captain James, be invited to act as a body-guard on the occasion of the reception of the remains of the late Dr. Kane, and escort the same to Independence Hall.

It was further *Resolved*, That the commanding officer of the First Division Pennsylvania Volunteers be requested to detail a brigade to act as a military escort on the occasion, in addition to the companies mentioned in the foregoing resolutions; and that all the officers of the Division not on duty be invited to attend the solemnities in uniform.

On learning that the remains of Dr. Kane had reached Baltimore, the Joint Committee of Arrangement despatched a delegation from their number, to proceed to that city and accompany them hither, the remains to be still in the care of the Committee of Baltimore.

The directors of the Philadelphia, Wilmington and Baltimore Railroad Company promptly and generously offered every facility for conveying the committee to Baltimore and bringing thence the body of Dr. Kane and those who should attend upon it; and, the kind offer having been thankfully accepted, the directors placed two cars at the disposal of the committee, who had declined accepting, as less sure and expeditious, the alternative of a "special train."

The remains of Dr. Kane were brought to the depôt at the corner of Broad and Prime Streets, at five o'clock on the afternoon of Monday, the 11th of March, accompanied by some members of the mourning family, and under the care of a committee consisting of the following-named gentlemen appointed by the Maryland Institute of Baltimore:—

JOHN DUKEHART,   JOHN RODGERS,
HUGH A. COOPER,   THOMAS TRIMBLE,
HON. JOSHUA VANSANT.

The Joint Committee proceeded to the depôt to meet the remains, and they caused them to be taken thence and conveyed to the Hall of Independence, in the following order:—

Officers of the Police.
First and Second Divisions of Police.
Washington Grays, Captain Parry.
Band.
The First City Troop, Captain James, acting as Guard of Honor.

City Troop.
Companions of Dr. Kane in the Arctic Expedition.
Committee of City Councils.
Committee from Maryland Institute.
Committee from Cincinnati.
Committees of various bodies from Wilmington and other places.
The Committee appointed by the Town Meeting.
The Committee from the Corn Exchange.
A body of the City Police, consisting of several hundred men, detailed by the Mayor.

The body of Dr. Kane, thus escorted, was placed in the Hall of Independence, the coffin resting on a pedestal and covered with a pall, and overlaid with the flag of the United States.

The committee were indebted to Mr. Peter Mackenzie for many splended wreaths, formed of the choicest flowers, decorating the covering of the remains.

When the coffin was properly disposed in the hall, Mr. Dukehart,

DR. KANE'S BODY LYING IN STATE,
In Independence Hall, Philadelphia.

DR. ELISHA KENT KANE.

the chairman of the delegation who attended the remains from Baltimore, resigned to the Philadelphia Committee the solemn charge, remarking :—

MR. CHAIRMAN :—In behalf of the citizens of Baltimore, I am now to deliver to your charge the remains of our deceased fellow-member, Elisha Kent Kane. I commit to you his remains in his native city, in his native State, in the hall consecrated to the cause of liberty, in this hall which may be truly termed the Mecca of all those who first promulgated the great truth that man was constituted for self-government.

I surrender to you, in his native city, the remains of our late brother. I may be permitted to say it is with deep regret, and that you cannot exclusively call him yours. We felt, whilst he was with us, whilst he was in our city, that we bestowed all the attention that was possible for us to do. Although this is his native city and his native State, his fame extends throughout the civilized world. In the icy regions where he sacrificed himself in the cause of humanity, even the wild Esquimaux will hand down, from father to son, the name of the deceased. Time will never obliterate the name of one who administered so much to their comfort, while himself suffering so much for the cause of humanity and science. Permit me now, gentlemen, on behalf of the city and of the citizens of Baltimore, in this hall consecrated to liberty, to commit to your charge the remains of Elisha Kent Kane, who sacrificed his life in the cause of humanity.

Mr. Chandler, as Chairman of the Joint Committee of Arrangements, received the sacred deposit with the following remarks :—

In the name of the corporation and citizens of Philadelphia, I receive from your committee these precious remains; and in their name I thank you and those whom you represent for the honors you have conferred upon one who has so honored his native city. While we know that it was from your abilities to appreciate excellence that you have distinguished yourselves by munificent consideration of the great departed, we, as Philadelphians, feel that, while our city enjoys a reflected lustre from the fame of our townsman, we must assume the obligations which your generous attentions create.

You have brought back to us the mortal remains of one who has achieved early immortality; and he returns in the fulfilment of the alternative of the Spartan mother's direction to her son,—"if not *behind*, at least *upon*, his shield." Nay, more: a Christian mother's cares are rewarded, and her hopes more than realized, in the life of a son devoted to science and philanthropy, and in that death whose hopes took hold on eternity.

Renewing to you the assurance of profound gratitude for the honors conferred upon these remains in your city and augmented by your presence here, this committee receive the sacred trust, and will watch over the body until it reaches its final resting-place in the grave.

Mr. Chandler then placed the remains under the care of the company of Washington Grays, who had volunteered to act as a guard of honor, and, addressing Captain Parry, their commander, he said:—

Captain Parry, on behalf of the Committee of Arrangements, I now announce to you that they have determined to place under your guard the remains of one so cherished by us all as a Philadelphian and a philanthropist. We trust that you will exercise a strict guardianship during the night, and restore to the committee the sacred trust which has been confided to your charge.

To which Captain Parry replied:—

I assure you, Mr. Chairman, on behalf of the corps which I have the honor to command, and which you have selected for the guardianship of the remains of the lamented Dr. Kane, that we are proud to accept your commission; and I need not say, on my own part, that I reply to you with all the emotion which may become a man. We will vigilantly guard the remains during the night, and return them to you in the morning as pure and unsullied as when we received them.

On Wednesday evening and on Thursday morning many hundred citizens were admitted to the Hall of Independence. At ten o'clock Captain Parry and his company were relieved from further duties as a guard of honor. Captain Parry, in a few appropriate remarks, resigned his charge, and received from Mr. Cuyler the thanks of the committee for the services which he and his corps had rendered. A splendid wreath of costly flowers was presented to the committee, accompanied by the subjoined note:—

"TO THE MEMORY OF DR. E. K. KANE."

FROM TWO LADIES.

These were deposited on the coffin with the rich offering of Mr. Mackenzie before noticed.

At noon precisely, the military, under Brigadier-General George Cadwallader, having been formed on Walnut Street, Chief-Marshal Ellmaker proceeded, with his aids and assistant marshals, to form the funeral procession according to the programme which had been adopted by the Committee of Arrangements.

The coffin was borne, by a detachment of seamen of the United States Navy, from the Hall of Independence down the centre-walk of Independence Square to Walnut Street, where it was received with appropriate honors by the military, and was then placed upon the funeral car prepared expressly for the occasion, twelve feet in length and five in breadth, set on low wheels concealed by the rich drapery suspended from the side of the car. On the four corners were upright spears with golden heads, and around these were entwined the American, the British, the Spanish, and the Danish flags, craped. Above the centre of the car was a dome of black cloth with white stripes, and from the canopy extended bands attached to the top of the spears at the four corners.

The dome was ornamented with white stars, and trimmed with white cord. The inside of the canopy was lined with white silk. The coffin being placed in the centre of the car, the American flag was thrown around it, and the garlands of flowers and the sword of the deceased were placed gracefully on the bier. The car was drawn by six black horses, each being attended by a groom appropriately attired.

FIRST DIVISION.

This division was headed by a strong body of police detailed by the Mayor to secure an unobstructed path to the cortège. The body was headed by the high-constables of the city, and, although the route of procession, covering a large extent of the central portion of the city, was densely packed with spectators, universal order prevailed. The police were also distributed along the line of the procession.

The military escort, consisting of the First Brigade, made an exceedingly creditable and imposing display. The Brigade comprised the following companies:—Squadron Cavalry, T. C. James; First City Troop, Captain James; First City Cavalry, Captain Baker; Artillery Battalion, Lieutenant-Colonel Biles, commandant; Washington Grays, Captain Parry; Philadelphia Grays, Captain Rush; Cadwallader Grays, Captain Breece; National Artillery, Captain Murphy.

First Regiment Infantry, Colonel Wm. D. Lewis, Jr., commandant:

State Fencibles, Captain Page; Washington Blues, Captain Gosline; National Guards, Captain Lyle; Independent Grays, Captain Braceland; *Independent Guards,* Captain Cromley; Washington Guards, Captain Wagner.

SECOND DIVISION

Was preceded by William H. Moore, undertaker. Then followed the funeral car and procession, in the following order:—

GUARD OF HONOR: 1st Troop Philadelphia City Cavalry.	PALL-BEARERS. Governor Pollock, Hon. Horace Binney, Commodore Stewart, Major C. J. Biddle, Bishop Potter, Chief-Justice Lewis, Doctor Dunglison, J. A. Brown, Esq.,	HEARSE.	PALL-BEARERS. Samuel Grant, Esq., Henry Grinnell, Esq., Commodore Read, Doctor Dillard, U.S.A., Rev. H. A. Boardman, D.D., Hugh L. Hodge, M.D., Hon. Wm. B. Reed.	GUARD OF HONOR: 1st Troop Philadelphia City Cavalry.

Comrades of the Deceased in the Arctic Expedition.
Committee of Arrangements.
Committee of the Authorities and Citizens of Baltimore.
Committee of the Common Council of the City of New York.
Reverend Clergy of the City.
Mayor and Recorder.
Heads of the several Departments.
Officers of Councils.
President of Select and Common Councils.
Select Council.
Common Council.
Ex-Members of Select and Common Councils.
Aldermen of the City.
Deputies and Clerks of the several Departments of the City.
Reporters of the Press.
Officers of the State Government.
The Societies of the Sons of St. George and Albion.
The Hibernian Society, the St. Andrew's and Scots Thistle Societies.
Officers of the United States Army, Navy, and Marine Corps.
Representatives of Foreign Governments and other Distinguished Strangers.
Judges and Officers of the United States and other Courts.
Officers and members of the American Philosophical Society.

Officers and Members of the Academy of Natural Sciences.
Wardens of the Port.
The remainder of the division paraded in the following order :—

THIRD DIVISION.

Marshal of the United States for the Eastern District of Pennsylvania,
His Deputies and Assistants.
United States District Attorney.
Collector, Naval Officer, and Surveyor of the Port, Post-Master, and other Officers of the United States Government.
Director and Treasurer, Officers, and Workmen of the United States Mint.
Members and Ex-Members of Congress.
High-Sheriff of the City and County, and other City and County Officers.
Physicians.
Members of the Bar.
Officers and Members of the Corn Exchange.
Officers of the Pennsylvania Militia not on duty.

FOURTH DIVISION.

Medical Faculty and Students of the University of Pennsylvania.
Medical Faculty, the Graduating Class, and the Students, of the Jefferson Medical College of Philadelphia.
Officers and Students of other Medical Societies.
Philadelphia County Medical Society.
Officers and Under-Graduates of the University of Pennsylvania.
President, Directors, and Officers of Girard College.
Principal and Faculty of the High School.
The Musical Fund Society.
Controllers of the Public Schools.

FIFTH DIVISION.

The Fire Department.
Independent Order of Odd-Fellows.
Young Men's American Club.
American Protestant Association.
Ancient Order of Druids.

SIXTH DIVISION.

Citizens.
Police.

The procession, which moved up Walnut Street to Seventeenth Street, up Seventeenth to Arch, down Arch to Seventh Street, terminated at the Second Presbyterian Church, North Seventh Street; and, as it was impossible for any considerable proportion of the procession to obtain admittance to the church, the public demonstration was considered as terminating on the arrival at this place. The remains were then taken from the hearse and conveyed, through the south gate of the enclosure, to the elevation in front of the church, and, while they lay in that position with the pall-bearers formed in a semicircle in the rear, the whole procession passed, uncovered, down Seventh Street, in view of the coffin. Few scenes have ever been presented of more solemn grandeur. The body then was conveyed into the church, accompanied on each side by the pall-bearers, and followed by the companions of Dr. Kane in the Arctic Expedition, the Committee of Arrangement, the Councils of the city, the Committees from other cities, the officers of the navy, and other citizens.

The exercises in the church commenced with the singing of an anthem from Mozart :—" I Heard a Voice from Heaven."

Then came the following beautiful and impressive invocation, delivered by the Rev. Charles Wadsworth, D.D. :—

"Holy, holy, holy, Lord God Almighty. The sinless and adoring seraphims veil their faces and cry, Holy! We are worms of the dust, sinful, miserable, unworthy, and to us thou art ever terrible in the glory of thy holiness, thou who hast thy way in the whirlwind, and around whose feet are thick clouds and darkness. And now, more than is thy wont, thou seemest terrible to us in thy forthgoings in judgment. We lift the eye, and behold a throne set in the heavens, and out of it proceed lightnings, and thunderings, and voices, and before it the pestilence and burning coals at its feet, and the smile seems gone from thine awful face; and thou seemest wroth with us, and thou art terrible in thine anger. Death, death, has cast its shadow on us; and this thy glorious Temple, this Bethel where the Heavenly ladder lifts, this altar-side where the Shekinah dwells, this blessed Father's house, where we have met thy Sabbath smiles,—alas! it is darkened now into a house of mourning. We are smitten, we are afflicted,—the spirit wounded, the heart broken. One we loved,—one we honored,—one, it may be, too dear to our affections,—one we parted with in fond hope,—

DR. ELISHA KENT KANE.

has come again to our sanctuary, the eye closed, the heart pulseless; and we stand by thine holy altar stricken, terrified, in the awful presence of God and death.

We think of thee, and are afraid. O thou Almighty! Thy ways are fearful. We are on the water, and the night is dark and the poor bark is tempest-tossed, and even the form of the Redeemer, walking the billows, seems phantom-like and dreadful, as it were a Spirit, and we stand back fearful and trembling from thine awful path, thou God of chastening; and yet, into thy presence, O our God, we come for comforting. Amid all thy stern and terrible manifestations, we know thou art merciful. With clouds and darkness around thee, and the pestilence and the burning coals at thy feet, thou art still our Father, our heavenly Father,—Father pitiful of thy children,—the bruised reed not breaking it, the smoking flax not quenching it. Thy glorious titles are Father, Redeemer, Comforter, and there is no sorrow thou canst not take away, no storm thou canst not still, no Marah in the wilderness thou canst not make sweet as the living water.

And in this our hour of chastening we come to thee for comfort. We have nowhere else to go. The world cannot comfort us. The glory of man seems a fading flower, and the voices of earth seem mournful in the shadow of the grave. But thou canst comfort; and we come to thee in trustful love and faith. We come to sit at thy feet, to look up into thy face, to cast ourselves, stricken and sorrowful, into thy gentle arms. Father, our Father, look upon us mercifully. Thou knowest where the thorn pierces. Oh, lift the load from the wounded heart; oh, bind up tenderly the wounded spirit.

We are here in thy temple, where thy voice is heard. Speak to us, O thou Eternal One, gently, tenderly, lovingly. Speak the words which man cannot utter,—the words of eternal life. Tell us of the resurrection, the immortality, the heaven. Make us to believe that, though this dear eye is shrouded, this dear heart cold in death, yet the beloved spirit that made the eye to sparkle and the heart to bound lives still, *lives still!* Thanks, thanks, for the hopes so glorious, so full of eternal life, that cluster around this shrouded dust,—hopes that our beloved one is even now more than conqueror through that Redeemer who died for him. Oh, give fuller power to our faith. Father, heavenly Father, utter with thy glorious voice thine own glorious oracles. Speak to us of the resurrection and the life. Tell us of the gates of pearl, and the trees of life in the midst of the garden; of the palms and white robes, and songs of victory; of the thrones of power, and the diadems of splendor; of the places prepared in the house of many mansions; "and the far more exceeding and eternal weight of glory." Father, our heavenly Father, we are listening for thy blessed voice. Oh, speak to us! Speak to us gently, joyfully, till faith grows strong in our stricken spirits; so that, time seeming the vapor and eternity the reality, we may look not down upon this sleeping dust, saying farewell, but rather upward to the risen spirit in the firmament, saying, All hail, redeemed one. Oh, comfort us, thou heavenly Comforter, thou merciful Savior, in whom "whosoever liveth and believeth shall never die." Thou Lamb of God, who takest away the sins of the world, fill our stricken hearts with thine own glorious grace, so that we may go forth as Mary, to find the grave of our beloved lustrous with the vision of angel, and write over it no sadder words than these :—" Blessed are the dead who die in the Lord!" whilst our song of triumphant faith, begun here in tears, shall go on in eternity :—" Unto Him who loved us, and washed us in his own blood, and hath made us kings and priests unto God and his Father," be glory and honor forever and ever. Amen.

The same divine also read the selection—

"I am the resurrection and the life; he that believeth in me, though he were dead, yet shall he live. Blessed are the dead who die in the Lord," &c.

The hymn "Hark to the Solemn Bell" was then sung by the choir.

REV. CHARLES W. SHIELDS,

Pastor of the Church, then delivered the following Funeral Discourse.

It is a noble instinct which prompts us to honor the dead. Humanity joins with religion in suppressing all earthly distinctions and passions at the mouth of the tomb. The mansion may be envied, the hovel may be scorned; but the grave is alike revered, whether it be adorned with sculptured marble or decked with a simple flower.

It would seem that in the mortal remains of a fellow-creature we respect a fate that we know must soon be our own, and, conscious of the worth of a soul, would do homage even to the ruined temple in which it was enshrined.

But when the object of such feelings concentrates in himself the best traits of our nature, and has been conducted by Providence to an eminence from which he illustrates them in the view of multitudes, the ordinary cold respect warms to admiration and melts into love. We behold the image of our common humanity reflected and magnified in him as a cherished ideal. Death, which makes sacred every thing it touches, throws a mild halo around his memory, and we hasten to bring to his grave—all that we now have to give—the poor tribute of our praises and tears.

We are assembled, my friends, to perform such comely though sad duties in honor of a man who, within the short lifetime of thirty-five years, under the combined impulses of humanity and science, has traversed nearly the whole of the planet in its most inaccessible places; has gathered here and there a laurel from every walk of physical research in which he strayed; has gone into the thick of perilous adventure, abstracting in the spirit of philosophy, yet seeing and loving in the spirit of poesy; has returned to invest the very story of his escape with the charms of literature and art; and, dying at length in the morning of his fame, is now lamented, with mingled affection and pride, by his country and the world.

Death discloses the human estimate of character. That mournful pageant which for days past has been wending its way hither, across the solemn main, along our mighty rivers, through cities clad in habiliments of grief, with the learned, the noble, and the good mingling in its train, is but the honest tribute of hearts that could have no motives but respect and love. To us belongs the sad privilege of at length closing the national obsequies in his native city and at the grave of his kindred. Fittingly we have suffered his honored remains to repose a few pensive hours at the shrine where patriotism gathers its fairest memories and choicest honors. Now, at last, we bear them—thankful to the Providence by which they have been preserved from mishap and peril—to the sacred altar at which he was reared.

I do not forget, my friends, the severer solemnities of the place and presence. I remind you of their claim. How empty the applause of mortals as vaunted in the ear of Heaven! How idle the distinctions among creatures involved in a common insignificance by death and sin! What a mockery the flimsy shows with which we cover up the realities of judgment and eternity! The thought may well temper the pride of our grief; yet it need not stanch its flow. No! I should but feel that the goodness of that God by whose munificent hand his creature was endowed had been wronged, did we not pause to reflect a while upon his virtues and drop some manly and Christian tears over his early grave.

Elisha Kent Kane—a name now to be pronounced in the simple dignity of history—was bred in the lap of science and trained in the school of peril, that he might consecrate himself to a philanthropic purpose to which so young he has fallen a martyr. The story of his life is already a fireside tale. Multitudes, in admiring fancy, have retraced his footprints. Now, that that brief career is closed in death, we recur to it with a mournful fondness, from the daring exploits which formed the pastime of his youth, to the graver tasks to which he brought his developed manhood. Though born to ease and elegance, when but a young student, used to academic tastes and honors, we see him breaking away from the refinements of life into the rough paths of privation and danger. Through distant and varied regions we follow him in his pursuit of scientific discovery and adventure. On the borders of China—within the unexplored depths of the crater of Luzon—in India and Ceylon—in the islands of the Pacific—by the sources of the Nile—amid the frowning sphinxes of Egypt and the classic ruins of Greece—along the fevered coast of Africa—on the embattled plains of Mexico—we behold him everywhere blending the enthusiasm of the scholar with the daring of the soldier and the research of the man of science.

Yet these were but the preparatory trials through which Providence was leading him to an object worthy his matured powers and noblest aims. Suddenly he becomes a centre of universal interest. With the prayers and hopes of his country following after him, he disappears from the abodes of men, on a pilgrimage of patience and love, into the icy solitudes of the North. Within the shadow of two sunless winters his fate is wrapt from our view. At length, like one come back from another world, he returns to thrill us with the marvels of his escape, and transport us, by his graphic pen, into scenes we scarcely realize as belonging to the earth we inhabit. All classes are penetrated and touched by the story so simply, so modestly, so eloquently told. The nation takes him to its heart with patriotic pride. In hopeful fancy, a still brighter career is pictured before him,—when, alas! the vision, while yet it dazzles, dissolves in tears. We awake to the sense of a loss which no contemporary, at his age, could occasion.

Of that loss let us not here attempt too studious an estimate. These sad solemnities may simply point us to the more moral qualities and actions in view of which every bereavement most deeply affects us.

As a votary of science, he will indeed receive fitting tributes. There will not be wanting those who shall do justice to that ardent thirst for truth which in him amounted to one of the controlling passions, to that intellect so severe in induction yet sagacious in conjecture, and to those contributions, so various and valuable, to the existing stock of human knowledge. But his memory will not be cherished alone in philosophic minds. His is not a name to be honored only within the privileged circles of the learned. There is for him another laurel, greener even than that which Science wreaths for her most gifted sons. He is endeared to the popular heart as its chosen ideal of the finest sentiment that adorns our earthly nature.

Philanthropy, considered as among things which are lovely and of good report, is the flower of human virtue. Of all the passions that have their root in the soil of this present life there is none which, when elevated into a conscious duty, is so disinterested and pure. In the domestic affections there is something of mere blind instinct; in friendship there is the limit of congeniality; in patriotism there are the restrictions of local attachment and national antipathy; but in that love of race which seeks its object in man as man, of whatever kindred, creed, or clime, earthly morality appears divested of the last dross of selfishness, and challenges our highest admiration and praise.

Providence, who governs the world by ideas, selects the fit occasions and men for their illustration. In an age when philanthropic sentiments, through the extension of Christianity and civilization, are on the increase, a fit occasion for their display is offered in the peril of a bold explorer, for whose rescue a cry of anguished affection rings in the ears of the nations; and the man found adequate to that occasion is he whose death we mourn.

If there was every thing congruous in the scene of the achievement,— laid, as it was, in those distant regions where the lines of geography converge beyond all the local distinctions that divide and separate man from his fellow, and among rigors of cold and darkness, and disease and famine, that would task to their utmost the powers of human endurance, —not less suited was the actor who was to enter upon that scene and enrich the world with such a lesson of heroic beneficence. Himself of a country estranged from that of the imperilled explorers, the simple act of assuming the task of their rescue was a beautiful tribute to the sentiment of national amity; while, as his warrant for undertaking it, he seemed lacking in no single qualification. To a scientific education and the experience of a cosmopolite he joined an assemblage of moral qualities so rich in their separate excellence, and so rare in their combination, that it is difficult to effect their analysis.

Conspicuous among them was that elementary virtue in every philanthropic mission,—an exalted yet minute *benevolence*. It was the crowning charm of his character, and a controlling motive in his perilous enterprise. Other promptings indeed there were, neither suppressed, nor in themselves to be depreciated. That passion for adventure, that love of science, that generous ambition, which stimulated his youthful exploits, appear now under the check and guidance of a still nobler impulse. It is his sympathy with the lost and suffering, and the duteous conviction that it may lie in his power to liberate them from their icy dungeon, which thrill his heart and nerve him to his hardy task. In his avowed aim, the interests of geography were to be subordinate to the claims of humanity. And neither the entreaties of affection, nor the imperilling of a fame which to a less modest spirit would have seemed too precious to hazard, could swerve him from the generous purpose.

And yet this was not a benevolence which could exhaust itself in any mere dazzling, visionary project. It was as practical as it was comprehensive. It could descend to all the minutiæ of personal kindness and gracefully disguise itself even in the most menial offices. When defeated in its great object, and forced to resign the proud hope of a philanthropist, it turns to lavish itself on his suffering comrades, whom he leads almost to forget the commander in the friend. With unselfish assiduity and cheerful patience, he devotes himself as a nurse and counsellor to relieve their wants and buoy them up under the most appalling misfortunes, and, in those still darker seasons when the expedition is threatened with disorganization, conquers them not less by kindness than by address. Does a party withdraw from him under opposite counsels? they are assured, in the event of their return, of "a brother's welcome." Are tidings brought him that a portion of the little band are forced to halt, he knows not where, in the snowy desert? he is off through the midnight cold for their rescue, and finds his reward in the touching assurance, "They knew that he would come." In sickness he tends them like a brother, and at death drops a tear of manly sensibility on their graves. Even the wretched savages, who might be supposed to have forfeited the claim, share in his kindly attentions; and it is with something of genuine human feeling that he parts from them at last, as "children of the same Creator."

In a cause of humanity like that which he had espoused, we feel that something more was needed than the diffuse and aimless philanthropy which is loud in panegyric upon human nature, while it disdains the details of practical well-doing; and, when in connection with such high, benevolent purpose we find a native goodness of heart disclosing such constant self-sacrifice, we are at no loss to recognise his vocation.

Then, as the fitting support of this noble quality, there was also the stauncher, but not less requisite virtue, of an indomitable *energy*. It was the iron column around whose capital that delicate lily-work was woven. His was not a benevolence which must waste itself in mere sentiment, for want of a power of endurance adequate to support it through hardship and peril. In that slight physical frame, suggestive only of refined culture and intellectual grace, there dwelt a sturdy force of will which no combination of material terrors seemed to appall, and, by a sort of magnetic impulse, subjected all inferior spirits to its control. It was the calm power of reason and duty asserting their superiority over mere brute courage, and compelling the instinctive homage of Herculean strength and prowess.

With what firm yet conscientious resolve does he quell the rising symptoms of rebellion which threaten to add the horrors of mutiny to those of famine and disease! And, all through that stern battle with Nature in her most savage haunts, how he ever seems to turn his mild front toward her frowning face, if in piteous appealing, yet not less in fixed resignation!

We instinctively exult in every triumph of mind over matter, in every fresh aggression of art upon nature, and cannot but feel, even while touched by their sufferings, a generous pride in those who enlarge our ideas of human endurance and strengthen our faith in moral as distinguished from material power. But when such intrepidity and fortitude are displayed in the pursuit of lofty, unselfish aims, it is as if we saw the olden romance of chivalry returning, in a practical age, to enlist the hardiest virtues in the service of the gentlest and purest charities. The heart must applaud in the midst of its pity, and smiles an approval even through its tears.

But if, in the conduct of that heroic enterprise, benevolence appeared supported by energy and patience, so, too, was it equipped with a most marvellous *practical tact*. He brought to his task not merely the resources of acquired skill, but a native power of adapting himself to emergencies, and a fertility in devising expedients, which no occasion ever seemed to baffle. Immured in a dreadful seclusion, where the combined terrors of nature forced him into all the closer contact with the passions of man, he not only rose, by his energy, superior to them both, but, by his ready executive talent, converted each to his ministry. Circumstances which would have whelmed ordinary minds in helpless bewilderment appeared only to enhance his self-collection and develop his versatile genius. Whether he had to deal with the humors of a sick and desponding crew, or to provide subsistence and amusement in the midst of a lifeless solitude, or to snatch the flower of opportunity at the dizzy brink of peril,—in every form of crisis he displayed the same keen perception of surrounding realities, with the same quick and nice adjustment of himself to their demands. Even the wild inmates of that icy world, from the mere stupid wonder with which at first they regarded his imported marvels of civilization, were at length forced to descend to a genuine respect and love, as they saw him outwitting their experience by his ingenuity and competing with them in the practice of their own rude, stoical virtues.

We love goodness; we admire courage; but when both are found armed for practice with an adaptive faculty which was as the skill of a strong hand that drew its pulse from a warm heart, there is nothing left us but to wonder at a combination so symmetrical and rare. From our contemplation of the man we revert to the occasion to which he is to be adjusted; and as we picture the genius of philanthropy leading forth her trained votary after a perilous prize which has been planted sheer beyond the boundaries of all local jealousy and pride, and at the magnetic centre of a universal sympathy, we know not whether more to admire the fitness of the scene to the actor, or of the actor to the scene. So does Providence, with poetical rectitude, arrange the drama of a good deed.

To such more sterling qualities were joined the graces of an affluent *cheerfulness*, that never deserted him in the darkest hours,—a delicate and capricious *humor*, glancing among the most rugged realities like the sunshine upon the rocks,—and, above all, that invariable stamp of true greatness, a beautiful *modesty*, ever sufficiently content with itself to be above the necessity of pretension. These were like the ornaments of a Grecian building, which, though they may not enter into the effect of the outline, are found to impart to it, the more nearly it is surveyed, all the grace and finish of the most exquisite sculpture.

And yet, strong and fair as were the proportions of that character in its more conspicuous aspects, we should still have been disappointed did we not find, albeit hidden deep beneath them, a firm basis of *religious sentiment*. For all serious and thoughtful minds this is the purest charm of those graphic volumes in which he has recorded the story of his wonderful escapes and deliverances. There is everywhere shining through its pages a chastened spirit, too familiar with human weakness to overlook a Providence in his trials, and too conscious of human insignificance to disdain its recognition. Now, in his lighter, more pensive moods, we see it rising, on the wing of a devout fancy, into that region where piety becomes also poetry:—

"I have trodden the deck and the floes when the life of earth seemed suspended,—its movements, its sounds, its colorings, its companionships; and, as I looked on the radiant hemisphere, circling above me, as if rendering worship to the unseen centre of light, I have ejaculated, in humility of spirit, 'Lord, what is man, that thou art mindful of him?'"

Again, in graver emergencies, it appears as a habitual resource, to which he has come in conscious dependence:—

"A trust, based on experience as well as on promises, buoyed me up at the worst of times. Call it fatalism, as you ignorantly may, there is that in the story of every eventful life which teaches the inefficiency of human means, and the present control of a Supreme Agency. See how often relief has come at the moment of extremity, in forms strangely unsought, almost at the time unwelcome; see, still more, how the back has been strengthened to its increasing burdens, and the heart cheered by some conscious influence of an unseen Power."

And at length we find it settling into that assurance which belongs to an experienced faith and hope:—

"I never doubted for an instant that the same Providence which had guarded us through the long darkness of winter was still watching over us for good, and that it was yet in reserve for us—for some; I dared not hope for all—to bear back the tidings of our rescue to a Christian land."

Those Arctic Sabbaths were "full of sober thought and wise resolve." We hear no profane oath vaunting itself from that little ice-bound islet of human life, where man has been thrown so helplessly into the hands of God; but rather, in its stead, murmured amid the wild uproar of the storm, that daily prayer, "Lord, accept our thanks, and restore us to our homes." And when at length that prayer is graciously answered, it is the same spirit which brings him whither now, alas! can only be brought these poor remains,—under the devout impulse, "I will pay my vows unto the Lord in the presence of all his people." Let us believe that a faith which supported him through trials worse than death did not fail him when death itself came.

Into that last tender scene both religion and delicacy alike forbid that we should too curiously intrude. Affection will prize its melancholy though sweet reminiscences, long after the more public grief has subsided. Enough only of the veil may be drawn to admit us to a privileged sympathy.

The disease by which Dr. Kane was prostrated was that terrible scourge of Arctic life, some seeds of which remained in his system on his return, but were afterward developed and aggravated by the exhausting literary labors incident to the narrative of the Expedition. Entirely under-estimating those labors, (of which but few of us are prepared to form an adequate conception,) he was quite too thoughtless of the claims of a body he had so long been accustomed to subject to his purpose, and only awoke to a discovery of the error when it was too late. With this melancholy conviction, he announced the completion of the work to a friend in the modest and touching sentence :—"The book, poor as it is, has been my coffin."

He left the country under a presentiment that he should never return. For the first time in his life, departure is shaded with foreboding. It was indeed an alarming symptom to find that iron nerve, which hitherto had sustained him under shocks apparently not less severe, thus beginning to falter. Yet it will enhance the interest that now gathers around his memory to learn that even then the great purpose of his life he had not wholly abandoned, but, in spite of the most serious entreaties, was already projecting another Arctic expedition of research and rescue. This object of his visit he was not destined to mature. Neither was it to be his privilege to enjoy the honors that awaited him. Successive and more virulent attacks of disease oblige him to recur to the last resorts of the invalid. In hope of repairing the wounds inflicted by the fierce rigors of the North, he is borne to the more genial South, where at length, beneath its ardent skies and amidst its fragrant airs, supported by the ministries of love and the consolations of religion, his life drew gently to a close.

In the near approach of death he was tranquil and composed. With too little strength either to support or indicate any thing of rapture, he was yet sufficiently conscious of his condition to perform some last acts befitting the solemn emergency. In reference to those whom he conceived to have deeply injured him, he expressed his cordial forgiveness. To each of the watching group around him his hand is given in the fond pressure of a final parting; and then, as if sensible that his ties to earth are loosening, he seeks consolation from the requested reading of such Scripture sentences as had been the favorite theme of his thoughtful hours.

Now he hears those soothing beatitudes which fell from the lips of

the Man of Sorrows in successive benediction. Then he will have repeated to him that sweet, sacred pastoral,—
"The Lord is my Shepherd : I shall not want. He maketh me to lie down in green pastures : he leadeth me beside the still waters. Yea, though I walk through the valley of the shadow of death, I will fear no evil; for thou art with me: thy rod and thy staff, they comfort me."

At length are recited the consolatory words with which the Savior took leave of his weeping disciples :—
"Let not your heart be troubled : ye believe in God; believe also in me. In my Father's house are many mansions : if it were not so, I would have told you. I go to prepare a place for you."

And at last, in the midst of this comforting recital, he is seen to expire, —so gently that the reading still proceeds some moments after other watchers have become aware that he is already beyond the reach of any mortal voice. Thus, in charity with all mankind, and with words of the Redeemer in his ear, conveyed by tones the most familiar and beloved on earth, his spirit passed from the world of men.

The heart refuses to deal with such a reality. Death never seems so much a usurper on the domain of life as at the grave of the young and the gifted. In fancy we strive to complete that brilliant fragment of a history so abruptly ended. We are carried forward into the future, in an effort to picture all that he might have been to his country and the world, until, drawn back again by these sad shows of our loss and sorrow, we pronounce nothing so visionary as this fleeting life, and nothing so empty as human glory.

And thus is it ever the same trite lesson we learn at each new-made grave. There was never any human life so complete that it could be finished on earth. There was never any human spirit so gifted that it could accomplish its destiny here. The most illustrious actions, the most varied attainments, the most disciplined virtues, are at best but crude, elementary trials of a novitiate state. Could we follow the regenerate spirit as it emerges from its earthly pupilage; could we trace its career from scene to scene of expanding effort and from accession to accession in knowledge, love, and joy; could we pause with it, at length, on some far-distant peak of high attainment, whence, as in retrospective fancy, it looks back upon rolling worlds with their changing climates and histories,—how would the science, the philanthropy, the heroism of this vanishing life have dwindled away to the merest playthings, the mimic smiles and tears, of the childhood of our immortality! Let the chaplet be woven, let the banner be shrouded, let the dirge be wailed, and, with fair, fond pageantry, let dust be rendered back to its kindred dust; but we shall not have soared to the highest moral of the elegiac spectacle, until, from that eternity which lies beyond this tomb of blighted hope and buried glory, we return to write upon it—This also is vanity.

Alas! the hand of the victor drops in death at the moment it is extended to grasp the laurel.

At the conclusion of the sermon the Rev. Dr. Boardman delivered the following impressive prayer:—

O Lord our God, from everlasting to everlasting thou art God; and besides thee there is none else. In the name of thy beloved Son, our Mediator, Jesus Christ, we come before thee, that we may obtain mercy and find grace to help in this time of need.

We acknowledge the righteousness of that sentence which has gone out against us,—"Dust thou art, and unto dust shalt thou return;" for we have sinned against thee and done evil in thy sight, and we are justly exposed to the penalty of thy holy law. It is of thy mercies that we are not consumed, because thy compassions fail not. Oh, deal not with us according to our desert, but according to the plenitude of thy grace and mercy in Christ Jesus our Lord.

We bow down under this afflictive dispensation of thy Providence, wherein thou art staining the pride of human glory and admonishing us of our frailty. All flesh indeed is grass, and all the glory of man as the flower of the field. We feel, as we gather, a stricken people, around these precious remains, that thou art a great God, and a great King above all Gods. Thou doest thy will in the army of heaven and among the inhabitants of the earth; and none can stay thine hand, or say unto thee, "What doest thou?"

We render thanks to thee for all thy goodness to thy servant departed. For the radiant gifts with which thou wast pleased to endow him, we praise thee. For that beneficent Providence in which he trusted, and which never forsook him, we praise thee. For all that he was enabled to do for humanity and for science, we praise thee. And above all do we praise thee for those divine supports and consolations which sustained him in sickness and in death.

And now, O Lord, we humbly beseech thee to heal the wound which thou hast made. Bind up the hearts of this afflicted household, and comfort them under their great bereavement. Help them to look, away from every earthly solace, to Him who is the resurrection and the life, and send the Holy Spirit, the divine Comforter, to assuage their grief, to inspire them with resignation, to fill them with the fulness of God, and to enable them to say, " The Lord gave, and the Lord hath taken away: blessed be the name of the Lord."

Be merciful also, we entreat thee, to thy servants, the surviving companions of our brother beloved, who shared his duties and his dangers. Comfort their hearts, and lead them to seek in Jesus Christ an enduring portion.

And may this mournful visitation be sanctified to this great community! Let it not be in vain that we are assembled to-day around the bier of one upon whom earth had so accumulated its honors and to whom so many hearts were drawn in loving confidence and affection. Especially may the monitory lessons of this event be impressed upon the hearts of those who, like him, are engaged in the pursuits of science. May the men of genius, and the men of skill, and the men of high renown, feel that the fear of the Lord is the beginning of wisdom, and that science is then fulfilling its noblest mission when it is unfolding the glories of the Creator in the works of his hands, and revealing to his creatures that beneficent Providence which is over all and in all! And may they joyfully and gratefully come with their gifts and their triumphs, and lay them at the feet of Jesus of Nazareth, who is over all, God blessed forever!

May it please thee to preserve us all from the idolatry of the world and from the neglect of things eternal! So teach us to number our days that we may apply our hearts unto wisdom. Enable us to follow those who through faith and patience have inherited the promises; and receive us at length into thy heavenly kingdom.

These and all other mercies needful to us we humbly ask, in the name and for the sake of Jesus Christ, our Mediator. Amen.

At the close of the prayer the beautiful and appropriate "Solo" composed by Dr. Calcott was sung by Prof. T. Bishop, with striking effect, as follows:—

"Forgive, blest shade, the tributary tear
 That mourns thy exit from a world like this;
Forgive the wish that would have kept thee here
 And stay'd thy progress to the seat of bliss.

"No more confined to grovelling scenes of night,
 No more a tenant pent in mortal clay;
Now we would rather hail thy glorious flight,
 And trace thy journey to the realms of day."

The dirge, "Unveil thy bosom, faithful tomb," was then performed; and, after a benediction by Rev. Mr. Shields, the large congregation commenced to disperse.

The imposing public demonstration necessarily terminated with the dismissal of the military escort and the civic societies at the church, and the subsequent solemnities were in some degree of a private character. Yet the Joint Committee considered that their appointment included directions to assist in the concluding rites, and to represent those by whom they were appointed even in conveying the remains of the deceased to the family vault. Thither also went the pall-bearers and the Arctic companions of Dr. Kane, and numerous citizens; and there, with a befitting service by the reverend clergy, the body of Elisha Kent Kane was laid at rest, amid the manifestations of grief and respect which have distinguished the burial of few men of his years in any country.

In reference to the formation of the funeral cortège, the committee deem it proper to state that they did not feel it incumbent upon them to issue invitations to any particular society to attend and participate in the ceremonies; and their confidence in the proper feeling of their fellow-citizens was justified in the numerous notices of societies, public institutions, scientific, literary, and philanthropic associations, and other bodies, of their intention to join in the services, and an expression of desire to have a place assigned them in the procession. All were accepted; and, though some notices were received after the completion and publication of the programme, yet it is believed that a place was assigned to all those who desired admittance to the ranks.

Of the distinguished gentlemen invited to act as pall-bearers, all not prevented by absence or illness accepted; and the terms of acceptance— or, where the necessity of the case rendered acceptance impossible, the expression of regrets—were such as to give additional proof of the high estimation in which Dr. Kane was held, and of the conviction of duty to make public demonstration of that estimation.

Only two persons resident beyond the limits of Pennsylvania were invited to act as pall-bearers. Those were Henry Grinnell, Esq., of New York, and George Peabody, Esq., a citizen of the United States resident in London, but now in this country. Both these gentlemen were so intimately connected with the Arctic Expeditions of Dr. Kane as to associate their names inseparably with the history of those great enterprises. It was to be regretted that Mr. Peabody had, before the arrangements for the obsequies were made, left Washington for the

DR. ELISHA KENT KANE. 383

Southern part of the Union, and did not even receive the invitation to be present. Mr. Grinnell came from New York, and assisted in the funeral services of one whom he so highly valued.

As it rarely happens that such civic honors are paid to the memory of those who have not been distinguished by lofty political places or some remarkable achievement in war, it may not be improper to add that the whole manifestation of respect by the corporation and citizens of Philadelphia to the remains of Dr. Kane seems to be remarkable from its expression of public feeling, which presented itself in a form and with a universality that demanded an extraordinary demonstration, and to sanction all that the Joint Committee could devise and execute under existing circumstances; and, while this same feeling was evident, and its utterance more remarkable, at Havana, where Dr. Kane breathed his last,—at New Orleans, where his remains first touched the shores of our country,—and all through the long "funeral march" from the mouth of the Mississippi to the banks of the Delaware,—it was most certainly appropriate that here, in Philadelphia, illustrated by his achievements, here, where his science and humanity had added new dignity to the distinction of his native city, his memory should be honored by those who can appreciate the excellence which he manifested, and who, though they mourn the loss to science and philanthropy which his early death has caused, can comprehend the merits of one who accomplished the work of ages in what was a short life in all respects save its usefulness. No city in the Union has a richer treasury in the fame of its sons than Philadelphia. In literature, in science, in the arts, in the achievements of war, in the beautiful works of peace, in enlarged provision for the destitute, and in general philanthropy, the examples of Philadelphians are beautiful precedents of all that is great in plan and ennobling in execution; and on the roll of their civic fame she now records the name of Elisha Kent Kane, and the whole civilized world attests the correctness of the appreciation and does homage to the merits that secured the record. At home the influence of the good example of those who have preceded us has been always operative for good: henceforth there will be an additional incitement to enterprise and philanthropy in the noble daring and self-sacrificing philanthropy of Dr. Kane; and Philadelphians abroad will have a new distinction in their civic relations with one whose actions have cast so much lustre on generous enterprise, and so magnified the value of practical benevolence.

Nor can the committee omit to remark that the generous courage and the unfailing urbanity of Dr. Kane awakened, even in the hearts of the *uncivilized* with whom he came in contact, a sense of lofty regard for the possession and practice of those qualities; so that, wherever Providence allowed him to gratify his desire for research, he excited feelings and left impressions that will keep alive profound admiration for his talents and secure ineffaceable gratitude for his kindness.

While it is understood that the same feeling of civic pride animated all who shared in the solemnities of the occasion, it is considered an act of justice to express gratitude to the chief-marshal, who assisted the committee in the arrangement of the plan of the procession, and who so successfully carried out the whole arrangement; while thanks are also due to his aids and assistants, who secured the most perfect fulfilment of his and the committee's arrangement in the details submitted to their care.

The procession derived much of its solemnity from the striking display of military, who, under Brigadier-General George Cadwallader, assisted as escort. The commanding officer was prompt in complying with the wishes of the committee; and the whole arrangement was a beautiful and meritorious tribute of respect by the citizen-soldiery to the citizen of arms and arts and sciences and generous impulses.

The company of Washington Grays, in addition to the escort-duties, earned the gratitude of the committee and of the public by the gentlemanly delicacy with which they discharged the duties of guard of honor to the body as it lay in state in the Hall of Independence. Where all the citizens seemed concerned to have the demonstration such as would be expressive of the deepest grief at the loss deplored and the most profound respect for the memory of the honored dead, it would seem unnecessary to make especial reference to the particular classes who joined in the manifestation of the day; but it is deemed due to the proper spirit of our citizens to say that the great mercantile interests of the city were represented not only by those who were invited to take some special part in the proceedings, but by a great body of merchants from the Corn Exchange, who did honor to their pursuits by the spirit and liberality with which they seconded the efforts of the Committee, and the numbers by which they were represented in the procession. Dr. Kane was not, in any of his various professional relations, directly connected with the commercial calling; but he was a man of enterprise, of science, of generous daring on the seas; he was a philanthropist; he was a Philadelphian; and the Association of the Corn Exchange showed its power to appreciate the honor which the fame of the deceased threw upon all professional pursuits, and they deserve the special thanks of the

DR. ELISHA KENT KANE.

committee for manifesting their generous sympathies for one who, as a Philadelphian, has thrown lustre upon nautical enterprise and invested the name and character of man with new and more beautiful attributes.

Claiming special proprietorship in the fame of Dr. Kane, the citizens of Philadelphia must feel that such honors as were in New Orleans, in Louisville, Cincinnati, Columbus, Baltimore, and other places, bestowed upon the remains of our townsman, devolved upon them the duty at least of public acknowledgment; and, while they know how spontaneous were these tokens of respect, and how specially paid to and deserved by the dead, the committee feel it incumbent upon them to express, in the name of those whom they represent, a profound gratitude for the striking manner in which the generous enthusiasm of their fellow-citizens at a distance found expression.

In the simple report of the proceedings of a committee, even on an occasion of such general interest, it is not necessary to incorporate any studied eulogy of him who was the object of those honors for the arrangement of which the committee was appointed. Everywhere the merits of Dr. Kane are acknowledged; everywhere his fame is regarded as a part of the distinction of this age; and the inspiration of the poet, the power of the pen and the press, and the voice of the public speaker, have been exercised to give utterance to those sentiments of admiration which all feel, and to which all respond when thus uttered. But, had such been a duty devolved upon the committee, that duty could not have been more gratifyingly discharged than it was by the Rev. Mr. Shields; and, to supply the deficiency of their own expressions, the committee adopt the language of that divine, and have incorporated into their statement of the proceedings of the day that most interesting part which, in the grandeur of simplicity, gave utterance to a well-prepared eulogy, and which held up for admiration the strong characteristics of the eulogized, and displayed those characteristics so blended with the beautiful and the good as to exhibit " a combination and a form indeed that gave the world assurance of a man."

In the opinion of the committee, the proceedings which marked the whole progress of the remains of Dr. Kane, from his death-bed to the sepulchre, were themselves one of the most distinguished eulogies that a people has ever pronounced upon one who claimed no distinction as a leader of armies or as a director in statemanship; and the single record of the outburst of public feeling, and the demonstration of general regard that had place in this country and are still to be noticed, will be the proudest monument that can be raised to the lofty and the gentle qualities, the enterprise, the philanthropy, the science, and the friendship, of Elisha Kent Kane.

But the committee are reminded of a subject submitted to one part of their body by the public meeting by which the committee from the citizens was appointed, viz.: the collection of funds to erect a monument, at some appropriate place, to the memory of Dr. Kane,—not simply to do him honor, but rather to do our community the justice to show that it could appreciate the noble character of their townsman; and, while the nation may possibly boast of the merits of the honored dead, our own citizens may proudly point to the recorded proof that he was of their own number.

It is not the opinion of the committee that the corporation of the city should be asked to assist in the erection of the proposed monument. The sum that would be worthy of the giver in such a case would deprive citizens of the opportunity of expressing their admiration of the character of the honored dead, and make the monument itself an emblem of civic pride rather than a token of popular admiration. The monument, if erected, must be the exponent of general sentiment individually expressed. And the young aspirant for fame and honor must learn, from that column, that greatness is the result of noble enterprise and self-abnegation, and that the virtues which secure permanent distinction and unfading honor are those that appeal to the affections of the people, and that no monument is so honorable or so enduring as that which records the triumphs of science by the aid of benevolence.

It is a part of the instructions of the solemnities and public proceedings which are here noticed, and the part most useful to the young and gratifying to all, that public sentiment in our country is most healthful, and that people of all pursuits and conditions can appreciate the merit that rests on the achievements of peace and the sacrifices to duty; and that the pomp and circumstance of war, or the distinction of lofty political station, appealing as they do to the patriotic pride of the people, are not the only claims to public applause. The young, by such demonstrations as have been made to the memory of Dr. Kane, see that there is a substantial worth in virtue and generous enterprise, and that the avenues to great distinction and to general gratitude are open to the man who can divest himself of calculations of selfish gain, and exercise the noblest sympathies of his nature in acts of public benefit, which call for the sacrifice of personal ease and safety to the comfort and convenience of others. And it is as much upon the character of the generous self-sacrificing philanthropy as upon that of a daring and *successful* contributor to science, that Dr. Kane has built his lofty reputation.

It is no inconsiderable portion of the great fame of Dr. Kane, that he had achieved the position which he must ever occupy in history, at an age when, in general, men are but undergoing the discipline which prepares them for the enterprise and endurance necessary to great success. And though he undoubtedly fell a sacrifice to his generous enterprise, and to his noble efforts to mitigate for others the consequences of perils and deprivations to which he and his companions were necessarily exposed, and suffered immensely from the voluntary assumption to himself of burdens that might have appropriately been left to others, yet it is not found that such manifest consequences led him to regret the sacrifice. On the contrary, his history exhibits not a single page of selfish thought or action, from the moment he entered upon the career which has given him the praise, sympathy, and gratitude of a world, to the hour when, afar from home, yet amidst cherished relatives and friends, he calmly yielded up all earthly ties, with a Christian's confidence and submission to his Creator's will. It is perfectly manifest that in all his undertakings, his privations and perils, and their obvious effect upon his system, he acted upon the ennobling sentiment that "the duties of life are greater than life."

The publishers would express their obligation to the Hon. Joseph R. Chandler for his admirable taste and skill in the preparation of the foregoing account of the obsequies of Dr. Kane. The various addresses, discourses, &c, have since been carefully revised and corrected by their authors.

CHILDS & PETERSON.

EULOGY

ON

DR. ELISHA KENT KANE,

PRONOUNCED BY

BRO. E. W. ANDREWS,

BEFORE THE GRAND LODGE OF THE ANCIENT AND HONORABLE FRATERNITY OF
FREE AND ACCEPTED MASONS IN THE STATE OF NEW YORK,

JUNE 5, 1857;

TOGETHER WITH THE

Opening Address

BY THE M. W. GRAND MASTER,

AND LETTERS RECEIVED ON THE OCCASION FROM

EDWARD EVERETT, WASHINGTON IRVING, GENERAL WOOL, JUDGE KANE,
COMMODORES PERRY, STEWART, AND READ,

AND MANY OTHER DISTINGUISHED GENTLEMEN IN VARIOUS PARTS
OF THE UNION.

OFFICE OF THE GRAND SECRETARY OF THE GRAND LODGE
OF FREE AND ACCEPTED MASONS OF THE STATE OF NEW YORK.
NEW YORK, June 22, 1857.

DEAR SIR AND BROTHER:—At the Annual Communication of the M.W. Grand Lodge of the State of New York, held in this city on the 6th of June, A.L. 5857, the following resolution was adopted:—

"Whereas, the members of the M.W. Grand Lodge of the State of New York, in Annual Communication assembled, having listened to the eulogy, pronounced on the evening of the 5th instant, to the memory of our distinguished and beloved brother Dr. E. K. Kane, do desire to express to our worthy and esteemed brother E. W. Andrews their high pleasure and satisfaction with the ability and fidelity with which he has discharged the duty imposed upon him: therefore,

"*Resolved*, That our brother E. W. Andrews be requested to place his manuscript in the hands of our R.W. Deputy Grand Master and R.W. Grand Secretary, to be published under their supervision, for distribution among the members of the Grand Lodge."

To enable us to carry out the wishes of the Grand Lodge, will you be kind enough to furnish us with a copy of said eulogy?

Very truly and fraternally, yours,

JAMES M. AUSTIN,
To Hon. E. W. ANDREWS.   *Grand Secretary.*

NEW YORK, June 24, 1857.

R.W. JAMES M. AUSTIN, *Grand Secretary*.

DEAR SIR AND BROTHER:—Your letter of the 22d instant, enclosing a copy of the resolution adopted by the New York Grand Lodge on the 6th of June last, was duly received, and is gratefully acknowledged.

In accordance with the wish embodied in the resolution, I herewith send you my manuscript and place it at your disposal.

Truly and fraternally, yours,

E. W. ANDREWS.

INTRODUCTION.

WHEN the painful intelligence of the death of Dr. Kane was received in the United States, the brethren of Arcana Lodge, in the city of New York, immediately adopted measures to pay suitable public honors to the memory of the illustrious deceased, as a worthy brother of the Fraternity of Free and Accepted Masons and an honorary member of that Lodge, by adopting the following preamble and resolutions :—

Whereas, In the removal of Bro. Kane from our midst we recognise a dispensation of the Great Architect of the Universe, to which we bow in humble submission, while as mortal beings we mourn the loss to mankind of so much worth beyond that with which Supreme Wisdom has endowed a large majority of His earthly intelligences; and

Whereas, In his decease we are sensible of the loss of a true and valued Brother; viewing it as an event of no ordinary sorrow, not to us alone as a Fraternity, but to the country in whose service his life has been sacrificed, after a short but brilliant career, to place a new and beautiful chaplet on her brow, and to the world, of which he was one of the brightest ornaments in science, bravery, and worth, having inscribed his name on the great scroll of time, to be read and respected by future generations; and

Whereas, His devotion to the Fraternity and to humanity was so nobly exhibited in his untiring efforts to rescue a lost brother, in the person of Sir John Franklin, and in planting, with the American flag, Masonic emblems to arrest the attention of travellers and voyagers in the desolate region of eternal ice: Therefore,

Resolved, That a Lodge of Sorrow be holden, at such time and place as may be hereafter designated, in honor of our cherished and lamented brother, Dr. Elisha K. Kane.

Upon subsequent consultation, however, with the officers of the Grand Lodge of the State, it was adjudged proper that this body, at its Annual Communication, to be held in June, should take the lead in giving expression to the profound grief of the brotherhood at the early death of one of its most distinguished members, and their respect and affection for his memory; and the following-named brethren were appointed a

COMMITTEE OF ARRANGEMENTS.

R. W. ROBT. MACOY, W. CHAS. S. WESTCOTT,
" JAMES M. AUSTIN, " THOMAS S. SOMMERS,
" CHAS. L. CHURCH, " THOMAS E. GARSON,
" JOHN W. SIMONS, " NEHEMIAH PECK,
W. WM. GURNEY, " ARTHUR BOYCE,
" CHAS. A. PECK, " GEO. C. WEBSTER,
" A. P. MORIARTY, " J. B. Y. SOMMERS,
" HENRY W. TURNER, " ANDRES CASSARD,
" CHAS. F. NEWTON, " JAMES B. TAYLOR,
Bro. SIDNEY KOPMAN.

The evening of the 5th of June was designated as the time when some appropriate public demonstration should be made, and the church of the Rev. Dr. Chapin, on Broadway, was selected as the place. Bro. E. W. Andrews, of New York, was invited to pronounce the eulogy on the occasion, which invitation he accepted. The music was placed under the direction of Bro. James B. Taylor; and other arrangements were made which the dignity and solemnity of the occasion demanded. When the appointed evening arrived, a large and most respectable audience assembled : the church was draped in mourning ; a fine bust of Dr. Kane was placed prominently in front of the pulpit, resting on a pedestal draped with the tattered flag of the two Arctic Expeditions, and in the rear of it was hung a beautiful banner, emblazoned with symbols of Free Masonry. The music, both vocal and instrumental, was in harmony with the mournfulness of the scene, and deepened the solemn impression it produced. The officers and members of the Grand Lodge appeared in full regalia and wearing badges of mourning. As in sad procession they entered the centre-aisle of the spacious church, and with slow and measured step passed up beneath its lofty arches toward the sacred altar, while the deep-toned organ pealed forth its solemn notes, and the voices of the choir, in the mournful dirge, seemed the breathings of bereaved hearts, the scene was deeply impressive. Every heart seemed touched with the spirit of sadness. When the music ceased, amidst the profound stillness that prevailed through the large and thoughtful assembly, the Grand Chaplain, R. W. and Rev. R. L. Schoonmaker, arose, and in a most fervent and touching prayer addressed the Throne of Grace. The following

ODE,

WRITTEN BY BRO. JAMES HERRING, WAS THEN
SUNG BY MRS. SPROSTON, MISS GEER, AND MESSRS. TAYLOR AND WILLIAMS.

> Here let the sacred rites decreed
> In honor of departed friends
> With solemn order now proceed,
> While living *faith* with sorrow blends.
>
> Now let the hymn, the humble prayer,
> From hearts sincere ascend on high,
> And mystic *evergreen* declare
> The *hope* within us cannot die.
>
> The mortal frame may be conceal'd
> Within the narrow house of gloom,
> But GOD in mercy has reveal'd
> Immortal life beyond the tomb.
>
> The friends we mourn we still may *love:*
> Then let our aspirations rise
> To that bright spirit-world above
> Where virtue lives, *love never dies.*

The M. W. Grand Master, John L. Lewis, Jr., then briefly addressed the audience upon the melancholy nature of the occasion which had brought them together.

ADDRESS.

BRETHREN OF THE MASONIC FRATERNITY,
 LADIES AND GENTLEMEN :—

A few hours since I was first informed, by reading the printed programme, that it was announced that I was to take an active part in the exercises of this evening. My Masonic brethren need not be told that my engagements elsewhere, till within the last hour, have prevented me from making any preparation, or reflecting upon the subject-matter of what I should here speak. But this consideration did not—could not—restrain me from being present and contributing my humble aid in this public testimonial to the services and worth of him who is wrapped in the silent slumber that knows no waking, in a distant city. I might indeed catch inspiration from the scene presented before and around me. This large and attentive assemblage, intent on doing homage to departed genius, the fervid and thrilling petition to the Throne of Grace, just offered, the rich harmony pealing from yonder skilled choir, all awaken deep emotions; but I will not attempt to give them utterance.

My simple duty will best be discharged by a brief allusion to the reasons that have brought us together.

This respectable and intelligent auditory scarcely require to be reminded of the cause of this assemblage. These emblems of Masonry, these drooping flags, these mute yet speaking evidences of sorrow, remind us that we are in the house of mourning. The Grand Lodge of the State of New York, now assembled in Annual Communication, have resolved to set apart a portion of their time to do public honor to the name and memory of Dr. Elisha K. Kane, as not only indicative of their own feelings, but as due to his character. And why should we thus honor his name and memory? He was not a citizen of our State, nor a regular member of any Lodge under this jurisdiction; and we have apparently only the feelings of sorrow entertained in common by the entire Craft, that a distinguished and beloved brother of our world-wide Fraternity has passed away. It would be sufficient to base our action alone upon this. While we claim that a connection with the Masonic Fraternity reflects credit upon each individual member, it frequently occurs that the character of its distinguished votaries also reflects a brighter renown upon our institution. Their fame becomes our fame; their honor is our honor, their renown our renown; and in this instance we feel that the achievements of Kane have shed a halo of glory around the Masonic brotherhood "bright as the mystic aurora of the clime he braved." The distinguished and eloquent brother from whose glowing lips we are to hear a truthful eulogy upon the life and character of Dr. Kane will tell how he loved our institution; how its lessons cheered the rigor and gloom of Polar night; and how, erecting his country's standard as at once a shield and a signal, he spread to the blast beneath it a flag bearing the peculiar devices of the Craft, that it might perchance catch the eye of some wanderer in that frozen clime and urge him by its mute appeal to more vigorous exertions to cheer and save. It is proper that I should remind you (as I have once already done at the opening of the Annual Communication) that the Grand Lodge of New York thus publicly pays tribute to his merits and genius because he was an honorary member of one of the Lodges under its jurisdiction, (Arcana Lodge,) and because his last spoken farewell, previous to his departure upon his latest perilous expedition, was to this Grand Lodge, assembled in special communication to exchange parting salutations and to cheer him onward in his hazardous enterprise of seeking for an eminent lost brother in the regions of perpetual wintry desolation.

DR. ELISHA KENT KANE.

It is as much the province of our ancient Fraternity to gather around the open grave and silent tomb of a brother as it is to meet upon festal or ceremonial occasions, where mutual smiles and innocent festivity denote the joyousness of the heart. We gather in our Lodges of Sorrow when the loved and honored have departed and sit in the chambers of death, to give expression to the emotions which stir our souls; and ours is the mournful duty of strewing the grave of a brother with the weeping acacia, as a token that, while we witness the mortality of the body, we also believe in the immortality of the soul, and lingering around the little mound of earth which crowns his last resting-place, while we speak of his virtues and our own bereavement. Ours is the mournful task of weaving chaplets for the sepulchre as well as garlands for the living brow, and of planting the shady cypress in the cemetery of the silent dead. We have thus met, as in a Lodge of Sorrow, to-night; and, while our spirits kindle at the recollection of what our distinguished brother has done for the cause of our common humanity and for the fresh honors he has shed upon our gallant navy, we mourn at the remembrance that he has passed away from earth forever, but yet in the fulness of his fame and the brightness of his early renown.

We do not mourn alone. Listen to what his former distinguished and gallant commander, Commodore Perry, that brave and renowned veteran, Commodore Stewart, the enlightened Maury, and others of high meritorious character, say of their lamented brother-officer. Nor alone does the voice of sorrow come up from the surges of the sounding sea. The gallant soldiery of the country delight to honor skill and daring, whether by sea or land. Hear the language of the distinguished and renowned second in command of the United States army, Major-General Wool. Hear also the voices of our statesmen and men of literature,—the accomplished Everett, Irving, Willis, Halleck, Lester, and a host of other celebrities, from the pulpit, the bar, and the mystic circle.

The Grand Master then read a number of letters which had been received in response to the following invitation :—

OFFICE OF THE GRAND LODGE OF
FREE AND ACCEPTED MASONS OF THE STATE OF NEW YORK,
NEW YORK, June 1, 1857.

DEAR SIR :—The fraternity of Free and Accepted Masons of the State of New York, desirous of testifying their high appreciation of the lamented and distinguished brother Dr. Elisha Kent Kane, have made arrangements for appropriate public honors to his memory. The ceremonies to take place on Friday evening, June 5, at the church of the Rev. Dr. E. H. Chapin, in Broadway, at half-past seven o'clock.

Eulogium by the Hon. Bro. E. W. Andrews, and other appropriate exercises. You are respectfully invited to attend and join in this tribute of respect to the memory of the departed.

CHAS. A. PECK,
ROBT. MACOY, } <i>Committee on Invitation.</i>
SIDNEY KOPMAN,

LETTERS.

(*From* CHARLES STEWART, *Senior Commodore, United States Navy.*)

PHILADELPHIA NAVY-YARD, June 3, 1857.

GENTLEMEN :—I have the honor to receive your kind invitation of the 1st instant, in behalf of the Honorable the Free and Accepted Masons of the State of New York, to attend in the contemplated public honors to the memory of the lamented and distinguished brother Dr. Elisha K. Kane.

Could I have been spared from the duties of this post, without public inconvenience, on the 5th instant, it would have afforded me the most grateful feelings to have united with our brethren of the State of New York by my attendance on the occasion of their tribute of respect to the memory of one so honorably distinguished and self-sacrificed for the benefit of the human family.

Accept, gentlemen, with the assurance of my regret, from inability on this occasion, to comply with your interesting wishes, that I have the honor to remain,

Most respectfully,
Your affectionate brother,

To Brothers   CHARLES STEWART.
   CHAS. A. PECK,
   ROBERT MACOY, } *Committee on Invitation.*
   SIDNEY KOPMAN,

(*From* COMMODORE PERRY, *United States Navy.*)

38 WEST THIRTY-SECOND STREET, NEW YORK, June 3, 1857.

GENTLEMEN :—I regret exceedingly that a protracted illness, which has confined me to my house for several weeks, will deprive me of the gratification of joining you in doing honor to the memory of our departed brother, "the lamented and distinguished" Dr. E. K. Kane.

Be assured, gentlemen, of my warmest sympathies being with you on the occasion of your melancholy ceremonies.

Most respectfully,
Your obedient servant,
M. C. PERRY.

(*From* COMMODORE READ, *United States Navy.*)

PHILADELPHIA, June 3, 1857.

GENTLEMEN :—I have the honor to acknowledge the polite invitation received from you to-day to attend and join in a ceremony the object of which is to bestow appropriate honors on the memory of the lamented Dr. Elisha K. Kane.

Allow me to say that I feel highly flattered by this mark of attention, and that I would with much pleasure attend and join in the tribute of respect to the memory of an old shipmate, were it not at present out of my power to do so.

I am, very respectfully,
Your obedient servant,
GEORGE READ.

(*From* LIEUTENANT MAURY, *United States Navy.*)

OBSERVATORY, WASHINGTON, June 3, 1857.

GENTLEMEN:—It will not, I regret to say, be in my power to participate with you in the melancholy satisfaction of rendering homage to the merits of our illustrious fellow-countryman, the late Dr. Kane.

Did not occupations and engagements which I am not at liberty to set aside prevent, I would surely be with you on Friday evening.

Respectfully, &c.,
M. F. MAURY.

(*From* MAJOR-GENERAL JOHN E. WOOL, *United States Army.*)

HEAD-QUARTERS, DEPARTMENT OF THE EAST,
TROY, N.Y., June 3, 1857.

GENTLEMEN:—I had the honor to receive your invitation of the 1st instant to join in the ceremonies intended as a testimony of the high appreciation entertained by the Free and Accepted Masons of the State of New York for their lamented and distinguished brother, Dr. Elisha K. Kane, to take place on Friday evening, June 5.

I deeply regret that my official duties will not permit me to avail myself of the opportunity of doing honor to the memory of your brother, who was no less distinguished than he rendered great and important services to his country.

I am, very respectfully,
Your obedient servant,
JOHN E. WOOL, *U. S. Army.*

(*From* HON. JUDGE KANE, P. M., *father of* DR. KANE.)

PHILADELPHIA, 6th June, 1857.

GENTLEMEN:—My absence from home when your note of invitation arrived prevented my receiving it till this morning; but I cannot omit to thank you for it, and to say how deeply I have been moved by the justly fraternal feeling which it represents. I believe I can speak of Dr. Kane as he was, for I knew him in the relations that determine the judgment as well as in those that affect the heart. I cannot suspect myself of a father's partiality when I say that our order never had a brighter representative,—that there was never a better son or brother, a truer friend, a purer man, or a more expanded and self-sacrificing philanthropist.

That his memory is honored by those who can emulate his virtues, and by that brotherhood especially which adopts them as its symbols, gives assurance that he did not live or die in vain. With grateful respect,

I am, gentlemen,
Your obedient servant,
J. K. KANE.

(*From* C. EDWARDS LESTER, ESQ.)

SPENCERTOWN, COLUMBIA COUNTY, NEW YORK, June 4, 1857.

GENTLEMEN AND BROTHERS :—I thank you for remembering me in connection with the honors you are to show to the memory and achievements of our beloved and heroic brother, Dr. Kane. I shall be with you if I can.

No more befitting or touching occasion could occur to call out our friendship or our grief. Thousands knew him as a *friend:* the uncounted hosts of the Masonic Fraternity knew him as a *brother*. His contributions to science laid the whole world under obligation ; his writings embellish literature ; while his whole life is radiant with the divine spirit of humanity. We should feel a new glow of gratitude and pleasure as we commemorate his virtues. He was a cherished member of a brotherhood on which the sun and the stars never go down ; and from the genial air of our lodge-rooms and firesides he carried our banner of peace to the frozen children of the Pole. Such are the men who have transmitted the torch of light from age to age.

Most faithfully, yours,
C. EDWARDS LESTER.

(*From* HON. EDWARD EVERETT, *Mass.*)

MEDFORD, MASS., June 4, 1857.

GENTLEMEN :—Your letter of the 1st has been forwarded to me at this place, inviting me to attend the commemoration-ceremonies in honor of the late lamented Dr. Kane, on the evening of the 5th, under the auspices of the " Free and Accepted Masons of the State of New York." I much regret that it is not in my power to be present on the interesting occasion.

I remain, gentlemen, with great respect,
Your obedient servant,
EDWARD EVERETT.

(*From* WASHINGTON IRVING, ESQ.)

SUNNYSIDE, June 5, 1857.

GENTLEMEN :—Your obliging invitation did not reach me until last evening. I regret to say that engagements which detain me in the country will prevent my attendance at the interesting ceremonies with which you propose to testify your high appreciation of the merits of our illustrious and lamented countryman.

Very respectfully,
Your obliged and humble servant,
WASHINGTON IRVING.

DR. ELISHA KENT KANE. 399

(*From* FITZ-GREENE HALLECK, ESQ.)

GUILFORD, CONNECTICUT, July 18, 1857.

GENTLEMEN :—I deeply regret that your letter, inviting me to be present on the 5th June ultimo, at the ceremonies, under your auspices, in remembrance of the late Dr. Kane, did not reach me in time to enable me to avail myself of its courtesy and to unite with you in doing public homage to the memory of a good and gallant brother of the brotherhood you represent, whose life was an honor to that Brotherhood and to humanity, and whose heroism of head and heart and hand was worthy of all homage.

With grateful acknowledgment of the compliment your invitation paid me, I am, gentlemen,

Your obedient servant,
FITZ-GREENE HALLECK.

(*From* JOSEPH D. EVANS, P. G. M.)

NEW YORK, June 5, 1857.

BRETHREN :—I have the honor of receiving your kind invitation to attend and join in the tribute of respect proposed to be paid to our lamented and distinguished brother, Dr. E. K. Kane, by the Masonic Fraternity of this State.

Although I find it impossible to be present this evening to participate in the ceremonies of the occasion, I nevertheless fully sympathize with you and the brotherhood generally in our irreparable loss.

Dr. Kane not only stood high in the estimation of his countrymen and with the world at large, but, by the noble traits of his social and moral character, won the affection and respect of his Masonic brethren.

It is due to his memory that the Fraternity generally should do honor to so estimable a gentleman and so true and warm-hearted a Mason.

With the highest respect, I remain, dear brethren,
Yours, truly and fraternally,
JOSEPH D. EVANS.

(*From* R. L. SCHOONMAKER, *Grand Chaplain.*)

GRAND LODGE ROOM, NEW YORK, June 4, 1857.

WORSHIPFUL BROTHERS :—I have received your kind communication of yesterday, inviting me to be present and officiate on the occasion of the funeral obsequies to be observed in memory of our beloved and deceased brother, Dr. E. K. Kane, in the church of the Rev. Dr. Chapin, of this city. It will afford me high satisfaction to be present with you on that occasion, so deeply interesting to us as American citizens, but especially as members of the great Masonic Fraternity. It is well thus to do honor to the memory of one who has so deservedly gained the respect and admiration of the world for his distinguished scientific attainments, for his indomitable energy and perseverance in the prosecution of those high purposes upon which his heart was fixed, for his sterling and excellent qualities as a man, and his warm devotion to the best interests of our beloved and cherished institution.

May it be our aim to emulate him in all those respects, and with him at last end our weary pilgrimage here on earth in a triumphant faith in God!

Truly and fraternally, yours,
R. L. SCHOONMAKER,
Grand Chaplain.

(*From* JOHN D. WILLARD, P. G. M.)

NEW YORK, June 4, 1857.

GENTLEMEN:—Should it be possible for me to remain in town, it will afford me very great satisfaction to accept the invitation with which I have been honored, and join in the Masonic tribute of respect to the memory of our departed brother, Dr. Elisha K. Kane.

There are few men of our age who, in my estimation, are so worthy of every public and every Masonic honor. His whole life was an exemplification of the beautiful tenets of our noble institution. The principles of our Order took deep root in his heart; they were entwined in all his affections, and they brought forth fruit in all his acts. How remarkably is this exhibited, to the eye of a Mason, in his last great contribution to the literature of our country,—his touching narrative of the Expedition that he commanded! How often, by little remarks and by the narration of little incidents, does he show his attachment to Free Masonry! How ready was he to peril life in the discharge of duty and *for the relief of a brother!* And how proud was he to bear the "Masonic Banner," beside the stars and stripes of our glorious Union, to the unknown regions of the North, and plant it, amid eternal ice and snows, where the footsteps of civilized man had never before trod!

But I am saying more than I intended. I meant simply to express this sentiment, which we all feel in our hearts:—that the rendering of these public Masonic honors is alike due to ourselves and to the memory of the illustrious dead.

Very respectfully and fraternally, yours,
JOHN D. WILLARD.

(*From* ROB MORRIS, *Kentucky.*)

LODGETON, KENTUCKY, June 5, 1857.

SIRS AND BROTHERS:—It is with profound regret that I have to express to you my inability to accept your kind invitation of the 1st instant. To join in a tribute of respect to one whose character I have so much admired as Dr. Kane's were a duty I should make any reasonable sacrifice to perform,—how much more to unite with so distinguished a body of the Masonic Fraternity as the Grand Lodge of New York; but other engagements render it impossible.

Allow me to say to you, gentlemen of the Committee, and through you to the illustrious body you represent, that we Western and Southern Masons have followed the body of Brother Elisha K. Kane from New Orleans, where it was landed, to the point which separates the Eastern from the Western States. At every landing on the great rivers, at every railway-station on our iron roads, crowds of loving Masons have gathered around that body, weeping that one so young should have thus passed beyond us, triumphing that his departure was not too soon for his own glory. Thus we claim that, though we cannot be with you in person, we will not be absent in admiration and respect.

For myself, my admiration for the intrepid navigator has made his history a familiar theme in my household. My children were taught to follow him upon his dangerous track, and they rejoiced with him upon his glorious return. As far back as 1853, I ventured to express that admiration publicly in these poor words. The prophecy truly has failed; but the sentiment is eternal. "Sir John Franklin, whose protracted absence upon an expedition to the northern coasts of America has aroused the solicitude of the world, is a Free Mason. Dr. E. K. Kane, the young and enthusiastic traveller, whose recent departure in search of Franklin has been chronicled throughout the land, is bound in the same holy communion, and in token thereof bears our symbol of the square and compass *upon his foresail.* What a meeting will it be, when, amidst Arctic night and desolation, these two Masons shall come together and grasp the brotherly hand!"

"Midst Polar snows and solitude,
   Eight weary years the voyager lies
Ice-bound upon the frozen flood,
   Till expectation vanishes.
Ah! many a hopeful tear is shed
For him thus number'd with the dead.

"Midst joys of home and well-earn'd fame,
   Young, healthful, honor'd, there is one
Who pines to win a nobler name,
   And feels his glory but begun:
His heart is with the voyager lost
Midst Polar solitude and frost.

"Is there some chain of sympathy
   Flung thus across the frozen seas?
Is there some strange, mysterious tie
   That joins these daring men? There is!
This, honor'd, healthful, free from want,
Is bound to *that* in covenant!

"For though these twain have never met,
   To press the hand or join the heart,
In unison their spirits beat,
   Brothers in the Masonic art!
One in the hour of joy and peace,
One in the hour of deep distress.

"The voice from off the frozen flood
   Appeals in trumpet-tones for aid :
'Tis heard, 'tis answer'd : swift abroad
   The flag is flung, the sail is spread,—
That flag, that sail, on which we see
The emblems of Free Masonry.

"Away on glorious errand now,
   Thou hero of a sense of right!
Success be on thy gallant prow,
   Thou greater than the sons of might!
Thy flag the banner of the Free,
Oh, may it lead to victory!

" And by that symbol, best of those
   Time-honor'd on our ancient wall,—
And by the prayer that ceaseless flows
   Upward from every mystic hall,—
And by thine own stout heart and hand
Known, mark'd, and loved in every land,—

" *Thou shalt succeed :* his drooping eye
   Shall catch thy banner broad and bright;
Those symbols he shall yet descry
   And know a *brother* in the sight.
Ah! noble pair, who happier then
Of those two daring, dauntless men?"

                 Very fraternally, yours,
                           ROB MORRIS.

(*From* N. P. WILLIS.)

                                IDLEWILD, June 4, 1857.

GENTLEMEN :—I received your polite and honoring invitation to-day, and am exceedingly sorry that it is out of my power to accept it. The ceremony is one which everyway interests my respect and sympathies ; and I rejoice in witnessing the tribute to such a man, paid by so estimable and honorable a society.

With thanks for the compliment to myself expressed in your valued invitation, I remain, gentlemen,

                 Yours, with highest respect,
                           N. P. WILLIS.

A HYMN,

WRITTEN BY BRO. GEO. P. MORRIS, WAS THEN SUNG
BY MRS. SPROSTON, MISS GEER, AND MESSRS. TAYLOR AND WILLIAMS.

"Man dieth and wasteth away,
   And where is he?" Hark! from the skies
I hear a voice answer and say,
   "The spirit of man never dies:
His body, which came from the earth,
   Must mingle again with the sod;
But his soul, which in heaven had birth,
   Returns to the bosom of God."

The sky will be burnt as a scroll,
   The earth, wrapt in flames, will expire;
But, freed from all shackles, the soul
   Will rise in the midst of the fire.
Then, brothers, mourn not for the dead,
   Who rest from their labors, forgiven:
Learn this, from your Bible, instead:—
   The grave is the gateway to heaven.

O Lord God Almighty! to thee
   We turn as our solace above;
The waters may fail from the sea,
   But not from thy fountains of love.
Oh, teach us thy will to obey,
   And sing, with one heart and accord,
"The Lord gives; the Lord takes away;
   And praised be the name of the Lord!"

The M. W. Grand Master then introduced the distinguished orator, Hon. Brother E. W. Andrews, who proceeded, for more than an hour, to delineate the life and portray the character of our lamented Brother Kane,—the audience testifying their deep interest in the theme by the most undivided and rapt attention, only broken by an occasional murmur of suppressed applause at the impassioned eloquence of the speaker.

At the close of the eulogy the benediction was pronounced by the Grand Chaplain, Rt. W. and Rev. John Gray, and the audience dispersed as the rich, full harmony of the Governmental Band resounded through the arches above in a sad requiem to the memory of Kane.

EULOGY.

BY HON. BROTHER E. W. ANDREWS.

Most Worshipful Grand Master, Brethren of the Grand Lodge, and of our Ancient and Honorable Fraternity generally.

LADIES AND GENTLEMEN :—We are assembled within these sacred walls to-night to render our humble tribute of affection and honor to the memory of our lamented brother, Dr. Kane. Rarely has a death occurred which has touched with so deep and universal a sorrow the heart of man. Cut down in the morning of his active life, and in the midst of a career which had already given him place among the most beloved and honored of men, and which was rich, almost beyond parallel, in its promise for the future, his untimely fall has called forth the strongest and tenderest expressions of grief throughout the civilized world.

Science mourns the loss of one of her most earnest and successful votaries; Philanthropy weeps the death of one who was ever eager to obey her heavenly behests; and Religion, sad at the necessary sacrifice of such a life, but joyful at the signal triumph of her own divine power in his peaceful death, stands by his tomb pointing to the skies.

And, brethren, *our own venerable Order*, whose mystic tie spans the earth, binding in sweet and sacred unison thousands of hearts in every clime,—*our own venerable Order*, ever the true friend and ally of Science, Philanthropy, and Religion,—everywhere bow their heads in grief, lamenting the early fall of a brother whose life, already illustrious by its beautiful harmony with our pure and exalted principles, promised to give them in the future even a brighter illustration, a more commanding power.

Under this impulse of grief, we meet in "a Lodge of Sorrow" to-night. We meet to spend this hour in the calm though mournful contemplation of a history crowded during its brief continuance with the most interesting events, marked by the noblest deeds, adorned by the purest virtues. We meet not to praise the dead: our praise could add not the faintest ray to the brightness that encircles his memory; we meet rather to study a life which we may safely imitate,—a character formed to give higher elevation and dignity to our nature,—a death that may teach us how to die.

*   *   *   *   *   *

[For want of space, a portion of this beautiful eulogy is necessarily omitted: the extracts which are here given will, we fear, scarcely do justice to the distinguished orator.—*Publishers.*]

A few days before the sailing of the Expedition, the fact was announced to Arcana Lodge, of this city, that Dr. Kane was a member of the Masonic Fraternity. This announcement produced a deep sensation among the members, and resolutions expressive of their high admiration of his character, and their profound sympathy with his generous self-sacrificing plans and labors for the rescue of a lost brother, were unanimously adopted and transmitted to him in Philadelphia. He returned the following reply:—

PHILADELPHIA, May 12, 1853.
DEAR SIR AND BROTHER :—I have received your eloquent letter enclosing the resolutions of the Free and Accepted Masons of Arcana Lodge. These resolutions, expressive of the sympathy of our brethren with the object of the expedition under my command, are to me especially pleasing. I shall communicate them formally to the officers and men, as an indication of valued sympathy at home, and a useful stimulus in the search after our lost brother, Sir John Franklin.
I have the honor to be,
Faithfully, your friend and brother,
E. K. KANE.
To SIDNEY KOPMAN, Sec'y Arcana Lodge.

On the evening of the 30th of May, 1853, being the night previous to his sailing, the members of the Grand Lodge of New York, and a large number of the personal friends of Dr. Kane, assembled in this city to testify their high appreciation of his character, and to express their deep sympathy with his heroic purpose of Christian philanthropy in again venturing forth amidst the perils of an Arctic voyage. Judge Kane, the father of Dr. Kane, Henry Grinnell, and other distinguished gentlemen, were present. Dr. Kane was seated, during the evening, by the side of the M. W. Grand Master; Masonic exercises of an appropriate and interesting character were performed. Among these was an address to Dr. Kane by the Deputy Grand Master, embodying, in the most eloquent and touching language, the sentiments which the body entertained toward their distinguished guest. To this address Dr. Kane replied in the following appropriate and beautiful terms :—

"In behalf of myself and my associates in the American Arctic Expedition, I thank you, sir, most cordially, for the tone and language of your very appropriate and feeling address, and the pleasure I have experienced in hearing it. With regard to your remarks directly associated with my name, I should be embarrassed could I not refuse to believe them addressed to me in any other capacity than that of the representative of a cause which perhaps may claim to associate Christian charity with American enterprise,—the attempt to save a gallant officer and his fellows from a dreadful death, without inquiring whether he or they and ourselves are citizens of the same or of another race, or clime, or nation. Worshipful, I have heard upon this floor to-night our party characterized as a Masonic expedition. And is it not this? And is its work not substantial Masonry? Are you, sir, or you, brothers, here, that are gathered around me, are we blindly attached to this or that ritual of this or that form or order of the Masonic institution? Say, is it not rather that we see reflected in Free Masonry the cause of free brotherhood throughout the world, and that our signs and our symbols, our tokens, legends, and pass-words, are only honorable in our eyes, and honored because they are a language in which affection can securely speak to sympathy, and humanity safely join hands with honor?

"Brethren, we are called in our day, perhaps, to make Masonry what it should be,—not a sectarian society, to garb, or rank, or enroll men, to separate them from their fellows, but a bond to unite the good and true in a common union for the common defence and welfare of all who are good and true men. Our brother Franklin, he was one who ruled his conduct by the compass and the square, and the accents of woe never for him fell on an unpitying ear. It may be he cannot hear your voice to-night, calling to him, 'Brother, be of good cheer.' But there are others living—other Franklins yet to live and to be born—whom your example and your sympathy will help to encourage and excite to emulate his example when they too peril their lives for the advantage and advancement of their species. These will not fall unnoticed; they shall not shrink while a brother's outstretched hand can save them. The Mason, the true man,—wherever is the Grand Lodge that the Most Worshipful has built up for our habitation, wherever is it that the cry of affliction is heard,—hastens to the rescue of the widow's son."

Such are the sentiments that reflect, in true colors, the character of Dr. Kane as a man, a Mason, a Christian!

At the close of this address, a delegation from the Grand Lodge of New Jersey was presented to Dr. Kane, who communicated to him resolutions which had been adopted by that body, expressing its warmest sympathies with the holy enterprise in which he was engaged, and giving to him, "*as a Mason*, on a worthy brother Mason's errand, and to his officers and men, an affectionate God-speed on their voyage." To this communication Dr. Kane made a brief but thrilling reply, and the meeting soon after adjourned. The whole scene was one of deep and tender interest,—one the impression of which can never fade from the hearts of those who had the privilege to witness it. As the brethren gathered around the departing hero to give him the farewell hand, many a manly breast heaved with deep emotion, and many a manly cheek was wet with the tears of brotherly affection. All felt that it was, *in truth*, the hand of a *brother* they grasped,—of a true man,—a faithful Mason,—a member of a family whose children are bound together "by a mystic cord, whose every thread is woven in the loom of Love."

The next morning he sailed. His departure was an event which, as you well know, excited a deep interest through the nation. From thousands of family altars and ten thousand silent hearts there went up that morning intense aspirations to the God of the sea and the land, invoking his watchful care over the fearless mariner. Vast crowds gathered on the Battery and on the wharves to take a parting look at the adventurous brig, her honored commander and gallant crew. The waters of our spacious bay everywhere swarmed with steamers and sailing-craft of every description, bearing the flags and emblems of Masonry, and bidding God-speed to the calm but determined and noble band. True, it was no novelty to see a vessel go forth from these secure and beautiful waters to a voyage upon the great deep. Ships of almost every nation of the earth are daily to be seen borne away, by the breezes of heaven, from this port to different seas and the remotest climes; but there was not one among the thousands who gazed that morning upon the little brig of one hundred and forty-four tons, manned by a crew of only eighteen men, as she slowly moved down the bay, who did not feel that the sight was noble and august; there was not one who was not conscious of unusual emotions at that hour and at that sight. There was moral sublimity in it. It was a triumph of what is great and pure and Godlike in our nature. It was the commencement of a voyage, not for the gains of commerce, nor for the crimson glories of war, nor yet for the advancement of science, but the commencement of a voyage of love,—a voyage for the rescue of a band of strangers of a distant nation from a dreary grave. It was a beautiful, an impressive recognition of the worth of man as man,—a noble tribute offered to the transcendent ties of our humanity,—a deed of lofty charity for coming ages to ponder upon and emulate.

At length, amid salutes and cheers of farewell, they cast off from the steamer, and were soon out upon the Atlantic, ploughing their way toward the eternal winters of the North. Their destination was to the highest penetrable point of Baffin's Bay, and from thence, by means of dog-sledges, to attempt a search for the missing expedition by following the trend of the coast.

* * * * * *

After gazing for some time in silence on the scene, [speaking of the open Polar sea,] and remembering that the hour was not only one of triumph for his noble commander, but for the Republic he represented, Mr. Morton raised upon the summit of the cliff where he stood the stars and stripes,—the flag of our Union. This flag Dr. Kane calls "THE GRINNELL FLAG OF THE ANTARCTIC,—a well-cherished little relic which had now followed me on two Polar voyages. This flag had been saved from the wreck of the United States sloop-of-war Peacock when she stranded off the Columbia River. It had accompanied Commander Wilkes in his far-southern discovery of an Antarctic continent. It was now its strange destiny to float over the highest northern land, not only of America, but of our globe. Side by side with this flag were placed our own Masonic emblems of the compass and the square. Here, mingling their folds, they floated from the black cliff over the dark, rock-shadowed waters which rolled up and broke in white caps at its base." By the kindness of Mr. Grinnell, I am able to-night to unfurl that memorable little flag in your presence,—"a flag which," in the language of Mr. Grinnell, in his note accompanying the flag when he sent it to me, "has been farther South and twice farther North than any other in existence." Here it is, [the flag was here unfurled by Mr. A.;] and I am authorized by its distinguished owner to say that whoever will plant this flag at any point farther north than that on which Dr. Kane planted it shall be entitled to its possession.

* * * * * *

I have thus traced in its faintest outline the life of our lamented brother. The prominent events of his career were of a nature fitted to develop and place in a strong light the leading traits of his character. That these traits, as combined in him, formed one of the most remarkable men of the age, is now universally acknowledged,—one of the truest and noblest whose name adorns the page of American biography. *The unconquerable energy of his nature* was one of his most prominent and striking traits. This element of power never failed him: from his early childhood it stamped his career. Although small in size, (his ordinary weight being about a hundred pounds,) and with an organization singularly delicate and refined, yet he exhibited an activity, physical and mental, a capacity for labor, a power of endurance, a resoluteness of purpose, and an iron will, such as the stoutest and strongest, the Goliaths of earth, have rarely shown. When an object was before him to the accomplishment of which duty pointed, he shrank from no labor, was disheartened by no obstacles, refused no sacrifices. If for the moment baffled, he seemed to rise from his defeat in renovated strength to renew the struggle. Whether toiling up the precipices of the Himalayas, or fighting his way through the ranks of the embattled hosts of Mexico, or contending amidst the wild war of elements on a stormy Arctic sea, or, from his ice-enchained little brig, going forth alone amid the darkness and dreariness of a Polar night to secure, if it may be, a mouthful of food that can minister to the strength of one of his dying crew,—*whatever* his purpose, *wherever* the scene of his efforts,—nothing seemed to daunt or discourage him: *onward, straight onward* to his object he directed his course, and, if within the compass of human power to reach it, success was the result. It has been truly said, "Our victory is in its nobility somewhat as are our enemies in their strength." The foes of an Arctic explorer are among the most terrible that man can encounter; and *triumphantly* to meet them demands a physical courage, a brave endurance, a *moral* heroism, higher and nobler than any battle-field whose scenes redden the page of history. Justly, therefore, to appreciate the mighty energy of his nature of whom we speak, we must follow him through the fearful conflicts to which he was called in that zone of mystery and terror. We must see how the mightiest powers of nature were arrayed against him; how the wildest elements encompassed him with fatal arms of death; how the sea raged, and the blinding snow fell, and the sun sank out of sight for months, and the mountain-icebergs are seen in the spectral twilight approaching to crush his little vessel in their mighty embrace. We must see "how contrivance was defeated by accident; how foresight proved insufficient to provide; how human strength was wasted in attempts that failed;" how bread was wanting and fuel was not found; how famine and disease came with ghastly terrors; how the strong man laid down despairingly and died; and then how *he* rose up against all this, and, asserting the supremacy of that nature which God had given him, triumphed over all, and bore back the remnant of worn and wearied men that was left him to the fair havens of their home in the South! Well has it been asked, "Are not the Arctic explorations a Christian Iliad, and is not our Achilles nobler than Thetis's son?"

But this controlling element of his nature, while it crowded his brief career with brilliant achievements and noble results, yet shortened his life. His constitution, never the most vigorous, yielded and finally gave way under the overwhelming burdens which his insatiate energy imposed upon it.

The intellect of Dr. Kane was of a high order. Quick in perception, rapid both in combination and analysis, sound in deduction, and powerfully retentive of memory, he acquired with great ease, and ever had his acquisitions at immediate disposal. In a high degree inquisitive, enthusiastic in pursuit, and favored as he was with abundant means of early discipline and culture, the range of his attainments was wide and varied, especially in the boundless fields of physical science,—his favorite sphere of intellectual effort. Although naturally impulsive, yet he exhibited in his career great prudence and calm self-reliance; and, when the emergency demanded new resources, his fertility of invention was wonderful. He was capable of the most intense mental concentration. No man, whenever investigation required it, was more laborious, patient, and unyielding. The paper he read before the American and Geographical Statistical Society, already alluded to, affords a fine illustration of his powers in this direction. His conclusions in regard to the existence of an open Polar sea, therein embodied, he had worked out by a chain of induction as severe as mathematical demonstration. He no more proceeded on mere conjecture than did the immortal discoverer of our hemisphere when, in the face of a scoffing world, he asserted its existence. Indeed, Dr. Kane may justly be styled the Columbus of the Arctic. His mind also was of that refined cast which rendered him alive to true grandeur and beauty, and would have enabled him, had he chosen, to range successfully the flowery paths and tempt the untrodden heights of the literary world. To nothing that unfolded the mysterious purposes and illustrated the exquisite perfection of nature's handiwork was he ever indifferent. Whether upon the ocean or the land, in the torrid or the frigid zone,—whether gazing in amazed delight upon the Arctic aurora with its startling and beautiful modifications of light in swiftly-varying succession, or penetrating the caves of his own Alleghanies, and there reading the history of earth among the hidden rocks and in the successive strata of her various formations,—whether watching the silent growth of the tiny flower that, under some overhanging cliff of eternal ice, opens its modest leaves to the pale beams of a Polar sun, or measuring the heavenly bodies in their distant spheres, and with mathematical accuracy marking out the paths along which they fly in their impetuous courses,—whether wandering amidst the pyramids of Egypt or through the classic ruins of lovely Greece,—no object of beauty, no scene of sublimity, no illustration of excellence, no proof of virtue, that ever met his eye, failed to minister pleasure to his soul. As we follow him in his Arctic wanderings, surrounded as he often was with horrors thick and dark enough to overwhelm an ordinary mind, we are astonished at the beautiful, glorious thoughts, invested often with the loftiest poetical imagery, which abound on the pages of his daily journal. Listen to his language on one occasion, after he had been pacing the deck of his little brig, as she lay motionless in her icy chains and surrounded by the unbroken silence of her mysterious solitude:—" The intense beauty of the Arctic firmament can hardly be imagined. It looks close above our heads, with its stars magnified in glory, and the very planets twinkling so much as to baffle the observations of the astronomer. I have trodden the deck when the life of earth seemed suspended,—its movements, its sounds, its coloring, its companionships; and, as I looked on the radiant hemisphere circling above me, as if rendering worship to the unseen Centre of Light, I have ejaculated, 'Lord, what is man, that thou art mindful of him?' And then I have thought of the kindly world we had left, with its revolving sunlight and shadow, and the other stars that gladden it in their changes, and the hearts that warmed to us there, till I lost myself in the memories of those who are not; and they bore me back to the stars again." Never have the beauties, the wonders, the terrors of that mysterious circle of earth's surface been so fully, graphically, and with such fascinating power of rhetoric revealed as they are in his "Arctic Explorations,"—a work which, while it will ever awaken the highest admiration for its gifted author, will ever be invested with a melancholy interest as the last monument of his genius, reared with his dying strength.

But the *moral qualities* of Dr. Kane constituted the governing power and the highest adornment of his nature; for they gave useful direction to his mighty energy, harmony and true wisdom to the workings of his lofty intellect, and brought his whole being into unison with the great law of Love.

Brethren, brightly and beautifully were the fundamental principles of our *venerable Order* displayed in the life of our lamented brother. Never, perhaps, were justice and truth more perfectly realized by man. Every foot of the wall which he built in the temple was in the strictest conformity to the square and the plummet. Deception, misrepresentation, unjust concealment, falsehood, oppression, wrong in every form, seemed his abhorrence. A beautiful instance of this may be found in his narrative of the first United States Grinnell Expedition. It seems that to a tract of land first discovered by Dr. Kane, while on this Expedition, lying to the north of Wellington Channel, Commander De Haven had given the name of Grinnell. A year afterward, this land appeared on the English maps inscribed with the name of "Prince Albert;" and the map from the hydrographer of the Admiralty not only inscribes "Albert Land" on this newly-discovered region, but pretends to explain the error of the American claim by stating, in a note, that "Baillie Hamilton Island is the Grinnell Land of the American squadron." Dr. Kane—after demonstrating from the journals of the English navigators themselves that the Americans were the actual discoverers of this region, and so demonstrating it that the hydrographer of the English Admiralty, in a letter to Mr. Grinnell, which I have had the pleasure of reading, has honorably acknowledged their mistake, and given assurance that hereafter their maps will be made to correspond with the facts—proceeds to say:—

"The controversy is perhaps of little moment. The time has gone by when the mere sighting of a distant coast conferred on a navigator or his monarch either ownership of the soil or a right to govern its people: even the planting of a flag-staff, with armorial emblazonments at the top and a record-bottle below it, does not insure nowadays a conceded title. Yet the comity of explorers has adopted the rule of the more scientific observers of nature, and holds it for law everywhere, that he who first sees and first announces shall also give the name. I should be sorry to withdraw from the extreme charts of Northern discovery any memorial, even an indirect one, of that Lady Sovereign whose noble-spirited subjects we met in Lancaster Sound." Mark now his ingenuousness, his honesty, his love of justice and truth. "*It was only by accident that we preceded them, under the guidance of causes that can assert for us little honor, since they were beyond our control, and we should have been glad to escape them.* But we did precede them; and the most northern land on the meridian of 94° West must retain, therefore, the honored name which it received from the American commander."

I have said that Dr. Kane was a man of justice. A British reviewer has, I am aware, charged him with an act of flagrant injustice toward Godfrey, one of his crew. This man had been disobedient and mutinous on previous occasions; now he was in the act of openly and boldly setting at defiance the authority of his commander, and fleeing from the ship. Dr. Kane, standing on the deck, raised his gun and fired upon him,— doing him, however, no injury. Subsequently Godfrey returned, and was restored to his place among the crew. Now, any man who, after reading the account of this matter as given by Dr. Kane and confirmed

DR. ELISHA KENT KANE.

by his officers and men,—after hearing the reasons which he believed rendered it his imperative though painful duty to adopt the course he did, for the maintenance of that discipline of the vessel which was vital to their safety,—will charge him with cruelty or injustice in this act, would blacken the memory of Washington for signing the death-warrant of the interesting André, although he firmly believed that the safety of the army—the welfare of the struggling Republic—that *unerring justice* —required it. No! never was a commander more just or generous toward those under his authority; and this is the testimony of the officers and men who shared with him the dangers and sufferings of the perilous voyage, and gathered around him, under the poor shelter they had, through those dismal and interminable winters; and with quivering lip, heaving breast, and moistened eye do they speak of his self-devotion, self-sacrifice, his never-failing regard for the welfare of his comrades, in that hazardous search for the lost.

Nor was he less distinguished by our other great principle of love. "Strong and binding was this cement of his edifice,—plastic and soft as the purest gem in its application, grasping and tenacious and abiding as the sculptor's adamant which it unites to form the whole outward aspect of his noble structure." Our brother fell a martyr to the benevolence of his nature. He died—*died out of time*—because he would rescue others from death. Human suffering, wherever he encountered it, in whatever accents he heard its moans, stirred up the deep fountains of love within him. His career was full of the most touching manifestations of this divine principle. Follow him through the scenes of his two Polar expeditions, and the streams of his kindness never ceased to flow. Yes! in an age of predominant avarice and mechanical routine, he has set us an example of as chivalrous self-devotion and as lofty, magnanimous enterprise as ever illumined the tracks of the holiest champions in the world's best day. See him during the long and dreary months of the second winter of their imprisonment in Rensselaer Bay, with every officer and man but one prostrate and helpless with disease. Day and night he gives himself no rest. With the tenderness and gentleness and assiduity of a mother's love he seeks to heal their diseases and alleviate their sufferings by his unceasing ministries of skill and compassion. Now we see him with his gun, going forth alone and toiling his way for hours through the snow-drifts and over the ice-covered rocks to secure food that will not aggravate the disease of the sick and dying; and now we see him seated by the side of the pale and desponding, speaking words of comfort and hope to sinking hearts. I know of no record of human kindness more beautiful, more touching, none which reveals a spirit in closer sympathy with His "who went about doing good," than does the record of this portion of the Arctic life of Dr. Kane.

Go with me at another time and visit that lonely brig. It is the month of March, 1855. The hour is midnight. A fearful storm is raging. The thermometer is at seventy-eight degrees below the freezing-point. Dr. Kane with a portion of his crew are in their moss-lined cabin below, their thoughts, it may be, far away with loved ones amid the comforts of home. Suddenly the noise of footsteps is heard on the deck, and the next moment three, of a party of eight who had gone forth two weeks before on an expedition of search and survey, enter the cabin. Their looks are startling: trembling with weakness, swollen, haggard, benumbed with cold, and but just able to utter a few broken words, their appearance tells of the terrible sufferings they have endured. Their story is short and frightful. Weak and faint with fatigue and hunger, their party were toiling their slow and painful way back to the brig, their only home amidst the mighty desolation around them, when they were overtaken by a storm of fierceness and power unusual even in that region of tempests. After battling against the enraged elements for hours, four of their number, exhausted and frozen, sank down on the ice to die. Of the remaining four, one remained with his dying comrades; the others, after many hours (how many they knew not) of wandering and struggle, half delirious, reached the brig. *Where* they have left their dying companions they cannot tell. But, notwithstanding the terrors of the night, and the faint prospect of success in their fearful search, and the probability of their own destruction in the apparently desperate attempt, yet the purpose of their leader is instantly formed, and immediate preparation for the rescue is ordered. Amid the darkness and howling tempest, the band, led by their master-spirit and commending themselves to the protection of Him who rides on the storm, start forth. Ignorant how to direct their course, yet they press forward. Hour after hour, through the mighty snow-drifts, in face of the blinding tempest, over the frozen and lacerating hummocks, they struggle on. Twice does the strength of their gallant commander give way, and he falls fainting upon the snow. At length, after twenty hours of constant and incredible toil and endurance, and just as they feel that they must yield and abandon their comrades to their sad fate, the keen eye of the Esquimaux boy, Hans, detects the faint, half-filled track of a sledge in the snow; following this, they soon perceive in the far distance a little signal fluttering in the wind; a nearer approach reveals the small tent of the lost party almost buried in the snow, and from the little flag-staff on the top floats the ensign of the Republic, and, underneath, *the Masonic flag.* Trembling with anxiety, they approach the silent tent. Their leader, dreading to realize his worst fears, slowly works his way through the surrounding drifts and enters the tent amid the darkness and ominous silence that prevail. There the lost party lay, prostrate and helpless, on the icy floor. He speaks; his voice is recognised: it gives new life to their benumbed and torpid senses, and, with reawakened hope and revived courage and swelling hearts, they exclaim, "We knew you'd come! we knew you'd come, brother!" And why did they "know he'd come"? Why were they sustained by this assurance when the cold arms of Death were encircling them? Ah, they knew that the divine principles symbolized by that little Masonic flag that fluttered over their sinking heads were the principles that ruled the heart and the life of their beloved and trusted leader, and that, under their power, no distance, no darkness of the night, no fierceness of the tempest, no terrors of the cold, no *obstacles* that human strength and skill *could* surmount, would prevent his flying to their rescue even at the expense of the last pulsation of his great and benevolent heart. "We knew you'd come!" Yes, frozen men just ready to die, he did come! Your faith in your noble brother, the true man, the faithful Mason, was no delusion. *He did come!* and kindly and gently he bore you back to your cabin-home; and, although one of your number fell a victim to the stern power of the frost-king of the North, and his body now lies entombed in sight of that "deserted hulk bound in the deathful ice," *you live* to tell with what constancy, fidelity, and beauty he illustrated the principle of love in his brief but immortal career.

Finally. Dr. Kane distinctly and constantly maintained the authority of religion, and with reverent faith sought its guidance and consolations. " Our honored Society, brethren, maintains this open profession, in carrying ever before us and in our midst, with solemn reverence, the holy Bible,—*an open Bible.*" Our lamented brother had faith in God and in his revealed word when faith meant something and cost much. Daily his little band knelt around him amid the Arctic darkness, and he led them in prayer to the Eternal Throne. He faithfully taught them the great truth of a Providence which presides over the course of events. He says, "Call it fatalism, as you ignorantly may, there is that in the story of every eventful life which teaches the inefficiency of human means and the present control of a Supreme Agency. See how often relief has come at the moment of extremity, in forms strangely unsought, almost at the time unwelcome! See, still more, how the back has been strengthened to its increasing burdens, and the heart cheered by some conscious influence of an unseen Power!" Such was his faith; and his life was in beautiful harmony with it. Strong and fearless before men, calm and intrepid amidst surrounding perils, yet he humbly asks God's help, and blushes not to declare his humble trust in Him. When hastily escaping from his vessel, which is threatened with instant destruction by the crushing ice, he grasps his "little home-Bible,"—inscribed, it may be, with a mother's hand,—as the treasure *first to be secured*. When about forsaking his little ice-enchained vessel, which had so long been his home in that mighty desolation, " he gathers all hands around" and lifts up their hearts to God. His faith ever sustained him. Guided by its rules, his work, brethren, from the time that he mounted the wall as an apprentice, to the glorious day when, as a wise master-builder, he set the key of his arch and brought forth the top-stone of the moral temple he built, his work was done and was well done.

Then, translated to a place of blessedness and dignity in that " temple not built with hands, eternal in the heavens," he still works, as angels do,—the great God of the Universe being the Grand Master-Builder.

Such, imperfectly, was the life, and such the character, of him to whose memory we have assembled to render this humble tribute of honor. He has gone to his grave, but in the fulness of his young renown. We shall see him here no more; but his noble life, his thrilling story, his beautiful example, his model character, and his precious memory, are our imperishable inheritance. Brethren, let us guard them well and emulate them as we may. Let us enshrine them in the deepest thoughts of our efforts; and, as he still works on the walls of the temple we build, let us be animated to greater diligence and high fidelity, that we too may enter in due time the portals of that Upper Temple, whose proportions of harmony, beauty, and infinite grandeur shall awaken our admiration and draw forth our increasing praises through eternal ages.

THE END.

STEREOTYPED BY L. JOHNSON & CO.
PHILADELPHIA.

From the LONDON ILLUSTRATED TIMES, Nov. 8, 1856.

"That portion of Dr. Kane's work which relates to personal adventure and experiences, will be warmly admired by such as read for amusement. But to those who concern themselves with weightier matters, the important discoveries he has made, will be in the highest degree instructive.

"In relating his adventures and developing his discoveries, Dr. Kane has written with the taste and judgment of a gentleman, and the modest pride so becoming in a man who has done his duty. The charm of his work is increased by hundreds of beautiful illustrations after his own drawings. We have gone through his volumes with real admiration, and have no doubt they will be in high favor with all who, perusing them, can appreciate patient endurance under fearful trials, and ardent zeal in the execution of duties in circumstances under which most men would inevitably sink. We congratulate Dr. Kane on having associated his name honorably and indissolubly with Arctic travel, and on having made discoveries which entitle him to the gratitude of the civilized world."

―――o―――

DR. KANE'S FIRST NARRATIVE.

THE UNITED STATES GRINNELL EXPEDITION IN SEARCH OF SIR JOHN FRANKLIN, during the years 1850—51. A Personal Narrative, by ELISHA KENT KANE, M. D., U. S. N. One volume 8vo., upwards of 550 pages, containing 200 steel plates and wood engravings, including a fine steel portrait of Sir John Franklin, being the only one ever engraved in America. Also, a BIOGRAPHY OF FRANKLIN, by S. AUSTIN ALLIBONE, Esq. $3.00.

This work is totally distinct from the second Arctic Expedition, and embraces much valuable and interesting matter never before published. It should be owned by all who have purchased the last Expedition as it makes Dr. KANE's works complete.

―――

IN PRESS,
COL. J. C. FRÉMONT'S EXPLORATIONS.
PREPARED BY THE AUTHOR, AND EMBRACING ALL HIS EXPEDITIONS.

Superbly Illustrated with Steel Plates and Wood Cuts, engraved under the immediate superintendence of COL. FRÉMONT, mostly from daguerreotypes taken on the spot, and will be issued in a style to match Dr. Kane's works. It will also contain a new Steel Portrait, being the only correct likeness of the author ever published.

TWO VOLUMES, OCTAVO—$6.00.

This work is being prepared with great care by COL. J. C. FRÉMONT, and will contain a résumé of the First and Second Expeditions in the years 1842, '43 and '44, and a detailed account of the Third Expedition during the years 1845, '46 and '47, across the Rocky Mountains through Oregon into California, covering the conquest and settlement of that country; the Fourth Expedition, of 1848-49, up the Kansas and Arkansas rivers into the Rocky Mountains of Mexico, down the Del Norte, through Sonora into California; the Fifth Expedition, of 1853 and '54, across the Rocky Mountains at the heads of the Arkansas and Colorado rivers, through the Mormon settlements and the Great Basin into California. The whole will embrace a period of ten years passed among the wilds of America.

The scientific portion of the work will be very complete, containing able articles from Professors Torrey, Hall, Guyot, Hubbard, and others, compiled from material furnished by the author.

The greatest possible care has been taken to insure the accuracy of the Maps, which will fully illustrate all the above-named Expeditions.

Brazil and the Brazilians.

By Rev. D. P. KIDDER, of the Methodist Episcopal Church.
" " J. C. FLETCHER, of the Presbyterian Church.

This new and splendidly-illustrated work (one large volume octavo, in uniform style with the superb volumes of Dr. Kane's *Arctic Explorations*) is the joint effort of the above-named gentlemen, who, as travellers and as missionaries, (and one in an official position as Acting Secretary of United States Legation at Rio,) have had a long and varied experience in a land full of interest, whether we regard it in a natural, commercial, political, or moral point of view.

There is no comprehensive book of recent date on the Empire of Brazil, and it is a great *desideratum* that the subject should be presented in its whole aspect.

It is the aim of "Brazil and the Brazilians" to lay before the public a popular and faithful account of the wonderful phenomena of the tropics, and with graphic pen and pencil to portray the gorgeous scenery, the history, peculiar manners and customs, and the political institutions of the country, and the general condition of the subjects of the enlightened Emperor Don Pedro II.

The naturalist should be interested in a region which, as Gardiner, the celebrated English botanist, has observed, "is richer than any other in the world in those objects to which he had devoted the study of his life."

The commercial man should know more of a land from whence are derived so many important staples,—which last year exported sixty million dollars' worth of her productions, and imported to the amount of fifty-three million dollars. Brazil is every year indebted to Europe, (which has seven lines of steamers to South America;) while the United States (with not a single steamer to the south of the equator) is behindhand each year with Brazil more than fourteen millions of dollars.

The Christian community should know more of the country where the banner of Protestant Christianity was first erected in the New World,—a land associated with the prayers, labors, and names of the French Huguenots, ministers of the Reformed Church of Holland, and of the devoted Henry Martyn,—a land open to Bible and missionary effort. This work treats of these topics, and contains deeply-interesting incidents of recent missionary tours.

A great interest attaches to this Empire, whose Constitution is liberal and tolerant, whose Government is strong, and whose material prosperity is ever advancing.

There are more than 130 engravings, on steel, wood, and stone, from original and other sketches, and by the pencils and gravers of the same artists who have so elegantly adorned the thrillingly-interesting narrative of Dr. Kane.

The publishers can only add that the style of letter-press and of the illustrations in the "Arctic Explorations" (which is from their establishment) is a sufficient guarantee for the rich typographical execution which characterizes "Brazil and the Brazilians."

☞ This work is sold exclusively by subscription, and can only be obtained from our authorized Agents. Price, $3.00 retail.

CHILDS & PETERSON, Publishers, *Philadelphia.*

Printed in Great Britain
by Amazon